Workers' Health, Workers' Democracy

Workers' Health
Workers' Democracy

The Western Miners' Struggle, 1891–1925

Alan Derickson

Cornell University Press   Ithaca and London

First published 1988 by Cornell University Press.

International Standard Book Number 0-8014-2060-1
Library of Congress Catalog Card Number 88-47722
Printed in the United States of America
Librarians: Library of Congress cataloging information
appears on the last page of the book.

The paper in this book is acid-free and meets the guidelines for
permanence and durability of the Committee on Production Guidelines
for Book Longevity of the Council on Library Resources.

For Peg

Contents

Map, Illustrations, and Tables

MAP

ILLUSTRATIONS

TABLES

Preface

Bowed by the weight of centuries he leans
Upon his hoe and gazes on the ground.
The emptiness of ages in his face,
And on his back the burden of the world.
Who made him dead to rapture and despair,
A thing that grieves not and that never hopes,
Stolid and stunned, a brother to the ox?
Who loosened and let down this brutal jaw?
Whose was the hand that slanted back this brow?
Whose breath blew out the light within this brain?

. . . . . .

O masters, lords and rulers in all lands,
Is this the handiwork you give to God,
This monstrous thing distorted and soul-quenched?
How will you ever straighten up this shape;
Touch it again with immortality;
Give back the upward looking and the light;
Rebuild in it the music and the dream;
Make right the immemorial infamies,
Perfidious wrongs, immedicable woes?
　　　　　　　　　　—Edwin Markham, 1899

On February 25, 1901, Joseph P. Langford recited this poem on
the wrong occasion. The evening on which the unions of DeLamar
and Silver City, Idaho, entertained Edward Boyce, president of the
Western Federation of Miners, was, according to the *Owyhee Avalanche*,
"the greatest social event in the history of DeLamar." An overflow
crowd of hardrock workers and the general public turned out to hear
speeches by Boyce and William D. Haywood, president of the Silver
City Miners' Union. Dancing "kept going continuously until 5 A.M."

ix

The only discordant note in the whole celebration sounded when Langford, a leader in the DeLamar organization, read "The Man with the Hoe." R. R. Thomas, another member of Local 53, immediately rose to take exception to this dismal stereotype of the hopelessly degraded laborer. In Thomas's view, the working class was "not so low as depicted by Mr. Markham." Whether he buttressed his argument by pointing to such accomplishments as the recent founding of the Silver City Miners' Union Hospital is, unfortunately, unclear. It is clear, however, that Langford learned a useful lesson about workers' capacity for self-improvement during his stint in southwestern Idaho. Shortly afterward, having migrated to the silver mines of Utah, Langford led the fight to establish the Park City Miners' Hospital.[1]

Organized metal miners at the turn of the century needed no enlightened "masters, lords and rulers" to fire their imaginations and uplift their conditions. Local hardrock unions throughout western North America established and controlled hospitals, administered nursing programs, regulated dangerous working conditions, and engaged in various other mutual aid endeavors. Taken together, these initiatives by members of the Western Federation of Miners embodied a distinctive strategy of grassroots self-help. This book traces the rise and fall of that strategy.

This is working-class history from an institutional perspective. Local unions in this period were built by rank-and-file workers to protect their fundamental interests. By focusing on local organizations, I hope to avoid, if not transcend, the dichotomy between workers' history and institutional studies of the labor movement.[2] My aim is to explain how unionism became a central factor in the lives of rank-and-file mine workers in the late nineteenth and early twentieth centuries. To this end, I illuminate diverse aspects of the thought, action, and experience of hardrock miners with respect to some of their biggest fears—illness, injury, disability, destitution, and death. More than

1. *Owyhee Avalanche* (Silver City, Ida.), Mar. 1, 1901; Press Committee [of DeLamar Miners' Union], "President Boyce Visits Locals Nos. 66 and 53," *MM*, Apr. 1901, pp. 29–33.
2. Recent scholarship has refreshed the institutional approach by exploring unionism at the local level. See, for example, Peter Friedlander, *The Emergence of a UAW Local, 1936–1939: A Study in Class and Culture* (Pittsburgh, 1975); Ronald W. Schatz, *The Electrical Workers: A History of Labor at General Electric and Westinghouse, 1923–60* (Urbana, Ill., 1983); Michael Kazin, *Barons of Labor: The San Francisco Building Trades and Union Power in the Progressive Era* (Urbana, Ill., 1987).

any other agency, the local union, through formal programs, tackled these problems.

Approaching unionism from the bottom up offers a fuller view of the Western Federation of Miners. The well-known militance of this organization resulted in part from bonds of solidarity forged by mutual assistance. In addition, my discussion of decades of avid, persistent political agitation by local and district affiliates for protective legislation shatters the syndicalist myth of the WFM. Thus it becomes plain that the Western Federation did much more than fight mine operators with dynamite and sponsor the Industrial Workers of the World.

Historians have given minimal attention to the mutual benefit work that Samuel Gompers and other pioneering unionists considered an integral part of the mission of their movement.[3] The WFM stood at one end of a continuum of labor involvement in mutual aid. Beginning with the railroad brotherhoods and other craft organizations in the mid-nineteenth century, most unions administered disability and death benefit programs.[4] In addition, around the turn of the century a number of organizations began to deliver health and welfare services, establishing old-age homes, sanitariums, clinics, and hospitals.[5] Unionists of all stripes understood not only the humanitarian value of such endeavors but also their instrumental value in recruiting and retaining members.[6] Although clearly exceptional in certain respects, the benevolent work of the Western Federation nonetheless represents a brand of fraternalism that prevailed widely within the North Amer-

3. Samuel Gompers, *Seventy Years of Life and Labor*, 2 vols., (New York, 1925), 1:42, 167; [idem], "The Next Step toward Emancipation," *American Federationist*, Dec. 1899, pp. 248–49.

4. James B. Kennedy, *Beneficiary Features of American Trade Unions* (Baltimore, 1908), pp. 7–83; U.S. Department of Commerce and Labor, Bureau of Labor, *Twenty-Third Annual Report of the Commissioner of Labor, 1908: Workmen's Insurance and Benefit Funds in the United States* (Washington, 1909), pp. 21–267; Canada, Department of Labor, "Trade Union Beneficiary Work," in *Sixth Annual Report on Labor Organization in Canada, 1916* (Ottawa, 1917), pp. 197–203; James M. Lynch, "Trade Union Sickness Insurance," *American Labor Legislation Review* 4 (1914): 82–91.

5. U.S. Bureau of the Census, *Benevolent Institutions, 1904* (Washington, 1905), pp. 222–23; idem, *Benevolent Institutions, 1910* (Washington, 1913), pp. 318–19; U.S. Bureau of Labor Statistics, *Beneficial Activities of American Trade Unions*, Bulletin 465 (Washington, 1928), pp. 45–84; *Polk's Medical Register and Directory of North America*, 13th ed. (Detroit, 1914), pp. 1739, 1749.

6. Gompers, *Seventy Years*, 1:166; Lloyd Ulman, *The Rise of the National Trade Union* (Cambridge, Mass., 1955), pp. 93–94, 182; Lynch, "Trade Union Sickness Insurance," p. 85; David Brody, *Steelworkers in America: The Nonunion Era* (1960; rpt. New York, 1969), p. 93.

ican labor movement in the era before the creation of the modern welfare system.

This book explores one aspect of the emergence of modern industrial relations. Indeed, workers' initiatives for health reform were inextricably embedded in a larger matrix of conflict between labor and capital. Accordingly, programs evolved dialectically. Miners' opposition to company doctors led them to found union hospitals. The success of union health services and of campaigns for mine safety and social insurance legislation, in turn, brought about elaborate corporate safety and benefit schemes. These programs form integral components of a welfare capitalism that has continued up to the present day.

The story of the hardrock hospitals fills gaps in the historical literature on the emergence of the general acute-care hospital in North America. It describes small institutions and small-town institutions that historians have largely neglected.[7] Moreover, this monograph complements previous work by exploring events in the Rocky Mountain region. During the late nineteenth and early twentieth centuries, the hospital moved from the periphery to the center of the health care system. That fundamental change appears to have proceeded furthest in western mining states: by 1920 Nevada, Arizona, Colorado, and Montana were among the seven leading states in per capita supply of hospital beds.[8] This book illuminates the process by which hospitalization supplanted home care in the West.

The historiography of occupational safety and health in North America is inadequate and misleading. There has been little analysis of the risks of work in the period before 1920.[9] Moreover, historians

---

7. Recent work has disentangled the complexities of the development of hospitals in Philadelphia, New York, and Boston. See Charles E. Rosenberg, "And Heal the Sick: The Hospital and the Patient in Nineteenth Century America," *Journal of Social History* 10 (1977): 428–47; idem, "Inward Vision and Outward Glance: The Shaping of the American Hospital, 1880–1914," *Bulletin of the History of Medicine* 53 (1979): 346–91; Morris J. Vogel, *The Invention of the Modern Hospital: Boston, 1870–1930* (Chicago, 1980); David K. Rosner, *A Once Charitable Enterprise: Health Care in Brooklyn and New York, 1885–1915* (New York, 1982). Unfortunately, there have been no comparable advances in understanding Canadian hospitals. See S. E. D. Shortt, "The Canadian Hospital in the Nineteenth Century: An Historiographic Lament," *Journal of Canadian Studies* 18 (Winter 1983–84): 3.

8. AMA, Council on Medical Education and Hospitals, "Hospital Service in the United States," *Journal of the American Medical Association* 76 (1921): 1083.

9. Exceptions include Walter Licht, *Working for the Railroad: The Organization of Work in the Nineteenth Century* (Princeton, 1983), pp. 181–97; Keith Dix, *Work Relations in the*

have virtually ignored workers' resistance to victimization by industrial illness and injury. My interpretation of early union advocacy of
improved working conditions and better health services for the casualties of production makes clear that miners were not merely abject
victims of hazardous technology.

Above all else, this is a study of the struggle to extend the frontier
of democracy. The movement for democratic control of health care in
mining communities challenged elitist arrangements for governing
hospitals and benefit plans. Similarly, workers' demands that they be
involved in the determination of working conditions confronted the
authoritarianism of mine management. Like other radicals of the period, WFM activists fought to expand the sphere of human affairs
subject to the rule of the majority.[10]

This book originated as a presentation at an occupational health
conference sponsored by the Butte Miners' Union in 1980. The early
work was done in the Department of the History of Health Sciences
at the University of California, San Francisco. I am happy to acknowledge the thorough criticism offered by Carroll Estes, Philip Lee, Daniel
Todes, Gert Brieger, and David Brody. I am especially grateful to
Professor Brody for helping to define and refine my arguments. Other
careful readers of various drafts of the manuscript were Dan Berman,
Tony Fels, Leon Fink, Jim Gregory, David Rosner, and George Silver.
In addition, I benefited from the insights and encouragement provided
by Abby Ginzberg, Alexis Rankin, Jamie Robinson, Sarah Samuels,
Glenn Shor, and Joan Trauner. My editor, Peter Agree, provided
expert guidance through the innumerable twists and turns along the
way to publication. I also acknowledge my debt to an inspiring teacher,
the late Herbert Gutman.

I am indebted to too many archivists and librarians to mention all
of them individually. I must, however, thank the staff of the Inter-
library Borrowing Service at the University of California, Berkeley,
Bette Eriskin at Berkeley's Graduate Social Science Library, and Jack

---

Coal Industry: The Hand-Loading Era, 1880–1930 (Morgantown, W.Va., 1977), pp. 67–
104; Carl Gersuny, *Work Hazards and Industrial Conflict* (Hanover, N.H., 1981), pp. 20–
67; Brody, *Steelworkers in America*, pp. 91–94, 99–102.

10. Lawrence Goodwyn, *Democratic Promise: The Populist Moment in America* (New
York, 1976); Leon Fink, *Workingmen's Democracy: The Knights of Labor and American Politics*
(Urbana, Ill., 1983); Nick Salvatore, *Eugene V. Debs: Citizen and Socialist* (Urbana, Ill.,
1982).

Brennan and his staff at the Western Historical Collections, University of Colorado, for their exceedingly helpful and patient service.

The Pew Memorial Trust gave me a fellowship through the Institute for Health Policy Studies and the Institute for Health and Aging at the University of California, San Francisco. A study award from the Bancroft Library facilitated my work there. I greatly appreciate this generous assistance.

My family made the greatest sacrifices and offered the most support for this undertaking. My wife, Peggy Spear, provided medical expertise, editorial insight, and much else. My daughters, Elizabeth and Katherine, helped by tolerating, up to a point, the parental lapses entailed by immersion in research and writing. They know that I am grateful to them not only for letting me work on this project but also for dragging me away from it occasionally.

ALAN DERICKSON

University Park, Pennsylvania

Abbreviations

AFL	American Federation of Labor
AMA	American Medical Association
ASARCO	American Smelting and Refining Company
BOM	U.S. Bureau of Mines
EMJ	*Engineering and Mining Journal*
IWW	Industrial Workers of the World
IUMMSW or Mine-Mill	International Union of Mine, Mill and Smelter Workers
MM	*Miners' Magazine*
MSP	*Mining and Scientific Press*
OBU	One Big Union
PHS	U.S. Public Health Service
RG	Record Group
UMW	United Mine Workers of America
WFM	Western Federation of Miners

Workers' Health, Workers' Democracy

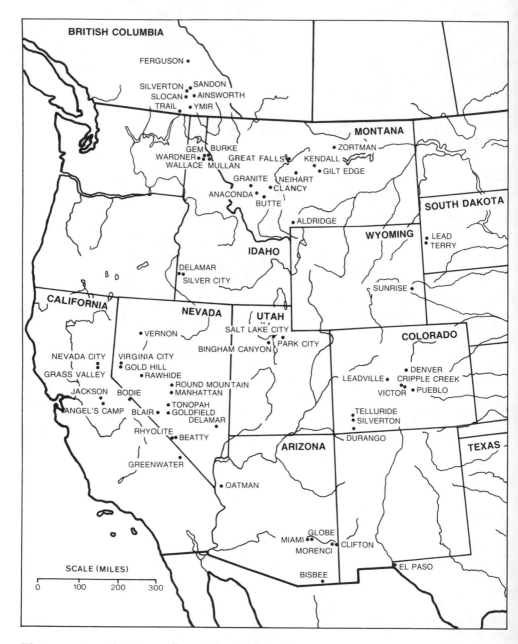

Western centers of mining, milling, and smelting metals

1 | *Declarations of Independence*

> Probably some of those who are opposed to the establishing of a hospital in Park City will tell us that we are weak and unable to cope with so large a proposition; but when shall we be stronger? When will there be a more opportune time for the launching and carrying out of this question to a successful issue? Will it be next week or next year? Brothers, allow me to suggest that now is the time for us to act. This is the time for us to assert our manhood; this is the time for us to show our enemies that we, poor miners as we are, are capable of doing noble things and not dreaming all day long. This is a glorious opportunity, let us grasp it, and show our independence.
>
> —Joseph P. Langford, 1903

The hardrock workers' health and welfare programs embodied deeply held ideals and customs of independent action. Craft work habits and beliefs, union traditions of self-organization and community development, and radical politics combined to provide the experiential, institutional, and ideological foundation for these initiatives. In a world of increasingly odious subordination to the mine owners, the miners' hospitals and other health and welfare plans reasserted old values and customs in new ways.

The creation of relationships of dependence is, of course, inherent in capitalist industrialization. Workers' resistance to proletarianization took many forms in North America in the nineteenth century. In recent years historians have analyzed strikes, boycotts, shopfloor struggles, political agitation, and other reactions to labor's deteriorating autonomy.[1] In this struggle, the western miners distinguished themselves

---

1. Herbert G. Gutman, *Work, Culture, and Society in Industrializing America* (New York, 1976); David Bensman, *The Practice of Solidarity: American Hat Finishers in the*

Table 1.1.   U.S. metals production, 1950–1920 (in thousands of ounces for gold and silver and in thousands of tons for copper and lead)

	Gold	Silver	Copper	Lead
1850	2,419	39	728	22,000
1860	2,225	116	8,064	15,600
1870	2,419	12,375	14,112	17,830
1880	1,742	30,319	30,240	95,725
1890	1,589	54,516	129,882	157,844
1900	3,830	57,647	303,059	367,773
1910	4,585	57,597	544,119	382,692
1920	2,383	56,537	612,275	496,814

SOURCE: U.S. Bureau of the Census, *Historical Statistics of the United States, Colonial Times to 1970*, 2 vols. (Washington, 1975), 1:602–4, 606.

from other groups of workers by their exceptionally militant and constructive stance. Self-help experiments formed but one part of a comprehensive strategy to counter the growing power of mine operators.

The extraction of metal-bearing ores became a leading industry in the western United States and Canada in the decades after 1850. Beginning with the California gold rush, a long succession of spectacular gold, silver, copper, and lead discoveries occurred throughout the mountainous wilderness west of the Great Plains. The total value added in metal mining in the United States more than quadrupled between 1860 and 1902, soaring from $37 million to $168 million. As indicated in Table 1.1, patterns varied for different metals, but the overall trend in output was explosive growth. Large-scale mining developed along the same lines in British Columbia after 1890 (see Table 1.2).[2]

Hardrock mining became a major employer in several western states

Nineteenth Century (Urbana, Ill., 1985); Alan Dawley, *Class and Community: The Industrial Revolution in Lynn* (Cambridge, Mass., 1976); Bruce Laurie, *Working People of Philadelphia, 1800–1850* (Philadelphia, 1980); David Montgomery, *Workers' Control in America* (New York, 1979), pp. 9–31.

2. Rodman W. Paul, *Mining Frontiers of the Far West, 1848–1880* (New York, 1963); William S. Greever, *The Bonanza West: The Story of the Western Mining Rushes, 1848–1900* (Norman, Okla., 1963); U.S. Bureau of the Census, *Historical Statistics of the United States, Colonial Times to 1970*, 2 vols. (Washington, 1975), 1:580, 602–4, 606; British Columbia Minister of Mines, "Annual Report," 1905, in British Columbia, *Sessional Papers, 1906* (Victoria, 1906), p. J10; idem, "Annual Report," 1913, in British Columbia, *Sessional Papers, 1914* (Victoria, 1914), 2:K12–13; idem, "Annual Report," 1921, in British Columbia, *Sessional Papers, 1922* (Victoria, 1922), 1:G12–13.

Table 1.2.   British Columbia metals production, 1890–1920 (in thousands of ounces for gold and silver and in thousands of tons for copper and lead)

	Gold	Silver	Copper	Lead
1890	25	70	0	0
1900	231	3,958	4,999	31,679
1910	295	2,450	19,122	17,329
1920	131	3,378	22,444	19,666

SOURCE: British Columbia Minister of Mines, "Annual Reports" (see note 2).

Table 1.3.   Metal miners in North America, 1890–1921

	1890	1900	1910	1920
Arizona	3,561	7,414	14,623	14,467
California	21,310	24,793	20,393	12,566
Colorado	16,476	22,793	13,477	8,273
Idaho	5,201	6,926	6,155	4,653
Montana	9,795	14,710	14,634	11,958
Nevada	4,844	2,637	9,062	5,406
Utah	3,120	5,624	6,822	5,097
United States	141,047	191,729	191,561	148,847
	1901	1911	1921	
British Columbia	4,694	4,605	2,415	

SOURCE: U.S. and Canadian census data (see note 3).

and in British Columbia (see Table 1.3). Western folklore obscures the fundamental fact that most prospectors discovered only that the probability of locating a bonanza was very low and decreasing all the time. The vast majority of miners in the late nineteenth century were employees earning a daily wage even though, as will be discussed below, some opportunities for independent production persisted.[3]

3. U.S. Census Office, *Report on Population . . . at the Eleventh Census: 1890*, pt. 2 (Washington, 1895), pp. 306–37; idem, *Twelfth Census . . . 1900*, Census Reports, vol. 2: *Population*, pt. 2 (Washington, 1902), pp. 514–45, 506; U.S. Bureau of the Census, *Thirteenth Census . . . 1910*, vol. 4: *Population, 1910, Occupation Statistics* (Washington, 1914), pp. 96–139, 91; idem, *Fourteenth Census . . . 1920*, vol. 4: *Population, 1920, Occupations* (Washington, 1923), pp. 56–111, 35; Canada, Census Office, *Fourth Census . . . 1901*, vol. 2: *Natural Products* (Ottawa, 1904), pp. 384–86; Canada, Census and Statistics Office, *Fifth Census . . . 1911*, vol. 6: *Occupations of the People* (Ottawa, 1915), p. 88; Canada, Dominion Bureau of Statistics, *Sixth Census . . . 1921*, vol. 6: *Occupations*

A diverse mix of first- and second-generation immigrants from northern and western Europe dominated the labor force before 1900. A substantial number came from Cornwall and the rest of England, Ireland, Scotland, Scandinavia, and Germany. By the turn of the century, a new wave of immigration was under way, bringing Italians, Finns, Serbs, and other southern and eastern Europeans into North American metal mining.[4]

Although other ethnic groups helped shape the miners' movement, Cornish immigrants played a unique role. The strong craft heritage of independence on the job which Cornishmen carried with them and imparted to their co-workers constituted a major underlying source of self-activism. Throughout the nineteenth century, a stream of new arrivals from the tin- and copper-producing region of southwestern England brought a wealth of mining knowledge to the western frontier.[5] Underground mining had been carried on in Cornwall since the sixteenth century so that, by the peak of immigration in the late nineteenth century, ore extraction had been a hereditary craft for many

(Ottawa, 1929), p. 816; Vernon H. Jensen, *Heritage of Conflict: Labor Relations in the Nonferrous Metals Industry up to 1930* (Ithaca, 1950), p. 4; Ronald C. Brown, *Hard-Rock Miners: The Intermountain West, 1860–1920* (College Station, Tex., 1979), pp. 99, 101.

4. Robert C. Chambers, "Testimony," Aug. 2, 1899, in U.S. Industrial Commission, *Report*, vol. 12: *Relations and Conditions of Capital and Labor Employed in the Mining Industry* (Washington, 1901), p. 588; U.S. Geological Survey, *Comstock Mining and Miners*, by Eliot Lord (Washington, 1883), pp. 382–86; Jensen, *Heritage of Conflict*, p. 4; Richard E. Lingenfelter, *The Hardrock Miners: A History of the Mining Labor Movement in the American West, 1863–1893* (Berkeley, 1974), pp. 4–7; Elliott West, "Five Idaho Mining Towns: A Computerized Profile," *Pacific Northwest Quarterly* 73 (July 1982): 111–12; Duane A. Smith, "The San Juaner: A Computerized Portrait," *Colorado Magazine* 52 (1975): 140–43; David M. Emmons, "Immigrant Workers and Industrial Hazards: The Irish Miners of Butte, 1880–1919," *Journal of American Ethnic History* 5 (1985): 41; U.S. Census Office, *Statistics of the Population . . . at the Tenth Census*, 1880, (Washington, 1883), p. 735; idem, *Twelfth Census . . . 1900*, vol. 1: *Population, Part I* (Washington, 1901), pp. 736–95; Canada, Census Office, *Fourth Census . . . 1901*, vol. 1: *Population* (Ottawa, 1902), pp. 284–85; H. F. Davis, "Labor in the Mines of Western America," *MSP*, Feb. 1, 1913, pp. 210–11; Thomas A. Michalski, "A Social History of Yugoslav Immigrants in Tonopah and White Pine, Nevada, 1860–1920" (Ph.D. dissertation, State University of New York at Buffalo, 1983), pp. 68, 77; Montana Department of Labor and Industry, *First Biennial Report, 1913–14* (Helena, n.d.), pp. 206–7.

5. John Rowe, *The Hard-Rock Men: Cornish Immigrants and the North American Mining Frontier* (N.p., 1974), pp. 38–296; Arthur C. Todd, *The Cornish Miner in America* (Truro, Eng., 1967); idem, "Cousin Jack in Idaho," *Idaho Yesterdays* 8 (Winter 1964–65): 2–11; William D. Haywood, *Bill Haywood's Book: The Autobiography of William D. Haywood* (New York, 1929), p. 57; Paul, *Mining Frontiers*, pp. 68–69, 122, 128, 180; P. B. McDonald, "The Cornish Miner in America," *MSP*, Sept. 25, 1915, p. 470; Ralph Mann, *After the Gold Rush: Society in Grass Valley and Nevada City, California, 1849–1870* (Stanford, 1982), pp. 142–45.

generations. Cornish expertise was indispensable to the rise of North American mining.[6]

Cornish miners brought with them not only technical knowledge but also traditional craft attitudes and beliefs. In particular, they believed firmly in the superiority of their own understanding of mining:

> Oh, oo's that chap in diggin' clothes,
>   Oo 'andles all tha h'ore;
> An' oo's tha chap oo naws 'is groun',
>   An' naws it all tha moor,
> Tha longer that 'e works un?
>   M'son, jus' listen 'ere,
> E's no bloody h'engineer,
>   But, tell e wot, e's on tha spot,
> An' wot 'e naws, 'e naws e's got,
>   An', dam-me, well e's learned un.[7]

Drawing on lessons taught them by their fathers or brothers and on personal experience, the Cousin Jacks insisted upon autonomy at work. No one was deemed qualified to interfere with "tha chap oo naws 'is groun'." Accordingly, Cornish immigrants did not tolerate direct supervision and refused to work while managers were present. Big Bill Haywood may have gotten his idea that the manager's brains were under the workman's cap from his association with such Cornishmen as Thomas Drew, one of the early leaders of the Silver City Miners' Union. Immigrant mining veterans not only trained new underground workers but also ingrained in them a strong sense of the pride and prerogatives of craftsmanship.[8]

This craft involved the exercise of formidable mental and physical skills. In the early days of the industry, miners customarily determined how to pursue meandering veins of ore through a mountain, which tools and materials to use, what pace of work to maintain, and how to safeguard working conditions. On every shift they made judgments

---

6. Rowe, *Hard-Rock Men*, pp. 2–3; Davis, "Labor in the Mines," p. 210.
7. D. E. Charlton, "The Cornish Miner," *EMJ*, Nov. 16, 1918, p. 889.
8. Raphael Samuel, "Mineral Workers," in Samuel, ed., *Miners, Quarrymen and Saltworkers* (London, 1977), p. 58; Todd, "Cousin Jack in Idaho," p. 6; Haywood, *Bill Haywood's Book*, p. 57; Otis E. Young, Jr., *Black Powder and Hand Steel: Miners and Machines on the Old Western Frontier* (Norman, Okla., 1976), p. 11; P. B. McDonald, "The Cornish Miner," *EMJ*, May 3, 1913, p. 882.

that were never routine because each work situation was unique. Common decisions, such as assessing the stability of the rock "roof" overhead or trouble-shooting a malfunctioning fuse, could mean life or death for the miner and his fellow workers. In the preindustrial era the basic manual tasks were hand drilling, loading the holes with blasting powder, and igniting the charges. The miner spent the largest share of his work time driving a steel drill through solid rock with a four- or eight-pound hammer. Like many other duties, hand drilling required strength and dexterity. Frank Crampton remembered performing this arduous task "from every position, excepting standing on one's head—in all directions—up, down, at an angle, or at one side." In a sense, the mining craftsman created his own workplace by continually blasting out new space, erecting timber roof supports, digging drainage ditches, and doing other maintenance chores. Skilled workers thus controlled the process of producing metal-bearing ores.[9]

Self-employment offered the greatest freedom to control production. Many miners spent time prospecting or running small mines on their own or with partners. Mining activity around Kendall, Montana, included not only several large firms but also "numberless small properties . . . owned by prospectors." In the Lardeau district of British Columbia in 1901, "dozens and dozens of claim owners [were] doing assessment and prospect work." These laborers were, as the *Lardeau Eagle* put it, "creating their own 'capital.'"[10] Although solitary individuals did most prospecting, partnerships and small collectives also carried out a substantial share of this work. As prospects developed, some independent producers became employers. Most, however, continued to function as one-man operations or partnerships, relying on their own labor.[11]

9. Frank A. Crampton, *Deep Enough: A Working Stiff in the Western Mine Camps* (1956; rpt. Norman, Okla., 1982), pp. 22 (quotation), 22–25; Otis E. Young, Jr., *Western Mining* (Norman, Okla., 1970), pp. 178–91; idem, *Black Powder*, pp. 30–40; Brown, *Hard-Rock Miners*, pp. 68–73; Harold Barger and Sam H. Schurr, *The Mining Industries, 1899–1939: A Study of Output, Employment and Productivity* (New York, 1944), p. 119; *MSP*, Dec. 31, 1910, p. 877; Malcolm Ross, *Death of a Yale Man* (New York, 1939), p. 38. Helpful studies of workers' control in the nineteenth century include Montgomery, *Workers' Control in America*, pp. 9–31; and Gregory S. Kealey, *Toronto Workers Respond to Industrial Capitalism, 1867–1892* (Toronto, 1980), pp. 64–82.

10. *Great Falls Daily Tribune* (Mont.), Dec. 4, 1905, p. 3; *Lardeau Eagle* (Ferguson, B.C.), June 27, 1901; *Fergus County Democrat* (Lewistown, Mont.), n.d., rpt. in *Kendall Miner* (Mont.), June 22, 1906; *Paystreak* (Sandon, B.C.), July 12, 1902; *Fairbanks Daily News-Miner* (Alaska), Aug. 26, 1909; *Idaho Avalanche* (Silver City), Jan. 29, June 25, 1897.

11. *Manhattan Post* (Nev.), Dec. 20, 1913, p. 4; *MSP*, Aug. 8, 1896, p. 107; *Great Falls*

The transplantation of Cornish contracting and leasing arrangements also helped foster and sustain a sense of independence. Under the Old World tutwork system, small groups of miners received a fixed payment for the completion of a specified amount of work. Leasing plans under which workers operated a mine or a section thereof and paid a share of their proceeds to the property owner derived from the ancient Cornish practice of tributing.[12]

Lease mining prevailed widely, especially in gold and silver districts. Although lessees often worked alone, with a partner, or in collectives, many were small employers. Yet class lines were not clearly drawn when the leaseholder, often a longtime miner and union member, toiled beside his employees and paid union wages. Lessees at Rawhide, Nevada, in 1908 paid generous wages ranging from $5.50 to $6.50 for eight hours' work.[13] Although miners' unions distrusted contracting because of the ever-present potential for employers to abuse any piecework scheme, they approved of leasing arrangements, which preserved autonomy on the job. For example, during the same week in 1913, Theodore Boak, a leader of WFM Local 26, the Silverton Miners' Union, both organized statewide support for striking coal miners and formed a leasing company to work part of a silver mine. Radicals largely because they loathed proletarianization, socialist miners leased property and employed wage labor.[14]

Daily Tribune, Aug. 29, 1901, p. 8; *Tonopah Bonanza* (Nev.), July 13, 1902; *Tonopah Daily Sun* (Nev.), Feb. 17, 1905, p. 1; *Slocan Drill* (B.C.), July 17, 1903; *Owyhee Avalanche*, May 15, 22, 1903; D. H. Gibson to Anthony Shilland, Aug. 12, 1903, International Union of Mine, Mill and Smelter Workers Papers (hereafter cited as Mine-Mill Papers), box 154, folder 5, Special Collections Division, University of British Columbia Library, Vancouver; *Little Rockies Miner* (Zortman, Mont.), June 26, 1909; *Kendall Miner*, Mar. 2, 1906.

12. Rowe, *Hard-Rock Men*, pp. 5, 200, 204; A. K. H. Jenkin, *The Cornish Miner*, 3d ed. (London, 1962), p. 285; Samuel, "Mineral Workers," pp. 48–49, 57–58. On the transmission of traditional practices of independent coal production from Scotland to Illinois, see John H. M. Laslett, *Nature's Noblemen: The Fortunes of the Independent Collier in Scotland and the American Midwest, 1855–1889* (Los Angeles, 1983), pp. 37–56.

13. W. Fay Boericke, "Rawhide, Nevada," *EMJ*, Mar. 14, 1908, p. 565; Nevada State Inspector of Mines, *Annual Report, 1910* (Carson City, 1911), pp. 20–54; *MSP*, Aug. 5, 1905, p. 100; *Neihart Miner* (Mont.), Sept. 1, 1898; Mark Wyman, *Hard-Rock Epic: Western Miners and the Industrial Revolution, 1860–1910* (Berkeley, 1979), p. 69; *Silverton Weekly Miner* (Colo.), Feb. 12, Sept. 3, 1909; Russell R. Elliott, "Tonopah, Goldfield, Bullfrog Mining Districts, 1900–1915: History of a Twentieth Century Mining Boom" (Ph.D. dissertation, University of California, Berkeley, 1963), p. 20; *San Miguel Examiner* (Telluride, Colo.), Nov. 20, 27, 1897; Thomas A. Rickard, *A History of American Mining* (New York, 1932), p. 56.

14. *MSP*, Aug. 19, 1899, p. 197; George G. Suggs, Jr., "Catalyst for Industrial Change: The WFM, 1893–1904," *Colorado Magazine* 45 (1968): 328–29; Executive Board, IUMMSW,

For most of those involved, prospecting and leasing only periodically complemented wage work, which always predominated. Prospectors generally took to the hills in the summer. Leasers operated when mines otherwise would have shut down because of low metal prices. A few struck it rich and escaped the working class; most eked out a modest existence and remained workers. For example, Neihart, Montana, and its Belt Mountain Miners' Union survived the collapse of silver prices in the 1890s although other silver centers became instant ghost towns. According to WFM organizer John C. Lowney, this local was "maintained intact by the leasers and prospectors, although at times there was not a wage worker in the camp."[15] Leasing kept Slocan, British Columbia, alive in 1904. "Company operation has largely given place to the lease system and the bulk of the wages earned today in the camp are being paid by lessees," observed the *Slocan Drill.* "In this way the people have revealed true independence and the good name of the dry ore belt has not been allowed to suffer."[16] These opportunities for self-employment not only reinforced a sense of self-reliance and self-confidence but also allowed miners to sink roots in a community.

In the late nineteenth and early twentieth centuries, hardrock mining became increasingly industrialized. The aggregate horsepower of metal-mining equipment increased from 171,000 to 1,408,000 between 1889 and 1919. Application first of steam and then of electrical energy to diverse underground operations transformed extractive technology in ways that undermined miners' control of the workplace. In particular, the advent of machine drilling after 1870, coupled with the adoption of dynamite as a blasting agent, brought about a crisis for craft methods of production. Power drills penetrated rock many times faster than did hand drills. Dynamite dislodged far more rock per explosion than did black powder. Combined with contemporaneous advances in ore-milling technology, these innovations led to reliance upon expanded gross output and economies of scale to achieve efficient production. Although innovations spread unevenly through

---

Minute Book, 4:122–23 (May 2, 1919), WFM-IUMMSW Archives, Western Historical Collections, Norlin Library, University of Colorado, Boulder, vol. 4; *Silverton Weekly Miner,* Oct. 25, 1907, June 25, 1909, Dec. 19, 1913; *Neihart Miner,* Feb. 3, 1898; *Rhyolite Daily Bulletin* (Nev.), Apr. 10, 1909; *Manhattan Post,* Jan. 6, 1912, p. 4.

15. J. C. Lowney, "Report from Montana," *MM,* Nov. 1920, p. 1; *Butte Bystander* (Mont.), July 15, 1893, Jan. 27, 1894; *Silverton Weekly Miner,* Dec. 2, 1910.

16. *Slocan Drill,* Jan. 1, 1904; British Columbia Minister of Mines, "Annual Report," 1905, p. J25.

the industry, they had largely superseded more precise but less productive craft methods by the turn of the century.[17]

The new technology devalued many traditional skills. Bill Haywood sardonically observed that "the machine is the apprentice of yesterday, the journeyman of today." Because no comparable technological breakthroughs occurred in ore loading and hauling in this period, the distribution of occupations underground shifted substantially. Before the onset of industrialization, a division of labor had already emerged in all but the smallest mines. Skilled miners drilled and blasted (strictly speaking, only those craftsmen who worked at the face of the mine were considered miners, but I have generally used "miner" to denote any underground mine worker), muckers shoveled broken rock into ore cars, and carmen moved the loaded cars through the mine. The immediate impact of industrialized methods was to increase markedly the proportion of unskilled muckers and carmen and to drive many skilled craftsmen down into unskilled jobs. Freedom on the job deteriorated; direct supervision proliferated. Laborers in particular were pushed harder to keep pace with drilling machines and dynamite.[18]

Metal mining became more capital-intensive. Heavy investment was necessary to purchase and maintain mining and milling equipment, acquire and consolidate claims, and meet other major expenses. Both the sensational success of some entrepreneurs and the general profitability of the industry drew a mob of investors. Metal-mining ventures took in such prominent stockholders as John D. and William Rockefeller, Charles Schwab, E. H. Harriman, and Andrew Mellon. With the infusion of eastern and foreign capital, many new corporations were formed. By the turn of the century these included giant integrated organizations such as the Amalgamated Copper Company (which held the Anaconda Copper Mining Company and much else) and the American Smelting and Refining Company. Absentee ownership became prevalent.[19]

17. U.S. Bureau of the Census, *Historical Statistics*, 1:580; Wyman, *Hard-Rock Epic*, pp. 84–117 and passim; Young, *Western Mining*, pp. 204–17; Paul, *Mining Frontiers*, pp. 64–68.

18. William D. Haywood, "Bell Signals," *MM*, June 29, 1905, p. 7; idem, *Bill Haywood's Book*, p. 80; Barger and Schurr, *Mining Industries*, pp. 115, 123–25, 130; Job Harriman, *The Class War in Idaho*, 3d ed. (New York, 1900), p. 3; D. E. Livingston-Little, "The Bunker Hill and Sullivan: North Idaho's Mining Development from 1885 to 1900," *Idaho Yesterdays* 7 (1963): 38; J. Cameron to Editor, Oct. 4, 1909, *MM*, Oct. 21, 1909, p. 11; Crampton, *Deep Enough*, p. 22.

19. Richard H. Peterson, *The Bonanza Kings: The Social Origins and Business Behavior of Western Mining Entrepreneurs, 1870–1900* (Lincoln, Neb., 1977), pp. 87–137; Michael

Investors reaped handsome rewards from metal mining. Despite inevitable risks and wild fluctuations in demand for some commodities, the average rate of return on mining capital in this period generally exceeded those for other North American industries. The Payne mine at Sandon, British Columbia, in 1898 alone produced net profits of $1.2 million on a capitalization of $1 million. From his office back in Pittsburgh, Thomas B. McKaig of the Trade Dollar Consolidated Mining Company kept his mine manager in Silver City, Idaho, apprised of the latest financial results. On May 14, 1898, McKaig crowed, "We have deposited in the bank here since April 1st, $159,123.57, and if that is not turning out money fast, nothing is." The mines of Park City, Utah, paid cumulative dividends of more than $5 million in 1901 and 1902. When the Bunker Hill and Sullivan Mining and Concentrating Company of Idaho paid its 177th dividend in June 1912, it had paid investors over $13 million on their aggregate investment of slightly more than $3 million. Although these examples are somewhat atypical in their extravagance, large surpluses were common.[20] These profits not only facilitated further technological progress but also armed capitalists with ample resources for dominating their employees economically and politically.

Hardrock miners responded to the burgeoning strength of capital by organizing unions. In the half-century after 1863, these organizations evolved through two stages. Commencing with the formation of local unions in the 1860s, workers first built a decentralized movement that was almost entirely defensive. The Western Federation of

P. Malone, *The Battle for Butte: Mining and Politics on the Northern Frontier, 1864–1906* (Seattle, 1981); Isaac F. Marcosson, *Anaconda* (New York, 1957), pp. 78–110; idem, *Metal Magic: The Story of the American Smelting and Refining Company* (New York, 1949), pp. 57–83 and passim; Clark C. Spence, *British Investments and the American Mining Frontier, 1860–1901* (Ithaca, 1958), pp. 219–20 and passim; Duane A. Smith, *Song of the Hammer and Drill: The Colorado San Juans, 1860–1914* (Golden, Colo., 1982), p. 98; James E. Fell, Jr., "Rockefeller's Right-Hand Man: Frederick T. Gates and the Northwestern Mining Investments," *Business History Review* 52 (1978): 537–61; *EMJ*, Feb. 20, 1897, p. 194, Mar. 22, 1913, p. 631, Dec. 26, 1908, pp. 1242–44; H. H. Langton, *James Douglas, A Biography* (Toronto, 1940), pp. 87–101.

20. Thomas B. McKaig to James Hutchinson, May 14, 1898, Trade Dollar Consolidated Mining Company Papers, box 3, Idaho State Historical Society, Boise; *Owyhee Avalanche*, Feb. 25, 1898; U.S. Bureau of the Census, *Fourteenth Census, 1920*, vol. 11: *Mines and Quarries, 1919* (Washington, 1922), p. 364; James R. Kluger, *The Clifton-Morenci Strike: Labor Difficulty in Arizona, 1915–1916* (Tucson, 1970), pp. 78, 24; *MSP*, Feb. 11, 1899, p. 147; *Park Record* (Park City, Utah), Dec. 27, 1902; *EMJ*, June 15, 1912, p. 1171; *Weekly Missoulian* (Missoula, Mont.), May 28, 1886.

Miners, however, went beyond a purely reactive opposition to employers' encroachments on wage standards and job autonomy. The WFM sought to expand workers' independence through cooperative projects that, union activists believed, planted seeds of socialism in mining communities. Underlying this movement was the fundamental assumption that independence for workers in industrial society primarily meant freedom from dictation by employers. Further, organized miners assumed that they could achieve true independence only by collective effort and interdependence.

The metal-mining labor movement began in the Comstock Lode of Nevada. The first significant union arose in 1864, when the silver workers of Gold Hill and Virginia City organized the Miners' League of Storey County. Threatened with a wage cut, the Nevada miners mounted the first strike in western mining. Their success preserved the $4 daily wage for all underground workers and put hardrock unionism on a solid footing.[21]

The Comstock pioneers set the pattern for the pre-WFM movement. Because chronic overproduction continually forced down metals prices in a highly competitive world market, operators frequently attempted to cut wages. Like most nineteenth-century North American unions, the western miners' organizations generally contested neither the implementation of new technology nor its control but rather the distribution of its fruits. Many, if not most, hardrock unions were organized in reaction to a wage cut or the imminent threat of one. Indeed, the primary function of virtually all early unions was to defend wage standards.[22]

The Comstock organizations insisted upon taking in all underground workers, rather than restricting membership to skilled craftsmen. This industrial unionism was prototypical, as was the concomitant egalitarian wage policy. As technological development forced more miners into less-skilled positions, their unions clung tenaciously to the principle of equal pay for all underground employees.[23] In ad-

21. Lingenfelter, *Hardrock Miners*, pp. 33–37; U.S. Geological Survey, *Comstock Mining and Miners*, pp. 182–87.

22. Irwin Yellowitz, *Industrialization and the American Labor Movement, 1850–1900* (Port Washington, N.Y., 1977), pp. 63–94; Lingenfelter, *Hardrock Miners*, pp. 39–65, 131–34, 157–68; Robert Randall, "Advises the Organization of a State Union," *MM*, Apr. 16, 1908, p. 7.

23. Lingenfelter, *Hardrock Miners*, pp. 44–45, 50, 84–88; U.S. Geological Survey, *Comstock Mining and Miners*, pp. 267–68.

dition, the Nevada organizations placed a strong emphasis on mutual benefit programs.[24] The migration of Comstock miners and their organizing efforts spread this model of unionism throughout the region. Numerous far-flung groups copied the Gold Hill and Virginia City constitutions practically verbatim.[25]

The organized miners played a prominent role in community development. Comstock unions contributed substantially to underwriting the erection of St. Mary's Hospital in Virginia City in the mid-1870s. Miners built large halls that commonly became the center of community social life. Union halls hosted theatrical and musical performances, government and other public meetings, church services, and educational programs. For many years the Virginia City Miners' Union library was both the only public library in the city and the largest collection of books in the state.[26] The culture of the workers' movement thus emphasized self-improvement and community involvement.

In the 1880s, Butte, Montana, site of an enormous copper boom, became the leading stronghold of hardrock unionism. By 1885 the Butte Miners' Union, with roughly eighteen hundred members, was the largest metal-miners' body in North America. Following the path broken by the Comstock organizations, this self-proclaimed "Gibraltar of Unionism" defended a uniform wage for all underground workers, won the closed shop, and administered disability and death benefits. Striving to build a broad labor movement in the northern Rockies, the Butte union and its former members organized numerous mining camps in Montana and Idaho, kept close ties with the Knights of Labor, and led the campaign to found the WFM. By 1893 this organization had over forty-six hundred members, making it the largest local union in the United States.[27]

---

24. Lingenfelter, *Hardrock Miners*, pp. 38, 51–52, 133; Jensen, *Heritage of Conflict*, pp. 13–14.

25. Paul, *Mining Frontiers*, pp. 70, 94; U.S. Geological Survey, *Comstock Mining and Miners*, p. 355; Jensen, *Heritage of Conflict*, p. 17; Lingenfelter, *Hardrock Miners*, pp. 85, 128, 131, 133; Mann, *After the Gold Rush*, p. 184.

26. Lingenfelter, *Hardrock Miners*, pp. 52–54, 131, 133, 185–87; Robert W. Smith, *The Coeur d'Alene Mining War of 1892* (Corvallis, Ore., 1961), p. 16; *Neihart Herald* (Mont.), July 17, Sept. 11, 18, 1891; *Territorial Enterprise* (Virginia City, Nev.), Dec. 23, 1877.

27. Lingenfelter, *Hardrock Miners*, pp. 132, 182–95; *Butte Daily Miner*, Mar. 8, 1889; Butte *Daily Inter Mountain*, Jan. 20, 1890, Apr. 11, 1891; *Butte Bystander*, July 21, 1894; Clancy Miners' Union (Mont., Local 30), Minute Book, p. 2 (Oct. 24, 1894), Small

The miners' union maintained a strong presence in Butte. In addition to operating its hall and library and leading lengthy, all-too-frequent funeral processions, the organization celebrated the anniversary of its founding, June 13, with all-out festivities. Miners' Union Day was a general holiday in the district. The proud membership customarily paraded through the city in a body, accompanied by flags and banners, marching bands, and delegations from other labor bodies. The parade was followed by an outpouring of florid oratory and a long night of dancing.[28] For many years, local hardrock unions throughout Montana celebrated this day. In Utah, June 13 became a statewide miners' holiday, on which union members and supporters converged on Salt Lake City for a parade, speeches, drilling matches, and other contests. In 1906, 1,150 people from Park City made the excursion to the Salt Palace. Seizing an opportunity to weed out union sympathizers, Utah Copper Company discharged 200 employees who had been absent from its Bingham Canyon operations on June 13, 1904.[29]

In May 1893, delegates from fifteen local groups in Colorado, Idaho, Montana, South Dakota, and Utah met in Butte to found the Western Federation of Miners. Recognizing that operators were growing ever more powerful and well organized, the hardrock workers united to defend wages, hours, working conditions, and other basic concerns. By stronger organization they hoped to prevent recurrence of the stinging defeat suffered by Coeur d'Alene miners the previous year in a bitter battle over a wage cut. After barely surviving the 1893 depression and its own internal difficulties, the WFM grew dramatically from the late 1890s up to 1911, reaching a peak of approximately fifty thousand members. In 1916 the union changed its name to the

Collection 270, folder 1, Montana Historical Society, Helena; Lem Kelly, T. H. Cole, and J. C. Duffy (Local 4) to Editor, Dec. 29, 1899, *MM*, Feb. 1900, pp. 28–29; Smith, *Coeur d'Alene War*, p. 14; WFM, *Official Proceedings of the Eleventh Annual Convention, 1903* (Denver, 1903), p. 17; Malone, *Battle for Butte*, pp. 76–77.

28. *Butte Daily Miner*, Oct. 8, 1889, June 14, 1887; Butte *Daily Inter Mountain*, Jan. 20, 1890; *Butte Bystander*, June 16, 1894.

29. *Neihart Herald*, May 28, 1892; *Great Falls Daily Tribune*, June 4, 1896, p. 1, June 11, 1902, p. 4, June 13, 1914, p. 3; *Little Rockies Miner*, July 4, 1907; Clancy Miners' Union, Minute Book, p. 49 (Apr. 30, 1895), Small Collection 270, folder 1; *Park Record*, June 18, 1904, May 12, June 16, 1906; *Tonopah Miner*, June 18, 1904; Bingham Miners' Union (Utah, Local 67), Minute Book, 2:4 (June 1, 1907), WFM and IUMMSW Records, box 2, Labor-Management Documentation Center, Catherwood Library, New York State School of Industrial and Labor Relations, Cornell University, Ithaca.

International Union of Mine, Mill and Smelter Workers (IUMMSW or Mine-Mill), in recognition of both its expansion beyond the West and its increasing efforts to organize workers in metallurgical plants.[30]

Although many locals were short-lived in this highly volatile industry, individuals often had a long-standing involvement with unionism. Because a large share of unionists migrated from boom camp to boom camp, Comstock and WFM veterans were everywhere in the West.[31] Further, many activists had belonged to miners' assemblies of the Knights of Labor. One union stalwart in British Columbia claimed in 1902 that "there are thousands of old line K. of L.'s in the W. F. of M."[32]

The Western Federation of Miners was, as Selig Perlman and Philip Taft put it, "the most militant [union] in the history of the United States." From its inception, local and district affiliates engaged in violent confrontations with employers. Disputes over ordinary labor-management issues repeatedly escalated into class war. Gunfights, dynamitings, declarations of martial law, vigilante actions, and whole-sale arrests and deportations occurred in numerous strikes and lock-outs. For instance, after strikebreakers and sheriff's deputies killed a union miner at Telluride, Colorado, on July 3, 1901, about 250 strikers shot it out with them for two hours. The battle left two dead and six wounded. When the strikebreakers finally surrendered, they were run out of the district. Just two years later the same local waged a protracted strike over ore-mill workers' hours that was ruthlessly broken by strikebreakers, the state militia, civilian authorities, and vigilantes. Although violent encounters were the exception, their fre-

30. WFM, "Proceedings of the First Annual Convention," 1893, p. 3, microfilm, Labor Collection, Graduate Social Science Library, University of California, Berkeley; Lingenfelter, *Hardrock Miners*, pp. 219–28; Leo Wolman, *Ebb and Flow in Trade Unionism* (New York, 1936), pp. 172–73, 192. In 1967 the IUMMSW merged into the United Steelworkers of America.

31. John E. Brinley, Jr., "The Western Federation of Miners" (Ph.D. dissertation, University of Utah, 1972), pp. 212–24; Jensen, *Heritage of Conflict*, pp. 2, 289, 355, 17–18; James C. Foster, "The Ten Day Tramps," *Labor History* 23 (1982): 608–23.

32. Lem Kelly, T. H. Cole, and J. C. Duffy (Local 4) to Editor, Dec. 22, 1899, *MM*, Feb. 1900, p. 28; "Slocan" to Editor, n.d., *MM*, Apr. 1902, p. 31; Bryan D. Palmer, *Working-Class Experience: The Rise and Reconstitution of Canadian Labour, 1800–1980* (Toronto, 1983), pp. 104, 179; Smith, *Song of the Hammer and Drill*, p. 59; Haywood, *Bill Haywood's Book*, pp. 63, 71; Jonathon Garlock, *Guide to the Local Assemblies of the Knights of Labor* (Westport, Conn., 1982), pp. 29, 33, 514; Jensen, *Heritage of Conflict*, p. 18; Wyman, *Hard-Rock Epic*, pp. 165–66.

quency nonetheless distinguished this industry and helped set the tone for industrial relations.[33] At the other extreme, in districts where the ore was rich and the mining companies were small, relations generally remained tranquil. In most locals, rudimentary collective bargaining (usually without formal contracts) channeled conflict over wages, hours, working conditions, and union rights.[34]

Miners prepared for militant action by creating strong locals. Many WFM affiliates were tightly organized, some maintaining strict union camps. The Belt Mountain Miners' Union proudly reported that only "good union men" worked in its jurisdiction. An editorial in the *Miners' Magazine* in 1903 praised the Silver City local as a stronghold: "The membership of No. 66 is always determined by the number of men employed." The Sandon Miners' Union also had its district completely organized. "We mean to keep it that way," swore the Press Committee of Local 81 in 1901.[35]

Miners built grassroots strength by various methods. Some locals used the threat of ostracism, placing nonmembers on a formal "scab

33. Selig Perlman and Philip Taft, *History of Labor in the United States, 1896–1932*, vol. 4: *Labor Movements* (New York, 1935), pp. 172–73 (quotation), 169–207; Jensen, *Heritage of Conflict*, pp. 25–53, 58–59, 72–95, 118–59, 219–35; Melvyn Dubofsky, "The Origins of Western Working Class Radicalism, 1890–1905," *Labor History* 7 (1966): 133–39; Suggs, "Catalyst for Industrial Change," pp. 328–30; idem, *Colorado's War on Militant Unionism: James H. Peabody and the Western Federation of Miners* (Detroit, 1972), pp. 118–45; Russell R. Elliott, "Labor Troubles at Goldfield, Nevada, 1906–1908," *Pacific Historical Review* 19 (1950): 369–84; James C. Foster, "Quantification and the Western Federation," *Historical Methods Newsletter* 10 (1977): 143.

34. *Owyhee Avalanche*, Feb. 25, 1898; *Lardeau Eagle*, Apr. 26, 1901, Jan. 1, 1904; Elliott, "Tonopah, Goldfield," p. 167; *Silverton Weekly Miner*, Mar. 6, 1903, July 12, 19, 1907; *Butte Bystander*, Apr. 27, 1894, p. 4; Charles E. Mahoney (Executive Board), Report, in WFM, *Official Proceedings of the Thirteenth Annual Convention, 1905* (Denver, 1905), pp. 246–48; idem, "Report of Acting President Mahoney," in WFM, *Official Proceedings of the Fifteenth Annual Convention, 1907*, Stenographic Report (N.p., n.d.), p. 33; *MM*, May 1903, p. 37; *Tonopah Sun*, June 22, 1907, Sept. 18, 1909; *Park Record*, Nov. 3, Dec. 15, 22, 29, 1906, Jan. 5, 1907; Great Falls Mill and Smeltermen's Union (Mont., Local 16), Minute Book, 4:230 (Mar. 12, 1907), WFM-IUMMSW Archives, vol. 244; *Seven Troughs Miner* (Vernon, Nev.), Apr. 11, 1908. Richard Peterson and James Foster have made apt criticisms of the preoccupation with spectacular struggles in a few localities. See Peterson, *Bonanza Kings*, pp. 66–86; Foster, "Quantification and the Western Federation," pp. 141–48.

35. Neihart No. 7, "Neihart Notes," *MM*, Jan. 1900, p. 33; [John M. O'Neill], Editorial, *MM*, Oct. 8, 1903, p. 5; Press Committee, No. 81, to Editor, Aug. 10, 1901, *MM*, Sept. 1901, p. 31; Thomas D. Tobin (Local 62) to Editor, Apr. 5, 1901, *MM*, May 1901, pp. 32–33; Press Committee, No. 63 (Telluride, Colo.), "Telluride Tidings," *MM*, Sept. 1901, pp. 40–41; *Great Falls Daily Tribune*, Mar. 27, 1902, p. 3; *Kendall Miner*, Dec. 21, 1906; Marion W. Moor, "Report," in WFM, *Proceedings, 1907*, p. 146; Fred G. Clough (Executive Board), "Report," *MM*, Nov. 26, 1908, p. 10.

list." Some deployed rank-and-file committees to enforce the union camp. In Silver City in 1897, Local 66 sent a committee "to wait on Mr. Deckert [and] give him 30 days to join the Union or leave the camp." The Greenwater Miners' Union claimed that "every member is a walking delegate and does his duty." Much recruiting was assigned to one of the union's officers. Joe Langford, walking delegate for the Park City local, brought in 120 new members during a single week in 1903, raising the organization's membership to a thousand.[36]

Fraternalism flourished in the WFM. Union halls remained the center of community social life, hosting concerts, lectures, religious services, and other events. The miners of Silverton, Colorado, spent over $35,000 on their building and dedicated it with two days of festivities. The Slocan Miners' Union opened its new hall with a concert at which union members performed songs, including one by Joe Purviance that reportedly "was a soul stirrer and nearly caused the collapse of the building."[37] Numerous locals maintained libraries.[38]

36. Silver City Miners' Union, Minute Book, pp. 138 (Aug. 2, 1897) (quotation), 141 (Aug. 9, 1897), 194–95 (Dec. 6, 1897), 203 (Dec. 25, 1897), Silver City Miners' Union Records, vol. 1, Bancroft Library, University of California, Berkeley; W. H. Culp (Local 207) to Editor, Feb. 2, 1907, *MM*, Feb. 14, 1907, p. 12; Central Executive Miners' Union of Coeur d'Alene, "By-Laws for Local Unions," *Constitution, By-Laws, Order of Business and Rules of Order* (Wallace, Ida., 1895), pp. 17–18; D. B. O'Neail (secretary, Local 62) to Editor, n.d., *MM*, Dec. 1901, p. 40; *Park Record*, Aug. 15, 1903; Great Falls Mill and Smeltermen's Union, Minute Book, 1:38 (Sept. 22, 1898), 48–49 (Oct. 22, 1898), WFM-IUMMSW Archives, vol. 241; Lead City Miners' Union, Minute Book, pp. 778–84 (Feb. 11–22, 1901), ibid., reel 53; C. W. Goodale to Frank Klepetko, Oct. 29, 1898, Anaconda Copper Mining Company Records, box 209, file 585–1, Montana Historical Society, Helena; *Great Falls Daily Tribune*, May 14, 1901, p. 8, May 15, 1901, p. 8, Aug. 3, 1906, p. 8, Aug. 4, 1906, pp. 2, 8.

37. *Slocan Drill*, Nov. 29, 1901; *Neihart Herald*, July 17, Sept. 11, 1891; Press Committee, "Sandon Miners' Union, No. 81, W.F.M.," *MM*, Dec. 1900, pp. 30–31; *Weekly News* (Nelson, B.C.), Mar. 6, 1911, p. 3; *Lardeau Eagle*, Mar. 6, 1902; *Goldfield News* (Nev.), Oct. 27, 1906; *Rhyolite Herald*, Nov. 24, 1905; *News-Record* (Terry, S.D.), Jan. 26, 1906; Lucile Berg, "A History of the Tonopah Area and Adjacent Region of Central Nevada, 1827–1941" (M.A. thesis, University of Nevada, Reno, 1942), p. 150; "Veritas" to Editor, Sept. 28, 1901, *MM*, Oct. 1901, pp. 34–36; *Park Record*, Jan. 3, 1903; *Silverton Weekly Miner*, Oct. 17, Dec. 12, 1903, Sept. 27, 1907, p. 53; *Fairbanks Daily Times* (Alaska), Mar. 1, 11, 1908.

38. *Phillipsburg Mail* (Mont.), n.d., rpt. in *Coeur d'Alene Miner* (Wallace, Ida.), Jan. 30, 1892, p. 6; *Butte Bystander*, Nov. 13, 1897, p. 5; Elizabeth Jameson, "Imperfect Unions: Class and Gender in Cripple Creek, 1894–1904," in Milton Cantor and Bruce Laurie, eds., *Class, Sex, and the Woman Worker* (Westport, Conn., 1977), p. 178; *Neihart Herald*, Feb. 12, 1892; *Tonopah Bonanza*, June 25, 1904; *Arizona Silver Belt* (Globe), Jan. 12, 1908, p. 6; U.S. Senate, *A Report on Labor Disturbances in the State of Colorado from 1880 to 1904 Inclusive*, 58th Cong., 3d sess., Senate Document 122 (Washington, 1905), p. 43; WFM, *Constitution and By-Laws*, 1896 (Butte, n.d.), p. 22; *Reese River Reveille* (Austin, Nev.), Feb. 11, 1911; Emma Langdon, "Anaconda's Activity," *MM*, Jan. 13, 1910, p. 8.

Like the anniversary of the founding of the Butte organization, Labor Day became a major holiday. Miners celebrated with parades, speeches, hand drilling contests, baseball games, and fireworks. The local in Jackson, California, fined members who lacked a good excuse for not marching in its parade.[39] Unions also took Independence Day and other holidays as opportunities to hold social events open to the general public.[40]

Along with incomplete proletarianization and fraternalism, a thoroughgoing radicalism helped to lay the groundwork for self-help in health matters. Believing that neither "pure and simple" unionism nor traditional political forces could check the growth of corporate power, the Western Federation experimented with cooperative economic enterprises and anticapitalist political activism. In their analysis of industrializing capitalism and in their attempts to create viable alternatives to it, the organized miners conceived independence in collective, and increasingly in class, terms.

The radical pursuit of political and economic independence held a special meaning for the Irish immigrants and their sons, who constituted perhaps the largest ethnic group within the mining work force in the decades up to 1910 and who dominated the leadership of early hardrock unions.[41] Throughout the late nineteenth century, these immigrants to the mining frontier followed closely and supported fervently the intertwined movements for Irish home rule and the expropriation of English landlords. When, for example, Michael Davitt of the Land League died in 1906, the WFM Executive Board hailed his exemplary life as "one long, ceaseless battle against wrong and oppression." This protracted struggle for self-determination shaped

39. *DeLamar Lode* (Delamar, Nev.), Sept. 2, 1902; Lead City Miners' Union (Local 2), Minute Book, p. 308 (July 18, 1894), WFM-IUMMSW Archives, reel 53; *San Miguel Examiner*, Sept. 3, 10, 1898, Sept. 12, 1903; *Kendall Miner*, Sept. 7, 1906; *Slocan Drill*, Sept. 5, 1902; *Little Rockies Miner*, Aug. 15, 1907; *Vernon Review* (Nev.), Aug. 31, 1907; *Rawhide Press-Times* (Nev.), Sept. 10, 1909; Jackson Miners' Union (Local 115), *Constitution and By-Laws*, 1903 (N.p., n.d.), p. 15.

40. *San Miguel Examiner*, Dec. 4, 25, 1897; *Seven Troughs Miner*, May 7, 1910; *Reese River Reveille*, Mar. 12, 1910; *Manhattan News* (Nev.), Mar. 10, 1907; *Goldfield News*, June 23, 1906. On diverse Independence Day celebrations by immigrant workers in Worcester, Massachusetts, in the late nineteenth century, see Roy Rosenzweig, *Eight Hours for What We Will: Workers and Leisure in an Industrial City, 1870–1920* (New York, 1983), pp. 65–90.

41. U.S. Census Office, *Tenth Census, 1880*, 1:735; U.S. Geological Survey, *Comstock Mining and Miners*, p. 383; Montana Department of Labor and Industry, *Report, 1913–14*, pp. 206–7; Emmons, "Immigrant Workers," p. 41; Lingenfelter, *Hardrock Miners*, pp. 6–7 and passim; West, "Five Idaho Mining Towns," p. 112.

the political and economic values and aspirations of Irishmen in North American mining centers.[42]

Western Federation leaders vigorously denounced the threat posed by the widening disparity between employers' and workers' power. In his report to the convention of 1897, Irish native Edward Boyce lamented the subservience resulting from the emergence of "vast combinations and corporations." "The American working man is no longer a sovereign," Boyce claimed, "he is a dependent supplicant, on bended knee, before the wealth he has created, but may not enjoy." Four years later, he concluded that exploitation precluded independence "because the wealth produced by [workers] is in the possession of those who are resisting their demands, and will be used to hold them in their present state of bondage."[43]

Miners contended that the wealth they had created was used against them through employers' domination of the political process and the government. Like other radical groups, the WFM frequently invoked the Declaration of Independence to protest the unresponsiveness of the state to workers' interests. In a 1903 appeal for funds to agitate for the eight-hour day, Boyce's successor, Charles Moyer, and Secretary-Treasurer Bill Haywood drew on the Declaration:

> The man who reads and thinks no longer entertains the opinion that there can be permanent peace and harmony between the capitalist and the laboring man, under an industrial system that demands profit at the expense of "life, liberty and the pursuit of happiness." The document of national liberty, the federal constitution and the organic law of every state of the Union seem to be helpless in placing the strong arm of protection around the rights and liberties of that great army of men and

42. Executive Board, WFM, Minute Book, 1:366–67 (June 15, 1906), WFM-IUMMSW Archives, vol. 1; [Michael Davitt], "Davitt on Imperialism," *MM*, Mar. 1902, pp. 49–51; Eric Foner, *Politics and Ideology in the Age of the Civil War* (New York, 1980), pp. 171, 176, 200; *Butte Daily Miner*, July 4, 1889, p. 1; Emmons, "Immigrant Workers," pp. 43–44. For useful discussions of the broad influence of Irish liberation movements on Irish immigrant workers in the United States, see Foner, *Politics and Ideology*, pp. 150–200; David Montgomery, *Beyond Equality: Labor and the Radical Republicans, 1862–1872* (New York, 1967), pp. 126–34.

43. Edward Boyce, "President Boyce's Report," *Butte Bystander*, May 15, 1897, p. 1; idem, "President's Report," in WFM, *Official Proceedings of the Ninth Annual Convention, 1901* (Pueblo, Colo., 1901), pp. 9–10; William D. Haywood to Officers and Delegates, May 24, 1906, in WFM, *Official Proceedings of the Fourteenth Annual Convention, 1906* (Denver, 1906), p. 19.

women who are camped on the industrial field, waging a ceaseless battle
for the right to exist.

The ease with which mine operators summoned the militia and blocked
labor legislation particularly galled western miners.[44]

Believing that only fundamental changes could prevent the rise of
a full-blown plutocracy, WFM leaders and rank-and-file activists became ardent supporters of radical political groups. In the United States,
hardrock miners were active in the Populist party in the 1890s and in
the Socialist party of America after 1900. In Canada, they successively
backed independent labor tickets, the British Columbia Socialist party,
the Socialist party of British Columbia, and the Socialist party of Canada.[45]

The Western Federation convention of 1902 officially endorsed socialism, urging members to "commence immediately the organization
of the Socialist movement in their respective towns and states, and
to co-operate in every way for the furtherance of the principles of
Socialism and the Socialist party." In the floor debate over this proposal, delegate John M. O'Neill amalgamated the Declaration of Independence and the Gettysburg Address to legitimate socialism. "The
government of the people, by the people and for the people has been
supplanted by government by injunction, which annuls the Declaration of Independence," raged O'Neill. "Socialism has written a declaration of independence which will gather together the scattered

44. Charles H. Moyer and William D. Haywood, "The Western Federation of Miners'
Appeal for an Eight-Hour Fund," July 11, 1903, Mine-Mill Papers, box 154, folder 4;
Salt Lake Tribune, n.d., rpt. in *Coeur d'Alene Miner*, Mar. 18, 1893, p. 5; Philip S. Foner,
ed., *We the Other People: Alternative Declarations of Independence by Labor Groups, Farmers,
Woman's Rights Advocates, Socialists, and Blacks, 1829–1975* (Urbana, Ill., 1976). On mining
capitalists' domination of Idaho's government, see Wyman, *Hard-Rock Epic*, pp. 191–
94, 220–22.

45. Dubofsky, "Origins of Western Working Class Radicalism," pp. 139–53; John H.
M. Laslett, *Labor and the Left: A Study of Socialist and Radical Influences in the American
Labor Movement, 1881–1924* (New York, 1970), pp. 244–46; *Neihart Herald*, Sept. 17, 1892;
Neihart Miner (Mont.), Sept. 15, 1898; *San Miguel Examiner*, Sept. 3, 1898; Stanley S.
Phipps, "From Bull Pen to Bargaining Table: The Tumultuous Struggle of the Coeur
d'Alene Miners for the Right to Organize, 1887–1942" (Ph.D. dissertation, University
of Idaho, 1983), pp. 68–78; A. Ross McCormack, *Reformers, Rebels, and Revolutionaries:
The Western Canadian Radical Movement, 1899–1919* (Toronto, 1977), pp. 18–34, 62–63;
Carlos A. Schwantes, *Radical Heritage: Labor, Socialism, and Reform in Washington and
British Columbia, 1885–1917* (Seattle, 1979), pp. 109, 121–22, 127–32, 182–83; Sandon
Paystreak, Sept. 22, 29, Oct. 6, 1900; J. A. Foley (Local 62) to Editor, n.d., *MM*, July
1901, pp. 33–34; David S. Ryan to Editor, Feb. 5, 1905, *MM*, Mar. 9, 1905, p. 12.

shreds of liberty and Lincolns would spring up in its defense."[46] If emancipation from wage slavery was indeed the issue, then only a radical approach would suffice.

In implementing this socialist policy, the locals forged a strategy of self-liberation. The predominant ideological tendency of this strategy was very clearly parliamentarian. Writing under the pen name "John Brown," a member of the Goldfield Miners' Union urged his comrades to help themselves: "We have had sufficient [sic] of the friends of the laboring man, we have got to become our own friends; we have got to depend upon ourselves, we have got to vote for ourselves." Accordingly, WFM socialists ran for local, state, and provincial political offices. A few won. Especially in British Columbia, where the commitment to electoral politics ran deepest, miners registered voters, raised funds, and seized educational opportunities offered by socialist campaigns.[47]

Generally quite nebulous and eclectic, miners' ideas of socialism emphasized equality and, of course, an end to economic exploitation. Thomas McCloughlin of Local 193 in Fairbanks, Alaska, declared that the movement aimed to "take and hold all the sources of wealth in America for the purpose of establishing a Co-operative Commonwealth where each man and woman shall have an equal independent right to the full proceeds of their labor." Former miner Ross Moudy illuminated the moderate nature of politics in the Cripple Creek district. "Every bill that passes the Legislature or that is presented to the

46. WFM, *Official Proceedings of the Tenth Annual Convention, 1902* (Denver, 1902), pp. 101 (endorsement quotation), 68 (O'Neill quotation), 100–104.

47. "John Brown" to Editor, June 13, 1906, *MM*, June 28, 1906, p. 13; *Slocan Drill*, Sept. 18, Oct. 9, 1903, Nov. 18, 1904; *Silverton Weekly Miner*, Nov. 14, 1902, Sept. 21, 1906; Vincent St. John, "A Challenge," *MM*, Nov. 1902, p. 47; *Manhattan Post*, Oct. 29, 1910; Schwantes, *Radical Heritage*, p. 179; Phipps, "Bull Pen," p. 74; Malone, *Battle for Butte*, pp. 208–9; Jerry Calvert, "The Rise and Fall of Socialism in a Company Town, 1902–1905," *Montana* 36 (Autumn 1986): 2–13; WFM, *Proceedings, 1907*, p. 372; *Lardeau Eagle*, Dec. 12, 1902; William Davidson to Officers and Members of Sandon Miners' Union, Dec. 19, 1904, Mine-Mill Papers, box 155, folder 11; George F. Dougherty (Local 22) to A. Shilland, July 22, 1903, ibid., box 154, folder 4; D. B. O'Neail (Local 62) to A. Shilland, Oct. 21, 1904, and J. H. Wilkinson to A. Shilland, Oct. 26, 1904, ibid., box 155, folder 9; "Subscription," Nov. 5, 1904, ibid., folder 10; Nelson *Weekly News*, Oct. 30, 1909. Of course, hardrock miners held diverse political views, and to determine precisely the proportions who were socialists and nonsocialists is beyond the scope of this study. See Alfred Parr (secretary-treasurer, District 6) to Officers and Members of Ymir Miners' Union, Jan. 2, 1902, Mine-Mill Papers, box 152, folder 10; *Lardeau Eagle*, Aug. 7, 1903; *Owyhee Avalanche*, June 3, 1898, Sept. 12, 1902; Wyman, *Hard-Rock Epic*, pp. 250–52; Laslett, *Labor and the Left*, pp. 267–68.

Legislature is read in the union and discussed, and if they are not satisfactory to the union they call upon their representatives to work against it," he observed. "Most of the union men are socialists, but they believe the change will come about gradually and not by revolution." Although reformism remained the dominant strain throughout this period, revolutionary syndicalism did attract a significant following among the most frustrated miners.[48]

Grassroots organizations emphasized political education during the formative years around 1900. The Silverton, Colorado, Socialist party, dominated by WFM Local 26, maintained in 1903 that its "first object is the education of the people." Joe Purviance of Slocan reported that the members of his branch of the Canadian Socialist League were "trying to enlighten one another on the important questions of the day." To this end, unions in British Columbia bought loads of socialist literature to pass the winters.[49]

Hardrock miners sponsored socialist lectures, debates, lyceum courses, and other propaganda activities.[50] Visiting speakers included WFM officials, party leaders, and other rabble-rousers.[51] Appearing at a Socialist party meeting in Park City, Mother Jones "talked Socialism straight from the shoulder" and "roasted President Roosevelt mildly, together with the existing government generally." Eugene Debs's supporters jammed the Sandon Miners' Union hall for his lecture "Unionism and Socialism" in 1902. The tireless J. Stitt Wilson gave Local 26 a sermon titled "The Impending Social Revolution, or the Trust Problem Solved."[52] John O'Neill, editor of the *Miners' Maga-*

---

48. Thomas McCloughlin to Editor, Oct. 1, 1907, *Tanana Miner* (Chena, Alaska), Oct. 7, 1907; Ross B. Moudy, "The Story of a Cripple Creek Miner," *Independent*, Aug. 18, 1904, p. 382; Wyman, *Hard-Rock Epic*, pp. 232–42.

49. *Silverton Weekly Miner*, Mar. 13, 1903; Joseph V. Purviance to Editor, n.d., *MM*, Feb. 1902, p. 35; *Slocan Drill*, April 6, 1900, Oct. 11, 1901; *MM*, Jan. 1902, p. 42; Press Committee, Telluride Miners' Union, to Editor, July 31, 1902, *MM*, Sept. 1902, p. 48.

50. Sandon *Paystreak*, Dec. 14, 1901; *Tonopah Miner*, Jan. 27, Feb. 3, 1912; Robert Randell, "Rights of Property versus the Rights of Man," *MM*, Feb. 7, 1907, p. 12; "A Socialist" to Editor, Feb. 12, 1903, *Park Record*, Feb. 14, 1903; M. L. Salter (Park City Socialist Club) to Editor, Nov. 11, 1902, *MM*, Dec. 1902, pp. 50–51; *Lardeau Eagle*, July 25, 1901.

51. *Park Record*, June 21, 28, Sept. 6, 1902; *Little Rockies Miner*, June 19, 1904; *Owyhee Avalanche*, July 24, 1903; Thomas E. Burke (Local 241) to Editor, n.d., *MM*, Sept. 6, 1906, p. 9; *Silverton Weekly Miner*, Mar. 27, 1903, Nov. 12, 1909; *San Miguel Examiner*, Feb. 7, 1903.

52. *Park Record*, Sept. 28, 1907; Sandon *Paystreak*, June 28, 1902; Tom L. Buckton (secretary, District Association 6, WFM) to A. Shilland, June 18, 1902, Mine-Mill Papers,

zine, exuded optimism before a crowd of two thousand in Telluride in 1902, declaring that "hopeless men become anarchists; hopeful men become Socialists." Heavy doses of radical ideology instilled in miners the conviction that they could not only understand but also make history. For example, Park City activists in 1903 boldly declared their readiness to shape the future: "Organized labor, studious of current history and prescient of future effects from present causes, realizes the irresistible approach of the crisis which has already wrapped the East in the twilight of its gloom, and is calmly and constantly preparing for its advent. The remedy is of labor's conception, and shall be only of labor's execution. The period of distress, however dire it may be, will be of briefer duration than in '93, for the soul of Marx has risen militant and triumphant from his grave."[53]

In the interim before the advent of socialism, the WFM supported producers' and consumers' cooperatives as alternatives to wage labor and company stores. Miners rejected employer-controlled health programs in part because they saw them as elements in a paternalistic strategy to exert systematic control over their whole lives. Calumet, Michigan, exemplified the domineering style to which many workers objected. *Mining and Scientific Press* reported in 1899 that the Calumet and Hecla Mining Company owned "the water works, smelting works, its docks, railroads, churches twenty-six in number, eight schools, hospitals and almost everything else" in this copper community. Although true company towns existed only in copper- and iron-mining areas, company stores, boardinghouses, and bunkhouses were commonplace in all types of hardrock mining districts.[54] Alfred Parr of

box 153, folder 4; *Silverton Weekly Miner*, Oct. 10, 1902; Press Committee, Telluride Miners' Union, to Editor, July 31, 1902, *MM*, Sept. 1902, p. 48; Terry *News-Record*, Sept. 16, 1909.

53. John M. O'Neill, "Telluride Celebrates," *MM*, Aug. 1902, pp. 38 (quotation), 36–42; Committee of Notification, Park City Miners' Union, to Editor, Feb. 2, 1903, *MM*, Mar. 1903, p. 43.

54. *MSP*, May 13, 1899, p. 509; James B. Allen, *The Company Town in the American West* (Norman, Okla., 1966), pp. xi, 33–49; idem, "The Company-Owned Mining Town in the West: Exploitation or Benevolent Paternalism?" in John A. Carroll, ed., *Reflections of Western Historians* (Tucson, 1969), pp. 177–78; Brown, *Hard-Rock Miners*, pp. 23–25; Arnold R. Alanen, "The 'Locations': Company Communities on Minnesota's Iron Ranges," *Minnesota History* 48 (1982): 94–107; Daniel S. McCorkle, "Testimony," in U.S. Commission on Industrial Relations, *Final Report and Testimony*, 64th Cong., 1st sess., Senate Document 415 (Washington, 1916), 9:8533–36; *Neihart Herald*, July 24, 1891; Smith, *Song of the Hammer and Drill*, pp. 93, 133; Trade Dollar Consolidated Mining

the Ymir Miners' Union viewed with alarm the rise of nonmining activity by the operators in his district. "Under the Truck system which some of the co[mpanie]s are trying hard to inauggurate," he warned, "we will have a company Doctor[,] co. store[,] co. Houses[,] Buy co. Wood or coal[,] Pay for co. Light and Heat and after a while have co. scrip so that then it would be impossible to Buy anything except from the co." Parr feared that this emerging pattern portended nothing less than a new form of corporate feudalism.[55]

Mine workers throughout western North America primarily resented company-owned commercial enterprises as a paternalistic infringement on their independence. Indeed, they seldom complained about the prices charged by these establishments. The preamble to the original Western Federation constitution stressed the need to "rid ourselves of the iniquitous system of spending our earnings where and how our employers or their officers may designate." The WFM convention in 1900 called for the abolition of company boardinghouses and stores "in the interest of the independence of our several localities."[56] Parr urged his comrades in British Columbia to achieve this end through boycotts: "I believe we should watch this business closely and crush it in its infancy by educating our members not to patronize a co. Doctor or a co. store or anything else of the kind." Like their brothers in Ymir, other WFM locals boycotted or otherwise actively opposed these enterprises, sometimes driving them out of business.[57]

Company Records, box 8, folder 8, Bancroft Library, University of California, Berkeley; Sandon *Paystreak*, Jan. 16, 1897, July 30, Sept. 24, 1898; *Little Rockies Miner*, July 4, 1907; *Blair Press* (Nev.), Mar. 26, 1909.

55. Alfred Parr to W. L. Hagler (secretary, Local 81), Feb. 25, 1901, Mine-Mill Papers, box 151, folder 14; "Convention Proceedings," *MM*, June 1900, p. 18; Samuel C. Dickinson, "A Sociological Survey of the Bisbee Warren District," 1917, p. 81, Special Collections Department, University of Arizona Library, Tucson. On the origins of the term "truck," see George Rosen, *The History of Miners' Diseases: A Medical and Social Interpretation* (New York, 1943), pp. 176–78.

56. WFM, "Proceedings," 1893, p. 4; WFM, "Proceedings," *MM*, June 1900, p. 18; San Juan District Union, WFM, *Constitution and By-Laws* (Telluride, Colo., n.d. [ca. 1900]), p. 3; *Butte Bystander*, Aug. 13, 1895; *MSP*, Nov. 6, 1920, p. 650; Harry Jardine (Local 63) to Editor, Mar. 16, 1903, *MM*, Apr. 1903, p. 67; *Park Record*, June 28, 1902; Davis, "Labor in the Mines," p. 211; Charles F. Willis, "Some Observations on Arizona Strikes," *EMJ*, Oct. 13, 1917, p. 643; John C. Sullivan (WFM member, Victor, Colo.), "Testimony," July 18, 1899, in U.S. Industrial Commission, *Report*, 12:348.

57. Alfred Parr to W. L. Hagler, Feb. 25, 1901, Mine-Mill Papers, box 151, folder 14; David Morgan (secretary, Local 119) to A. Shilland, Oct. 5, 1903, ibid., box 154, folder 7; *Slocan Drill*, Aug. 23, 30, 1901; *Owyhee Avalanche*, Aug. 23, 1901; Charles E. Mahoney, "Report of Acting President Mahoney," in WFM, *Proceedings, 1907*, p. 33; J. C. Lowney,

Miners' commitment to consumers' and producers' cooperatives reflected the influence of the Knights of Labor, which administered cooperative grocery stores, boardinghouses, laundries, and coal mines. These undertakings also drew on the examples of Debs's Brotherhood of the Cooperative Commonwealth and similar communitarian schemes of the late nineteenth century.[58] A "Declaration of Principles" by the WFM in 1900 began with this sweeping endorsement: "We believe that the wage system should be abolished and the production of labor be distributed under the co-operative plan." In addition, the new socialist radicalism reinforced the old. Socialist partisans in the Western Federation contended that they sought simply "organized co-operation," "co-operative ownership," "a rational co-operative system," or "the co-operative commonwealth."[59] The proclamations of the Park City socialists notwithstanding, it would appear that it was Laurence Gronlund, not Karl Marx, who had "risen militant and triumphant from his grave."

Guided perhaps less by these formulations than by the practical success of the Rochdale model, several locals set up cooperative grocery and general stores, laundries, and fuel plans.[60] Reflecting on the accomplishments of these enterprises, the convention of 1908 concluded that "this co-operative store system holds promises of unlim-

"Report," in WFM, *Official Proceedings of the Sixteenth Annual Convention, 1908* (Denver, 1908), p. 278; *Butte Bystander*, Aug. 2, 23, 1896; *Idaho Avalanche*, May 1, 29, 1896; *EMJ*, Apr. 11, 1891, p. 453, Apr. 25, 1891, p. 503; Paul A. Frisch, "Labor Conflict at Eureka, 1886–97," *Utah Historical Quarterly* 49 (1981): 153; *MM*, Mar. 1901, pp. 12–14; *MSP*, Sept. 8, 1894, p. 147.

58. David Brundage, "The Producing Classes and the Saloon: Denver in the 1880s," *Labor History* 26 (1985): 38; John R. Commons et al., *History of Labour in the United States*, 4 vols. (New York, 1918), 2:352; *Labor: Its Rights and Wrongs* (1886; rpt. Westport, Conn., 1975), p. 33; *Butte Bystander*, Jan. 12, 1895; Charles LeWarne, "Labor and Communitarianism, 1880–1900," *Labor History* 16 (1975): 393–407; Bernard J. Brommel, "Debs's Cooperative Commonwealth Plan for Workers," *Labor History* 12 (1971): 560–69; Salvatore, *Eugene Debs*, p. 162. In 1889, the organization established the Knights of Labor Free Clinic in Cleveland, Ohio. See *Medical and Surgical Register of the United States*, 2d ed. (Detroit, 1890), p. 881.

59. WFM, "Declaration of Principles," *MM*, Sept. 1900, p. 13; *Lardeau Eagle*, Mar. 13, 1902; Harry Jardine (Local 220) to Editor, Oct. 3, 1906, *MM*, Oct. 18, 1906, p. 13; *Silverton Weekly Miner*, Feb. 19, 1909.

60. Executive Board, WFM, Minute Book, 1:82 (Dec. 1, 1903), 85 (Dec. 2, 1903), 121 (Dec. 10, 1903), 145 (May 20, 1904), 156 (June 2, 1904), 327 (Dec. 12, 1905), 2: 103 (Jan. 21, 1909), WFM-IUMMSW Archives, vols. 1–2; *MM*, Sept. 24, 1908, p. 4; *Tonopah Daily Sun*, Aug. 31, 1907; *Terry News-Record*, Oct. 16, Nov. 6, 1908; People's Co-operative Company to Officers and Members of Organized Labor, May 5, 1912, *MM*, May 16, 1912, p. 10; *Arizona Labor Journal* (Phoenix), July 27, 1917, p. 1; Emma Langdon, "Anaconda's Activity," *MM*, Jan. 3, 1910, p. 8.

ited possibilities for the betterment of the working class, by fostering a spirit of independence, self-respect, and concerted action."[61]

The same enthusiasm surrounded cooperative mining plans, under which the WFM would locate, buy, and develop mining properties. President Boyce broached the issue in 1897, asserting that cooperation offered "the solution of the labor question among the miners."[62] Secretary-Treasurer Haywood added fuel to the fire with an article titled "Co-operative Ownership of Mines" in the *Miners' Magazine* of February 1902. Haywood held that although cooperation was not in itself socialism, it nonetheless "would mean that the members of the organization would be independent of any company, corporation or syndicate and we would be in a position to assist others to better their conditions." This man:festo brought a flood of letters to the magazine which were virtually unanimous in their support for cooperation. One correspondent suggested that part of the surplus from union mining be used for "the care of our aged brothers and of those upon whom the hand of misfortune had been heavily laid."[63] Despite widespread interest among the rank and file, these loose proposals did not develop into a viable program. The conventions of 1902 and subsequent years killed a series of self-employment plans involving the general organization; local projects also aborted.[64] Although cooperative production did not work, it did contribute to the ferment of self-help within the movement.

In April 1900 the WFM unveiled a new charter. It featured the three stars—education, independence, and organization—that would re-

61. WFM, *Proceedings, 1908*, pp. 355–56. Support for the Rochdale system resulted largely from the experience of the Cripple Creek district strike stores. See Executive Board, "Report," in WFM, *Official Proceedings of the Twelfth Annual Convention, 1904* (Denver, 1904), p. 171.

62. Edward Boyce, "President Boyce's Report," *Butte Bystander*, May 15, 1897, p. 4; idem, "President's Report," in WFM, *Proceedings, 1901*, pp. 11–12.

63. William D. Haywood, "Co-operative Ownership of Mines," *MM*, Feb. 1902, p. 8; Dercy W. Johnston to Editor, n.d., *MM*, June 1902, p. 39 (quotation); *MM*, Mar. 1902, pp. 12–13; Jeff White to Editor, n.d., ibid., pp. 24–27; W. T. Hubbell to Editor, n.d., *MM*, Apr. 1902, p. 38; Chris Hansen to Editor, n.d., ibid.; J. A. Foley (Local 62) to Editor, n.d., *MM*, May 1902, pp. 39–40.

64. WFM, *Proceedings, 1902*, pp. 70, 83–85, 163–65; Charles H. Moyer, Report, in WFM, *Proceedings, 1903*, pp. 33–34; WFM, *Proceedings, 1906*, pp. 246–48; WFM, *Official Proceedings of the Nineteenth Annual Convention, 1911* (Denver, 1911), p. 264; *MSP*, June 13, 1903, p. 378; Executive Board, WFM, Minute Book, 1:307 (Dec. 8, 1905), WFM-IUMMSW Archives, vol. 1; *San Miguel Examiner*, June 20, 1903; *Tonopah Miner*, June 18, 1904.

Western Federation of Miners' charter. First developed in 1900, tri-star symbolism remained part of the union's regalia for decades. (Courtesy of Western Historical Collections, University of Colorado)

main part of the union emblem for decades.[65] That the star of independence was central, elevated, and radiating light clearly indicates the paramount value of independence to hardrock workers. That independence was symbolized by a distant star, however, suggests that wrenching changes had left miners far from freedom.

If the immediate opportunities to escape the status they often called "wage slavery" were small and dwindling, the western miners could find in experiments such as their hospitals some refuge from the dictation of their employers. Participants in a movement whose culture fostered self-reliance and innovation, these workers were strongly predisposed to undertake ambitious self-help programs in health and welfare.

65. *MM*, Apr. 1900, frontispiece; Haywood, *Bill Haywood's Book*, p. 82; Joseph Ulmer (Local 99), "Our Emblem," *MM*, Nov. 1901, p. 44: "Independence is our morning star, / The other two I quote: / It's educate and organize— / These three are worthy of note."

2 | *Occupational Hazards*

> The life of the miner is a hazardous one. He knows not the day nor the hour when in his living tomb in the bowels of the earth, cruel fate demands a sacrifice of his health, or he comes to the surface maimed for life, mangled through a fall of rock or a treacherous explosion. The local unions of the Western Federation of Miners have expended vast sums of money, not only in the erection of beautiful buildings in which to hold meetings of the unions, but hospitals have been erected where the sick and crippled have felt the fraternal hand of that brotherhood, that smoothes the pillow of pain and suffering.
>
> —John M. O'Neill, 1905

More than any other factor, the hazards of the job drove hard-rock miners to create and maintain health and welfare programs. Accidents crippled and killed countless workers. Debilitating industrial diseases took a heavy toll. Industrialization exacerbated old risks and generated new ones. In particular, silicosis became rampant in the wake of the technological revolution of the late nineteenth century.

Paradoxically, injuries, a relatively less severe problem, proved more influential than disease in stimulating local unions to take action. Occupational diseases were somewhat underrecognized by miners and others in mining communities, but the mayhem caused by work accidents was readily apparent to all. In the course of a typical shift of work, a miner encountered a great variety of safety hazards.

Merely reaching the collar of the mine could involve a perilous journey. During the winter months, avalanches occasionally swept away miners on their way to work. Charles Nelson never had a chance when a snowslide swallowed him while he was walking to the Trade Dollar in Silver City in January 1906. Above-ground laborers were

28

constantly at risk. An avalanche in April 1897 near Sandon, British Columbia, crashed down on three men working at a tramway that conveyed ore to a concentrating mill. The victims took shelter in a nearby shed, but a wall of snow demolished the building, and they were crushed.[1]

In mines lacking power hoisting equipment, miners descended into the shaft by ladders or were lowered by means of a windlass. This preindustrial technology led to frequent fatal falls.[2] Steam, electric, or gasoline engines controlled the cages or ore buckets that took workers down into larger and more advanced mines. Although by the turn of the century Colorado law required installation of cages in all shafts more than 200 feet deep, one miner complained of flagrant noncompliance in the Cripple Creek district: "I do not know one hole two hundred feet deep that has a cage, and know of lots that are from four to six hundred that have nothing but a bucket." The common practice of riding the bucket by standing on its rim and grasping the cable meant literally taking one's life in one's hands every day. When Stephano Rossi missed his step boarding an ore bucket in the Iowa-Tiger near Silverton, Colorado, he plunged 150 feet to his death. Cages operated by electric power not only occasionally plummeted to the bottom of the shaft but also suffered short circuits that electrocuted passengers.[3] In addition, malfunctioning hoisting equipment threatened miners working at the bottom of the shaft. Mat Anderson lost his life in a Rhyolite, Nevada, mine when the hoist clutch slipped and dropped a bucket full of ore on his head.[4]

Miners and muckers extracted ore in a stope, that is, a working face that followed a vein of ore at an oblique angle. Arriving at a worksite altered by the previous shift's detonation of charges, miners used picks or bars to pry down chunks of rock loosened by blasting. This task sometimes brought slabs of rock down on the workers. One Silver

1. Emmet Morrow and R. J. Hanlon (Local 66), "In Memoriam," Feb. 1, 1906, *MM*, Feb. 8, 1906, p. 14; Sandon *Paystreak*, Apr. 10, 1897; Nelson *Weekly News*, Jan. 9, 1913, p. 4; *Park Record*, Jan. 31, 1903.
   2. *Rhyolite Herald*, Sept. 7, 1906; *Silverton Weekly Miner*, Sept. 3, 1915; *Fairbanks Daily Times* (Alaska), Oct. 15, 1907.
   3. Moudy, "Cripple Creek Miner," p. 382; *Silverton Weekly Miner*, Feb. 5, 1909; *EMJ*, Sept. 4, 1897, p. 272; *Tanana Leader* (Alaska), Aug. 26, 1909; *Carthage Press* (Mo.), Nov. 18, 1915; John C. Sullivan, "Testimony," July 18, 1899, in U.S. Industrial Commission, *Report*, 12:356–57.
   4. *Rhyolite Herald*, Feb. 23, 1906; *Tonopah Miner*, Mar. 5, 1904; *Goldfield News*, Sept. 28, 1907; *Park Record*, Aug. 9, 1902; British Columbia Minister of Mines, "Annual Report . . . , 1898," in British Columbia, *Sessional Papers, 1899* (Victoria, 1899), p. 1161.

City miner narrowly escaped death when he tore out a loose rock and inadvertently tapped into a reservoir of underground water, which washed him down the tunnel.[5] Breaking away rock also detonated unexploded portions of dynamite sticks which remained hidden in the face. When Alonzo Mason picked into a missed hole at the Silver King in Park City, he was "instantly blown into eternity." Muckers breaking boulders and shoveling muck ran similar risks.[6]

Miners spent the largest part of their shift drilling the holes into which explosives were inserted. Machine work predominated, but certain circumstances required drilling with hand tools. Driving a steel drill into granite or other hard rock with a hammer sent splinters of rock and metal into miners' eyes. Errant swings of these heavy hammers pounded hands and fingers holding drills in place.[7] Power tools posed different problems. Miners unavoidably lost some rounds in their daily wrestling matches with cumbersome machinery that sometimes outweighed them. At the Reco mine near Sandon, Tom Woods "was running a machine drill . . . [when it] suddenly tipped and crushed his ribs into his lungs." The kickback from these drills ruptured intestines and inflicted other internal injuries. Moreover, the vibration of drilling equipment precipitated the fall of rocks, sometimes with fatal results.[8]

The worst hazard of drilling was the possibility of accidentally striking dynamite that had failed to explode in a previous round of charges. Poor visibility underground, defective explosives and fuses, pressure to speed up production, and errors in judgment and communication combined to create extreme danger. When Eric Cook drilled into a missed shot near Telluride, Colorado, he was destroyed instantly by the blast.[9] Although their duties kept them farther from the point of

5. *Blair News* (Nev.), Jan. 11, 1908; Arizona Copper Company, Department of Mine Safety, "Report of Mine Inspector for Year Ending September 30, 1917," Arizona Copper Company Records, box 110, folder 1, Special Collections Department, University of Arizona Library, Tucson; *Owyhee Avalanche*, Apr. 27, 1900; *San Miguel Examiner*, May 2, 1903.

6. *Park Record*, May 12, 1906; *Wardner News*, Feb. 28, Mar. 7, 1891; *San Miguel Examiner*, July 15, 1899, Sept. 7, 1901; Nelson *Weekly News*, Feb. 23, 1911, p. 5; *Silverton Weekly Miner*, Nov. 26, 1915.

7. *Slocan Drill*, June 8, 1900; *Neihart Herald*, Feb. 19, 1892; Terry *News-Record*, Mar. 9, 1906.

8. Sandon *Paystreak*, Dec. 10, 1898; *Owyhee Avalanche*, May 10, 1901; British Columbia Minister of Mines, "Report . . ., 1899," in British Columbia, *Sessional Papers, 1900* (Victoria, 1900), p. 816; Nye County Recorder, "Record of Deaths, 1914–1923," p. 24, Nye County Records, vol F., Nye County Courthouse, Tonopah, Nev.

9. *San Miguel Examiner*, Nov. 20, 1897; *Silverton Weekly Miner*, Mar. 4, 1910; British

explosion, muckers and other underground workers were also killed and injured in these accidents. When Charles Lee struck an unde-tonated charge at the War Eagle near Sandon, two other miners and a mucker perished along with him: "Lee[']s head was blown off clean and the bodies of the other three were filled with splinters of rock and their bodies crushed beneath the large masses of rock that came down with the blast."[10]

After a set of holes had been drilled to sufficient depth, the miner prepared an explosive charge, usually of dynamite (then commonly called "giant powder"). During cold weather, it was necessary to thaw dynamite to make it work. After forty sticks exploded while Rhyolite miner Chris Jorgenson was heating them, "there was little left of the unfortunate man but the trunk."[11] In addition to exploding, powder occasionally ignited and burned those using it.[12]

Filling holes with blasting powder and tamping it down were del-icate procedures. After they had affixed fuses to the charges and lit them, miners tried to leave their workplace before it exploded. Many failed. Workers engaged in sinking shafts were especially vulnerable to premature blasts. When Park City miner William Eisenman had problems with a fuse, he called to the windlass operators to retrieve him immediately from the bottom of the shaft. But the primitive hand-cranked hoist had lifted Eisenman only six feet when the charge exploded, peppering him with rock and breaking his eardrum. Some shaft sinkers were expected to climb the cable to escape the impending blast.[13] Not surprisingly, many hardrock workers did not survive these close encounters with dynamite. Following the explosion that obli-terated John Schaeffer near Silverton, Colorado, "pieces of [the remains] had to be gathered up in sacks."[14] These unexpected explo-

Columbia Minister of Mines, "Annual Report . . ., 1902," in British Columbia, *Sessional Papers, 1903* (Victoria, 1903), p. H259.

10. Sandon *Paystreak*, June 24, 1899; *Douglas Island News* (Alaska), Feb. 19, 1908; *Owyhee Avalanche*, Sept. 13, 1901; *San Miguel Examiner*, Jan. 8, 1898, Jan. 28, 1899; *Silverton Weekly Miner*, Oct. 2, 1908.

11. *Rhyolite Herald*, Dec. 15, 1905; *Manhattan News* (Nev.), Apr. 14, 1906; *San Miguel Examiner*, Feb. 8, 1902; *Tonopah Miner*, Feb. 13, 1904.

12. *Idaho Avalanche*, July 16, 1897; Haywood, *Bill Haywood's Book*, p. 69; *San Miguel Examiner*, Sept. 3, 1898; *Blair Press*, Feb. 4, 1910.

13. *Park Record*, Aug. 30, 1902; British Columbia Minister of Mines, "Annual Report . . ., 1902," in British Columbia, *Sessional Papers, 1903*, p. H258; Montana Industrial Accident Board, *Fifth Annual Report . . . for the Twelve Months Ending June 30th, 1920* (Helena, n.d.), p. 256; *Industrial Worker* (Spokane, Wash.), Apr. 6, 1911.

14. *Silverton Weekly Miner*, July 6, 1906, Feb. 13, 1903; *Rhyolite Herald*, July 7, 1905; *Great Falls Daily Tribune*, Dec. 12, 1895.

sions sometimes struck down several workers at once. The detonation of the powder magazine and subsequent spread of toxic gases through the Daly-West and Ontario mines at Park City annihilated thirty-four men on July 16, 1902. A blast at the Broadwater mine in Neihart, Montana, killed seven and injured fifteen others in 1896.[15]

In addition to the possibility of being blasted, the carmen or trammers who pushed ore cars or drove trains of cars faced a myriad of other safety risks. Moving loads of ore through the semidarkness on makeshift rail systems led to collisions, falls, and other accidents. Cars carrying a ton or more of rock tipped over on trammers or ran them down. Jack Fitzgerald of Kendall, Montana, was one of many who were crushed into tunnel walls by loaded cars. Most horizontal underground transportation remained primitive throughout this period. The introduction of electric locomotives, however, meant that workers traded the risk of being kicked by mules for the increased risk of being squashed against mine walls by large engines. Running loads of ore through the mine occasionally set off roof cave-ins such as the one that did in Alex Fraser at the Last Chance near Sandon in 1902.[16]

Because they were continuously moving through the labyrinthine underground workings, carmen frequently fell accidentally. Poor visibility led trammers to push cars into empty shafts, usually pulling the unfortunate worker with them. Charles Foley plunged with a car from the nine-hundred-foot level to the fourteen-hundred-foot level in the Tennessee mine at Chloride, Arizona, and "was picked up in pieces." Many falls of less than five hundred feet had similar results. Tom Koustas died in a Tonopah, Nevada, mine after falling only seven feet. Besides tumbling down shafts, trammers and other mine workers hurtled down unguarded ore chutes and raises between levels of mines and fell from aerial tramways between mines and ore mills.[17]

---

15. *Park Record*, July 19, 1902; *Butte Bystander*, Apr. 21, 1896; *Silverton Weekly Miner*, June 19, 1903; *MM*, Mar. 2, 1905, p. 4.

16. Butte *Daily Inter Mountain*, Jan. 15, 1887; *Neihart Miner* (Mont.), Apr. 28, 1898; *Kendall Miner*, Apr. 16, 1909; L. M. Banks, "Report of Mine Inspector for Six Months Ending Mar. 31, 1914," p. 2, Arizona Copper Company Records, box 110, folder 1; *Blair Press*, Dec. 10, 1909; *Silverton Weekly Miner*, Apr. 5, 1907; Sandon *Paystreak*, Feb. 1, 1902. The division of labor in this period was often fluid; muckers' jobs could include haulage tasks. See *Great Falls Daily Tribune*, Aug. 19, 1905, p. 6.

17. *Arizona Labor Journal*, July 13, 1916, p. 1; John A. Church, "Accidents in the Comstock Mines and Their Relation to Deep Mining," in American Institute of Mining Engineers, *Transactions* 8 (1880): 91; Nye County Recorder, "Record of Deaths, 1914–

Falling rocks and cave-ins constituted the greatest safety hazard of hardrock mining. Timbermen, whose job it was to brace the ceiling of newly hewn cavities, worked under the most perilous conditions. On November 22, 1903, timberman L. M. Scheid became the fourth man to die that month in the Daly-Judge mine at Park City when a thousand pounds of rock crushed him. In smaller operations with less division of labor, craftsmen did their own timbering and braved possible disaster on every shift. Needless to say, the pieces of rock that rained down on underground workers inflicted innumerable bruises and broken bones, as well as fatal injuries.[18] The collapse of large sections of roof or wall could bring many tons of rock down on a group of miners in an instant. Such calamities left little chance for either escape or survival. A cave-in at the Anna Lee mine in the Cripple Creek district killed eight men in 1896. The massive rock slab that landed on John Mullan and Anton Scheffler in the Bunker Hill and Sullivan mine left them "crushed almost beyond recognition." For most victims of cave-ins, the first accident was also the last.[19]

Some managers sent workers in to clear jammed ore chutes. Frank Crampton narrowly escaped death performing this treacherous chore in Bingham Canyon, Utah. "Just as I made the opening of the chute a dribble of muck started to come down," recalled Crampton. "Then larger pieces, and I was no more than clear of the chute-mouth, and in the drift, when the whole thing let go and came down. I cleared the chute opening, and the chute-set timbers, before the mess hit and took everything out, and before it could bury me." George Curry had worse luck. Curry crawled down into a clogged chute at the Barnes-King in Kendall, Montana, and was swallowed up in the ensuing cascade of rock. Co-workers shoveled out seven carloads of ore before they reached his body.[20]

23," p. 44, Nye County Records, vol. F; *Weekly Missoulian* (Missoula, Mont.), May 21, 1886; *Manhattan News*, Sept. 23, 1906; *Silverton Weekly Miner*, May 1, 1908, Sept. 17, Nov. 5, 1909, Apr. 22, 1910; *Tanana Mine Worker* (Fairbanks, Alaska), Apr. 8, 1907.

18. *Park Record*, Nov. 28, 1903, Mar. 10, 1906; *Idaho Avalanche*, July 10, 1896, June 25, 1897; *Silverton Weekly Miner*, Aug. 7, Sept. 18, 1908; *Butte Bystander*, June 16, 1894.

19. *Coeur d'Alene Miner* (Wallace, Ida.), Feb. 18, 1893, p. 5, Feb. 24, 1894, p. 1, Oct. 27, 1894, p. 1; *EMJ*, Jan. 8, 1896, p. 68; *San Miguel Examiner*, Sept. 24, 1898, May 16, 1903; *Daily Arizona Silver Belt* (Globe), Jan. 14, 1912, p. 1; *Fairbanks Daily Times* (Alaska), Sept. 1, 1907; *Butte Bystander*, June 9, 1894; *Goldfield News*, Sept. 28, 1907; *Tanana Miner* (Chena, Alaska), July 28, 1907.

20. Crampton, *Deep Enough*, p. 70; *Kendall Miner*, Oct. 15, 1909; *Silverton Weekly Miner*, Nov. 13, 1903; *San Miguel Examiner*, Apr. 30, 1904.

Fortunately, underground fires were infrequent in metal mines. Unfortunately, they proved catastrophic whenever smoke or flames blocked escape routes. The first western conflagration killed 45 employees of the Yellow Jacket mine in Gold Hill, Nevada, in 1869. On November 20, 1901, buildings at the mouth of the Smuggler-Union tunnel at Telluride caught fire, sending smoke into the workings and suffocating 24 men. In 1911, the Belmont disaster in Tonopah, Nevada, took 17 lives, 13 by asphyxiation and 4 by falls from the cage caused by partial asphyxiation. The worst holocaust of this period occurred on June 8, 1917, when 163 miners perished in the Speculator mine in Butte.[21]

Fatigue contributed to accidents at the end of the shift. Richard Prout fainted and toppled from an ascending cage in the Mountain View mine under Butte, landing in the sump a thousand feet below. "The body was found," reported the *Butte Bystander*, "mangled out of all human semblance." Miners bore the same increased risks riding buckets and climbing ladders after eight or ten hours of hard labor.[22] Fatigued hoisting engineers made disastrous miscalculations that dashed cages or buckets full of workers into the framework at the top of the shaft. Fifteen died at the Independence mine in Victor, Colorado, in 1904 when they were hoisted into the sheaves.[23]

Avalanches jeopardized not only miners leaving work but even some of those at home. Especially at risk were employees who were required to live in company housing, which was often situated precariously close to the mine. Near Nelson, British Columbia, a snowslide killed nine miners and injured ten others on Christmas Day of 1902 in the bunkhouse of the Molly Gibson mine, perched at an eight-thousand-foot elevation directly below a glacier. Sixteen employees of the Liberty Bell at Telluride perished under similar circumstances in the winter of 1901–2. In the Britannia Beach disaster in British

21. DeQuille, *Big Bonanza*, pp. 126–31; U.S. Geological Survey, *Comstock Mining*, pp. 269–77; *MM*, Dec. 1901, pp. 1–3; Vincent St. John (Local 63) to Editor, Dec. 19, 1901, *MM*, Feb. 1902, pp. 39–40; Nevada State Inspector of Mines, *Annual Report, 1912* (Carson City, 1913), pp. 40–55; Arnon Gutfeld, "The Speculator Disaster in 1917: Labor Resurgence at Butte, Montana," *Arizona and the West* 11 (1969): 27–30; U.S. Bureau of Mines, *Metal-Mining Accidents in the United States during the Calendar Year 1918*, by Albert H. Fay, Technical Paper 252 (Washington, 1920), pp. 71–73.

22. *Butte Bystander*, Apr. 21, 1894; *Tonopah Sun*, Apr. 3, 10, 1909; *Owyhee Avalanche*, Apr. 15, 1898; *Tanana Miner*, Feb. 23, 1908.

23. *MM*, Feb. 11, 1904, pp. 3, 7–10; *EMJ*, May 20, 1893, p. 470; *Owyhee Avalanche*, Nov. 16, 1900; Church, "Accidents in Comstock Mines," p. 93.

Columbia on March 22, 1915, a massive landslide came down on the bunkhouses along with the snow, killing fifty-six.[24]

Workers in ore-processing mills ran a different daily gauntlet. Unguarded machinery posed a constant threat. The death of Mike Vranes, an employee of the Kittimac mill near Silverton, Colorado, illustrates the consequences of small mishaps: "He was . . . feeding the crusher and in some manner became overbalanced, falling backward into the big fly wheel which crushed his head against the timbers with such force that he never knew what happened to him."[25] Other safety hazards of milling included falls, falling equipment, and accidents with ore cars.[26]

Molten metal caused the most spectacular accidents in smelting plants. When liquified copper exploded on contact with water in the Boston and Montana smelter at Great Falls, Montana, in 1896, "hot copper was thrown around in showers like a hail storm," killing one employee and injuring two others. The explosion of a ladle containing seven tons of copper at the Washoe plant in Anaconda, Montana, ended the life of Anton Mercel, who was "fairly bathed by the flying molten metal." Acids and other chemicals used in metallurgical processes also inflicted burns on smelter workers.[27]

Gears, belts, pulleys, and other inadequately shielded mechanical devices had a voracious appetite for smelter workers' fingers, hands, and arms. While adjusting a drive belt in the Canadian Pacific Railway smelter in Trail, British Columbia, George Grandy "got his left hand

24. Sandon *Paystreak*, Nov. 20, 1897, Mar. 10, 1900; *Slocan Drill*, Jan. 2, 1903; *San Miguel Examiner*, Apr. 20, 1901, Mar. 1, 1902; Idaho State Inspector of Mines, *Nineteenth Annual Report, 1917* (Boise, n.d.), pp. 11–12; *Silverton Weekly Miner*, Mar. 23, 30, 1906, Jan. 7, 1910; *MM*, Apr. 1, 1915; Charles H. Moyer, Report, in WFM, *Proceedings, 1903*, p. 34.

25. *Silverton Weekly Miner*, Apr. 29, 1910; *Coeur d'Alene Miner*, Dec. 10, 1892, p. 2; *San Miguel Examiner*, Apr. 1, 1899; *Neihart Herald*, Aug. 14, 1891; *DeLamar Lode*, May 14, 1901; *Terry News-Record*, Oct. 11, 1907.

26. *Little Rockies Miner*, Apr. 29, 1909; *Silverton Weekly Miner*, Mar. 19, 26, 1909; *Owyhee Avalanche*, June 16, 1899; *Blair Press*, June 20, 1908; Montana Industrial Accident Board, *Third Annual Report . . . for the Twelve Months Ending June 30th, 1918* (Helena, n.d.), p. 230; U.S. Bureau of Mines, *Accidents at Metallurgical Works in the United States during the Calendar Year 1920*, by William W. Adams, Technical Paper 297 (Washington, 1922), pp. 14, 17, 22–24.

27. *Great Falls Daily Tribune*, May 1, 1896, Aug. 12, 1915, p. 3, Oct. 17, 1901, p. 8, Oct. 22, 1906, p. 8, June 6, 1907, p. 4, June 7, 1907, p. 8; Great Falls Mill and Smeltermen's Union, Minute Book, 8:155 (May 20, 1918), 186 (Aug. 19, 1918), WFM-IUMMSW Archives, vol. 248; *Safety Review* (ASARCO), Aug. 1915, Oct. 1915; *Anode*, Nov. 1917, p. 15; Earle Strain (physician, Great Falls smelter), "Outside Report . . . [on] Accidental Injuries," Dec. 1897, Anaconda Records, box 195, file 32.

entangled in the machinery and had his arm torn off near the elbow." Less fortunate was William J. Breen, an employee of the Great Falls smelter, who was "crushed to death by being dragged between a revolving belt shaft and the concentrator floor." The noise inside smelting works often drowned out the cries of those being pulled into machinery, preventing a quick rescue and less serious injuries.[28] Workers were also caught beneath malfunctioning cranes, run over by locomotives, and injured by other mechanical equipment in and around smelters.[29]

Incomplete mechanization left much lifting and other arduous work to be done by hand in metallurgical plants. As late as 1915, "hand labor," not machinery, accounted for the majority of accidents in the American Smelting and Refining Company plants. Hernias and back injuries were common. Workers who dropped castings or other heavy objects crushed bones in their feet. More than five hundred workers at the Great Falls copper smelter suffered injuries to their legs and feet in the period 1903–7.[30] In addition, falls disabled or killed many metallurgical workers.[31]

Aggregate data on accidents unequivocally confirm the impression created by these anecdotal reports that hardrock mining was an exceedingly dangerous industry. Although available statistical evidence is profoundly flawed by numerous biases and pervasive underreporting,[32] it nonetheless provides a rough estimate of the magnitude

28. *Slocan Drill*, Mar. 25, 1904; *Great Falls Daily Tribune*, May 16, 1908, p. 5, Jan. 31, 1900, p. 3, June 20, 1901, p. 6, Sept. 15, 1908, p. 5; *Anode*, Feb. 1918, p. 15; ASARCO *Safety Review*, Nov. 1915.

29. *Great Falls Daily Tribune*, Mar. 7, 1902, p. 8, Feb. 25, 1913, p. 6, Sept. 8, 1913, p. 2; *Arizona Silver Belt*, Aug. 18, 1907, p. 4; *Anode*, Nov. 1917, p. 15, June 1918, p. 15; U.S. Bureau of Mines, *Accidents at Metallurgical Works*, 1920, pp. 9, 11, 14, 17, 22–24.

30. ASARCO *Safety Review*, Sept. 1915; Great Falls Mill and Smeltermen's Union, Minute Book, 9:1 (July 7, 1919), 7 (July 21, 1919), 8 (July 21, 1919), 63 (Jan. 5, 1920), 82 (Feb. 23, 1920), WFM-IUMMSW Archives, vol. 249; C. W. Goodale (manager, Great Falls smelter) to C. F. Kelley, Mar. 17, 1908, Anaconda Records, no box, file 153; Earle Strain, "Outside Report . . . [on] Accidental Injuries," Dec. 1897, box 195, file 32, ibid.; *Great Falls Daily Tribune*, Sept. 23, 1900, p. 8; *Anode*, Apr. 1918, p. 15.

31. ASARCO *Safety Review*, Sept. 1915; Great Falls Mill and Smeltermen's Union, Minute Book, 8:84 (Nov. 19, 1917), 99 (Dec. 31, 1917), WFM-IUMMSW Archives, vol. 248; *Anode*, Feb. 1918, p. 15, Oct. 1918, p. 15. In Durango, Colorado, in 1903, undertaker A. F. Hood complained that the smelter strike was ruining his business. See [no first name] Copley to Editor, Sept. 8, 1903, *MM*, Sept. 17, 1903, p. 10.

32. Frederick L. Hoffman, "Fatal Accidents in Metal Mining in the United States," *EMJ*, Jan. 14, 1904, p. 79; idem, "Fatal Accidents in American Metal Mines," *EMJ*, Mar. 5, 1910, p. 511; U.S. Bureau of Mines, *Metal-Mine Accidents in the United States during the Calendar Year 1920*, by William W. Adams, Technical Paper 299 (Washington, 1922), p. 9. Most BOM data came from employers' self-reports, a notoriously flawed source.

of the threat of injury. Concentrating on fatality data minimizes to some extent the problems of underreporting and noncomparable classification of accidents.

In the years 1894–1908, U.S. metal miners succumbed to occupational accidents at the average rate of 3.1 deaths per 1,000 employees per year. After 1910 the federal Bureau of Mines (BOM) calculated fatality statistics on a different basis, taking short-term unemployment into account. With this adjustment, U.S. death rates averaged 3.8 per 1,000 three-hundred-day workers for 1911–20.[33] Hardrock miners in British Columbia perished from injuries at a mean annual rate of 4.2 per 1,000 during the interval 1898–1908 and 3.3 per 1,000 for 1909–20.[34] Metal and coal mining were the most hazardous industries in North America in the early twentieth century. A hardrock worker was, for example, more than ten times more likely to be killed by an accident on the job in 1910 than a worker in manufacturing.[35]

The leading causes of fatal injuries changed little in the three decades after 1890. Because there are no comprehensive national data for the period before 1911, the precise trend in causes of accidental deaths remains unknown. Tables 2.1 and 2.2 nonetheless make clear that falling rock, explosives, and miners' falls remained the most frequent causes of traumatic death. The diffuse distribution of causes of fatal

33. Hoffman, "Fatal Accidents in American Metal Mines," pp. 511–12; U.S. Bureau of Mines, *Metal-Mine Accidents, 1920*, pp. 73–75.

34. Hoffman, "Fatal Accidents in American Metal Mines," p. 512; British Columbia Minister of Mines, "Annual Report . . ., 1909," in British Columbia, *Sessional Papers, 1910* (Victoria, 1910), p. K156; idem, "Annual Report . . ., 1910," in British Columbia, *Sessional Papers, 1911* (Victoria, 1911), p. K169; idem, "Annual Report . . ., 1911," in British Columbia, *Sessional Papers, 1912* (Victoria, 1912), p. K216; idem, "Annual Report . . ., 1912," in British Columbia, *Sessional Papers, 1913* (Victoria, 1913), p. K241; idem, "Annual Report . . ., 1913," in British Columbia, *Sessional Papers, 1914* (Victoria, 1914), 2:K328; idem, "Annual Report . . ., 1914," in British Columbia, *Sessional Papers, 1915* (Victoria, 1915), 2:K399; idem, "Annual Report . . ., 1915," in British Columbia, *Sessional Papers, 1916* (Victoria, 1916), 2:K374; idem, "Annual Report . . ., 1916," in British Columbia, *Sessional Papers, 1917* (Victoria, 1917), 2:K444; idem, "Annual Report . . ., 1917," in British Columbia, *Sessional Papers, 1918* (Victoria, 1918), 1:F376; idem, "Annual Report . . ., 1918," in British Columbia, *Sessional Papers, 1919* (Victoria, 1919), 2:K17–18, K396–97; idem, "Annual Report . . ., 1919," in British Columbia, *Sessional Papers, 1920* (Victoria, 1920), 2:N293; idem, "Annual Report . . ., 1920," in British Columbia, *Sessional Papers, 1921* (Victoria, 1921), 2:N17–18, N253. Unfortunately, the "hard" evidence on nonfatal accidents in British Columbia is virtually worthless.

35. Hoffman, "Fatal Accidents in American Metal Mines," p. 512; U.S. Bureau of the Census, *Historical Statistics*, 1:607; U.S. Bureau of Labor Statistics, *Industrial Accident Statistics*, by Frederick L. Hoffman, Bulletin 157 (Washington, 1915), p. 6: "Metal mining ranks as most hazardous [of seventeen major industries and groupings of industries in 1910], with a fatality rate of 4.0 per 1,000, and manufacturing industries in general rank lowest, with a rate of 0.25 per 1,000."

Table 2.1. Causes of fatal accidents in U.S. metal mining, 1893–1902

	Montana		Colorado	
	Deaths	Percent	Deaths	Percent
Falls of rock, etc.	92	28.7	166	22.8
Falls down shaft, etc.	77	24.0	176	24.2
Explosion	63	19.6	192	26.4
Other shaft accidents	26	8.1	74	10.2
Asphyxiation	21	6.5	62	8.5
Other causes	42	13.1	58	8.0
TOTALS	321	100.0	728	100.1*

*Total exceeds 100 because of rounding.
SOURCE: Frederick L. Hoffman, "Fatal Accidents in Metal Mining in the United States," *Engineering and Mining Journal*, Jan. 14, 1904, pp. 79–80.

Table 2.2. Causes of accidents in U.S. metal and nonmetallic mineral mining, 1911–1920

	Fatal accidents	Percent	Nonfatal accidents	Percent
Underground				
Fall of rock	1,902	30.5	70,739	19.8
Explosives	617	9.9	4,465	1.2
Falls down chute, etc.	417	6.7	9,006	2.5
Falls down shaft	370	5.9	838	0.2
Haulage	310	5.0	38,879	10.9
Cage or skip	291	4.7	2,624	0.7
Ore loading	80	1.3	37,290	10.4
Timber or hand tools	47	0.8	30,811	8.6
Drilling	16	0.3	17,712	5.0
Other causes	1,015	16.3	70,043	19.6
Surface, all causes	551	8.8	43,245	12.1
Open pit, all causes	623	10.0	31,647	8.9
TOTALS	6,239	100.2*	357,299	99.9*

*Figures do not add to 100 because of rounding.
SOURCE: U.S. Bureau of Mines, *Metal-Mine Accidents in the United States during the Calendar Year 1920*, by William W. Adams, Technical Paper 299 (Washington, 1922), pp. 76–83.

injuries for 1911–20 supports the popular view that a myriad of hazards jeopardized mine workers' safety.[36]

Unlike fatal accidents, nonfatal mishaps were largely ignored by government statisticians. Montana officials identified 1,064 mine fatalities between 1893 and 1916 but reported only 733 disabling acci-

36. Hoffman, "Fatal Accidents in Metal Mining," pp. 79–80; U.S. Bureau of Mines,

dents during this interval. Federal data were somewhat more complete. According to the Bureau of Mines, more than one worker in five suffered a nonfatal injury each year in the typical U.S. metal mine in the decade 1911–20. But given the incentives for employers to overlook "minor" accidents, this report of 357,299 nonfatal injuries undoubtedly understates the magnitude of the problem.[37]

Most occupational diseases developed insidiously. Nevertheless, it is clear that work-induced illnesses posed a larger problem for miners than did traumatic injuries. One disorder in particular, silicosis, took the lives of more metal miners in this period than did all mine accidents combined.

Silicosis is a chronic respiratory disease that results from the inhalation of free silica (SiO_2), one of the primary constituents of the earth's crust. Rock formations containing high proportions of free silica, such as quartzite and granite, are found throughout the mining regions of North America. In the mines around Kendall, Montana, for instance, the ore was over three quarters silica.[38] As a result, a large share of mine and mill workers incurred daily exposure to this hazard. Inhaling microscopic silica particles (of less than ten microns in diameter) for many years led to fibrotic scarring of the lungs. Fibrosis, in turn, led to impaired respiratory function and a predisposition to pulmonary tuberculosis and pneumonia.[39]

Although miners and other workers had contracted this disorder

Metal-Mine Accidents, 1920, pp. 76–83; Larry D. Lankton, "Died in the Mines," *Michigan History* 67 (Nov.-Dec. 1983): 35–39; Brown, *Hard-Rock Miners*, p. 173. Quantitative data on the causes of fatal accidents in British Columbia reveal a similar pattern.

37. Montana Department of Labor and Industry, *Second Biennial Report, 1915–16* (Helena, n.d.), p. 70; Nevada State Inspector of Mines, *Annual Report, 1912*, pp. 65–71; idem, *Biennial Report, 1913–14* (Carson City, 1915), pp. 26–51; U.S. Bureau of Mines, *Metal-Mine Accidents, 1920*, pp. 74–75; idem, *Accidents at Metallurgical Works, 1920*, p. 27.

38. U.S. Bureau of Mines, *Review of Literature on Effects of Breathing Dusts with Special Reference to Silicosis*, by Daniel Harrington and Sara J. Davenport, Bulletin 400 (Washington, 1937), p. 113; James C. Foster, "Western Miners and Silicosis: 'The Scourge of the Underground Toiler,' 1890–1943," *Industrial and Labor Relations Review* 37 (1984): 372n; Walter H. Weed, *The Mines Handbook*, vol. 12 (New York, 1916), passim.

39. Morton Ziskind, Robert N. Jones, and Hans Weill, "Silicosis: State of the Art," *American Review of Respiratory Disease* 113 (1976): 647–61; Kaye H. Kilburn, Ruth Lilis, and Edwin Holstein, "Silicosis," in John M. Last, ed., *Maxcy-Rosenau Public Health and Preventive Medicine*, 11th ed. (New York, 1980), pp. 602–7; Anthony Seaton, "Silicosis," in William K. Morgan and Seaton, *Occupational Lung Diseases* (Philadelphia, 1975), pp. 88–89.

for centuries,[40] silicosis became a widespread occupational health problem only as a result of the profound technological changes of the nineteenth century. The development of power drills greatly exacerbated the dust hazard. Between 1880 and 1902, the number of drills used in gold and silver mining in the United States driven by steam, compressed air, or electricity rose from 257 to 3,329. By 1902, power drills were used in extracting about three-quarters of precious-metal ore and about six-sevenths of copper ore. These tools were constantly improved to become ever faster, lighter, more durable, and more adaptable to varied conditions. Mechanical drilling thus became both technically feasible and economically advantageous in more situations. More than anything else, the industrialization of metal mining meant the substitution of power drilling for hand drilling.[41]

In general, power drills were more widely employed to cut tunnels and shafts to develop a mining property than to extract ore in a working stope. When in 1905 electric drills replaced "'Armstrong' power" in driving the Yukon tunnel at Silverton, Colorado, the *Weekly Miner* commented that "drill thumping by hand has for a long time fallen far short of the go aheaditiveness essential to the furtherance of a great enterprise." A power drill tested at the Payne mine at Sandon in 1901 cut through forty-three inches of hard rock in only sixteen minutes, a rate of productivity several times that of hand drilling. Not surprisingly, small and marginally profitable mines mechanized less rapidly and less thoroughly than did larger and richer operations. Nonetheless, by the early twentieth century, the new drilling technology had spread throughout western North America.[42]

40. R. R. Sayers and Anthony J. Lanza, "History of Silicosis and Asbestosis," in Lanza, ed., *Silicosis and Asbestosis* (New York, 1938), pp. 3–4; Rosen, *History of Miners' Diseases*, pp. 6–7, 125, 128.

41. U.S. Census Office, *Tenth Census, 1880*, vol. 13: *Statistics and Technology of the Precious Metals*, by S. F. Emmons and G. F. Becker (Washington, 1885), p. 151; U.S. Bureau of the Census, *Special Reports: Mines and Quarries, 1902* (Washington, 1905), pp. 529–30, 477; U.S. Work Projects Administration and Bureau of Mines, *Rock Drilling*, by C. E. Nighman and O. E. Kiessling, Report No. E–11 (Philadelphia, 1940), pp. 12–13, 18–34; *MSP*, Apr. 14, 1888, p. 238, Dec. 5, 1896, p. 459, Nov. 25, 1905, p. 360; *EMJ*, May 16, 1891, p. 585; Montana-Tonopah Mining Company, *Report for Fiscal Year 1909–1910* (N.p., n.d.), p. 6; Treve Holman, "Historical Relationship of Mining, Silicosis, and Rock Removal," *British Journal of Industrial Medicine* 4 (1947): 9–13; Wyman, *Hard-Rock Epic*, pp. 84–90; Larry D. Lankton, "The Machine *under* the Garden: Rock Drills Arrive at the Lake Superior Copper Mines, 1868–1883," *Technology and Culture* 24 (1983): 1–37.

42. *Silverton Weekly Miner*, Jan. 13, 1905; C. W. Tolman to Messrs. Siemens and Halske, Mar. 4, 1898, Silver Lake Mines, Letter Book, p. 260, Bancroft Library, University

Machine drills and other concomitant facets of industrialization dramatically intensified the dust hazard. Boring through rock at a terrific rate, the drills generated far greater quantities of dust than did hand drilling. They also pulverized the broken rock into smaller particles, capable of reaching the alveoli of the worker's lungs. "Now, these buzzy machines, they grind the dust up extra fine," complained Butte miner Joe Shannon, "and you inhale every bit of that dust as it comes out. The dust settles in your lungs and you can't get away from it. You are right there facing it, and it is pumped into you, the same as the hose turned on you. And the man down below you shoveling, he inhales it just as bad as you." Shannon clearly recognized that the silica threat crossed occupational lines, placing craftsmen and laborers in common peril.[43]

Faster drilling meant more frequent blasting, which filled the workplace with dust and toxic gases. The editors of the *Engineering and Mining Journal* lamented that "in the hurry to push forward exploitation, insufficient time is given for the dust to settle after blasting." Other practices that raised dust included blowing out clogged holes with compressed air, blasting boulders, removing ore from chutes, and other ore-handling tasks. Speedup, which was particularly intense for the ore shovelers, who had to keep pace with the new drills, forced workers to breathe harder and faster, thereby increasing their dose of silica. In mills, processes in which ore was crushed or conveyed dry contaminated the working environment. Poor ventilation left dust particles suspended in the air for hours.[44]

Mine operators undertook no systematic industrial hygiene pro-

---

of California, Berkeley; *MSP*, Jan. 21, 1899, p. 59; Sandon *Paystreak*, Oct. 26, 1901; *Neihart Herald*, Aug. 14, 1891; Haywood, *Bill Haywood's Book*, pp. 80, 89; William M. McCutcheon (Ingersoll-Sergeant Drill Co.) to Frederic Irwin, Dec. 27, 1902, Trade Dollar Consolidated Mining and Milling Company Papers, box 4, Idaho State Historical Society, Boise.

43. Joe Shannon, "Testimony," Aug. 8, 1914, in U.S. Commission on Industrial Relations, *Final Report and Testimony* (Washington, 1916), 4:3857; Samuel C. Hotchkiss, "Occupational Diseases in the Mining Industry," *American Labor Legislation Review* 2 (1912): 138; *MSP*, May 9, 1903, p. 303; Alice Hamilton, *Exploring the Dangerous Trades* (Boston, 1943), p. 217; Ed Rosevear, "A Mucker's Dream of Paradise," *MM*, July 1918.

44. *EMJ*, June 2, 1904, p. 870; U.S. Bureau of Mines, *Miners' Consumption in the Mines of Butte, Montana*, by Daniel Harrington and Anthony J. Lanza, Technical Paper 260 (Washington, 1921), p. 9; idem, *Siliceous Dust in Relation to Pulmonary Disease among Miners in the Joplin District, Missouri*, by Edwin Higgins, Anthony J. Lanza, F. B. Laney, and George S. Rice, Bulletin 132 (Washington, 1917), pp. 13–21; idem, *Ventilation in Metal Mines, A Preliminary Report*, by Daniel Harrington, Technical Paper 251 (Washington, 1921), pp. 28–29; *DeLamar Lode*, Apr. 15, 1895.

grams in this period, so there was little measurement of the silica hazard. Only the exceptional Bureau of Mines-Public Health Service studies in Joplin, Missouri, and Butte, Montana, in the 1910s drew numerous air samples to monitor dust levels. Both evaluations found silica in average concentrations approximately one hundred times higher than the current (1988) federal limit on exposure. For example, eighty air samples taken in a wide spectrum of worksites in the Anaconda mine in Butte during 1916 yielded an astronomical mean value of 55.7 milligrams of dust (which was at least 60 percent free silica) per cubic meter of air.[45] Even if we assume that conditions in Joplin and Butte were far worse than those in normal hardrock mines, this evidence suggests strongly that dangerous dust contamination existed in any workings where dry mechanized drilling took place. Mines that were, for instance, ten times less dusty than those in Butte or Joplin still harbored a serious silica risk.

Anecdotal evidence of the severity of the hazard further supports this assessment. In 1911, Dr. Samuel C. Hotchkiss of the Public Health and Marine Hospital Service reported that "it was impossible to see the strong light of a carbide lamp fifty feet away" in Colorado metal mines that used machine hammer drills. Malcolm Ross recalled observing a power drill operator enveloped in "a cloud of white dust." An employee of the Silver King mine at Park City described returning to work after a blast as "a vision of Dante's Inferno" in which "it was impossible to see one's hand held out at arm's length."[46] Informal evaluations indicated that conditions in ore mills were equally bad. In Delamar, Nevada, Dr. William Betts found that the crushing of roughly three hundred tons of gold-bearing quartz per day produced dust "so dense that one can not be recognized a few feet away."[47]

After the turn of the century, miners became increasingly aware that mechanization generated more dust than did hand drilling and that, in turn, this dust caused respiratory disease. They often referred

45. U.S. Bureau of Mines, *Siliceous Dust in Joplin*, pp. 33–43; Anthony J. Lanza to Surgeon General, Dec. 27, 1916, Report on Anaconda mine, Butte, Montana, pp. 39, 40, 44, U.S. Public Health Service Records, RG 90, General Files, 1897–1923, file 5153, box 500-L, National Archives; Lanza and Harrington, "Report of Investigation of Mountain View Mine, Butte, Montana," 1916, pp. 19, 20, 26, ibid.

46. Hotchkiss, "Occupational Diseases," p. 138; Ross, *Yale Man*, p. 39; A Miner, "The Crying Need of Utah," *MM*, June 8, 1911, p. 10; *Owyhee Avalanche*, Feb. 1, 1901.

47. William W. Betts, "Chalicosis Pulmonum or Chronic Interstitial Pneumonia Induced by Stone Dust," *Journal of the American Medical Association* 34 (1900): 70; *DeLamar Lode*, June 13, 1899; "Drill Runner" to Editor, Sept. 24, 1910, *MSP*, Oct. 15, 1910, p. 511.

Early dust-monitoring equipment. Federal officials used this apparatus to collect more than two hundred samples of rock dust from lead-zinc mines around Joplin, Missouri, during 1914 and 1915. (Reprinted from U.S. Bureau of Mines, *Siliceous Dust in Joplin*)

Power drilling. Both the machine miner (left) and his chuck-tender incurred substantial exposure to silica dust while working in tight places underground. (Reprinted from *Mining and Scientific Press*)

to power drills as "widow makers" and "orphanisers." In Butte, where Larry Dugan was a prominent undertaker, the stoper drill was known as "Larry Dugan's friend." One of the many colloquial terms for silicosis was "the jackhammer laugh." Most miners, therefore, did not accept the specious argument that exhaust from compressed air drills effectively controlled rock dust by ventilation. Workers called the conveyor room at the Delamar mill the "death trap." Particularly dusty mines acquired similar reputations.[48]

The characteristic symptoms of silicosis usually became manifest only after the passage of a latency period of several years. The most prominent symptoms were cough and shortness of breath. Mabel Barbee Lee recalled hearing her father, a Cripple Creek prospector and miner, returning home "coughing the hard, dry, body-wracking cough that always frightened me" and going out to find him "slumped against a woodshed, gasping for breath." As the disease progressed, coughing came in violent episodes, disrupting sleep and digestion. Some silicosis victims were forced to sleep sitting up. Others tried to work in the mines after coughing spells had made them regurgitate their breakfasts.[49]

The health of silicotic miners followed an irreversible downward course. This incurable, progressive disorder slowly eroded the breathing capacity and vitality of its victims: the unrelenting toxic effect of silica particles trapped in the lung led first to nodular lesions and then

48. E. M. Weston, "Mine Dust Prevention on the Rand," *EMJ*, May 13, 1911, p. 952; U.S. Public Health Service, *Miners' Consumption: A Study of 433 Cases of the Disease among Zinc Miners in Southwestern Missouri*, by A. J. Lanza and S. B. Childs, Bulletin 85 (Washington, 1917), pp. 6–7; John Fahey, *The Days of the Hercules* (Moscow, Ida., 1978), p. 23; A Miner, "The Crying Need of Utah," *MM*, June 8, 1911, p. 10; Lanza to Surgeon General, Dec. 27, 1916, Report on Anaconda mine, p. 19, U.S. Public Health Service Records, file 5153, box 500-L; R. R. Pearson, *The Philosophy of a Mucker* (Ridgecrest, Calif., 1960); *Salt Lake Tribune*, Jan. 1, 1900, rpt. in *DeLamar Lode*, Jan. 16, 1900; "Drill Runner" to Editor, Sept. 24, 1910, *MSP*, Oct. 15, 1910, p. 511; Smith, *Song of the Hummer and Drill*, pp. 133–34, 148; Haywood, *Bill Haywood's Book*, p. 82. Larry Lankton argues that the new drills "improved underground ventilation" by releasing compressed air ("Machine *under* the Garden," p. 31). The dust measurements cited above from Joplin and Butte refute this contention. Further, although the air exhausted from drills somewhat diluted the silica contamination at the mine face (though certainly not to a harmless level), this was done by blowing dust into areas where it increased the hazard to other workers. See Daniel Harrington, "Efficient Ventilation of Metal Mines," in American Institute of Mining and Metallurgical Engineers, *Transactions* 68 (1923): 411; U.S. Bureau of Mines, *Effects of Breathing Dusts*, p. 114; *MSP*, May 28, 1904, p. 360; Edward Ryan, "Mine Accidents and Their Prevention," *MSP*, June 22, 1912, p. 862. For a full discussion of the limitations of dilution ventilation, see John E. Mutchler, "Principles of Ventilation," in National Institute of Occupational Safety and Health, *The Industrial Environment—Its Evaluation and Control*, 3d ed. (Washington, 1973), pp. 573–82.

49. Mabel Barbee Lee, *Cripple Creek Days* (Garden City, N.Y., 1958), pp. 62 (quotation), 68, 184; *Silverton Weekly Miner*, Aug. 18, 1911; U.S. Public Health Service, *Miners' Consumption*, pp. 8–24, 36–38; U.S. Bureau of Mines, *Siliceous Dust in Joplin*, p. 70.

to gradual coalescence of these nodules into masses of fibrotic scarring. Dr. Anthony Lanza of the Public Health Service (PHS) delineated three stages in this deterioration:

> In the first stage of miners' consumption are included those cases in which the sufferers showed a slight or moderate tendency to shortness of breath and some diminished expansion of the chest. Generally there was some pain in the chest, coughing, and expectoration, but no marked impairment of working ability. The second stage includes cases in which the sufferers showed moderate or moderately severe shortness of breath on exertion, diminished expansion of the chest, and well-defined impairment of working ability, with or without other symptoms. Those sufferers classed as being in the third stage showed a severe shortness of breath, with more or less total disability and aggravated symptoms of various kinds.

Of course, lay terminology lacked scientific precision. A miner with an advanced case was "almost a walking shadow," "a continual sufferer," or "worn out with suffering."[50]

Lanza's classification scheme is misleading in one important respect. Neither a "well-defined impairment of working ability" nor "more or less total disability" stopped sick miners from trying to work. Through a combination of economic necessity and psychological denial, they clung to their jobs as long as possible. Of the 433 silicosis victims Lanza examined in the Joplin study in 1915, 310 (71.6 percent) were still working at the time of the examination, including more than one-third (54 of 141) of those in the third stage of the disorder. The Butte investigation disclosed a comparable pattern of desperate tenacity. Disabled miners abandoned extremely strenuous work such as shoveling ore for less demanding jobs like driving mules. Some stayed on the job until the day they died.[51]

Most silicosis victims, however, eventually had no choice but to quit the mines. The disabled sought easier jobs above ground. Joe Duffy from Butte sang of leaving mining for lighter work:

50. U.S. Bureau of Mines, *Siliceous Dust in Joplin*, p. 70; *DeLamar Lode*, Feb. 8, 1898; *Silverton Weekly Miner*, Feb. 7, 1913; *Park Record*, Apr. 19, 1902.

51. Lanza, "Silicosis and Pulmonary Tuberculosis," 1915, p. 5, U.S. Public Health Service Records, RG 90, General Files, 1897–1923, file 5153, box 500-L; U.S. Bureau of Mines, *Pulmonary Disease in Joplin*, p. 39; U.S. Public Health Service, *Miners' Consumption*, pp. 15–24, 36–39; U.S. Bureau of Mines, *Miners' Consumption in Butte*, p. 11; *Silverton Weekly Miner*, Dec. 10, 1915.

> But soon I got weary,
> My eyes got getting bleary;
> My lungs they wheezed most all the time.
> So to dodge the undertaker
> I turned a moonshine maker,
> And gave up the deep, dark mine.[52]

When dyspnea made walking even short distances impossible, the sick miner became bedridden. Alvin Churchill's case took a typical trajectory: "He has been ill for a long time, but has only been confined to his bed for a few weeks. During the summer he was out most of the time and was able to do some light work, but lately the ravages of the disease have prostrated him." Some lingered on for months or years in a state of disability.[53] Of these, a sizable share fled to lower elevations and milder climates, often on the California coast.[54] Many immigrants returned to their native countries, refugees from the industrial revolution.[55]

Death often followed disability. Silicotics believed that they were doomed. The obituary of Silverton, Colorado, miner Hugh Kennedy characterized him as "a long and patient sufferer with no hope at any time of recovery." The editor of the *Engineering and Mining Journal* stated that silicosis was "commonly looked forward to by the underground man as his ultimate end." WFM organizer J. C. Lowney complained that "this deadly plague is so prevalent among the miners of Butte that it is looked upon with stoical indifference, the majority

52. Joe Duffy, "When I Was a Miner, a Hard-Rock Miner," in Wayland D. Hand, Charles Cutts, Robert C. Wylder, and Betty Wylder, "Songs of the Butte Miner," *Western Folklore* 9 (1950): 44; *Park Record*, Feb. 17, 1906; J. C. Lowney to Editor, May 4, 1909, *MM*, May 13, 1909, p. 9; Brown, *Hard-Rock Miners*, p. 94.

53. *Silverton Weekly Miner*, Oct. 2, 1903, Dec. 15, 1905, Sept. 22, 1911; *Park Record*, July 20, 1907; *DeLamar Lode*, Feb. 12, 19, 1901.

54. Dennis Sullivan to Officers and Delegates, May 31, 1904, in WFM, *Proceedings, 1904*, pp. 247–48; Harrington to Lanza, Apr. 3, 1918, Lanza to Harrington, Apr. 15, 1918, U.S. Bureau of Mines Records, RG 70, General Records, 1910–50, box 364, file 71317, Washington National Records Center, National Archives and Records Administration, Suitland, Md.; *Coeur d'Alene Miner*, Jan. 13, 1894; *San Miguel Examiner*, Oct. 5, 1901, May 16, 1903; *Tonopah Miner*, May 7, 1904; *Rhyolite Daily Bulletin*, Feb. 1, 1908.

55. Holman, "Mining, Silicosis, and Rock Removal," p. 10; M. McCusker, "Testimony," Aug. 8, 1914, in U.S. Commission on Industrial Relations, *Final Report and Testimony*, 4:3837; *Silverton Weekly Miner*, May 3, 1912; Dan DeQuille, *Mining Industry*, n.d., rpt. in *MSP*, Feb. 18, 1893, p. 106. For a comparative analysis of this phenomenon, see Alan Derickson, "Industrial Refugees: The Migration of Silicotics from the Mines of North America and South Africa in the Early Twentieth Century," *Labor History* 29 (1988): 66–89.

taking it for granted that it is the inevitable doom of all who remain long enough at work in the mines."[56] Accordingly, although some victims grew despondent, most bore their illness with fortitude and perseverance. These men looked to death as a "welcome relief."[57] Whereas cardiorespiratory failure took some victims "peacefully over the great divide," others succumbed violently when a coughing spell precipitated massive hemorrhaging.[58]

Disease victims met their fate in various settings—alone in cabins or hotel rooms, surrounded by family or friends, or in hospitals. Hardly news in mining towns, these fatalities were cursorily dismissed in newspaper reports. This untitled obituary lay buried among miscellaneous items in the *Rhyolite Herald*: "N. N. Rogers died Tuesday at the [miners' union] hospital of miners' consumption. He was buried Thursday afternoon in the local cemetery by Bonanza Miners' Union. The deceased had no relatives in this section."[59] Industrial disease was not a facet of economic development that served the booster aims of mining-town journalism.

Complications frequently hastened death. The disorder was called "miners' consumption" because it fostered a strong predisposition to pulmonary tuberculosis. In the Joplin study, only 8 of 128 first-stage silicotics had tuberculosis as well, but 73 of 141 third-stage subjects had this complication. As the name implies, consumption consumed its victims, often with startling speed.[60]

Silicosis also set up those who contracted it for pneumonia. The demise of Louis Johnson illustrates the vulnerability to infection. "Mr. Johnson had been in poor health for more than a year past, suffering

56. *Silverton Weekly Miner*, Oct. 14, 1910; *EMJ*, June 13, 1914, p. 1211; J. C. Lowney to Editor, Nov. 23, 1908, *MM*, Dec. 10, 1908, p. 11; *Tonopah Miner*, Apr. 16, 1904, Sept. 9, 1911.

57. *Park Record*, Sept. 27, 1902; *MM*, May 1918; *Silverton Weekly Miner*, May 29, 1903, May 20, 1910; Terry *News-Record*, Oct. 30, 1908.

58. *Park Record*, Apr. 15, 1905; Nye County Recorder, "Record of Deaths, 1912–1917," pp. 167, 198, Nye County Records, vol. D; idem, "Record of Deaths, 1914–23," p. 34, Nye County Records, vol. F; *MM*, May 1919; *Tonopah Daily Sun*, Sept. 22, 1905; Nevada County Recorder, "Register of Deaths, 1916–25," p. 72, Nevada County Records, vol. 4, Rood Administrative Center, Nevada City, Calif.

59. *Rhyolite Herald*, Sept. 21, 1906; *Park Record*, Jan. 31, 1903, Jan. 9, 1904, July 7, 1906; *San Miguel Examiner*, Feb. 24, 1900, May 18, 1901, Apr. 11, 1903; Nevada County Recorder, "Register of Deaths, 1873–1905," pp. 339–40, Nevada County Records, vol. 1; *Tonopah Bonanza*, Mar. 18, 1905; *Daily Arizona Silver Belt*, Jan. 3, 1912, p. 2.

60. U.S. Public Health Service, *Miners' Consumption*, pp. 16–24, 6, 13–14; Nye County Recorder, "Record of Deaths, 1914–1923," pp. 39, 140, 151, Nye County Records, vol. F; *EMJ*, Mar. 28, 1908, p. 643.

from miners' consumption," reported the *Silverton Weekly Miner*, "but had never been confined to his bed or unable to attend to his work until about nine days before his death, when he was seized with an acute attack of pneumonia." In April 1918, BOM engineer Daniel Harrington informed his colleague Anthony Lanza that pneumonia was responsible for a substantial proportion of the mortality in Butte during the preceding month. "This apparently bears out your idea," noted Harrington, "that a miner affected by miners' consumption even to a very slight degree becomes extremely susceptible to pneumonia and kindred diseases and very much inclined to succumb to them."[61]

Silicosis became an acute disorder when the hazard was extraordinary. The epidemic in Delamar, Nevada, at the turn of the century demonstrated the disastrous consequences of short-term exposure to severe dust contamination. Built in a remote desert area far from water, the Delamar mill crushed quartz ore in a dry state, without any real hazard controls. Within five years, an accelerated pathological process had killed more than one hundred workers (as in the Gauley Bridge disaster, a precise toll cannot be determined). Dr. William Betts found that among a group of thirty deceased employees the mean duration of employment was only fourteen months. After leaving the mill, these workers survived less than eight months on average. The mean age at death was thirty years.[62] This outbreak became infamous. In a Labor Day speech in Silver City, Idaho, in 1899, Dave Farmer of WFM Local 66 declared (somewhat hyperbolically) that more men had died in the Delamar mill than in the war in the Philippines.[63]

61. *Silverton Weekly Miner*, May 19, 1911; Harrington to Lanza, Apr. 3, 1918, U.S. Bureau of Mines Records, RG 70, General Records, 1910–50, box 364, file 71317; Nevada County Recorder, "Register of Deaths, 1905–09," p. 16, Nevada County Records, vol. 2; *Tonopah Miner*, Sept. 23, 1911.

62. *DeLamar Lode*, Apr. 1, 1895, Feb. 8, 15, 1898, June 13, Sept. 5, Oct. 3, 1899; Betts, "Chalicosis Pulmonum," pp. 70–74; *MSP*, Apr. 21, 1900, p. 435; *EMJ*, Dec. 14, 1918, p. 1038; John M. Townley, "The Delamar Boom: Development of a Small, One-Company Mining District in the Great Basin," *Nevada Historical Society Quarterly* 15 (1972): 8–12. Townley fails to differentiate the silicosis epidemic from a preceding outbreak of some infectious disease. This infectious condition was plainly not tuberculosis complicating silicosis. Instead, its timing, symptoms, and apparent transmission by water suggest typhoid fever. See ibid., pp. 10–12; *DeLamar Lode*, Sept. 16, Oct. 21, 1895, Sept. 6, 1897, Oct. 2, 1900. For evidence that miners suffered acute silicosis as well, see Robert T. Legge, "Miners' Silicosis: Its Pathology, Symptomatology and Prevention," *Journal of the American Medical Association* 81 (1923): 809. On the myriad difficulties of estimating mortality in acute silicosis outbreaks among migrant workers in remote areas, see Martin Cherniack, *The Hawk's Nest Incident: America's Worst Industrial Disaster* (New Haven, 1986), pp. 89–170.

63. *Owyhee Avalanche*, Sept. 8, 1899; *Tonopah Bonanza*, June 14, 1902.

Even the casualties of silicosis in its chronic form died relatively young. In Joplin the mean age at death for 198 fatal cases was 36.7 years. More than a quarter of these miners succumbed before reaching the age of thirty. The mortality pattern in southwestern Missouri included multiple premature deaths within the same family: "Mrs. C. lost two husbands, aged 32 and 48, one son, aged 28, and one son-in-law, aged 34; Mrs. L. lost four brothers, aged 40, 42, 44, and 40; Mrs. T. lost two brothers, aged 30 and 28, a half brother aged 30, a husband aged 29, and a brother-in-law aged 28." Dr. Lanza concluded that the typical silicotic in this district died within ten years of his initial exposure to rock dust.[64]

Western miners survived somewhat longer because they started mining at a later age, generally worked in rock less hazardous than the Joplin formations, which were 95 percent silica, and had unions to press for improved working conditions. Nonetheless, miners' consumption cut short lives in the Rocky Mountain region as well. Data for eighty-one fatalities in Park City, Tonopah, and Silverton suggest that the typical silicotic died in his late forties. In the United States in 1910 the average life expectancy for white males at age twenty was 62.7 years, so the metal miners who fell prey to silicosis lost a significant share of their lives to the disease.[65] An angry miner claimed that silicosis was the reason why "Butte is very conspicuous for its absence of gray-haired men." Further commentary on life expectancy on the "richest hill on earth" came from J. C. Lowney: "The time required to bring about this condition is so short that the natural heritage of mankind, a serene old age, the evening of life, is almost unknown among the miners." The consensus was that victims died in "the prime of life."[66]

Silicosis prevailed widely, if not universally, in hardrock mining

64. U.S. Public Health Service, *Miners' Consumption*, pp. 26 (quotation), 15–27.

65. *Tonopah Bonanza*, 1901–2; *Tonopah Daily Sun*, 1905; *Tonopah Miner*, 1902–5, 1911–13; Nye County Recorder, "Births and Deaths, 1887–1906," "Births and Deaths, 1906–1909," "Record of Deaths, 1912–17," and "Record of Deaths, 1914–23," Nye County Records, vols. A, B, D, and F; *Silverton Weekly Miner*, 1902–16; *Park Record*, 1902–7; Michalski, "Yugoslav Immigrants," p. 122; U.S. Bureau of the Census, *Historical Statistics*, 1:56.

66. A Miner, "Butte—Montana's Hell," *Industrial Worker*, Oct. 24, 1912, p. 7; J. C. Lowney to Editor, Nov. 23, 1908, *MM*, Dec. 10, 1908, p. 11; Guy E. Miller, Gus Larson, and John Briardy, "In Memoriam," Nov. 29, 1917, *MM*, Dec. 1917; *EMJ*, July 2, 1910, p. 11.

areas by the early twentieth century. Samuel Hotchkiss discovered that in one Colorado district "this preventable disease was recorded as the chief or contributory cause of 30 per cent of the deaths which had occurred among miners . . . during the past nine years." The principal finding of the BOM-PHS research in Joplin was that 433 of the 720 miners examined (60.1 percent) had miners' consumption. Taking into consideration the self-selection bias inherent in such screenings and other available information, Anthony Lanza estimated the prevalence of the disorder in the Joplin area to be 30 to 35 percent, or more than a thousand cases.[67] Lanza diagnosed 432 of 1,018 Butte miners (42.8 percent) as silicotic. Because of the self-selection problem and other confounding factors in this study, he cautiously refused to quantify the prevalence in this district. Amateur epidemiologists were less circumspect. Testifying before a state investigating committee in 1911, two veteran Butte miners expressed the belief that roughly one-third of the career copper workers in the vicinity had miners' consumption.[68] The BOM diagnosed 244 of 303 Tonopah miners (80.5 percent) as silicotic in 1921. In the final federal studies of this period, 45 of 181 California gold miners (24.8 percent) were found to have silicosis in 1921–22, and 33 of 112 (29.5 percent) hardrock workers in the Oatman, Arizona, district examined in 1922 were deemed to be "affected" by silica dust.[69]

By today's standards these investigations are hardly rigorously designed epidemiological research. They nonetheless provide the best extant evidence that a significant proportion of North American metal miners suffered from silicosis. In addition, numerous informal observations on western miners' health status buttress their findings.[70]

67. Hotchkiss, "Occupational Diseases," p. 134; U.S. Public Health Service, *Miners' Consumption*, pp. 14–26, 30.

68. U.S. Bureau of Mines, *Miners' Consumption in Butte*, pp. 10–12; John Vickers and John Driscoll, Testimony, Jan. 30, 1911, "Proceedings of the Joint Committee of the Senate and the House of [Montana] . . . to Investigate . . . Ventilation of the Mines," rpt. in U.S. Commission on Industrial Relations, *Final Report and Testimony*, 4:3925, 3939.

69. E. R. Sayres [R. R. Sayers], E. R. Hayhurst, and A. J. Lanza, "Status of Silicosis," *American Journal of Public Health* 19 (1929): 636; *Tonopah Mining Reporter* (Nev.), Dec. 10, 17, 24, 1921; Cleve E. Kindall to R. R. Sayers, July 29, 1922, U.S. Bureau of Mines Records, RG 70, Records of the Office of the Chief Surgeon, 1916–33, box 84, file 032.1; D. Harrington to E. D. Gardner, Apr. 25, 1922, transmitting "Dr. Saunders' Oatman [Ariz.] reports," ibid., box 84, file: "Dust and Ventilation—District 'J,' 132.1, General Correspondence, 1922," and file: "Dust and Vent., 032.1, Dr. Saunders."

70. U.S. Public Health Service, *Miners' Consumption*, p. 6; Alice Hamilton, "Dean

Whereas self-selection in mass screenings tended to overstate the prevalence of silicosis, virtually all other confounding variables served to understate greatly the extent of the problem. The true rate of prevalence was obscured by primitive or nonexistent vital statistics programs, vague or incorrect diagnoses by physicians, popular misconceptions, cover-ups by employers and by the victims themselves, and the migration of silicotics. Throughout this period, the most important source of misunderstanding was the pervasive failure to differentiate silicosis from tuberculosis.[71] Therefore, it seems reasonable to conclude that in the early twentieth century at least 20 percent of North American metal miners suffered from this condition, or at least thirty thousand cases at any time.

Reflecting on four years of personal experience studying silicosis in six states, BOM engineer Harrington in 1920 estimated that the disease killed at least a thousand hardrock miners per year in the United States. In Colorado from 1917 through 1920, metal miners died from silicosis at the annual rate of 6.1 per thousand.[72] Hence the death rate from silicosis appears to have exceeded that for all mine accidents by over 50 percent.

Taken together, prevalence and mortality data show that silicosis

Scarlett, Phoenix," Jan. 12, 1919, Notes on trip to Arizona, Alice Hamilton Papers, box 2, folder 37, Schlesinger Library, Radcliffe College, Cambridge, Mass.; *Arizona Labor Journal*, n.d., rpt. in *MM*, July 1918; *Tonopah Miner*, Feb. 27, 1904; Legge, "Miners' Silicosis," p. 810; M. P. Villeneuve, "In Memoriam," *MM*, May 1918.

71. Harrington to Lanza, Apr. 3, 1918, U.S. Bureau of Mines Records, RG 70, General Records, 1910–50, box 364, file 71317; James H. Cassedy, "The Registration Area and American Vital Statistics: Development of a Health Research Resource, 1885–1915," *Bulletin of the History of Medicine* 39 (1965): 223–29; Editorial, "Occupational Diseases," *Journal of the Missouri State Medical Association* 13 (1916): 286; Alice Hamilton, "[Notes on trip to] Miami Copper Co. Mine," Jan. 18, 1919, and "Phelps-Dodge Corporation, Clifton-Morenci, Yankie Mine," Jan. 23, 1919, Alice Hamilton Papers, box 2, folder 37; Montana State Board of Health, *Sixth Biennial Report . . ., 1911 and 1912* (N.p., n.d.), p. 17; U.S. Bureau of Mines, *Miners' Consumption in Butte*, p. 12; idem, *Pulmonary Disease in Joplin*, pp. 9–10; *EMJ*, Jan. 16, 1915, p. 168; W. W. Boardman, "Pneumonoconiosis," *American Journal of Roentgenology* 4 (1917): 292; *Lyon County Times* (Yerington, Nev.), July 27, 1907; Betts, "Chalicosis Pulmonum," p. 74; Lee, *Cripple Creek Days*, pp. 63, 168–69. The problem of underrecognition persists. See Bill Keller, "U.S. Health Aide Asks Logging of Job Injuries," *New York Times*, June 21, 1984, p. 13; Rose Kaminski, John Brockert, John Sestito, and Todd Frazier, "Occupational Information on Death Certificates: A Survey of State Practices," *American Journal of Public Health* 71 (1981): 525–26.

72. U.S. Bureau of Mines, *Metal Mine Ventilation*, p. 5; idem, *Silicosis among Miners*, by R. R. Sayers, Technical Paper 372 (Washington, 1925), p. 4; Nevada State Inspector of Mines, *Annual Report, 1912*, p. 10; Alice Hamilton, "[Notes on meeting at] Headquarters of Miners' Union, Morenci," Jan. 1919, Alice Hamilton Papers, box 2, folder 37.

by itself posed a greater threat to miners' well-being than did all safety hazards combined. Indeed, contemporary observers espoused just this viewpoint. H. I. Young, a manager for American Zinc, Lead and Smelting Company, and Dr. Lanza saw silicosis as far and away the leading hazard. "For every man killed or disabled by injury in hard rock mines, twenty-five have been victims of hard rock dust," Young and Lanza overstated in 1917. "The history of hard rock mining districts throughout the world is predominantly overshadowed by the spectre of miners' consumption."[73] Clearly, silicosis deserved its reputation as the "dread disease."

Lead poisoning was the second most important occupational disease afflicting hardrock miners. Inhalation of lead dust generated by various tasks led to gastrointestinal, neurological, and other symptoms of intoxication. When John Murphy ingested a lethal dose of lead, the pain he suffered was reportedly "simply excruciating." Unlike silicosis, lead poisoning was generally an acute but reversible disorder. Not surprisingly, its victims tended to return to work too soon after an episode of illness, only to contract a recurrence of the condition. Although significant hazards existed in the Coeur d'Alenes, the Sandon area, and other lead centers, conditions in the district surrounding Park City were perhaps the worst in the industry. More than seven thousand Park City miners were "leaded" badly enough to seek medical attention in the period 1872–1903.[74]

Lead also wrecked the health of countless smelter workers. Preparing ore, operating furnaces, handling metal and slag cars, and other tasks led to deleterious doses of dust and fume. John Wright of the Denver Smeltermen's Union identified drawing out furnaces

73. H. I. Young and A. J. Lanza, "Underground Mine Sanitation," in National Safety Council, *Proceedings of the . . . Sixth Annual Safety Congress, 1917* (N.p., n.d.), p. 1350; U.S. Bureau of Mines, *Pulmonary Disease in Joplin*, p. 40; J. C. Lowney, Testimony, "Ventilation of Mines," Jan. 24, 1911, rpt. in U.S. Commission on Industrial Relations, *Final Report and Testimony*, 4:3918; John L. Boardman (chairman, Bureau of Safety, Anaconda Copper Mining Co.), "Safety in Mining—Other Than Coal," *Annals of the American Academy of Political and Social Science* 123 (1926): 102.

74. *Park Record*, Jan. 16, May 21, 1904; Ralph Richards, *Of Medicine, Hospitals, and Doctors* (Salt Lake City, 1953), pp. 126–38; Samuel Norman to Anthony Shilland, Feb. 25, 1903, Mine-Mill Papers, box 153, folder 12; Frisch, "Labor Conflict at Eureka," p. 153; Hotchkiss, "Occupational Diseases," p. 135; U.S. Bureau of Mines, *Relation of Lead Poisoning in Utah to Mining*, by Arthur L. Murray, Report of Investigation 2274 (N.p., 1921), pp. 1–7; U.S. Census Office, *Tenth Census, 1880*, 13:174–75, 175n; George Kislingbury (assistant state inspector of mines, Colo.) to Editor, n.d., *MSP*, Feb. 8, 1890, p. 92.

and cleaning dust chambers as two particularly hazardous procedures.[75] In 1912, Alice Hamilton found that of approximately 7,400 workers in nineteen major U.S. smelters and refineries, 1,769 suffered from lead intoxication. Less systematic studies and observations corroborated the high incidence of this disorder. PHS physician R. R. Sayers discovered that 299 poisoning cases had occurred at the smelter in Northport, Washington, between October 1916 and March 1918.[76] Immediate causes of death included gastritis, kidney disease ("Bright's disease"), and cirrhosis of the liver.[77]

Mining induced a host of other acute and chronic disorders. Toxic gases, mainly produced by the detonation of explosives, killed and injured both directly by acute poisoning and indirectly by causing intoxication, which, in turn, led to fatal falls. Near Ferguson, British Columbia, three members of WFM Local 119 died in 1903 from inhaling gases created by blasting without adequate ventilation.[78] Hookworm disease plagued the gold miners of California. In 1916, federal and state examiners found that 444 of 1,440 miners (30.8 percent) in the Mother Lode were infected with this debilitating parasite.[79] Additional

75. John R. Wright, "Testimony," July 15, 1899, in U.S. Industrial Commission, *Report*, 12:307–8; U.S. Bureau of Labor Statistics, *Lead Poisoning*, pp. 6–8; James O. Clifford, "Industrial Lead Poisoning," *MSP*, July 6, 1912, p. 10; Hamilton, *Exploring the Dangerous Trades*, p. 147.

76. U.S. Bureau of Labor Statistics, *Lead Poisoning*, pp. 58–61; Hamilton, *Exploring the Dangerous Trades*, pp. 143–54; idem, "Lead Poisoning in Illinois," *American Labor Legislation Review* 1 (1911): 19; idem, "Lead-Poisoning in Illinois," *Journal of the American Medical Association* 56 (1911): 1240–44; R. R. Sayers to E. H. Laws (superintendent, Northport smelter), July 29, 1918, U.S. Bureau of Mines Records, RG 70, General Records, 1910–50, box 364, file 70606; Lanza to George S. Rice, May 10, 27, 1918, ibid.; Edward Crough to Editor, May 24, 1912, *MM*, May 30, 1912, p. 11; Albert E. Wiggin (general superintendent, Great Falls smelter) to Dr. H. C. Ernst, Dec. 16, 1921, Anaconda Records, box 219, file 1002–1; Great Falls Mill and Smeltermen's Union, Minute Book, 8:150 (May 6, 1918), 186 (Aug. 19, 1918), WFM-IUMMSW Archives, vol. 248; *Coeur d'Alene Sun* (Murray, Ida.), Mar. 29, 1895.

77. Clifford, "Industrial Lead Poisoning," p. 10; U.S. Bureau of Labor Statistics, *Lead Poisoning*, p. 64; *Great Falls Daily Tribune*, Feb. 15, 1898.

78. *Lardeau Eagle*, Mar. 13, 1903; Hotchkiss, "Occupational Diseases," pp. 134–35; *Kendall Miner*, Aug. 27, 1909; *MSP*, Oct. 17, 1914, p. 608; *Mining Congress Journal*, Apr. 1922, p. 692; Terry *News-Record*, Apr. 13, 1906; Peter Fisher (Local 109) to Editor, n.d., *MM*, Dec. 19, 1907, p. 13; Idaho State Inspector of Mines, *Fifteenth Annual Report, 1913* (N.p., n.d.), p. 31.

79. U.S. Bureau of Mines, *Control of Hookworm Infection at the Deep Gold Mines of the Mother Lode, California*, by James G. Cumming and Joseph H. White, Bulletin 139 (Washington, 1917), pp. 5–9, 39; Herbert Gunn, "Hookworm Disease Infection in the Mines of California," *California State Board of Health Monthly Bulletin* 6 (1910): 408–13. On the contemporaneous epidemic of this disease among southern textile workers, see John Ettling, *The Germ of Laziness: Rockefeller Philanthropy and Public Health in the New South* (Cambridge, Mass., 1981).

health hazards included extremes of heat and cold, ergonomic risk factors, and the psychological stress of working in constant danger.[80] Ore milling generated risks of chlorine, cyanide, and mercury poisoning.[81] Smelting and refining workers were exposed to arsenic and zinc oxides, arsine, sulfur dioxide, and other toxic dusts, fumes, and gases.[82]

As with silicosis, these health hazards arose largely as by-products of the industrial revolution. Machine drilling generated higher levels of lead dust. It also led to increased use of explosives that produced toxic gases. Ongoing mechanization and other technological advances in milling and smelting also tended to exacerbate exposure to toxic substances.[83] Whereas in 1850 the primary threat to employees in mines, mills, and smelters was the possibility of an accident on the job, by the turn of the century these workers had more to fear from a wide range of work-induced diseases.

On balance, industrialization caused working conditions to deteriorate. To be sure, there is no conclusive evidence that the new technology fostered an overall rise in the accident rate. For instance, a higher proportion of exhausted men may have fallen to their deaths from crude, often wet, ladders while climbing out of mines at the end of their shift than were killed in the more dramatic mishaps involving

80. F. G. Clough (WFM Executive Board), "Report," n.d., *MM*, Mar. 3, 1910, p. 10; William E. Gomm, Physician's Certificate of Disability, July 11, 1903, Mine-Mill Papers, box 154, folder 4; Bingham Miners' Union, Minute Book, 2:43 (Aug. 23, 1907), WFM and IUMMSW Records, box 2, Cornell University; *Butte Daily Miner*, Feb. 12, 1887; *Park Record*, Feb. 6, 1904; A Miner, "Butte—Montana's Hell," *Industrial Worker*, Oct. 24, 1912, p. 7.

81. *DeLamar Lode*, Apr. 8, 1895, Sept. 7, 1896; *Little Rockies Miner*, Oct. 10, 1907; *Manhattan Post*, June 24, 1911, p. 1; *Idaho Avalanche*, Nov. 13, 1896; Haywood, *Bill Haywood's Book*, p. 62.

82. Great Falls Mill and Smeltermen's Union, Minute Book, 8:217 (Dec. 2, 1918), 219–20 (Dec. 9, 1918), 9:3 (July 14, 1919), WFM-IUMMSW Archives, vols. 248–49; Montana Industrial Accident Board, *Fourth Annual Report, 1919* (Helena, n.d.), p. 93; Richard Terhune, "Testimony," Aug. 3, 1899, in U.S. Industrial Commission, *Report*, 12:592; *EMJ*, July 1, 1911, p. 24; Charles H. Fulton to Editor, Aug. 18, 1915, *EMJ*, Aug. 28, 1915, p. 363; *MSP*, May 16, 1914, p. 811. Apparently, no one in the nonferrous metals industry recognized the carcinogenicity of arsenic at this time.

83. John R. Wright, "Testimony," July 17, 1899, in U.S. Industrial Commission, *Report*, 12:314; Anthony J. Lanza to George S. Rice, May 27, 1918, U.S. Bureau of Mines Records, RG 70, General Records, 1910–50, box 364, file 70606; Young, *Western Mining*, pp. 212–13, 217–18, 231–33, 274, 283–85; U.S. Bureau of the Census, *Fourteenth Census, 1920, 10: Manufactures, 1919* (Washington, 1922), p. 851. The health effects of industrialization on smelting were more equivocal than on mining and milling. Alice Hamilton observed a decline in the lead hazard in most smelting and refining plants. See U.S. Bureau of Labor Statistics, *Lead Poisoning*, pp. 5–6.

power hoisting equipment. Dan DeQuille detected no trend toward fewer accidents during the initial phase of industrialization: "In the early days, when the miners worked in a primitive way with a hand-windlass and sunk a small round shaft resembling an ordinary well, they quite as frequently broke legs, arms, and ribs, or were instantly killed, as at the present day." The extant data offer no reason to romanticize preindustrial working conditions with respect to safety from injury.[84]

On the other hand, mechanization and the application of inanimate sources of power to ore extraction and processing unquestionably created unprecedented risks of occupational disease. It is also plain that by the early twentieth century the problem of disease dwarfed that of trauma. *Mining and Scientific Press* expressed the consensus in 1910: "The insidious undermining of health through the breathing of dust from machine drills, vitiated air, poisonous gases from explosives and from the rocks, exposure to water, etc., is of far more real importance than deaths and broken limbs from falls of ground or the various more obvious dangers." The magnitude of the silicosis epidemic alone settles this issue.[85]

The labor process thus grew more threatening to the well-being of mine, mill, and smelter workers in the late nineteenth and early twentieth centuries. The only course of action available to unorganized laborers was to quit work before they were victimized.[86] Unionized workers had other alternatives.

---

84. DeQuille, *Big Bonanza*, p. 145; R. W. Raymond, "The Hygiene of Mines," in American Institute of Mining Engineers, *Transactions* 8 (1880): 109–10; *Weekly Missoulian*, Aug. 6, 1886; *Slocan Drill*, Oct. 23, 1903; Gates, *Michigan Copper*, p. 103; Brown, *Hard-Rock Miners*, pp. 81–82; cf. Wyman, *Hard-Rock Epic*, pp. 84–117. In a detailed examination of one mining district, Larry D. Lankton and Jack K. Martin present considerable evidence that the probability of fatal injury on the job actually decreased during the industrializing era. Unfortunately, this study does not address the larger issue of work-related disease. See "Technological Advance, Organizational Structure, and Underground Fatalities in the Upper Michigan Copper Mines, 1860–1929," *Technology and Culture* 28 (1987): 42–66.

85. *MSP*, July 2, 1910, p. 11; George Kislingbury to Editor, n.d., *MSP*, Feb. 8, 1890, p. 92.

86. *Coeur d'Alene Miner*, Feb. 24, 1894; *Idaho Avalanche*, Nov. 22, 1895; Wyman, *Hard-Rock Epic*, pp. 127–28. Conservative economists contend that through labor market forces individual decisions to quit dangerous jobs bring about the amelioration of hazardous working conditions. For an incisive critique of this contention, see James C. Robinson, "Worker Responses to Workplace Hazards," *Journal of Health Politics, Policy and Law* 12 (1987): 665–82.

3 | *Mutual Aid*

Miners came to one another's aid in sickness and injury. They attempted to prevent occupational hazards and rescued co-workers injured on the job. Through the WFM, they disbursed disability benefits and provided medical services. Their local unions made sure that deceased members received a respectable burial. Mutual dependence for survival and security strengthened solidarity in the ranks of the Western Federation.

An ethos of mutualism shaped the lives of union miners. Their shared struggles to cope with misfortune were of a piece with the other collective endeavors of their movement. This comprehensive fraternalism differed markedly from the circumscribed commitments of other fraternal bodies. In fact, secret societies like the Masons, which sealed fraternal impulses in exotic compartments removed from their members' working lives, reinforced values and practices of individualism. Although some helped members to find employment, most mutual benefit societies organized along ethnic or religious lines confined themselves to social activities and administering insurance programs.[1] Union mutualism, in contrast, integrated protective measures on the job with benevolent activities outside the workplace.

1. Wilson C. McWilliams, *The Idea of Fraternity in America* (Berkeley, 1973), p. 379; Albert C. Stevens, *The Cyclopedia of Fraternities*, 2d ed. (1907; rpt. Detroit, 1966), pp. v, xx–xxi, 112–22, 160–68, 262, and passim; Alvin J. Schmidt, *Fraternal Organizations* (Westport, Conn., 1980), pp. 3–20 and passim; Anthony D. Fels, "The Square and Compass: San Francisco's Freemasons and American Religion, 1870–1900" (Ph.D. dissertation, Stanford University, 1987), pp. 589–667. A significant share of union miners joined a wide variety of fraternal organizations. The Independent Order of Odd Fellows—"the

Taking safety precautions constituted an essential part of the traditional craft of mining. With characteristic self-assurance, a Cornish
immigrant boasted of his mastery over these matters:

> Oh, oo's tha chap o' girth an' brawn,
>   Oo naws tha set that's needed —
> Oo naws jus' 'ow a stull is put,
>   An' wot groun' should be 'eeded
> When caves do start a-workin'?
>   M'son, jus' 'ark to me,
> Min' I tellin' this to thee.

Timbering expertise—knowing "tha set that's needed" and "jus' 'ow
a stull is put"—came with training and experience. Frank Crampton
recalled his informal apprenticeship:

> A hard-rock mining stiff had to know how to do everything that was
> to be done underground, so the boys gave me the works. I was taught
> to lay track, test the roof and walls for loose ground, and to stand clear
> of rock falls while I was doing it.
>
> After I had learned the things I needed to hold a job, and keep alive
> while doing it, there came a course in timbering, cutting hitches for stulls,
> framing for chutes and raises, and putting in tunnel or drift sets.

Peter Fisher of Douglas Island, Alaska, believed that it took "years of
practice" to "learn how to preserve your dear self from injuries, which
is three-fourths of a first-class miner's mining knowledge." Workers
learned to drill overhead holes from an angle that sent any falling
slabs of rock away from the driller. They relied on the "candle test"
for air contamination, knowing that an atmosphere in which a candle
could not burn contained too little oxygen to work in.[2] They devised
diverse methods of controlling silica dust, including pouring water

---

Apr. 21, 1894; *Slocan Drill*, July 11, 1902; *Rhyolite Daily Bulletin*, Mar. 8, Apr. 27, 1909;
Silverton Weekly Miner, Sept. 27, 1907, p. 53, Dec. 9, 1910; Mario T. Garcia, *Desert
Immigrants: The Mexicans of El Paso, 1880–1920* (New Haven, 1981), pp. 223–27; Smith,
Rocky Mountain Mining Camps, pp. 189–91.

2. D. E. Charlton, "The Cornish Miner," *EMJ*, Nov. 16, 1918, p. 889; Crampton,
Deep Enough, p. 23; Peter Fisher to Editor, n.d., *MM*, Dec. 19, 1907, p. 13; Albert Willis
to Editor, n.d., *MM*, Feb. 2, 1911, p. 10; George W. King, "First Aid to the Injured,"
paper presented at the International Mining Congress, Sept. 1902, rpt. in Montana
Inspector of Mines, *Fourteenth Annual Report, 1902* (Helena, n.d.), p. 89.

into drill holes and improvising dust hoods around drills from the legs of discarded overalls.[3]

Metal miners had to entrust their lives to their comrades every day. Working as a young mucker, Malcolm Ross quickly learned the value of an experienced partner. "You are alone with your partner for eight hours, dependent on him to be alert for danger, whether small hurts or death," observed Ross. "The rock is always treacherous. It is good to be working with an old-timer whose miner ear catches the secret shifting in the disturbed load overhead." Underground workers routinely warned one another of impending danger. Unfortunately, not all those so warned took the advice. In 1914 the Idaho state inspector of mines reported that William Wallace had been crushed to death by a mule train of loaded cars, "having failed to get out of the way or to find a sufficiently wide place between the timbers to protect himself, although he was advised to do so by a companion." As the division of labor underground became finer, miners had to rely increasingly on the capabilities of hoist engineers, timbermen, and other specialists. Constant dependence on the vigilance of co-workers forged deeper solidarity among the hardrock men. As Malcolm Ross put it, "There is a brotherhood among miners knit by an unspoken pact against the rock."[4]

Workers were able to avert some risks through militant collective action. The first major strike over occupational hazards occurred in 1869, when the Miners' League of Grass Valley, California, walked out over the introduction of dynamite and single-handed drilling. After a three-month shutdown, mine owners agreed to the union's demands. But because of the clear superiority of dynamite over black powder as a blasting agent, this victory proved to be short-lived. The decision to replace candles with oil lamps led to a spontaneous strike by two hundred employees of the Daly-West mine at Park City, Utah, on May 31, 1906. The *Park Record* reported the grievances of Local 144: "The miners claim that the lamps . . . are unhealthful, dirty and inconvenient, and believe they are being imposed upon when asked

3. Raymond, "Hygiene of Mines," p. 113; G. E. Wolcott, "Stoping with the Air-Hammer Drill," *EMJ*, July 20, 1907, p. 117; Foster, "*Western Dilemma*," pp. 272–73.

4. Ross, *Yale Man*, p. 31; Idaho State Inspector of Mines, *Sixteenth Annual Report, 1914* (N.p., n.d.), pp. 9–10; idem, *Fifteenth Annual Report, 1913*, p. 33; *Silverton Weekly Miner*, Feb. 27, 1903; Lingenfelter, *Hardrock Miners*, pp. 7–8; Wyman, *Hard-Rock Epic*, pp. 99–102.

to use them." The issue was settled about a week later on the union's terms after management determined that candles were cheaper than the objectionable lamps. Whether or not they ultimately won their strike demands, miners prevented some accidents whenever they stopped work and abandoned situations involving imminent danger.[5]

When catastrophe struck, workers who were themselves in danger aided their fellows. The Belmont fire of 1911 demonstrated the extent of rank-and-file mutualism: "When the smoke and gas were so bad that men were falling all around, men stayed . . . to assist their less fortunate companions who were compelled to climb ladders. The weak were encouraged by the strong. 'Come on, boys, we are going up,' frequently came from the lips of the few who were able to talk, in order to encourage others. In one instance one [miner] unable to stand crawled onto the cage and pulled on a companion who was overcome." Manus Duggan became a hero in Butte for his role in the Speculator disaster of 1917. Duggan convinced a group of trapped miners to barricade themselves in a dead-end tunnel and to stay there for a day and a half until lethal gases had dissipated. His efforts saved twenty-five lives.[6]

Rescue teams boldly descended into burning mines. Gold Hill miners fought for the right to go to the aid of those caught in the Yellow Jacket mine. During the Belmont fire, "relay rescue parties were immediately formed from the hundreds of willing miners." When a blaze cut off the escape of four workers in the Eclipse mine near Silverton, Colorado, two hundred men freed them by boring a twenty-foot tunnel in only two hours. Many died in these labors. In 1906 three members of the Globe Miners' Union perished fighting a fire in the Old Dominion workings.[7]

Miners also undertook perilous missions to retrieve victims of explosions, cave-ins, and other mishaps. An early explosion on Hooligan Hill in Rawhide, Nevada, injured Tom Shannon, but "he probably

5. *Park Record*, June 2, 9, 1906; Mann, *After the Gold Rush*, pp. 183–86, 193; *MM*, June 1903, p. 33; Wyman, *Hard-Rock Epic*, p. 186; F. Szymounske (Local 190), "Stay Away from Whitcomb and Zortman," *MM*, Jan. 12, 1911, p. 10.

6. Nevada State Inspector of Mines, *Annual Report, 1912*, p. 45; *Tonopah Miner*, Feb. 25, 1911; Josiah James, "Lone Butte Survivor of 1917 Fire Recalls Heroic Manus Duggan," WFM-IUMMSW Archives, box 221.

7. *Tonopah Miner*, Feb. 25, 1911; DeQuille, *Big Bonanza*, pp. 128–29; *Silverton Weekly Miner*, Dec. 3, 1909; F. H. Little, J. J. Croal, and William Wills (Local 60), Mar. 27, 1906, "In Memoriam," *MM*, Apr. 12, 1906, p. 15.

would have been killed had his partners . . . not faced the shots and [run] back in the tunnel and carried him out." The only hope for those buried by cave-ins was that fellow workers would dig them out before they suffocated. As with fires, some rescuers died or suffered injuries aiding their comrades.[8] Heroic efforts came to be expected among these workers.

Union benefit programs grew out of traditional generosity. From the first days of the mining frontier, disabled miners and the widows and orphans of deceased miners benefited from informal collections. Hardrock workers customarily donated part of their earnings on the first payday following an accident. When Bill Haywood broke his hand at the Blaine mine before the formation of WFM Local 66, his fellow employees raised enough money to enable him to buy a small house and provide for his family until he recovered. Even after formal union programs were established, miners and their organizations continued to provide donations, loans, and other ad hoc forms of assistance to unfortunate fellows and their dependents. According to the Terry, South Dakota, *News-Record*, the miners' local took immediate action when it learned of the "needy condition" of Sophia Johnson and her three children: "With customary open-handedness, the union at once made a donation to support the destitute widow and it was also decided to give a ball for her benefit."[9]

The family was the most important institution providing for health and welfare in the nineteenth century. Hardrock miners who were bachelors and peripatetic workers, however, were largely cut off from familial support in times of misfortune. Reviewing the admissions records of St. Vincent's Hospital in Leadville, Colorado, for the quarter-

8. *Yerington Times* (Nev.), Dec. 28, 1907; *Manhattan News*, Jan. 6, 1907; Sandon *Paystreak*, Oct. 23, 1897; Frank Treanor (Local 119) to A. Shilland, Apr. 14, 1903, Mine-Mill Papers, box 154, folder 1; *Owyhee Avalanche*, June 21, 1901; *EMJ*, May 5, 1917, p. 812; *Tonopah Sun*, June 22, 1907.

9. Terry *News-Record*, Feb. 16, 1906; Haywood, *Bill Haywood's Book*, p. 61; DeQuille, *Big Bonanza*, p. 340; Charles H. Shinn, *Mining Camps: A Study in American Frontier Government* (1884; rpt. New York, 1965), p. 114; Robert V. Hine, *Community on the American Frontier: Separate but Not Alone* (Norman, Okla., 1980), p. 78; *Wallace Press*, May 20, 1896; *Kendall Miner*, Nov. 5, 1909; *Lardeau Eagle*, Aug. 22, 1901; Silver City Miners' Union, Minute Book, pp. 94 (Mar. 29, 1897), 98 (Apr. 5, 1897), 255 (June 6, 1898), Silver City Miners' Union Records, vol. 1; Bingham Miners' Union, Minute Book, 1:363–64 (Mar. 16, 1907), 2:108 (Feb. 8, 1908), WFM and IUMMSW Records, box 2; M. A. Whitney to Secretary, Miners' Union No. 47, Nov. 29, 1898, Gold Hill Miners' Union Organizational Papers, folder 1, Bancroft Library, University of California, Berkeley.

century up to 1913, Alice Hamilton concluded that it had served "a camp full of men, young men mostly." In Silver City, a union committee reported in 1897 that single men outnumbered married by well over two to one at a prominent mine in its jurisdiction. In 1901 there were roughly three males for every female in the Slocan Riding of British Columbia and more than two to one in the Nelson Riding. These ratios were typical of mining districts in western North America at the turn of the century.[10] Immigrants were least likely to have access to a familial refuge. Among foreign-born men in their twenties in four leading mining states—Colorado, Idaho, Montana, and Nevada—in 1900, not one in five was married. Moreover, the wives and daughters of many married immigrants remained in the old country.[11]

Without families to fall back on, sick or injured miners faced the grim prospect of public relief. Because mining communities tended to be small and culturally diverse, relatively few private charity agencies were organized on an ethnic or religious basis.[12] Hence the county hospital-poorhouse was often the only alternative to union mutual assistance.

Throughout this period, the county hospital served as a general welfare institution into which unfortunate people were dumped. "The county institutions of the far West, especially California, combine the functions of hospital and almshouse," observed the U.S. Bureau of Labor Statistics in the mid-1920s. "They are known as 'county hospitals' and their inmates consist of the temporarily sick or injured poor as well as the permanently dependent chronic sick and indigent." In Fergus County, Montana, for example, the facility was formally

10. Hamilton, *Exploring the Dangerous Trades*, p. 151; Silver City Miners' Union, Minute Book, p. 192 (Dec. 6, 1897), Silver City Miners' Union Records, vol. 1; Canada, Census Office, *Fourth Census of Canada, 1901*, 1: *Population* (Ottawa, 1902), pp. 26–27; U.S. Census Office, *Twelfth Census . . ., 1900*, 1: *Population, Part I* (Washington, 1901), pp. 496, 499, 511, 512; idem, *Twelfth Census . . ., 1900*, 2: *Population, Part II* (Washington, 1902), p. 253; Margaret S. Woyski, "Women and Mining in the Old West," *Journal of the West*, 20 (Apr. 1981): 44; Malcolm J. Rohrbough, *Aspen: The History of a Silver-mining Town, 1879–1893* (New York, 1986), p. 203. Prostitutes delivered some health care to miners. See Marion S. Goldman, *Gold Diggers and Silver Miners: Prostitution and Social Life on the Comstock Lode* (Ann Arbor, 1981), pp. 88, 71.

11. U.S. Census Office, *Twelfth Census . . ., 1900*, 1:575, 576, 579, 591, 593, 604, 2:261, 268, 283, 285; Michalski, "Yugoslav Immigrants," p. 77; Rowe, *Hard-Rock Men*, p. 32; *San Miguel Examiner*, Jan. 14, 1899.

12. Frederick C. Luebke, "Ethnic Minority Groups in the American West," in Michael P. Malone, ed., *Historians and the American West* (Lincoln, Neb., 1983), p. 394. Sizable cities such as Butte could of course support ethnic mutual aid societies. See Emmons, "Immigrant Workers," pp. 41–64.

named the County Poor Farm and Hospital. Miners forced by destitution into these institutions encountered primitive conditions. The *San Miguel Examiner* in 1903 expressed facetious concern that patients might infect "innocent rats, mise [sic], beetles, bugs, lizards and various other helpless creatures that have taken up their permanent homes in the bedding" of the county facility. Inmates surrendered all independence. The hospital serving Butte boasted a washhouse "where the matron can enforce her ideas of personal cleanliness on all the patients." Institutionalization meant disgrace. A sympathetic obituary for an old Black Hills prospector fumbled for excuses for his demise. "It was through no fault of his own apparently that he was finally taken to the county hospital, as he was unable to work," claimed the Terry *News-Record*. "He [was] never known as intemperate and did his best to keep body and soul together." Miners feared and loathed these places.[13]

Hardrock unions endeavored to keep their members out of the hospital-poorhouse and, indeed, free from dependence on any form of charity. The silver miners' organizations of the Comstock Lode set the pattern for decades of self-help. The preamble to the Gold Hill constitution of 1866 began with an emphatic declaration: "Experience has taught us . . . that the dangers to which we are continually exposed are, unfortunately, too fully verified by the serious and often fatal accidents that occur in the Mines, and that Benefits in many of these cases are positively necessary." After reflecting on the "fearfully hazardous nature of our vocation," silver workers in Virginia City resolved to organize to "enable the miner to be his own benefactor." These pioneering unions spent more time and money on mutual aid than on any other activity, including collective bargaining. Between 1867 and 1920, the Virginia City Miners' Union paid its sick and injured members over $450,000.[14]

13. U.S. Bureau of Labor Statistics, *The Cost of Almshouses*, by Estelle M. Stewart, Bulletin 386 (Washington, 1925), p. 4; *San Miguel Examiner*, Feb. 7, 1903; Terry *News-Record*, Oct. 25, 1907; *Butte Daily Miner*, Nov. 29, 1888, Feb. 11, 1887; AMA, *American Medical Directory*, 6th ed. (Chicago, 1918), p. 944; California State Board of Charities and Corrections, *Second Biennial Report . . . from July 1, 1904, to June 30, 1906* (Sacramento, 1906), p. 120; idem, *Fourth Biennial Report . . . from July 1, 1908, to June 30, 1910* (Sacramento, 1910), p. 105; Nevada County Recorder, "Register of Deaths, 1916–25," p. 161, Nevada County Records, vol. 4; *Manhattan Post*, Nov. 18, 1913, p. 1; *Arizona Silver Belt*, Dec. 8, 1907, p. 8; *Blair Press*, Dec. 10, 1909. Some Cornish miners came to North America to avoid the humiliation of accepting charity. See Young, *Black Powder*, p. 4.

14. Gold Hill Miners' Union, *Constitution, By-Laws, Order of Business, and Rules of*

This model of welfare unionism proved to be portable as well as durable. When miners in Globe, Arizona, formed a union in 1884, they borrowed language directly from the Gold Hill and Virginia City constitutions. Newly formed locals of the WFM throughout the West in the 1890s and 1900s proclaimed it their policy to "enable the miner to be his own benefactor" and adopted the Comstock benefit provisions with only minor variations.[15]

While disabled, sick or injured union members received from $7 to $10 per week, that is, between one-third and one-half of lost wages. Benefit payments were essential because what made incapacitated miners destitute was not heavy medical expenses but rather simple loss of income. Accordingly, union programs sought to ensure bare subsistence during temporary disability.[16]

Benefits for the disabled were virtually universal among WFM locals. Like their predecessors in the Comstock, Western Federation affiliates considered sickness and accident compensation an essential responsibility of unionism. When miners in Clancy, Montana, organized in 1894, they set up an insurance plan even before they drafted a constitution. Such plans consumed a large share of financial and other resources. By the mid-1890s, the Butte organization distributed

---

Order, 1866 (Virginia City, Nev., 1871), p. 3; Virginia City Miners' Union, *Constitution, By-Laws, Order of Business, and Rules of Order*, ca. 1867 (Virginia City, Nev., 1879), p. 3; Gold Hill Miners' Union, Minute Book, passim (1866–68), Gold Hill Miners' Union Records, box 1, folder 1, Special Collections Department, University of Nevada Library, Reno; idem, Financial Records, 1886–99, Gold Hill Miners' Union Organizational Papers, vols. 2 and 3; Lingenfelter, *Hardrock Miners*, pp. 51–52; Jensen, *Heritage of Conflict*, p. 14; Ben Goggin, "Come on Now!" *MM*, Apr. 1921, p. 3. The origins of the Comstock model remain obscure. Discussing the Gold Hill constitution, Lingenfelter states that "it seems very likely that it was rather closely modeled after that of some other organization. But what that organization might have been remains a mystery." He speculates that it may have been an eastern coal miners' union. See *Hardrock Miners*, p. 45.

15. Globe Miners' Union, *Constitution and By-Laws* (Globe, Ariz., 1884), pp. 2–3, 16–19; Central Executive Miners' Union of Coeur d'Alenes, *Constitution, By-Laws, Order of Business, and Rules of Order* (Wallace, Ida., 1895), pp. 2, 21–22, 24–25; Butte Miners' Union, *Constitution, By-Laws, Order of Business, and Rules of Order* (Butte, 1902), pp. 7, 18–20; Park City Miners' Union, *Constitution, By-Laws, Order of Business, and Rules of Order* (Park City, Utah, 1902), pp. 2, 9–10; Grass Valley Miners' Union, *Constitution, By-Laws and Rules of Order* (Grass Valley, Calif., 1903), pp. 3, 14–15; Cloud City Miners' Union, *Constitution, By-Laws, Order of Business and Rules of Order*, 1895 (Leadville, Colo., n.d.), pp. 12, 15; Trail Mill and Smeltermen's Union, *Constitution and By-Laws*, 1907 (Trail, B.C., n.d.), pp. 20–23; Lingenfelter, *Hardrock Miners*, pp. 27, 52, 133.

16. *MM*, Jan. 27, 1910, p. 3; *Daily Territorial Enterprise*, Sept. 22, 1877; Sandon Miners' Union, Minutes, unpaginated (July 21, 1900), Mine-Mill Papers, box 151, folder 11; Harry Jardine, "Some Suggested Changes," *MM*, Jan. 30, 1908, p. 13; WFM, *Proceedings, 1903*, pp. 194–95. See sources listed in note 15 for amounts and durations of benefits.

about $20,000 per year. For the WFM as a whole, indemnities reported to the international headquarters grew to $157,502 by 1907.[17]

Disability benefits were financed mainly by union dues. When epidemics or other catastrophes drained the treasury, some locals generated revenue from nonmembers through fund-raising social events. Most, however, managed to build a large enough surplus during good times to survive periods of increased claims or decreased revenue. When, for example, silicosis was decimating the Delamar mill workers, their union muddled through by liquidating its treasury. Only in dire emergencies, such as protracted strikes or economic depressions, did locals suspend benefits. The sacrifice made by Jim Hill exemplified the strenuous efforts that beleaguered organizations made to maintain their programs. As secretary of the moribund Mackay Miners' Union of Idaho, Hill paid $185 (more than a month's wages) to sick and injured members out of his own pocket.[18]

Many North American unions of this period developed centralized disability programs,[19] but the WFM plans remained strictly under local control. As its name plainly indicates, this labor organization was a decentralized federation of local unions, some of the most important of which had been formed as autonomous bodies long before the creation of the WFM. Accordingly, the general office administered only a minimal program for tramp members who had no local.[20] The

17. Clancy Miners' Union, Minute Book, p. 2 (Oct. 24, 1894), Small Collection 270, folder 1; *Butte Bystander*, June 7, 1896; Ernest Mills, "Financial Report of Secretary-Treasurer," in WFM, *Proceedings, 1908*, pp. 216–21.

18. A. E. Wheeler (superintendent, Great Falls smelter), "Memorandum," Dec. 31, 1908, Anaconda Records, box 203, file 237–6; Committee, Tonopah Miners' Union, to A. Shilland, Feb. 6, 1902, Mine-Mill Papers, box 152, folder 11; Sandon Miners' Union, Minutes, unpaginated (Mar. 10, 31, 1900), ibid., box 151, folder 11; *DeLamar Lode*, Sept. 12, 1899; T. O'Keefe (Local 72) to Editor, n.d., *MM*, July 1901, p. 34; Gold Hill Miners' Union, Minute Book, pp. 326 (Apr. 10, 1893), 332 (May 1, 1893), 336 (May 29, 1893), Gold Hill Miners' Union Records, Nevada Historical Society, Reno; Executive Board, WFM, Minute Book, 3:30 (Jan. 6, 1910), WFM-IUMMSW Archives, vol. 3.

19. U.S. Bureau of Labor, *Annual Report of the Commissioner, 1908*, pp. 21–195. According to this report (p. 24), the Brotherhood of Locomotive Engineers in 1867 became the first U.S. union to establish a national benefit program, providing indemnities for death and permanent disability. In many organizations the general secretary-treasurer took charge of administering the insurance plan. The degree of centralization varied considerably among organizations.

20. Edward Boyce, "President's Report," in WFM, *Proceedings, 1901*, p. 13; WFM, *Proceedings, 1903*, pp. 197–98, 214; Executive Board, WFM, Minute Book, 1:401 (Dec. 10, 1906), WFM-IUMMSW Archives, vol. 1. For a very helpful discussion of the union at large, see James C. Foster, "The Ten Day Tramps," *Labor History*, 23 (1982): 615–18. The WFM Executive Board inconsistently granted some desperate pleas for donations and denied others. See Executive Board, WFM, Minute Book, 1:279 (May 13, 1905),

international executive board did its best to avoid becoming entangled in disputes over individuals' eligibility for benefits.[21]

Indeed, the administration of disability insurance presented a thicket of problems. The limits of fraternal obligation were always difficult to define and enforce. The most fundamental conflict was simple: the needs of the disabled were overwhelming, but the resources of the union were finite. In addition to workplace injuries and illnesses, a wide range of nonoccupational disorders plagued hardrock miners. Numerous cases of typhoid fever, influenza, pneumonia, heart disease, and other conditions put a heavy burden on local funds.[22] Many needy brothers had to be refused assistance.

Formal rules governed benefit eligibility. Incorporated into local constitutional by-laws, these requirements reflected Comstock customs and basic values. Waiting periods kept members from collecting benefits for the first week or two of disability. The total indemnity for any episode was limited to a specified number of weeks of benefits, usually ten. The miners, however, were always ambivalent about enforcing such rigid limits. Accordingly, locals often adopted loophole clauses, permitting the organization to vote to extend insurance for an additional five weeks to members "receiving great bodily injury." Not immune to Victorian moralism, organized miners denied aid when "the sickness or accident was caused by intemperance, imprudence or immoral conduct." The Silver City Miners' Union bluntly stated that it granted no benefits for venereal disease. Some locals barred payments for any chronic disease. All unions required that applications be accompanied by a physician's certificate delineating the facts of the case.

Other restrictions sought to protect the collectivity against claims by those who had not contributed their share to the fund. Assistance was unavailable during the first months after one joined the union.

---

296 (May 25, 1905), 2:95 (Jan. 18, 1909), 104 (Jan. 21, 1909), WFM-IUMMSW Archives, vols. 1–2.

21. Executive Board, WFM, Minute Book, 1:101 (Dec. 5, 1903), 218 (Dec. 7, 1904), 356 (May 23, 1906), WFM-IUMMSW Archives, vol. 1.

22. Ernest P. Orford to Hugh Limbeer, Oct. 20, 1897, Ernest P. Orford Letter Book, Idaho State Historical Society, Boise; W. A. Holt, "Cleanliness and Health," *State Safety News* (Arizona State Mining Bureau), May 1917, p. 11; *Park Record*, Jan. 14, 1905; *Fairbanks Daily Times* (Alaska), Mar. 4, 1908; *Little Rockies Miner*, Jan. 30, 1908; Nevada State Board of Health, *Biennial Report . . . 1903–04* (Carson City, Nev., 1905), p. 8; *Manhattan News*, Dec. 30, 1906; Brown, *Hard-Rock Miners*, pp. 42–44.

All locals prohibited benefits for any conditions that had existed before initiation, thereby thwarting those who hastily joined the union to collect benefits. Similarly, members whose delinquency in paying dues and assessments put them in bad standing were barred from receiving assistance. Further, most local by-laws forbade reversing bad standing after the occurrence of an injury or illness.[23] These provisions sought not only to block inequitable claims but also to expand membership and thereby increase the funds available.

Determining the rights of itinerant members to benefits was an administrative nightmare with which WFM conventions repeatedly wrestled. A series of amendments to the international union constitution created membership cards, traveling cards, transfer cards, and withdrawal cards, as well as detailed regulations for their use. Yet none of these devices entirely succeeded in providing immediate aid to the migratory worker while ensuring that only the local in which he was currently in good standing bore the expense.[24]

Making rules, of course, proved to be easier than applying them. Face to face with hardship, bureaucratic reason often yielded to fraternal emotion. The case of Isaac Myers illuminates one common way of accommodating this conflict. When Myers suffered a "rupture" and applied to the Silver City Miners' Union for benefits in January 1897, he was found to be delinquent. To bypass this obstacle, the local membership voted that "Bro Myers be declared in good standing."

23. Gold Hill Miners' Union, *Constitution*, 1871, pp. 8–9; idem, *Constitution, By-Laws, Order of Business, and Rules of Order*, rev. 1885 (Virginia City, Nev., 1885), pp. 15–16, 18; Virginia City Miners' Union, *Constitution*, 1879, pp. 16–17; Central Executive Miners' Union of Coeur d'Alenes, *Constitution*, pp. 21–22, 24–25; Silver City Miners' Union, *Constitution*, pp. 16–17; Park City Miners' Union, *Constitution*, pp. 9–10; Butte Miners' Union, *Constitution*, pp. 7, 19–20; Trail Mill and Smeltermen's Union, *Constitution*, pp. 20–23; Grass Valley Miners' Union, *Constitution*, pp. 14–15; Tonopah Miners' Union, *Constitution and By-Laws* (Tonopah, Nev., n.d.), pp. 15, 17; San Juan District Union (Colo.), *Constitution and By-Laws* (Telluride, Colo., n.d.), p. 27; WFM, *Proceedings, 1903*, pp. 194–95; Lead City Miners' Union, Minute Book, p. 136 (Feb. 23, 1892), WFM-IUMMSW Archives, reel 53; Silverton Miners' Union, Minute Book, p. 69 (Apr. 3, 1920), ibid., vol. 59. With minor variations, similar eligibility rules and procedures prevailed among other North American unions in this period. See U.S. Bureau of Labor, *Annual Report of the Commissioner, 1908*, pp. 28–30, 53, 205–13.

24. WFM, *Constitution and By-Laws*, rev. 1896 (Butte, Mont., n.d.), pp. 19–25; WFM, membership card, transfer card, and traveling card, Silver City Miners' Union Records, envelope 2; WFM, *Proceedings, 1901*, pp. 58–59, 96; WFM, *Constitution and By-Laws*, rev. 1901 (N.p., n.d.), pp. 15–19; WFM, *Proceedings, 1903*, pp. 224–25; WFM, *Proceedings, 1904*, pp. 251–52, 298–99; L. E. Higley (Local 4) to A. Shilland, Oct. 1, 1904, Mine-Mill Papers, box 155, folder 9; Executive Board, WFM, Minute Book, 1:310 (Dec. 9, 1905), WFM-IUMMSW Archives, vol. 1; WFM, *Proceedings, 1908*, pp. 426–27; WFM, *Constitution*, rev. 1914 (Denver, n.d.), pp. 23–24; Foster, "Ten Day Tramps," pp. 611–12.

But this maneuver failed to impress the union's finance committee, which rejected the invalid claim. Undeterred, the members of Local 66 settled the dispute by passing a motion that the matter "be taken from the hands of the Finance Committee and the amount of one week benefit allowed." This episode led directly to a more lenient eligibility policy. At the next weekly meeting it was resolved that "when a member is sick or injured his dues be remitted for the period covered by his illness or injury, but that when in arrears prior to his sickness the same be deducted from his allowance." If rules could not be broken, they could sometimes be circumvented. Locals frequently approved special donations and collections for members denied regular benefits.[25]

Although bureaucracy never completely constrained miners' generosity, the general trend in this period was to rationalize the administration of disability insurance. Too much easygoing openhandedness threatened not only solvency but also solidarity. Favoritism and other inevitable inconsistencies in bending rules divided local unions. Hence, presentation of a detailed physician's certificate and strict adherence to other eligibility criteria became real necessities.[26] Through such painful experiences as the sudden disappearance of the secretary of the Jerome Miners' Union, "leaving nothing behind but thirty cents in postage stamps," the WFM learned the value of bonding requirements and tighter auditing procedures. Grudgingly, locals adopted a more businesslike approach to benevolence.[27]

25. Silver City Miners' Union, Minute Book, pp. 65–66 (Jan. 18, 1897), 68 (Jan. 25, 1897), 55–56 (Dec. 14, 1896), 199–200 (Dec. 6, 20, 1897), Silver City Miners' Union Records, vol. 1; John Pozzi to Officers and Brothers, Bodie Miners' Union, Aug. 21, 1900, Bodie Miners' Union Records, vol. 2, folder: "Incoming Letters, 1890–1913," Bancroft Library, University of California, Berkeley; Clancy Miners' Union, Minute Book, p. 107 (Dec. 31, 1895), Small Collection 270, folder 1; Bingham Miners' Union, Minute Book, 1:6 (Dec. 3, 1904), 2:21 (July 13, 1907), 50 (Aug. 30, 1907), 78–80 (Nov. 23, 30, 1907), 87 (Dec. 14, 1907), WFM and IUMMSW Records, box 2; *MM*, Aug. 28, 1913, p. 9.
26. Sandon Miners' Union, Minutes, unpaginated (Oct. 13, 1900), Mine-Mill Papers, box 151, folder 11; Philip Nolan to Officers and Members of the Twelfth Annual Convention, May 17, 1904, in WFM, *Proceedings, 1904*, pp. 283–84; Silver City Miners' Union, Minute Book, p. 64 (Jan. 11, 1897), Silver City Miners' Union Records, vol. 1; Bingham Miners' Union, Minute Book, 2:195–96 (Nov. 28, 1908), WFM and IUMMSW Records, box 2.
27. W. J. T. to Editor, Dec. 8, 1900, *MM*, Jan. 1901, p. 43; *MM*, July 1903, p. 53; L. Roberts (Local 199), "An Embezzler and Absconder," *MM*, Oct. 22, 1903, p. 8; [Edward Boyce], "Honesty Is Good When Practiced," *MM*, June 1901, p. 3: "Labor organizations should be run on strictly business principles, and no man, however honest he may

Paradoxically, in at least one respect bureaucracy fostered fraternity. Benefit applications increasingly consisted of physicians' reports sent directly to the local union officers. Executive board members or other local leaders investigated most questionable claims. Thus, rank-and-file visiting committees had to devote less time to policing claims while aiding the sick.[28]

Friendly visiting was a hardy union tradition. The early Comstock organizations required their presidents to appoint committees each month, "whose duty it shall be to visit the sick and those injured in the mines." The order of business of union meetings invariably included the question, "Does any one know of a member sick, or injured in a mine?"[29] Even when the 1893 depression forced the Gold Hill union to suspend sick benefits, rank-and-file delegations continued to visit the disabled and report on their status.[30] The psychosocial support offered by these visitors to homes and hospitals no doubt prevented mental illness and hastened recovery in some cases.[31]

Visiting committees also aided the sick and injured in material ways.

---

be, should be placed at an advantage where he can defraud the union at will"; John Murphy, "Concerning Surety Bonds," *MM*, Nov. 1901, pp. 21–22.

28. Silver City Miners' Union, Minute Book, pp. 119 (June 7, 1897), 183 (Nov. 22, 1897), 241–42 (Apr. 18, 1898), 297 (Sept. 19, 1898), Silver City Miners' Union Records, vol. 1; Bingham Miners' Union, Minute Book, 1:2–3 (Nov. 26, 1904), 2:165 (Aug. 15, 1908), WFM and IUMMSW Records, box 2. In contrast, it appears that visiting committees in most other labor unions at this time remained preoccupied with monitoring claims to detect malingering, excessive drinking, or other improper behavior. See U.S. Bureau of Labor, *Annual Report of the Commissioner, 1908*, pp. 53, 55, 57, 71, 85, 109, 115, 139–40, 145, 152, 179, 211.

29. Gold Hill Miners' Union, draft constitution, in Minute Book, p. 12 (Dec. 1866), Gold Hill Miners' Union Records, box 1, folder 1, University of Nevada; idem, *Constitution*, 1871, pp. 8–9; Virginia City Miners' Union, *Constitution*, 1879, pp. 15, 18; Lead City Miners' Union, Minute Book, pp. 32–33 (Oct. 6, 1890), WFM-IUMMSW Archives, reel 53. For evidence of the universal creation of visiting committees in WFM locals, see sources cited in note 15.

30. Gold Hill Miners' Union, Minute Book, pp. 362 (Aug. 28, 1893), 380 (Oct. 16, 1893), 383 (Oct. 23, 1893), Gold Hill Miners' Union Records, Nevada Historical Society. Similarly, the Butte Miners' Union sick committee persevered during the Great Depression though it had no benefits to disburse. See Reid Robinson (Local 1), "Monthly Report," Sept. 1930, WFM-IUMMSW Archives, box 1, folder 48.

31. Silver City Miners' Union, Minute Book, pp. 50 (Nov. 9, 1896), 296 (Sept. 19, 1898), Silver City Miners' Union Records, vol. 1; Great Falls Mill and Smeltermen's Union, Minute Book, 2:2 (July 29, 1899), 32 (Oct. 28, 1899), 499 (Dec. 20, 1902), 6:237 (Nov. 1, 1910), WFM-IUMMSW Archives, vols. 242, 246; Wyman, *Hard-Rock Epic*, p. 180; Berton H. Kaplan, John C. Cassel, and Susan Gore, "Social Support and Health," *Medical Care* 15, Suppl. (May 1977): 47–58; Ramsay Liem and Joan Liem, "Social Class and Mental Illness Reconsidered: The Role of Economic Stress and Social Support," *Journal of Health and Social Behavior* 19 (1978): 139–56.

Besides distributing benefit payments, visitors saw to it that those immobilized by disability received the necessities of life. Instructed to "call on Brother Frank Puigatore and to see of what he is in need . . . and to purchase same," the Sick Committee of the Hibbing, Minnesota, Miners' Union gave Puigatore food and clothing. The Great Falls committee found A. W. Parker "in Bad condition from long continued sickness" and nearly out of coal in January 1907. Local 16 donated two tons of coal to Parker and his family and advised the committee that "if anything further was needed to furnish it." Such mutual aid helped union members to stay out of the poorhouse.[32]

Emergencies forced hardrock workers to improvise first-aid and ambulance services for their fellows. Under the infernal working conditions in the Comstock, miners administered aid for heat stroke: "When the pain was so great that men began to rave or talk incoherently their companions would quickly take them up and carry them to the coolest place on the level, where they were subjected to a vigorous rubbing on all parts of the body, but particularly on the pit of the stomach. When these so-called 'stomach-knots' disappeared under the friendly hands, the checked perspiration again began to flow, and the men regained their senses." After Joseph Tresh and Fred MacDowell were blasted at the Rambler mine near Sandon, "a party of miners at once went to their rescue and bore Tresh to the boarding house and cared for him as well as possible until Dr. Gomm [of the Miners' Union Hospital] arrived." In other circumstances, workers transported the sick or injured to care. Eight men used a toboggan to bring pneumonia victim William Summerville down from King Solomon mountain near Silverton, Colorado, in a snowstorm.[33]

When professionals were unavailable, miners provided lay nursing services. Working partners in particular took responsibility for each other. Joseph Rogers's poem recalled this bond:

32. Hibbing Miners' Union (Local 191), Minute Book, pp. 9–10 (Mar. 23, 30, 1919), WFM-IUMMSW Archives, vol. 58; Great Falls Mill and Smeltermen's Union, Minute Book, 4:208–9 (Jan. 29, 1907), 215 (Feb. 5, 1907), 225 (Feb. 26, 1907), WFM-IUMMSW Archives, vol. 244; J. B. McGinnis, Report, July 7, 1890, Gold Hill Miners' Union Organizational Papers, folder 8, Bancroft Library; Silver City Miners' Union, Minute Book, p. 299 (Sept. 26, 1898), Silver City Miners' Union Records, vol. 1.

33. U.S. Geological Survey, *Comstock Mining and Miners*, pp. 394–95; *Silverton Weekly Miner*, Feb. 10, 1905; Sandon *Paystreak*, Aug. 14, 1897, Oct. 5, 1901; *Rhyolite Herald*, July 27, 1906.

> The southern heat, the arctic's chill
> Have taxed the nature from our blood
> For oft alarmed—sternly still,
> We've at each other's sick bed stood
> Ah! when disease arranged a deadly war,
> Bill acted nurse a dozen times or more.

The exigencies of frontier life demanded that mutual assistance encompass a great deal of care.[34]

Formal union programs grew out of these informal customs. When an unexpected blast shattered Jack McTaggart's kneecap near Ferguson, British Columbia, ten comrades immediately carried him into town on a stretcher. There the Ferguson Miners' Union "took him in charge" and "every attention possible was given him." During Joseph Nesbitt's attack of typhoid fever in 1898, fellow members of Local 72 "watched with him through the long, lonely nights." The editor of the *Tonopah Bonanza* admired the exceptional mobilization by the local miners' organization during the pneumonia outbreak of 1901–2: "Every member . . . has constituted himself a committee of one to aid and nurse the sick of the town."[35]

Although much nursing went uncompensated, some locals paid members their lost wages. In attending to Alexander Morris, the Silver City Miners' Union paid for forty-two shifts of nursing by five different members. Four lay nurses took turns with another patient in this local, with successful results: "Bro Andrew Bell reported as suffering from mental derangement, he is under the care of the Union and at the present time improving." Needless to say, the efforts of unskilled practitioners did not always bring about a recovery. In the case of James T. Scanlon, nurses submitted their bills to Local 66 shortly after Scanlon's funeral.[36]

Following no consistent policy, the Great Falls Mill and Smelter-

---

34. Joseph Rogers, "My Partner," *MM*, June 27, 1907, p. 14; Deadwood Pioneer, "Just from Dawson," *MM*, Nov. 1901, p. 20; Richard Dunlop, *Doctors of the American Frontier* (Garden City, N.Y., 1965), p. 119; Shinn, Mining Camps, p. 111.

35. *Lardeau Eagle*, Aug. 15, 1901; *DeLamar Lode*, Nov. 15, 1898; *Tonopah Bonanza*, Jan. 11, Feb. 8, 1902; *Tonopah Miner*, July 2, 1904.

36. Silver City Miners' Union, Minute Book, pp. 57–58 (quotation), 57–60 (Dec. 21, 28, 1896), 83 (Mar. 1, 1897), 171 (Oct. 25, 1897), 174–75 (Nov. 1, 1897), 177 (Nov. 8, 1897), 180 (Nov. 15, 1897), Silver City Miners' Union Records, vol. 1; Telluride Miners' Union, "Report of Secty-Treas for Quarter Ending Sept 30th, [19]03," Oct. 3, 1903, WFM-IUMMSW Archives, box 1, folder 19; Moudy, "Cripple Creek Miner," p. 381.

men's Union relied upon both rank-and-file members and outsiders to deliver nursing services. In 1907, this local sent a nurse to care for "Bro Smarich for a Few Nights, as he was a Very Sick Man . . . whos [sic] wife had also been sick and died." Although bachelors and widowers needed the most help, married workers also required nurses in certain dire situations. In 1915 the Great Falls sick committee reported "Bro Jos Bartlett almost gone and family tired out taking care of him." The membership instructed the financial secretary to "secure Nurse to attend to him in order to give the family a chance to rest up."[37]

Some locals created more comprehensive health care plans. The earliest attempt to provide prepaid medical services occurred in 1864. The original constitution of the Miners' League of Storey County, Nevada, called for a salaried physician "to give all necessary medical attention." At its first meeting, however, the league postponed this ambitious plan, substituting a more modest indemnity program. At the turn of the century, Local 53 in DeLamar, Idaho, regularly elected a physician, who was paid a per capita monthly fee and expected to deal with all medical problems of the membership. Local 5 in Terry, South Dakota, decided in January 1907 to hire its own physician so as to reduce the cost of medical care.[38]

At least two Western Federation affiliates set up comprehensive prepaid health plans with local hospitals. Local 193 in the Tanana Valley surrounding Fairbanks, Alaska, began in 1907 with a fund that paid members' hospital bills. Faced with mounting expenses under this arrangement, the union commenced plans for erecting its own inpatient facility. The impending threat of a major loss of revenue drove three Fairbanks hospitals to offer to deliver services on a capitation basis. Thus miners were free to choose among Catholic, Episcopalian, and Scandinavian institutions, and ruinous competition was averted. Local 193 also elected physicians to provide not only

37. Great Falls Mill and Smeltermen's Union, Minute Book, 5:34–35 (Aug. 13, 1907), 7:96 (June 15, 1915), 1:64 (Dec. 3, 1898), 119 (Apr. 29, 1899), 124–25 (May 13, 1899), 2:113 (Apr. 28, 1900), 115 (May 5, 1900), 212 (Dec. 22, 1900), 9:92 (Mar. 8, 1920), WFM-IUMMSW Archives, vols. 245, 247, 241–42, 249; H. L. Lane to Members of the Twelfth Annual Convention, June 2, 1904, in WFM, *Proceedings, 1904*, p. 267; Lead City Miners' Union, Minute Book, p. 4 (July 14, 1890), WFM-IUMMSW Archives, reel 53.

38. *Gold Hill Daily News*, Sept. 16, 1864, quoted in Lingenfelter, *Hardrock Miners*, p. 38; *Owyhee Avalanche*, Aug. 3, 1900, July 19, 1901, Feb. 19, 1904; *Great Falls Daily Tribune*, Oct. 18, 1902, p. 8; *Reese River Reveille*, Jan. 14, 1911; Terry *News-Record*, Jan. 18, 1907.

inpatient services but also outpatient care for outlying camps. In Austin, Nevada, the miners' local expanded its medical plan in 1911 by entering into an arrangement with the Lander County Hospital.[39]

The primary purpose of union death benefits was to avoid burial in a potter's field. Public supervisors of the poor unceremoniously interred many immigrant miners and others separated from family and kin. The *Silverton Weekly Miner* called attention to the "large number of unmarked graves" in the local cemetery and observed that "graves are not marked, unless some lodge has marked them." Across the ridge in San Miguel County, a similar situation existed. "There seems to be another epidemic of sickness among the scabs, for they are bringing down from one to two every day and are bringing them to the graveyard about as regular," noted a striking member of the Telluride Miners' Union in 1904, with no pretense of sadness. "They do not have funerals, but get a cheap coffin, put them in an express wagon and drive them out. The county pays the bills." No miner wanted his own or his comrade's life to end with this indignity.[40]

Union funerals also spared miners from the ignominious disposal procedures used by some employers. At the Treadwell mine on Douglas Island, Alaska, Charles Puckett reported in 1908 that "if they killed a man (and the statistics show they have averaged a man a day for the last ten years) he was wrapped in canvas and carried away to the cemetery and buried by the company and by company men, not giving his relatives or the shift a chance to lay off in respect to their brother or fellow-workman." Across the continent in Mineville, New York, the same efficiency prevailed: "It has frequently occurred that bodies of men killed in the morning at these works have been buried on the same afternoon, and in cases of men not belonging to the union, no notice given of the interment." Employers in this way prevented not only interruptions of production for funeral attendance but also trou-

39. *Tanana Miner*, Sept. 29, Oct. 14, 28, Nov. 3, Dec. 8, 1907; *Fairbanks Daily Times*, Dec. 3, 1907; *Miners' Union Bulletin* (Local 193, Fairbanks, Alaska), Mar. 1, Oct. 4, Dec. 6, 1909; *Reese River Reveille*, Feb. 11, 1911. For an informative study of Local 193, see James C. Foster, "Syndicalism Northern Style: The Life and Death of WFM No. 193," *Alaska Journal* 4 (1974): 130–41.

40. *Silverton Weekly Miner*, July 22, 1904; "Lex et Pax" (Local 63) to Editor, May 28, 1904, *MM*, June 9, 1904, p. 14; *Goldfield News*, Jan. 5, 1906, p. 6; *Great Falls Daily Tribune*, Feb. 20, 1901, p. 6.

blesome post mortem examinations that might produce information useful in damage suits.[41]

Union aid to the deceased and their families derived from personal commitments as well as constitutional requirements. Miners serving as nurses pledged to fulfill deathbed requests. When Alexander Gardner of Local 193 sensed that the end was near, he "called some of his fellow unionists to his bedside and instructed [them] as to his desires in case of death." Tonopah Miners' Union president John O'Toole "closed the dead men's eyes" during the pneumonia epidemic of 1901–2. Union representatives retrieved bodies, informed families of their loss, and transported the deceased to the undertaker or to relatives. In March 1903, twenty-five members of the Ferguson Miners' Union volunteered to deliver the remains of two fellow members to relatives waiting across Arrow Lake. The miners pulled a sled twelve miles across the frozen lake through "water and snow, mixed, eighteen inches deep."[42]

Funeral and burial benefits were provided through formal programs. Like many commercial insurance carriers and fraternal societies of this period, the WFM refused to underwrite miners' risk of death to the extent of paying sizable life insurance indemnities. Instead, locals limited payments to an amount deemed sufficient to cover a respectable burial. This allowance seldom exceeded $100. Nonetheless, in the year that ended on March 31, 1911, Local 1 in Butte paid over $12,000 in funeral benefits for 140 deaths. If next of kin could be located nearby, they received the benefit. When no relatives were available, the local president saw to it that the deceased received a decent funeral and burial.[43]

41. Charles Puckett, "Striking at the Bayonet Point," *MM*, Apr. 30, 1908, p. 14; *MM*, Feb. 6, 1913, p. 11. During the colonial era, workers who died in the Bolivian tin mines were buried in the mines. See June C. Nash, *We Eat the Mines and the Mines Eat Us: Dependency and Exploitation in Bolivian Tin Mines* (New York, 1979), p. 26.

42. *Tanana Miner*, Dec. 8, 1907; Carl B. Glasscock, *Gold in Them Hills: The Story of the West's Last Wild Mining Days* (Indianapolis, 1932), p. 50; *Lardeau Eagle*, Mar. 20, Sept. 18, 1903; *Park Record*, Sept. 26, 1903; *Territorial Enterprise*, Dec. 23, 1877; *San Miguel Examiner*, Mar. 14, July 25, 1903.

43. *Owyhee Avalanche*, Nov. 17, 1899; John H. Murphy, "Life Insurance for the W.F. of M.," *MM*, May 1900, p. 15; Silver City Miners' Union, *Constitution*, p. 17; Park City Miners' Union, *Constitution*, pp. 10–11; Bodie Miners' Union, *Constitution*, pp. 21–22; Grass Valley Miners' Union, *Constitution*, p. 16; Butte Miners' Union, *Constitution*, pp. 20–21; Trail Mill and Smeltermen's Union, *Constitution*, p. 23; Ernest Mills, "Financial Report of the Secretary-Treasurer . . . for the Fiscal Year Ending June 30, 1911," in WFM, *Proceedings, 1911*, p. 197; Sandon Miners' Union, Minutes, unpaginated (Apr.

Whereas some locals let undertakers take charge of funeral plans, others handled the arrangements themselves. After Charles Wright was killed in the Poorman mine in the Coeur d'Alene, his body lay in the Burke Miners' Union hall for viewing before burial. Lead City miners prepared for obsequies by holding special meetings to appoint chief marshals, honor guards, pallbearers, and color bearers.[44] Funerals frequently were held in WFM halls. The service for five members of Local 26 killed in an avalanche in January 1906 was held in the miners' hall because it was the only building in Silverton large enough to accommodate the crowd. In some instances funerals were conducted solely by the union, led by the local president.[45]

More often, however, the union played a limited role. Clergymen conducted most miners' funerals in churches, commercial funeral parlors, lodge halls, private homes, or cemeteries. Frequently, the WFM and another fraternal society jointly ran the ceremony. For example, the Butte Miners' Union, the Ancient Order of United Workmen, and the Sons of Saint George together conducted Sam Rundle's funeral in 1894.[46]

On the mining frontier, where many went to their graves accompanied only by the undertaker, funerals were judged mainly by their size. Unions showed respect for the deceased by attending funerals en masse as required by local by-laws: "It shall be the duty of all members of the union to attend funerals, upon notice from the president, and they shall assist in escorting the remains to the outskirts of the town." Some locals fined those who failed to participate.[47]

7, 1900), Mine-Mill Papers, box 151, folder 11. Most other unions at the turn of the century paid a death benefit that covered only funeral and burial costs. Only the railroad brotherhoods, the cigar makers, and the letter carriers paid over $500 in 1907. See U.S. Bureau of Labor, *Annual Report of the Commissioner, 1908*, pp. 42–47.

44. *Wallace Press*, Apr. 25, 1891; Lead City Miners' Union, Minute Book, pp. 5–6 (July 15, 1890), 108 (Oct. 5, 1891), WFM-IUMMSW Archives, reel 53; Great Falls Mill and Smeltermen's Union, Minute Book, 2:13–14 (Aug. 19, 26, 1899), 260–61 (Mar. 2, 1901), WFM-IUMMSW Archives, vol. 242; *Lardeau Eagle*, Mar. 13, 1903; Terry *News-Record*, Sept. 7, 1906.

45. *Silverton Weekly Miner*, Jan. 26, 1906; *Neihart Herald*, Dec. 18, 1891; *Rhyolite Herald*, Oct. 20, 1905; *Kendall Miner*, Oct. 26, 1906; Butte *Daily Inter Mountain*, Feb. 14, 1887; Sandon *Paystreak*, Mar. 10, 1900.

46. *Butte Bystander*, June 16, 1894; Mar. 11, 1893; *Lardeau Eagle*, Mar. 27, 1903; *Tonopah Sun*, July 20, 1907; *Great Falls Daily Tribune*, Mar. 8, 1903, p. 3; *Little Rockies Miner*, Nov. 28, 1907; *Rhyolite Herald*, Oct. 20, 1905.

47. Central Executive Miners' Union of Coeur d'Alenes, *Constitution*, p. 23; Two Bit Miners' Union, *Constitution and By-Laws* (Deadwood, S.D., 1898), p. 30; Sandon Miners' Union, Funeral Notice, Nov. 1913, Mine-Mill Papers, box 157, folder 8; *San Miguel*

The common practice was for the rank and file to meet at the union hall and put on black armbands, then proceed to the funeral in a body. When Dan Kelliher died in Delamar, sixty members of the Lincoln Miners' Union assembled on fifteen minutes' notice to follow his remains to the cemetery. In most cases, miners had to leave work to attend funerals. During services for John Leary, a member of the North Moccasin Miners' Union, "work at both mines was suspended so that members of the union might attend the funeral." In Zortman, Montana, all businesses closed during services for members of Local 190. Because smelters could not shut down so easily, the Great Falls Mill and Smeltermen's Union proposed only the "suspension of all work that is possible."[48]

Solemn processions accompanied the deceased to the cemetery. "The largest funeral processions ever witnessed in Butte, or for that matter, in all Montana," observed the *Bystander*, "are those formed by the Butte Miners' Union." On February 27, 1911, after the Tonopah Miners' Union conducted services for fourteen victims of the Belmont fire, more than two thousand men marched through a blizzard to the graveyard. When the merchants of Silverton, Colorado, strayed from the custom of drawing their shades while a procession passed, a committee from the Trades and Labor Assembly led by WFM activist Roderick MacKenzie responded indignantly:

> We are willing to put up with all the snubs, rebuffs and abuse that you may deem advisable to dole out to us during our lives, but when death has at last closed our eyes in eternal sleep and our hearts are freed from evil thoughts and our hands from worse deeds we humbly ask that your contempt, snubs and abuse cease. And this is how we wish you to show it: We don't ask you to shed any tears; nor do we expect many of you to join us at church, hall or anywhere else the carcass of our dead is being clumsily prepared for burial. No, gentlemen, we haven't the gall to expect much less to ask you to do any of these things. But we do ask without a preface of any "ifs" or "ands" that you pull down the window

---

Examiner, Jan. 13, 1900; see also sources cited in note 42. Similarly, the Atlantic Coast Seamen's Union required all members in port to attend funerals. See U.S. Bureau of Labor, *Annual Report of the Commissioner, 1908*, p. 160.

48. *Kendall Miner*, Oct. 26, 1906; Great Falls Mill and Smeltermen's Union, Minute Book, 1:49 (Oct. 22, 1898), WFM-IUMMSW Archives, vol. 241; *DeLamar Lode*, Aug. 2, 1898; *Little Rockies Miner*, Nov. 28, 1907; *Wallace Press*, Oct. 25, 1890. Some slaveholders permitted their slaves to stop work for daytime funerals; others refused. See Eugene D. Genovese, *Roll, Jordan, Roll: The World the Slaves Made* (New York, 1972), p. 197.

shades of your place of business when the funeral of a working man is passing your doors; and this we ask irrespective of nationality, because even among foreigners there might be an odd one who is human.

Thus funeral processions displayed class solidarity as well as respect for the dead. Further, when hundreds or thousands participated, the miners made a public show of strength.[49]

Local presidents performed burial ceremonies in accordance with WFM ritual. Wallace Johnson of Local 66 read a passage from the Bible and "gave an able discourse thereon" at the grave of R. T. Owens in 1901. Belt Mountain Miners' Union leader George Gunn delivered a "touching oration and eulogy" to Robert Weaver at the Neihart, Montana, cemetery. The editor of the *Neihart Herald* was moved to remark that "the ritualistic service of the Union is as fine as it can be." Services ended with each union member depositing a sprig of evergreen in the grave as he marched past it.[50]

Some locals had their own cemeteries. The Miners' Union Cemetery outside Wallace, Idaho, served the organizations in the Coeur d'Alene. Defiant to the end, Mack Devine asked to be buried beneath union ground as he lay dying in the infamous Coeur d'Alene bullpen in 1899. The Belt Mountain local elected a sexton to administer its grave-yard. Some groups designed their own grave markers.[51]

Miners composed resolutions to honor departed brothers. The union sent these declarations to the family of the deceased and published them in community newspapers and in the *Miners' Magazine*. Upon the death of Maurice Odella, Local 47 in Confidence, California, ex-tended condolences by having its resolution translated into Italian and sent to Odella's relatives in Savona, Italy. In the traditional rhet-oric of the movement, a committee of the Granite Miners' Union paid

49. *Butte Bystander*, June 7, 1896; *Silverton Weekly Miner*, Mar. 28, 1913, Feb. 26, 1904, June 12, 1908; *Tonopah Miner*, Mar. 4, 1911; *Park Record*, May 2, 1903; Haywood, *Bill Haywood's Book*, p. 98; Phipps, "Bull Pen," pp. 52, 57–58; E. J. Flanagan to Editor, Sept. 16, 1900, MM, Oct. 1900, pp. 35–37.

50. *Owyhee Avalanche*, July 26, 1901; *Neihart Herald*, Dec. 18, 1891; *Tonopah Sun*, July 31, 1909; Haywood, *Bill Haywood's Book*, p. 98; IUMMSW, *Ritual* (Chicago, n.d.), pp. 15–16.

51. *Wallace Press*, Aug. 22, 1891, Feb. 13, 1895; Edward Boyce, "Address," in WFM, "Convention Proceedings," MM, June 1900, p. 7; *Neihart Herald*, May 29, 1891, Dec. 3, 1892; Executive Board, WFM, Minute Book, 1:307–8 (Dec. 8, 1905), WFM-IUMMSW Archives, vol. 1; William D. Haywood, "Notice," MM, Jan. 11, 1906, p. 13; Telluride Miners' Union, "Report of Secretary-Treas for Quarter ending June 30th, [19]03," WFM-IUMMSW Archives, box 1, folder 19.

"just tribute to the memory" of John Darby by praising his "services as a union man and his merits as a man." Local 72 remembered Thomas Hislington as "faithful to his obligation, brave, cheerful, kindly and generous of disposition, fearless and outspoken in the cause of right and justice." The resolutions grasped for the meaning of apparently meaningless deaths. Most committees concluded that these events reflected a divine plan. The deceased was usually deemed to have ended a life of hard labor and gone off to an eternity of rest. Early resolutions thus emphasized fraternalism and fatalism.[52]

Besides generosity and loyalty to the union, resolutions also celebrated other mutualistic values. For example, the miners' movement cherished the self-sacrifice displayed by participants in mine-rescue efforts. The Telluride WFM affiliate singled out one victim of the Bullion fire:

Whereas, The grim reaper has taken from our midst Brother Hugh O'Neil, who lost his life trying to save those of his fellow man at the Bullion tunnel fire; and

Whereas, Brother O'Neil was a loyal and faithful member of the 16 to 1 Miners' Union who, while living, sought to better the conditions of the wage earners and went to a hero's death in his efforts to save the lives of his fellow workmen; Therefore, be it

Resolved, by the 16 to 1 Miners' Union, that we extend to the sorrowing relatives and friends of Bro. O'Neil our heartfelt sympathy in their bereavement for we who knew him so well in life feel his loss most keenly and realize the loss to his relatives and friends; and be it further

Resolved, That the life and heroic death of Bro. O'Neil is worthy of emulation, "For greater love hath no man than he who lays down his life for another," and be it further

Resolved, That a copy of these resolutions be mailed to the relatives and friends; and a copy be sent to the Miners' Magazine, Courier, and Chronicle and Examiner, and the same be spread on the minutes of our

52. D. D. Good et al. (Local 4), "Resolutions of Condolence," *Butte Bystander*, July 1, 1893; Brothers Dees, Castles, and O'Keefe, "Resolutions," May 2, 1901, *DeLamar Lode*, May 7, 1901; A. F. McCormick and Fred E. Moyle (Local 47), "In Memoriam," Oct. 25, 1902, *MM*, Dec. 1902, pp. 55–56; Lead City Miners' Union, Minute Book, p. 8 (July 21, 1890), WFM-IUMMSW Archives, reel 53; W. B. Easterly et al. (Local 19), "Communications," Jan. 29, 1901, *MM*, Mar. 1901, p. 37; James Gibson, P. R. McDonald, and J. A. McKinnon (Local 38), "In Memoriam," Mar. 21, 1906, *MM*, Apr. 12, 1906, p. 15; Nick Comes, Henry Young, and Alex Robertson (Local 151), "Resolution of Condolence," *Tintic Miner*, n.d., rpt. in *Park Record*, Aug. 2, 1902.

meeting and our charter be draped [in black] for sixty days in memory of the heroic sacrifice of Brother Hugh O'Neil.

Death resolutions afforded a unique opportunity not only to reaffirm basic values within the union but also to proclaim them to the general public.[53]

After 1905 resolutions of condolence began to comment on the causes of death. In 1909 members of Local 235 in Rhyolite, Nevada, denounced the silica hazard that did in Harry Egan and declared their commitment "to strive for the better ventillation [*sic*] of mines and overcoming of the dust evil." This committee also resolved to disseminate its statement to the press "so that a wider publicity may be achieved in our efforts to wrest from a ruthless system a fair working condition." In Elk Lake, Ontario, Local 140 asserted that the life of Vincent McGillvary had been "unnecessarily sacrificed through a premature explosion for the maintenance of production and to satisfy the insatiable greed of the exploiting class."[54] Determination to eradicate hazards and the system that fostered them increasingly replaced fatalistic resignation.

Other commemorative activity expressed workers' grievances as well. The funeral for Joe Sukovich, killed in the Treadwell in 1908, became the scene of a demonstration at which thirty members of Local 109 were arrested for disturbing the peace. Coeur d'Alene miners observed as a major holiday the anniversary of the deaths of three union men in a gun battle with strikebreakers on July 11, 1892. In 1894 the procession of seven hundred to the union cemetery included delegations from the Knights of Labor, the American Railway Union, and the Cigar Makers Union. Orators at these exercises reiterated the contention that the three unionists were victims of corporate tyranny

53. V. St. John, O. M. Carpenter, and K. A. McLean (Local 63), "Resolutions of Respect," rpt. in *San Miguel Examiner*, Dec. 7, 1901; Butte *Daily Inter Mountain*, Nov. 29, 1889; F. H. Little, J. J. Croal, and William Wills (Local 60), "In Memoriam," Mar. 27, 1906, *MM*, Apr. 12, 1906, p. 15.

54. George T. Phillips, L. M. Davis, and John J. Kelly (Local 235), "Resolutions of Respect," Jan. 25, 1909, *Rhyolite Daily Bulletin*, Jan. 28, 1909; James McGuire, Charles H. Lowthian, and Gerald Desmond (Local 140), "In Memoriam," Oct. 18, 1909, *MM*, Oct. 28, 1909, p. 14; Harry Jardine, C. W. Neihart, and J. P. Cosgrove (Local 220), "Resolutions of Sympathy," Oct. 5, 1905, *Goldfield News*, Oct. 6, 1905, p. 4; Owen McCabe, Charles Manhire, and E. B. Coolidge (Local 111), "Resolution of Condolence," *Kendall Miner*, Aug. 30, 1907.

and martyrs to the labor movement. When martial law returned to the district in 1899, military authorities suppressed this celebration.[55]

Mutual assistance programs strengthened the miners' movement in several ways. Insurance helped induce men to become union members and to remain in good standing. Ross Moudy joined a WFM local in Cripple Creek "for protection in case of accident or sickness." Itinerant workers outside any local jurisdiction maintained membership in their home local in large part to preserve their eligibility for benefits. By enforcing eligibility rules, unions prevented delinquency and tightened organizational discipline. Although members promoted to management lost their right to participate in all deliberations, locals permitted foremen and shift bosses to pay dues and maintain insurance coverage. In the Coeur d'Alene, which had such a provision, foremen helped unionists circumvent an elaborate blacklisting system. Of course, the hardrock organizations won the gratitude of all beneficiaries of aid. Upon receiving a disability insurance payment, Gold Hill miner Peter Farrell sent his "best wishes for the welfare of the Union."[56]

Benefit programs enabled WFM locals to continue to serve members at times when they lacked the leverage to raise wages or shorten hours. In an industry subject to both wild cyclical fluctuations and ongoing pressure to cut labor costs to meet stiff competition in the world market, the miners' movement often found itself in a weak, defensive stance. The organization barely survived the depression of 1893, for example, taking wage cuts in most districts. Indeed, re-

55. *Douglas Island News,* Apr. 29, Mar. 11, 1908; *Spokane Review,* July 13, 1893, p. 6; *Coeur d'Alene Sun,* n.d., rpt. in *Butte Bystander,* July 21, 1894; *Idaho State Tribune* (Wallace), n.d., rpt. in *Pueblo Courier* (Colo.), July 15, 1898; U.S. House of Representatives, Committee on Military Affairs, *Coeur d'Alene Labor Troubles,* 56th Cong., 1st sess., Report 1999 (Washington, 1900), p. 106; *San Miguel Examiner,* July 5, 1902, July 4, 1903; Wyman, *Hard-Rock Epic,* pp. 47–49. On the tactical uses of commemorative activity by coal miners, see Alan Derickson, "Down Solid: The Origins and Development of the Black Lung Insurgency," *Journal of Public Health Policy* 4 (1983): 28–29, 38.

56. Moudy, "Cripple Creek Miner," p. 381; Peter Farrell to President and Members of the Gold Hill Miners' Union, Dec. 16, 1887, Gold Hill Miners' Union Organizational Papers, folder 1; *Butte Daily Miner,* June 14, 1888; J. M. Hill (Local 10) to "My Dear Brothers [convention delegates]," June 27, 1908, in WFM, *Proceedings, 1908,* p. 367; WFM, *Constitution,* 1914, p. 21; Butte Miners' Union, *Constitution,* pp. 8–9; Central Executive Miners' Union of Coeur d'Alene, *Constitution,* p. 12; Phipps, "Bull Pen," p. 47; Great Falls Mill and Smeltermen's Union, Minute Book, 3:27 (Mar. 14, 1903), WFM-IUMMSW Archives, vol. 243; *Manhattan Post,* Jan. 13, 1912, p. 1.

cruiting and holding membership were highly problematic for the Western Federation throughout this period. In these hard circumstances, insurance payments and friendly visiting were sometimes about all that hardrock unions could offer prospective members.[57]

In this regard, the WFM, which angrily quit the American Federation of Labor (AFL) in 1897, shared the same approach to institutional maintenance taken by Samuel Gompers's Cigar Makers International Union and other stodgy craft organizations that the hardrock militants despised. Comparing the collapse of the labor movement during the panic in the 1870s with its relative success in weathering the depression twenty years later, Gompers and other AFL leaders heralded benefit arrangements as an important means of preserving strength during periods of adversity. In an article titled "True Trade Unionism" in the *American Federationist* of October 1894, Cigar Makers president George Perkins boasted that amid economic disaster his union had "not only retained its membership, but has actually increased, and, in addition, has had to suffer no reductions of wages." To Gompers, these programs represented a practical alternative to "the chimerical schemes advocated by would-be social revolutionists." But to self-help advocates in the Western Federation, many of whom considered themselves social revolutionists, insurance benefits and other forms of mutual aid did not foreclose broader reforms. Hardrock activists undoubtedly would have concurred with this analysis by David Montgomery: "Socialism grows from the work and living patterns of working people. Its tap root is the mutualism spurred by their daily struggle for control of the circumstances of their lives."[58] In any case, radical industrial and conservative craft unionists agreed that

57. U.S. Bureau of the Census, *Historical Statistics*, 1:602–6; Gold Hill Miners' Union, Minute Book, pp. 362–598 (Aug. 28, 1893-Dec. 21, 1896), Gold Hill Miners' Union Records, Nevada Historical Society; Lem Kelly, T. H. Gale, and J. C. Duffy (Local 4) to Editor, Dec. 22, 1899, *MM*, Feb. 1900, pp. 29–30; Emma F. Langdon, "Anaconda's Activity," *MM*, Jan. 13, 1910, pp. 8–9.

58. George W. Perkins, "True Trade Unionism," *American Federationist*, Oct. 1894, p. 168; [Samuel Gompers], "Establish Union Benefits," ibid., Jan. 1900, pp. 10–11; David Montgomery, "Spontaneity and Organization: Some Comments," *Radical America* 7 (Nov.-Dec. 1973): 77; [Samuel Gompers], "A Model Union," *American Federationist*, Mar. 1895, p. 14; [idem], "The Next Step toward Emancipation," ibid., Dec. 1899, pp. 248–49. During the period when trade unions were illegal in Britain, benefit societies frequently served as fronts for illicit collective activities. See E. P. Thompson, *The Making of the English Working Class* (New York, 1963), pp. 166, 181; Sidney Webb and Beatrice Webb, *The History of Trade Unionism* (New York, 1920), pp. 24, 27n, 39–41, 70–71, 75, 77.

welfare plans helped their organizations to survive to fight another day.

Mutual aid programs also attracted conservative miners to a radical movement. Welfare unionism was perhaps the only form of collectivism that could attract individualistic Cornishmen. According to Sidney and Beatrice Webb, unions were "absolutely unknown" to the miners of Cornwall. But friendly societies flourished throughout southwestern England in the nineteenth century. By the 1860s, some groups of Cornish tin workers had also taken control of mine accident and funeral clubs. This experience prepared immigrants to join unions that emphasized mutual benefit activity. Beginning with the Comstock organizations, the Cousin Jacks not only joined but influenced the development of the hardrock labor movement.[59]

Mutual aid programs also helped transcend some of the ethnic divisions among miners. Uniting workers of many different nationalities and religions was, of course, a fundamental, often intractable, task facing all working-class organizations. In addition to the abiding antagonism between the Cornish and the Irish, prejudice against immigrants from Mexico and southern and eastern Europe often festered within locals.[60] But when disaster struck, cultural differences shrank into insignificance. More than 350 members of the Silverton Miners' Union followed the bodies of Peter Carlson, Nels Gustafson, and Luigi Rosadas in a single procession from the union hall after their funeral. W. S. Reid of Local 55 in Angel's Camp, California, reported the deaths of "three good men" in 1909:

> Without the slightest warning fifteen tons of rock crashed down, killing three men instantly, and seriously injuring one. It took about eight hours' hard work to extricate the bodies, one of which was horribly mangled beyond all recognition. A joint funeral was held from Calaveras Miners' Union hall at 2 P. M., Monday, February 22nd, and No. 55 outdid itself

59. Webb and Webb, *History of Trade Unionism*, p. 434; Jenkin, *Cornish Miner*, p. 267; P. H. Gosden, *The Friendly Societies in England, 1815–1875* (Manchester, Eng., 1961), pp. 22–24, 31, 42, 45; Rowe, *Hard-Rock Men*, pp. 244–46; Lingenfelter, *Hardrock Miners*, pp. 43–44, 51–52.

60. Wyman, *Hard-Rock Epic*, pp. 42–46; Malone, *Battle for Butte*, p. 77; Rowe, *Hard-Rock Men*, pp. 246–47; "John Brown" to Editor, May 6, 1905, *MM*, May 18, 1905, p. 12; Thomas A. French, Fred Oliver, and James F. Healy (Local 247), "Vigorous Resolutions from Round Mountain, Nevada," *MM*, Apr. 9, 1908, p. 11. Racist antipathy toward the Chinese also persisted. See George T. Kane (Local 69) to A. Shilland, Sept. 11, 1902, Mine-Mill Papers, box 153, folder 7; Wyman, *Hard-Rock Epic*, pp. 38–41.

in paying the last sad tribute to their deceased brothers, John Rasca, Marko Maslash, and Angelo Cariniano.

The weather was fine and there were about seven or eight hundred men in the procession headed by the local band. Two of the deceased were Austrians, and one was an Italian, but it was really gratifying to see the way in which all thoughts of nationality were swept into the background—a happy indication of the fast disappearing artificial barriers which the exploiting class would be glad to maintain between the workers of different nationalities.[61]

Visiting the sick and injured also brought workers together in new ways. Yet even the best intentions failed to surmount certain obstacles. A committee from Local 16 visiting Steve Kruzich found that he had sustained a severe eye injury, but the delegation was frustrated by its inability to communicate with Kruzich and recommended that "a committee of his own countrymen be appointed to persuade him to undergo an operation."[62] Thus fraternal activities could contribute relatively little to overcoming such formidable impediments to inter-ethnic solidarity as the language barrier.

The miners' organizations actively cultivated a benevolent image in the community. The Lead City Miners' Union was chartered by South Dakota as a charitable body. WFM locals in British Columbia publicized their incorporation under the Benevolent Societies Act. The Telluride miners' body identified itself as "a benevolent and fraternal society." Before a huge crowd at Miners' Union Day festivities in Butte in 1900, WFM president Boyce extolled Local 1 as "the husband of the widow and the father of the orphan."[63] Local unions regularly published statistics on their cumulative benefit expenditures. The *Daily Inter Mountain* observed that "more sick benefits are paid out from

61. W. S. Reid to Editor, Feb. 26, 1909, *MM*, Mar. 11, 1909, p. 9; *Tonopah Miner*, Mar. 4, 1911; *Silverton Weekly Miner*, Mar. 30, 1906; *Owyhee Avalanche*, Mar. 9, 1900; Bingham Miners' Union, Minute Book, 1:following 166 (Sept. 30, 1905), WFM and IUMMSW Records, box 2.

62. Great Falls Mill and Smeltermen's Union, Minute Book, 4:175 (Nov. 6, 1906), 6:298 (June 6, 1911), 8:2 (June 18, 1917), 88 (Nov. 26, 1917), WFM-IUMMSW Archives, vols. 244, 246, 248; Visiting Committee, Bodie Miners' Union, Reports, Sept. 10, 1895, Apr. 24, June 19, July 3, 1900, Bodie Miners' Union Records, vol. 2, folder: "Reports on Sickness, 1890–1900"; Hibbing Miners' Union, Minute Book, pp. 9 (Mar. 23, 1919), 10 (Mar. 30, 1919), WFM-IUMMSW Archives, vol. 58.

63. Telluride Miners' Union, Deed, Oct. 1901, WFM-IUMMSW Archives, box 1, folder 19; Edward Boyce, "Miners' Union Day at Butte, Montana," *MM*, Mar. 1900, p. 39; Jensen, *Heritage of Conflict*, p. 249; *Slocan Drill*, Sept. 7, 1900; *Lardeau Eagle*, Sept. 5, 1901; Lingenfelter, *Hardrock Miners*, pp. 43–44.

the Butte Miners' Union than by all the [other] organizations in the state put together."[64] Like many enlightened capitalists of this period, hardrock unionists recognized the value of prominent good works as a means to obtain public support.

This quest for respectability often succeeded. Although violence tarnished the WFM's reputation in some areas, in many mining districts the local union was considered a pillar of the community. The *Lardeau Eagle* unsparingly praised Local 119: "When one of their number is injured . . ., how willingly do we see them come to their injured brother's assistance with money and sympathy. The workers may lack polish, but they are genuine. Among them the real heart-throb of humanity is felt." Even the previously antiunion editor of the *Tanana Miner* in Fairbanks came to view the Tanana Mine Workers' Union as a responsible organization, in part because of its mutual assistance work.[65] At the height of the silicosis epidemic at the turn of the century, the *DeLamar Lode* considered Local 72 "an institution that the camp should be and is proud of."[66]

A generous reputation served the organized miners well in their dealings with recalcitrant nonmembers and employers. Pointing to a recent episode when members of Local 119 carried an injured worker twenty-six miles to medical care, the *Lardeau Eagle* urged nonunion miners to see the light. At the Poorman mine in the Coeur d'Alene, foreman Simon Healey fired an employee who refused to join the Burke Miners' Union. Healey praised the union as a benevolent body. The *Wallace Press* agreed: "The wage worker who will not unite with his fellows in honorable comradeship for counsel, advise [sic], and mutual aid in case of sickness or distress, is more of a stubborn animal than a reasoning man, and is not only unworthy of confidence, but is also unfit to work alongside of honorable men. Miners' Unions are practically beneficiary societies, and it is an honor for all competent miners to belong to them." Some locals combined visiting the sick with visiting nonmembers to induce them to enter the organization.

64. Butte *Daily Inter Mountain*, Jan. 18, 1890; *Directory of Owyhee County*, p. 61; Terry *News-Record*, July 13, 1906; *San Miguel Examiner*, Jan. 24, 1903.

65. [R. P. Pettipiece], Editorial, *Lardeau Eagle*, Oct. 24, 1901; *Tanana Miner*, Oct. 28, Nov. 10, Dec. 22, 1907; *Silverton Weekly Miner*, Jan. 2, 1903; *Directory of Owyhee County*, p. 61.

66. *DeLamar Lode*, Mar. 14, Apr. 4, 11, 1899, Mar. 19, 1901; *Tonopah Bonanza*, Jan. 11, 1902; *Coeur d'Alene Miner*, Jan. 14, 1893, p. 5; Mr. and Mrs. J. Hewitt, "Card of Thanks," *San Miguel Examiner*, May 9, 1903.

In this way, benevolent activity legitimated even the process of organizing. In addition, in disputes over economic issues with employers, miners sometimes justified their position in part by their expenditures on benefits. Locals drawn into strikes, lockouts, and other disputes often enjoyed the advantage of favorable public sentiment.[67]

In 1913 the Butte Miners' Union proudly reported that during the thirty-five years of its existence, not one of its members had been buried in a pauper's grave.[68] Given the harsh realities of working-class life and death during the industrializing era, this was surely an achievement worth boasting about. In contrast, no hardrock union claimed that its disability benefit programs had kept every disabled member out of the county hospital-poorhouse. To provide adequate assistance to the sick and injured, miners would have to build their own hospitals.

67. *Wallace Press*, Dec. 20, 1890; *Lardeau Eagle*, Aug. 15, 1901; Haywood, *Bill Haywood's Book*, p. 65; A Miner, "That Granite Trouble," Butte *Daily Inter Mountain*, Jan. 15, 1890; *Daily Territorial Enterprise*, Aug. 30, 1877; Silver City Miners' Union, *Constitution*, pp. 13–14; Colorado City Mill and Smeltermen's Union (Local 125) to Mill Managers, n.d., rpt. in *MM*, Apr. 1903, pp. 10–11.
68. *MM*, Aug. 28, 1913, p. 9; William Lakeland (Local 22) to Editor, Aug. 26, 1913, *EMJ*, Sept. 13, 1913, p. 512.

4 | *The Coeur d'Alene Miners' Union Hospital*

Hardrock unions planned, built, and controlled general hospitals throughout the western United States and Canada. Workers in northern Idaho established the first, the Coeur d'Alene Miners' Union Hospital, in 1891. Like many other grassroots democratic initiatives, this institution was the product of hard struggle. Miners had to strike the largest operator in the district to found their hospital. The Coeur d'Alene hospital won considerable community support for the miners' movement and inspired many other local unions to establish similar facilities.

Metal mining boomed in the Coeur d'Alene in the 1880s. The discovery of rich deposits of lead and silver suddenly transformed a remote wilderness in the panhandle of Idaho into a major mining center. Shoshone County had become the third leading lead-producing county in the United States by 1889. The value of all ore extracted in the district in 1890 was estimated to be $10 million.[1]

Although numerous small operations successfully tapped lead-silver veins in the Coeur d'Alene, only large companies had sufficient capital to exploit these resources fully. Aggressive entrepreneurs moved quickly to develop this wealth. Upon securing the most promising

---

1. Paul, *Mining Frontiers*, p. 149; U.S. Census Office, *Report on Mineral Industries in the United States at the Eleventh Census: 1890* (Washington, 1892), p. 164; Smith, *Coeur d'Alene Mining War*, p. 8.

properties for $650,000 in 1887, Simeon G. Reed incorporated the Bunker Hill and Sullivan Mining and Concentrating Company for $3 million. Reed immediately built a 150-ton-per-day ore concentrator and made other major improvements. The gross output of the company's workings tripled in the year following consolidation, making Bunker Hill by far the largest firm in the district. With eastern, western, and midwestern capitalists investing heavily in other nearby properties, absentee ownership became predominant throughout the area.[2]

A handful of small towns grew up around the mines along the Coeur d'Alene River and its tributary creeks. The *Wardner News* announced in June 1888 that "experienced miners from all directions are commencing to appear." The newspaper hailed the arrival of "that class most desirable in a mining country." Veteran craftsmen converged on the Coeur d'Alene from the Comstock Lode, Butte, and other mining areas. By 1891 the district employed more than twelve hundred mine workers.[3] The vast majority were unmarried men. A substantial proportion were immigrants from Ireland, Canada, Germany, Sweden, Italy, England, and elsewhere.[4]

Operators initially paid the Butte wage of $3.50 per day to all underground workers. In June 1887, however, Bunker Hill cut the pay of miners to $3.00 and that of carmen and muckers to $2.50. After workers resisted this reduction, the firm restored miners' wages to $3.50 but raised the laborers' pay to only $3.00. In November 1887 the miners of Wardner organized a union to prevent further cuts and to press for a uniform standard. Independent local unions, comprised of both skilled and unskilled workers, formed in 1890 in the other principal camps of the district—Gem, Mullan, and Burke.[5]

2. Smith, *Coeur d'Alene Mining War*, p. 4; John Hays Hammond, *The Autobiography of John Hays Hammond*, 2 vols. (New York, 1935), 1:181; U.S. Census Office, *Mineral Industries: 1890*, p. 81; John M. Henderson, William S. Shiach, and Harry B. Averill, *An Illustrated History of North Idaho* (N.p., 1903), pp. 996–1000, 1052–57; Thomas A. Rickard, *The Bunker Hill Enterprise* (San Francisco, 1921), pp. 75–76; D. E. Livingston-Little, "The Bunker Hill and Sullivan: North Idaho's Mining Development from 1885 to 1900," *Idaho Yesterdays* 7 (1963): 36–39; *EMJ*, June 6, 1891, p. 663.

3. *Wardner News*, June 1, 1888, rpt. in *MSP*, June 23, 1888, p. 397; Smith, *Coeur d'Alene Mining War*, pp. 6–12; Job Harriman, *The Class War in Idaho*, 3d ed. (New York, 1900), p. 3.

4. U.S. Census Office, *Report on Population of the United States at the Eleventh Census: 1890*, vol. 1 (Washington 1895), pp. 494, 618; U.S. Senate, *Coeur d'Alene Mining Troubles*, 56th Cong., 1st sess., Document 24 (Washington, 1899), p. 13; *EMJ*, Mar. 3, 1894, p. 193; A. C. Todd, "Cousin Jack in Idaho," *Idaho Yesterdays* 8 (Winter 1964–65): 2–11.

5. Edward Boyce (charter member, Wardner Miners' Union), "Crime of the Century,"

The unions' egalitarian wage policy became increasingly precarious. In the late 1880s companies began to introduce machine drills into their operations. By 1891 electricity as well as steam was being used to raise drilling productivity. According to one observer, "with a few machines, the same force of men would turn out almost twice as much rock as before. The shovelers were driven much harder than formerly." With displaced miners providing an ample supply of labor for unskilled jobs, more operators adopted a two-tier pay scale. As a growing share of their fellows was forced into shoveling and tramming jobs and their traditional skills became obsolete, the Coeur d'Alene workers saw their power evaporating.[6]

Stronger organization was imperative. Accordingly, the four local unions formed a district federation in January 1891. This body was officially named the Central Executive Miners' Union of Coeur d'Alene but known most commonly as the Coeur d'Alene Miners' Union. Its primary purpose was to restore and defend the $3.50 wage. By mid-1891 the miners' organizations had won a series of strikes which set the Butte rate for all underground workers at all mines except those of Bunker Hill. The district union had postponed the inevitable.[7]

This new structure permitted joint undertakings beyond the means of any individual local. Immediately upon its formation, the Coeur d'Alene Miners' Union set out to establish a hospital. Having failed to interest the Sisters of Mercy in building a facility in the area, the miners decided to proceed with this unprecedented project on their own. The Idaho union thus sought to give fresh meaning to the old Comstock policy of enabling the miner to be his own benefactor.[8]

The silver-lead workers considered the company doctor to be something less than a benefaction. Mines throughout the district participated in an arrangement under which a physician delivered care under a contract with the employers paid for by mandatory payroll deduc-

in U.S. Senate, *Coeur d'Alene Mining Troubles,* 56th Cong., 1st sess., Document 25 (Washington, 1899), pp. 1–2; Phipps, "Bull Pen," pp. 10–14; Smith, *Coeur d'Alene Mining War,* pp. 17–18; *Spokane Review,* Mar. 31, 1892, p. 2; *Wallace Press,* Nov. 15, 1890.

6. Harriman, *Class War,* p. 3; Livingston-Little, "Bunker Hill and Sullivan," p. 38; *Wallace Press,* Apr. 4, 1891; *Spokane Review,* Apr. 25, 1891, p. 3, Aug. 13, 1891, p. 3; *EMJ,* Feb. 21, 1891, p. 241, July 11, 1891, p. 49.

7. *Wallace Press,* Jan. 10, July 25, 1891; *Wardner News,* Aug. 8, 1891; Smith, *Coeur d'Alene Mining War,* pp. 19–20; Harriman, *Class War,* pp. 3–4.

8. Central Executive Miners' Union of Coeur d'Alene, *Constitution,* rev. 1895, p. 2; *Wallace Press,* Jan. 10, 1891; *Spokane Review,* Mar. 31, 1892, p. 2.

tions. This system generated over $1,000 per month by 1891. John Sweeney, president of the Wardner Miners' Union, summarized the criticism of this plan: "One dollar per month was deducted from each man's pay as a hospital fee, but no hospital was provided. This money was paid over to a doctor, who gave medical attendance when called upon. This plan was very unsatisfactory to the miners." Although workers made no specific allegations of malpractice, James Drennin of the Wardner union asserted that "proper care and treatment . . . [was] something we never received from company doctors."[9]

Workers also objected to the company doctor as a matter of principle. They resented being unable to select their own physician and believed that the doctor felt responsible only to the mine owners who had hired him, not to the employees who paid his salary. The actions of one physician in particular bore out the validity of this belief. When martial law was declared in the district during a violent strike in 1892, Dr. William Sims zealously served the operators' interests. Appointed acting sheriff of Shoshone County, Sims personally identified numerous union activists for arrest. The *Spokane Review* reported that the employers' physician was "cordially hated by every union man in the county."[10]

Miners also opposed the company doctor as one representative of an expanding quasi-feudal system. As elsewhere, Coeur d'Alene employers either explicitly required or implicitly coerced workers to patronize company stores, bunkhouses, and boardinghouses. According to James Sovereign, editor of the *Idaho State Tribune* in Wallace, "The employee who does not trade at the company store usually . . . is soon discharged from the service of the company for some imaginary cause." A desire for independence from employers' dictation was a major factor underlying the hospital initiative.[11]

9. John W. Sweeney to Editor, Mar. 29, 1892, *Spokane Review*, Mar. 31, 1892, p. 2; James A. Drennin to Editor, Aug. 8, 1891, *Wardner News*, Aug. 8, 1891; Lew Roberts et al. (Executive Board, Coeur d'Alene Miners' Union), "The Miners' Appeal," *Spokane Review*, Aug. 20, 1891, p. 5; Harriman, *Class War*, p. 3.
10. *Spokane Review*, July 16, 1892, p. 2; John W. Sweeney to Editor, Mar. 29, 1892, ibid., Mar. 31, 1892, p. 2; Harriman, *Class War*, p. 9; James A. Drennin to Editor, Aug. 8, 1891, *Wardner News*, Aug. 8, 1891; Smith, *Coeur d'Alene Mining War*, p. 81.
11. James R. Sovereign, "Testimony," July 26, 1899, in U.S. Industrial Commission, *Report*, 12:407, 410; F. P. Matchette, "Testimony," July 26, 1899, in ibid., 435–36; Bartholomew R. Creedon (miner, Wallace, Ida.), "Testimony," July 28, 1899, in ibid., 525; Boyce, "Crime of the Century," p. 1; *Spokane Review*, Mar. 27, 1892, p. 5, May 12, 1892, p. 2, May 13, 1892, p. 1; Sweeney to Editor, ibid., Mar. 31, 1892, p. 2; "Pioneer" to Editor, n.d., *Wallace Press*, June 11, 1892.

The growing number of occupational accidents gave urgency to the proposed reform. In March 1889 the *Coeur d'Alene Sun* recounted a mine tragedy at Mullan in which John Murphy was "badly cut and bruised" and John Waters was killed, his head "literally torn to pieces" by a premature blast. An avalanche smashed the boardinghouse at the Custer mine in February 1890, killing six. When in September 1890 a box of blasting caps exploded in George Peters's hands, it was found that "a large portion of the left hand, together with pieces of fuse and caps, had been blown into the abdomen." During the following month two more Coeur d'Alene miners lost their lives in accidents on the job. The mounting toll of death and disability created increased demand for improved health care services and facilities.[12]

Building plans proceeded rapidly. A planning committee made up of two representatives from each local union entertained proposals from communities offering to donate tracts of land for the institution. After reviewing several prospective sites, the planners submitted two to a referendum. The rank-and-file membership selected the centrally located town of Wallace as the site for the hospital. On April 8, 1891, the Coeur d'Alene central union signed a formal agreement with a citizens' committee of Wallace to build there.[13]

Construction funds came from many sources. The unions allocated money from their treasuries and levied a special assessment on their six hundred members. In addition, to broaden their financial base, the locals increased their efforts to recruit new members. The central union held a dance on St. Patrick's Day, which brought in over $400. Civic leaders in Wallace raised additional funds from the general public by subscription.[14]

In April the unions and mine owners agreed upon a role for the latter in the project. A five-member hospital governing board was constituted, consisting of one representative from each local union and one from the operators' association. In return for participation in governance, the employers promised to remit to the union hospital the dollar per worker per month being deducted for the company

12. *Coeur d'Alene Sun* (Murray, Ida.), Mar. 9, 1889; *Wallace Press*, Sept. 21, 12, Oct. 25, 1890; Henderson, Shiach, and Averill, *History of North Idaho*, p. 999; *Wardner News*, Jan. 24, 1891.

13. *Wardner News*, Mar. 7, 1891; *Wallace Press*, Apr. 4, 11, June 13, 1891; *Spokane Review*, Apr. 15, 1891, p. 4.

14. *Wallace Press*, Apr. 4, 11, May 9, Aug. 8, 1891.

doctor. Under this arrangement the unions gave up only a modicum of policy-making freedom in exchange for a large measure of financial security. Soon every operator in the district except Bunker Hill and Sullivan had agreed to support the new institution. Bunker Hill persisted in making a compulsory deduction and retaining its own physician.[15]

While plans for a larger permanent building were being drawn up, the Coeur d'Alene Miners' Union Hospital began operations on May 8, 1891, in temporary quarters. Facilities included a ward of six beds, an operating room, and a vacant room "capable of holding four or five beds at a moment's notice." The dispensary contained "enough chemicals . . . to furnish bane or antidote for any number of people in any man's country." The resident staff initially consisted of a superintendent and "a most experienced nurse." Two "new men," Drs. William F. Herrington and Franklin P. Matchette, were selected to care for patients. (Both of these practitioners would remain loyal to the miners' movement throughout the turbulent decade to come. Each won election as county coroner on the Populist ticket.) Among the many sick and injured workers who descended on the hospital was Dan O'Coner, who was admitted on May 25 after being "blown up in Granite mine."[16]

Before a month had passed, the hospital superintendent suddenly resigned. The miners turned to the Sisters of Charity of Providence for assistance. A Roman Catholic order that ran hospitals in the Pacific Northwest, the Sisters of Providence agreed to take charge of nursing and administration. The union, however, remained financially responsible for maintaining the temporary facility and erecting a more substantial permanent one.[17]

These financial obligations increased the need to bring the sizable number of Bunker Hill and Sullivan employees into the union health program. On June 29 a committee of miners presented Bunker Hill general manager Victor M. Clement with a petition signed by a majority of his mine workers requesting that the company participate in

15. *Spokane Review*, Apr. 29, 1891, p. 5; Lew Roberts (president, Wardner Miners' Union) to "A Generous and Justice Loving Public," Aug. 12, 1891, ibid., Aug. 14, 1891, p. 1; *Wallace Press*, May 16, 1891.

16. *Wallace Press*, May 16, Aug. 8, Apr. 25, June 27, 1891; Henderson, Shiach, and Averill, *History of North Idaho*, pp. 1022–25.

17. *Wallace Press*, June 6, 13, 20, July 11, 1891; Mary McKernan, "Mother Joseph: Pioneer Nun," *American West* 18 (Sept.-Oct. 1981): 20–21.

the new hospital plan: "Your employees respectfully ask that one dollar per month be deducted from each man's pay and turned over to the Miners' Union Hospital in Wallace, where our sick and injured will be cared for in the future." The union offered to open a dispensary near the Bunker Hill mine to meet management criticism of the distance (of about ten miles) from the Wardner operations to the Wallace hospital. Clement rejected this proposition in a letter of July 9. "We cannot be privy to a collection of fees or contribution from the entire body of our employees in behalf or in support of any foreign body or association," he argued, "specially so as we cannot know that the distribution and use of it is made solely for the purpose intended for it." Ignoring the presence of a mine operator on the hospital board, Clement implied that fees would be diverted for other activities. In response, a group of the firm's workers sent management written authorization for payroll deductions to the union facility.[18]

Shortly thereafter, Bunker Hill made a counterproposal for a company-supported hospital near Wardner, control of which was described in nebulous terms. On the morning of August 6, the union offered a compromise, a strictly voluntary arrangement under which each individual could choose either to have a deduction made for the union facility or to have nothing taken from his wages.[19] Later the same day, management held a referendum on the issue. Three alternatives, none of which embodied either of the union proposals, appeared on the ballot. The choices were: 1) continuation of the company doctor plan, 2) establishment of a company hospital, and 3) cessation of deductions for health care, contingent upon "signing a contract with the Bunker Hill and Sullivan Mining Co., releasing them from all liabilities for sickness or injury while in their employ."[20] Underground workers boycotted what the Wardner union president called a "fake election." Nonunion ore mill employees, however, chose to take part. That evening, management posted a notice announcing the results in favor of the company hospital option and declaring that

18. William Powers and J. W. Glass (Wardner Miners' Union) to V. M. Clement, June 29, 1891, in *Wardner News*, Aug. 8, 1891; V. M. Clement to F. W. Bradley (assistant manager, B. H. and S.), July 9, 1891, in ibid.; [Employees] to Manager of the Bunker Hill and Sullivan Mining Co., n.d., in ibid.

19. V. M. Clement to Miners and Employees, n.d., in *Spokane Review*, Aug. 9, 1891, p. 1; Wardner Miners' Union to Manager of the Bunker Hill and Sullivan Mines, Aug. 6, 1891, *Wardner News*, Aug. 8, 1891.

20. *Wallace Press*, Aug. 8, 1891.

henceforth one dollar per month would be taken from every employee to support this scheme. The notice urged those who objected "to call at the company's office for their time."[21]

The miners answered this challenge forcefully. Not long after Bunker Hill posted its ultimatum, all but a handful of underground workers on the night shift spontaneously walked out. An impromptu union meeting followed at which the miners formally decided to strike. Upon adjournment, a large crowd returned to the Bunker Hill and induced the remaining four or five workers there to join them. Three hundred miners marched from the mine in an orderly procession, leaving it shut down.[22]

The next day a union delegation met with management and made two demands. First, they reiterated the proposal to have deductions to their hospital or no deductions at all. Second, the union called for a fifty-cent raise for carmen and muckers, so that all underground workers would be paid $3.50 per day. On August 8, Wardner management received a telegram from the firm's newly appointed president, John Hays Hammond, which dismissed the demands as "unjust" and "preposterous."[23] During the preceding year, Hammond, a prominent mining engineer and entrepreneur, had put together a syndicate that was in the process of buying out Simeon Reed. On August 8 the *Wardner News* published an appeal by union secretary James Drennin, asking the community to "support a union composed of men who act as their motto dictates: 'Act justly and fear not.'" Because Bunker Hill was the largest corporation in the district and the new group of investors now in command included such formidable capitalists as Chicago reaper magnate Cyrus McCormick II, San Francisco banker William Crocker, and New York financier Darius Mills, the Wardner miners surely had plenty to fear.[24]

Following the initial walkout, the strike was relatively uneventful and totally effective. At the request of Bunker Hill management, Sher-

21. Lew Roberts to Editor, Aug. 10, 1891, *Spokane Review*, Aug. 12, 1891, p. 1; V. M. Clement, "Notice to Employes," in *Wallace Press*, Aug. 8, 1891; *Wardner News*, Aug. 8, 1891.
22. *Wallace Press*, Aug. 8, 1891; *Wardner News*, Aug. 8, 1891; *Spokane Review*, Aug. 9, 1891, p. 1, Aug. 12, 1891, p. 1.
23. John Hays Hammond to F. W. Bradley, telegram, Aug. 8, 1891, in *Wardner News*, Aug. 8, 1891.
24. James A. Drennin to Editor, Aug. 8, 1891, *Wardner News*, Aug. 8, 1891; Hammond, *Autobiography*, 1:186–87; Rickard, *Bunker Hill Enterprise*, p. 77; *Spokane Review*, Apr. 16, 1891, p. 3.

iff R. A. Cunningham appointed thirty special deputies to protect company property at the firm's expense. But Cunningham found that the strikers were conducting themselves in a "quiet and orderly manner." After receiving a pledge from union leaders that no damage would be done, he refused to deploy the deputies. The strikers received a symbolic expression of solidarity on August 10, when workers at the nearby Granite mine struck in sympathy, vowing that they would not return until the Bunker Hill dispute was settled.[25]

On August 14 the company announced that it would immediately resume operations. Bunker Hill claimed that it had seventy-five miners ready to return to work, including some "discontented strikers," and was advertising "broadcast" for more. This tactic was either a bluff or a fiasco. The following day the *Wallace Press* reported that "the Bunker Hill and Sullivan strike remains unchanged and no men are working in the mine." Union president Lew Roberts took the opportunity to point out that "the scab who enlists on the side of capital against the just demands of his brothers is despised of all honest men and held in contempt even by those who hire him."[26]

Throughout the strike the union attempted not only to discourage potential strikebreakers but also to recruit striking nonunion miners. By August 12, Roberts claimed that "with the exception of eight or ten all men working underground were union men, and the exceptions had promised to join."[27] Although unionists tried to persuade recalcitrant local workers to join them, they made no such effort with outsiders drawn to Wardner by Bunker Hill's inducements: "The Miners' Union . . . held an impromptu meeting last night and conducted two non-union men to the junction in a manner that indicated in no uncertain tone that the union men will not permit cut-rate artists to locate here. The procession presented a novel appearance as it moved down Main street with the scabs on a rail. The newcomers had offered their services for $2 per day. The sympathy of the citizens was with the union men in this instance." Hammond soon complained that the strikers had extended their demands to include the firing of all foremen

25. *Spokane Review*, Aug. 12, 1891, p. 1, Aug. 13, 1891, p. 3.

26. Ibid., Aug. 14, 1891, p. 1; *Wallace Press*, Aug. 15, 1891; Lew Roberts to "A Generous and Justice Loving Public," Aug. 12, 1891, in *Spokane Review*, Aug. 14, 1891, p. 1.

27. Roberts to "Public," in *Spokane Review*, Aug. 14, 1891, p. 1; ibid., Aug. 9, 1891, p. 1.

who were working during the dispute.[28] This was another clear indication of who had the upper hand in the conflict.

Negotiations on August 21 settled the strike. The agreement provided for an optional system of deductions: employees could choose either the company doctor or no deduction. For those who selected the latter option, Bunker Hill gained relief only from liability for medical expenses, not the blanket release from "all liabilities" it had sought. Injured miners thus preserved the right to sue for lost wages, a small but significant concession. The company granted the $3.50 wage to all underground laborers, a clear-cut victory for the union. Bunker Hill agreed to rehire strikers without any discrimination.[29]

At a meeting between labor and management on September 24, the terms of this settlement were revised. The new agreement gave the union exactly what it had sought: "Beginning October 1 next, this company will collect from every employee who has worked one day, one dollar per month, to be paid to the Miners' Union Hospital fund." In return for this capitulation, the union accepted the obligation to "furnish a resident physician and to assume all responsibility of furnishing necessary medical attendance to anyone injured or becoming ill while contributing to this fund."[30] The Wardner miners had decisively won the hospital battle of 1891. Thus assured of broad financial support, the unions erected and transferred to the Sisters of Providence a sixty-bed facility, which served as a community hospital until 1967.[31]

The miners prevailed in large part because the community sympathized with their mutual assistance programs. The union called attention to its charitable work throughout the course of the strike, consciously covering itself with a mantle of respectability. The exec-

28. *Wallace Press*, Aug. 22, 1891; *Spokane Review*, Aug. 21, 1891, p. 3.

29. *Spokane Review*, Aug. 22, 1891, p. 1.

30. Ibid., Sept. 26, 1891, p. 2.

31. *Wallace Press*, June 13, July 11, Aug. 29, 1891, Feb. 20, 1892; *Polk's Medical Register and Directory of the United States and Canada*, 7th ed. (Detroit, 1902), p. 481. By 1893 the facility had been renamed Providence Hospital. The unions continued to take financial responsibility for the institution until at least 1905, at which time the original construction cost of $50,000 had been paid. See H. E. Bonebrake, Paul M. Ellis, and E. J. Fitzgerald, *Medical History of Wallace Area* (N.p., n.d. [1966]); Sister Anselma Mary Price (archivist, Sisters of Providence) to author, Jan. 28, 1982.

utive board of the Coeur d'Alene Miners' Union reminded the general public that self-help saved the taxpayers money:

> We care for our sick and alleviate the pains of our injured with a brotherly spirit. Our dead are laid to rest with all the respect and propriety becoming such sad occasions, and surely thus . . . we also relieve corporations and the public at large. Many will ask, in what manner? In answer we can say that our members suffering from sickness or injury and pecuniarily embarrassed are not thrown upon the public or [left to] die by the wayside as heretofore, nor do they find a pauper's grave as in the past. . . . In this charitable mission we also lessen the taxes of the taxpayer, and in return ask only their sympathy, which we have every reason to expect, when they closely study our position and object.[32]

The strikers sorely needed to trade on public gratitude. With traditional skills rapidly becoming outmoded, union power depended less on a monopoly of craft knowledge and more on community goodwill. Industrialization had enlarged the pool of potential strikebreakers to include most able-bodied men. On the day Bunker Hill planned to begin its back-to-work movement, union president Roberts appealed to "a Generous and Justice Loving Public." After reviewing the history of the decision to construct "a first-class miners' union hospital," Roberts asked that "all friends of labor . . . assist us to win this fight by notifying those in search of work to keep away from Wardner until the strike is won."[33] Locked in a fight for its life, the miners' movement drew on its good reputation to gain concrete assistance from the community.

The union also emphasized its commitment to local control of community development. Roberts pointed out that the hospital was governed by a bipartisan board composed of Coeur d'Alene residents. He also noted that "the miners' union is a much more domestic institution than the corporation which seeks its destruction[,] whose headquarters are over a thousand miles away." Criticism of the company's refusal to allow its employees to spend their earnings in the way they chose undoubtedly struck a responsive chord with small businessmen threatened by company stores and boardinghouses.[34]

---

32. Lew Roberts et al., "The Miners' Appeal," *Spokane Review*, Aug. 20, 1891, p. 5; *Boise Statesman*, June 8, 1892, rpt. in *Coeur d'Alene Miner*, June 11, 1892.
33. Roberts to "Public," in *Spokane Review*, Aug. 14, 1891, p. 1.
34. Ibid.; Roberts to Editor, Aug. 10, 1891, ibid., Aug. 12, 1891, p. 1.

These arguments worked. "The sympathy of the public," declared the *Wallace Press*, "is quite generally with the miners." In such a favorable climate of opinion, local residents refused to serve as strikebreakers, potential strikebreakers from outside the area were run off, and the county sheriff failed to deploy company-financed deputies. Several months later, when the Coeur d'Alene miners entered another dispute, the *Spokane Review* asserted that the work of their organizations was "of a very charitable and benevolent nature, and they have become one of the institutions of the country."[35]

Benevolent work also bolstered claims for equal pay, explaining in part why this issue was interjected after the strike had begun. The establishment of the hospital, together with numerous union-conducted funerals, drew public attention to the extraordinary hazards that mining craftsmen and laborers shared. Beginning with the strikes at the Granite and Custer mines in July 1891, the miners asserted that "the shovelers have as hard and dangerous work underground as the miners and are entitled to the same pay." In addition, union supporters argued that the introduction of "labor-saving machinery" had created equivalent risks for miners and mine laborers, which justified uniform pay.[36]

The Miners' Union Hospital produced strong evidence of the occupational dangers faced by mine laborers. On August 8 (the day after the Bunker Hill workers demanded equal pay) the *Wallace Press* published the hospital's first quarterly report. Among the conditions treated were "rheumatism with lead poisoning" and "bruised legs by ore car running on him." One advocate of equal pay acknowledged the institution's role in illuminating the lead hazard to muckers:

A shovel full of lead-silver ore will weigh three and four times as much as a shovel full of white quartz, and to inhale the lead dust is the very essence of poison. Of course none of our mine owners have ever been "leaded," except politically, but the hospital records will show that sickness from that cause is quite prevalent. There is perhaps no harder task

35. *Wallace Press*, Aug. 15, 22, Jan. 10, 1891, Dec. 20, 1890; *Spokane Review*, Apr. 5, 1892, p. 8; *Wardner News*, Aug. 8, 1891; Smith, *Coeur d'Alene Mining War*, pp. 38–39, 55, 60. Many corporations met similar opposition in small towns. See Herbert G. Gutman, "The Worker's Search for Power: Labor in the Gilded Age," in H. Wayne Morgan, ed., *The Gilded Age: A Reappraisal* (Syracuse, N.Y., 1963), pp. 38–68.

36. *Wallace Press*, July 25, 1891; "Pioneer" to Editor, n.d., ibid., June 11, 1892. Union sympathizers in Butte used the same logic. See *Butte Bystander*, Apr. 29, 1893.

alloted [*sic*] to man than to shovel lead-silver ore for ten hours. We believe in grading employment about a silver-lead mine, but the underground workers should receive a uniform rate.

Throughout the recurrent skirmishes over this issue in the 1890s, the Coeur d'Alene unions stressed that equal risk merited equal reward.[37]

Industrial peace proved to be short-lived. Early in 1892, operators imposed a wage cut throughout the district. In the ensuing strike, violence escalated following the introduction of strikebreakers. Warfare culminated in a confrontation in Gem on July 11, 1892. No one was injured when strikers dynamited the mill at the Frisco mine, but three union men died in a lengthy gun battle at the Gem mine. A declaration of martial law brought hundreds of federal and state troops to the Coeur d'Alene. Union supporters were arrested wholesale and imprisoned in a crude bull pen. Labor's benevolent accomplishments made no impression on General James Curtis and his soldiers. The strike was smashed.[38]

This defeat scattered union partisans throughout the region. As Vernon Jensen observed, "Men from the Coeur d'Alenes traveled far when their union was broken. They added color to the story of unionism in many places." In addition to the "bitterness and animosity" of the "heritage of conflict" which Jensen emphasized, the Coeur d'Alene veterans carried with them the knowledge of how to build their own hospital.[39]

The largest contingent fled north. Many, if not most, union leaders found their way to the Slocan district of British Columbia. Rank-and-file unionists emigrated there as well. In March 1893, the *Coeur d'Alene Miner* observed that "every outgoing train . . . carries away quite a number of miners, the objective point being the Slocan country." The neighboring Kootenay district of British Columbia was described in 1894 as "really a continuation of the Coeur d'Alene"; most workers were from the United States.[40] These miners soon organized local

37. *Wallace Press*, Aug. 8, 1891, May 28, 1892; *Spokane Review*, Mar. 27, 1892, p. 5; *Coeur d'Alene Miner*, Oct. 7, 1893, p. 4.

38. Smith, *Coeur d'Alene Mining War*, pp. 31–105; Jensen, *Heritage of Conflict*, pp. 25–37.

39. Jensen, *Heritage of Conflict*, p. 26. Jensen also viewed conflict over the union hospital as a significant factor in the spiral of conflict (p. 37).

40. *Los Angeles Mining Review*, n.d., rpt. in Nelson *Weekly News*, June 18, 1910;

affiliates of the WFM. Beginning with the Sandon Miners' Union in 1899, six British Columbia locals established hospitals. The success of the Sandon institution encouraged not only other groups of metal miners but also coal miners and lumber workers to set up their own medical facilities.[41]

Other Coeur d'Alene veterans spread the idea throughout western North America. Upon assuming the presidency of the WFM in 1896, Edward Boyce devoted most of his time to forming new locals. This indefatigable organizer strongly emphasized benevolence in explaining unionism to new recruits. When, for instance, Boyce organized the coal miners of Aldridge, Montana, in April 1897, he remarked unhappily that "between $1.50 per month doctor's fees, company store and saloon, almost every cent [of miners' earnings] passes back to the company." By the end of the year, this camp had a union hospital. The Silver City Miners' Union began to plan its own health care center immediately after Boyce organized the local in 1896.[42] This local, in turn, produced several activists who disseminated information on their successful venture. Shortly after he helped found the Silver City hospital, Big Bill Haywood became a general officer of the federation. James McCambridge and Alex Main became early leaders of the Tonopah Miners' Union, the first local in Nevada to build a hospital.[43]

Coeur d'Alene Miner, Mar. 18, 1893, p. 4; *EMJ*, June 30, 1894, p. 610; W. M. Brewer, "British Columbia, IX—The Sandon District," *EMJ*, June 18, 1898, p. 731.

41. Alfred Parr (Local 85) to W. L. Hagler (Local 81), Jan. 3, 1901, Mine-Mill Papers, box 151, folder 13; William H. Bambury (Phoenix [B.C.] Trades and Labor Council) to Secretary, Sandon Miners' Union, Feb. 23, 1901, and W. J. Adcock (Local 62) to W. L. Hagler, Feb. 18, 1901, ibid., folder 14; S. M. Chisholm (matron, Sandon Miners' Union Hospital), "Suggestions for Building a Small Hospital," Mar. 24, 1902, ibid., box 153, folder 1; W. Edwin Newcombe (physician, Lardeau Miners' Union Hospital) to A. Shilland, Dec. 10, 1902, ibid., folder 10; Frank Treanor (secretary, Local 119) to A. Shilland, Feb. 1, 1903, and D. B. O'Neail (Slocan Miners' Union General Hospital) to A. Shilland, Feb. 5, 1903, ibid., folder 12; George Keeling (secretary, Eureka [Calif.] Federated Trades Council) to Anthony Shilland, Oct. 30, 1905, ibid., box 156, folder 2; James Williams (Roslyn-Cle Elum [Wash.] Beneficial Association) to Anthony Shilland, May 15, 1904, ibid., box 155, folder 3; *Lardeau Eagle*, Mar. 6, 1902; *MM*, May 1900, p. 33.

42. Boyce quoted in *Butte Bystander*, Apr. 24, 1897, p. 5; *Polk's Medical Register and Directory of North America*, 9th ed. (Detroit, 1906), p. 1263; Silver City Miners' Union, Minute Book, pp. 2–5 (Aug. 8, 1896), 28 (Sept. 7, 1896), Silver City Miners' Union Records, vol. 1; Edward Boyce, Travel Diaries, 2 vols., passim (May 20, 1896-May 27, 1902), Edward Boyce Papers, box 1, folder 2, Eastern Washington State Historical Society, Spokane.

43. *Idaho Avalanche*, Mar. 5, 1897; Haywood, *Bill Haywood's Book*, pp. 64–65, 88, 91–121; Sandon *Paystreak*, Sept. 30, 1899; *Owyhee Avalanche*, July 12, Mar. 1, Feb. 1, 1901; Silver City Miners' Union, Minute Book, p. 176 (Nov. 8, 1897), Silver City Miners' Union Records, vol. 1; *Tonopah Bonanza*, July 6, 1901; *Tonopah Sun*, June 22, 1907.

In 1903 the *Miners' Magazine* serialized Job Harriman's *Class War in Idaho*, which included an account of the Coeur d'Alene hospital dispute of 1891. Harriman's polemic provided few of the concrete details useful to those seeking to establish their own institutions.[44] By this time, however, numerous miners' hospitals were available to guide locals seeking to take control of health services. With the republication of this tract, the Coeur d'Alene Miners' Union Hospital passed into the mythology of the WFM. For an organization militantly opposed to all forms of employer paternalism, the pioneering institution remained a symbol of fundamental values.

---

44. Harriman, *Class War*, rpt. in *MM*, Oct. 8, 1903, p. 8.

5 | *Founding Hospitals*

At least twenty-five local affiliates of the WFM established their own hospitals. Between 1897 and 1918, groups of miners in Montana, Idaho, Colorado, Utah, Nevada, California, and British Columbia set up health care facilities in their communities[1] (see Table 5.1). Miners planned the construction of facilities and raised funds to meet building costs. Democratic decision making and rank-and-file participation, customary in the miners' movement, guided the founding of these institutions.

Democracy not only shaped the process by which these enterprises were realized; it was one of their primary aims. Although union activists had many reasons for establishing their own hospitals, the most important was deep-seated resentment of the autocratic nature of company health plans. Extraordinary health and safety risks only partially explain the emergence of these institutions. Severe occu-

---

1. *Great Falls Daily Tribune*, Sept. 11, 1898, p. 3, Mar. 22, 1909, p. 3; *The Standard Medical Directory of North America, 1903–4* (Chicago, 1903), p. 1165; *MM*, June 10, 1909, p. 4, June 5, 1913, p. 4; AMA, *American Medical Directory*, 2d ed. (Chicago, 1909), p. 666; idem, *American Medical Directory*, 3d ed. (Chicago, 1912), pp. 1349, 717; *Slocan Drill*, June 7, 1901; *San Miguel Examiner*, Oct. 18, 1902; *Owyhee Avalanche*, Oct. 29, 1897; Sandon Miners' Union, *By-Laws and Sketch of Sandon Miners' Union Hospital* (N.p., n.d. [1905]), p. 7; Alfred Parr, Con Robinson, and Archie McDougall (Local 85) to Officers and Members of Sandon Union, June 16, 1902, Mine-Mill Papers, box 153, folder 4; Marcus Martin (president, District 6), "B.C. District Convention Report," *MM*, Mar. 1919; *Polk's Medical Register*, 9th ed., p. 1263; *Lardeau Eagle*, Sept. 26, 1902; *Tonopah Bonanza*, Dec. 7, 1901, Feb. 8, 1902; *Park Record*, Oct. 1, 1904; W. H. Culp (Local 207) to Editor, Feb. 2, 1907, *MM*, Feb. 14, 1907, p. 12; *Polk's Medical Register and Directory of North America*, 12th ed. (Detroit, 1912), p. 1058; Press Committee, Local 235, to Editor, Dec. 7, 1905, *MM*, Dec. 21, 1905, p. 11; *Rawhide Daily Press*, Feb. 1, 1908; *Rhyolite Herald*, Apr. 26, 1907; Berg, "History of Tonopah," p. 158; *Goldfield News*, Feb. 9, 1907; *Blair Press*, Apr. 18, 1908; *Seven Troughs Miner*, Jan. 4, 1908.

Table 5.1.   Hospitals of the Western Federation of Miners

Year founded	Local	Miners' union	Location
1897	57	Aldridge	Aldridge, Mont.
1897	66	Silver City	Silver City, Idaho
1898	7	Belt Mountain	Neihart, Mont.
1899	81	Sandon	Sandon, B.C.
1900	85	Ymir	Ymir, B.C.
1901	62	Slocan	Slocan, B.C.
1901	107	Judith Mountain	Gilt Edge, Mont.
1901	121	Tonopah	Tonopah, Nev.
1902	63	Telluride	Telluride, Colo.
1903	111	North Moccasin	Kendall, Mont.
1903	119	Lardeau	Ferguson, B.C.
1904	144	Park City	Park City, Utah
1904	220	Goldfield	Goldfield, Nev.
1905	235	Bonanza	Rhyolite, Nev.
1906	241	Manhattan	Manhattan, Nev.
1907	207	Greenwater	Greenwater, Calif.
1907	245	Beatty	Beatty, Nev.
1907	247	Round Mountain	Round Mountain, Nev.
1907	253	Silver Peak	Blair, Nev.
1907	256	Vernon	Vernon, Nev.
ca. 1907	190	Zortman	Zortman, Mont.
1908	244	Rawhide	Rawhide, Nev.
1909	26	Silverton	Silverton, Colo.
1911	96	Nelson	Ainsworth, B.C.
1918	95	Silverton	Silverton, B.C.

SOURCE: See note 1.

pational and nonoccupational health problems were present in every hardrock mining district, but in only a relatively small number of localities were union health care facilities built.[2]

Most metal-mine and smelter operators maintained health plans for their employees. Employers generally insisted upon exercising unilateral control over these plans. Although some allowed workers to choose their doctor, most considered the selection of a medical practitioner to be the sole prerogative of management. Relatively few firms

2. Mark Wyman's contention that the locals that established hospitals were "usually those most pressed by large-scale disasters" is wrong. In both cases he cites (Telluride and Tonopah), the union had already commenced hospital construction before catastrophe struck. See Wyman, *Hard-Rock Epic*, pp. 182 (quotation), 182–83; *San Miguel Examiner*, Aug. 24, Oct. 12, Nov. 9, 1901; *Tonopah Bonanza*, Oct. 19, Nov. 23, Dec. 7, 1901, Feb. 8, 1902.

at the turn of the century either directly employed their own staff physicians or built company hospitals. Instead, mine and smelter superintendents usually entered into agreements with local practitioners, who not only delivered medical services but maintained their own hospitals. Hence physicians remained (often only nominally) independent medical professionals and businessmen. Workers were denied any formal role in drafting and administering these contracts. At least one company gave its foremen the power to decide whether miners injured under their supervision should be admitted to the hospital.[3]

In the vast majority of plans, employee participation was mandatory. Management automatically deducted a fee, usually one dollar per month, from every worker's pay and transmitted the sum collected to the doctor. Individual grievances against these compulsory assessments were futile. According to WFM president Moyer, "If a complaint is made against the checking off of the hospital fee, . . . the company finds a way to dispense with the services of the individual."[4]

Hardrock miners throughout North America opposed the arrogant principles underlying this system. Workers particularly resented being denied the right to determine how to spend their own wages. Aware

3. U.S. Industrial Commission, *Report*, 12:xiii, 233, 298, 307; Montana Industrial Accident Board, *First Annual Report, 1916* (Helena, n.d.), p. 25; New Denver (B.C.) *Ledge*, n.d., rpt. in Sandon *Paystreak*, Sept. 25, 1897; Owen W. Parker, "Pioneer Physicians of the Vermilion and Missabe Ranges of Minnesota," *Minnesota Medicine* 21 (1938): 332–35, 424–27; Ben Goggin to Editor, Feb. 26, 1917, *MM*, Mar. 1917; *Butte Daily Miner*, Mar. 3, 1887, July 18, 1889, p. 4; James Opie (Local 73), "Protection and Benefits of Unionism," *MM*, Dec. 1900, p. 32; Marlene H. Rikard, "An Experiment in Welfare Capitalism: The Health Care Services of the Tennessee Coal, Iron and Railroad Company" (Ph.D. dissertation, University of Alabama, 1983), p. 133 and passim; Louis S. Reed, *The Medical Service of the Homestake Mining Company* (Chicago, 1932), pp. 4–5; B. F. Tillson, "Accident Prevention by the New Jersey Zinc Co.," *EMJ*, Dec. 12, 1914, p. 1038. On autocratic programs in this industry in subsequent years, see Laurel Sefton MacDowell, *"Remember Kirkland Lake": The Gold Miners' Strike of 1941–42* (Toronto, 1983), p. 104. During this period contract practice prevailed not only in many other industries but also through various arrangements unrelated to employment. See George Rosen, *The Structure of American Medical Practice, 1875–1941* (Philadelphia, 1983), pp. 98–108.

4. Charles H. Moyer, Testimony, Oct. 9, 1917, in U.S., President's Mediation Commission, "[Transcript of Hearing] Sessions at Globe, Arizona," p. 132, Henry S. McCluskey Collection, box 4, Arizona Collection, Arizona State University Library, Tempe; U.S. Industrial Commission, *Report*, 12:xiii, 298, 317, 578, 585, 608–9; Alfred Parr to W. L. Hagler, Feb. 25, 1901, Mine-Mill Papers, box 151, folder 14; see also the sources cited in note 3. Company programs in North America had their origins in the "bal surgeon" system of eighteenth-century Cornwall. See Jenkin, *Cornish Miner*, p. 141. The Cornish plan first appeared on this continent around 1860 in the Michigan copper mines. See Todd, *Cornish Miner in America*, p. 120; Gates, *Michigan Copper*, p. 104.

that they were demanding a new right, Sandon unionists argued that "it is in line with the highest trend of modern thought . . . that it should be the privilege of the man who pays for the service to say how the service should be conducted, and to have a voice in the selection of the persons by whom such service should be rendered." When operators in Park City opposed union hospital plans, Local 144 president Joseph Langford seized the high ground. "What we contend for is the right to dispose of the hospital fee, which come [*sic*] out of our wages, as we see fit," declared Langford. "The companies have no moral right to dispose of a portion of our wages on the grounds that they can use it to a better advantage than we can." Opposition to paternalism thus rested on bedrock values of independence and self-reliance.[5]

Miners also had practical reasons for seeking reform. Workers throughout the industry echoed complaints first voiced in the Coeur d'Alene. Company doctors were accused of negligence or incompetence. On the Mesabi Range of northern Minnesota, union organizer Teofila Petriella claimed that "the list of the injured who die for lack of assistance is long, despite the fact that the men pay $1.00 a month for doctor and hospital care." The *Miners' Magazine* cynically reported that some physicians had found the panacea: "Many cases have come under our observation where company doctors had a standing prescription, it mattered not whether the miner had a mangled foot, was blasted or had some internal trouble—the prescription went for all." Engineer Mark Lamb made a quick survey of widely held stereotypes: "Many companies provide a doctor grudgingly, usually a recently graduated student, who will work for a small salary and experience— the latter not furnished by the company—and who will keep the books and run the store. In other cases he is a dipsomaniac, a drug fiend, or a horse doctor available on account of his misfortunes and satisfactory on account of his being willing to work for low pay." Lack of confidence in the professional skill of company physicians was widespread among miners at the turn of the century.[6]

5. Sandon Miners' Union, *By-Laws of Hospital*, p. 5; Langford quoted in *Park Record*, Dec. 19, 1903; *Idaho Avalanche*, Apr. 16, 1897; A. Shilland to Membership of Sandon Miners' Union, Nov. 20, 1910, Mine-Mill Papers, box 157, folder 5. In addition to broadening the ideological attack on employers' paternalism, radical miners offered an anticapitalist conception of their own initiatives. The Sandon local maintained that its hospital embodied the "principle of operation for use rather than profit." See Sandon Miners' Union, *By-Laws of Hospital*, pp. 5 (quotation), 4–6.
6. Teofila Petriella, "Report," in WFM, *Proceedings, 1907*, p. 186; MM, Aug. 1917;

Other practices seemed to confirm that the company doctor considered the company, not the worker, to be his patient. Mine and
smelter physicians tended to find their employers blameless in occupational accident cases. Hence lawsuits brought by victims or their
surviving dependents lacked essential corroborating medical evidence. At one prominent smelting firm Alice Hamilton encountered
"a hard-boiled man, a good servant to the company but with an
attitude of contemptuous hostility toward his charges. When an accident occurred, . . . he was always ready to fend off a damage suit
by certifying that the victim had heart disease and it was an attack of
heart failure on his part, not negligence on the part of the company,
that had injured or killed him." In 1915 Reverend Daniel McCorkle
described for the U.S. Commission on Industrial Relations the mu-
tually advantageous arrangement between the Colorado Fuel and Iron
Company and the physician at its iron mine in Sunrise, Wyoming.
Dr. W. C. Foster staunchly upheld the company's repressive labor
policies, at one point explaining to McCorkle that "the company wants
you in Sunrise to help keep the Greek and Italian people down, not
to stir them up. If you do not help the company keep them down
. . ., it does not want you here at all." In return for serving as a labor
relations expert, Foster not only received the usual capitation payments but also had the right to charge additional fees for his services,
which the company took directly out of employees' paychecks.
McCorkle reported that this practice engendered "much bitter feeling"
among the iron miners. Thus a long list of objectionable practices led
to a general distrust of company health care programs.[7]

Mark R. Lamb, "The Gentle Art of Appreciation," *EMJ*, Feb. 11, 1911, p. 326; Lead
City Miners' Union, Minute Book, p. 451 (Nov. 23, 1896), WFM-IUMMSW Archives,
reel 53; Louis Hughes to Editor, June 14, 1907, *MM*, June 27, 1907, p. 12. Negative
views of company doctors help explain why miners initiated health reforms. Hence
assessing the validity of these beliefs is beyond the scope of this study (and virtually
impossible to do). To be sure, there is countervailing evidence of diligent, competent
company physicians. See Arthur C. McMillan, "Granite's Glittering Glory," *Montana*
14 (July 1964): 67.

7. Hamilton, *Exploring the Dangerous Trades*, pp. 152–53; Daniel S. McCorkle, "Testimony," May 20, 1915, in U.S. Commission on Industrial Relations, *Final Report and
Testimony*, 9:8549 (quotation), 8543 (quotation), 8548–50; Louis Hughes to Editor, June
14, 1907, *MM*, June 27, 1907, p. 12; E. R. Fouts (company physician) to M. W. Krejci
(assistant manager, Great Falls smelter), May 4, 1918, Anaconda Records, box 219, file
1002–1; *MM*, Feb. 16, 1911, p. 8; Press Committee, Local 44, "History of Randsburg
Strike," *MM*, Dec. 10, 1903, p. 13; Alfred Parr to W. L. Hagler, Feb. 25, 1901, Mine-
Mill Papers, box 151, folder 14; U.S., National War Labor Board, "Award in re Employees
vs. Sloss-Sheffield Steel and Iron Co.," rpt. in IUMMSW, *Official Proceedings of the Twenty-
Third Consecutive and Third Biennial Convention, 1918* (Denver, n.d.), p. 112.

Some groups of miners set out to establish hospitals because existing programs provided patently inadequate facilities. As had been the case in the Coeur d'Alene before the founding of the union hospital, mine workers in Silver City paid a "hospital fee," but no hospital existed. Instead, the company doctor treated the sick and injured in their homes. Similarly, in the Lardeau district of British Columbia, one dollar per month was deducted from all workers, but neither the operators nor their physicians maintained any facility for even rudimentary inpatient services.[8]

In Silverton, Colorado, competition in the local health care market left miners with expensive as well as inadequate facilities. In August 1905 Dr. W. W. Wilkinson established Silverton's first hospital, with eight beds and a Turkish bath guaranteed to make users "feel five years younger." Within a matter of weeks, Mrs. B. Kemp set up a rival facility. "My hospital will not be run as an advertising scheme for the purpose of bolstering up the practice of any Doctor," insinuated Kemp. "It will be a strictly Ethical Hospital, open to all Ethical Physicians." Besides moral superiority, she promised "reasonable" prices and a prepayment plan aimed at capturing a share of the lucrative check-off business from the mines. Wilkinson responded by adopting an open medical staff policy and renaming his establishment the Silverton Hospital. By granting other physicians access to his facilities, Wilkinson by one move ran Mrs. Kemp out of business and appeased his professional competitors. This accommodation led to the creation of the San Juan Medical Association. In March 1908 Wilkinson and his colleagues sought to take advantage of their control over the supply of health care services:

> After a careful investigation the San Juan Medical Association finds that a hospital fee of one dollar per month does not give adequate compensation to the doctors in addition to paying hospital expenses and have decided to increase the hospital fee to $1.50 per month.
>
> Under the new arrangement the men may have the services of any doctor in Silverton, and should indicate in their order on the company to hold out [the] hospital fee, which doctor they wish, in case of sickness

8. *Idaho Avalanche*, Oct. 25, 1895, Sept. 25, 1896; Silver City Miners' Union, Minute Book, p. 122 (June 14, 1897), Silver City Miners' Union Records, vol. 1; *Revelstoke Herald* (B.C.), n.d., rpt. in *Lardeau Eagle*, Apr. 24, 1902; *Lardeau Eagle*, May 15, 1902, Feb. 6, 1903.

or accident. The men will be taken care of for the present at the Silverton Hospital.

Faced with these sharp business practices and the limited capacity of Wilkinson's hospital, the Silverton Miners' Union immediately embarked on a campaign to establish an institution "not . . . conducted for revenue but to meet a necessity."[9]

The leading proprietary hospital in the Slocan district engaged in a different form of overreaching. Established in New Denver in 1895 by Dr. J. E. Brouse, the Slocan Hospital soon had "all the mines in the division [as] subscribers." To serve outlying camps, Brouse maintained dispensaries at which physicians treated minor problems and stabilized serious cases for the trip to New Denver. The harsh climate, rugged terrain, and primitive transportation system of the area combined to make this plan unacceptable to many hardrock workers. The Sandon union observed that "at certain seasons of the year it was by no means a light task for even a healthy man to undertake the journey." In addition, Local 81 criticized the inherent unreliability of such profit-making ventures: "It is not unreasonable to presume that they were operated in the interests of their owners, nor was it to be expected that, should the camp fail to realize expectations, a continuance of their service would be maintained." Besides the Sandon workers, two other groups in the district—the Slocan Miners' Union and the Silverton Miners' Union—rejected Brouse's system and set up facilities more accessible to their members.[10]

The transience of hospital proprietors pulled other WFM locals into the health care field as well. In 1892 Dr. B. F. Sandow offered to open an inpatient facility in Neihart, Montana, if mine owners agreed to take $1.50 per month from each of their employees and remit the sum collected to him. When the operators accepted this proposal, Sandow remodeled a house and named it Belt Mountain Hospital. The collapse of silver prices and the general economic depression beginning in 1893

9. *Silverton Weekly Miner*, Nov. 10, Oct. 6, 1905, Mar. 13, 1908, Mar. 7, 1913, Aug. 25, 1905, Oct. 18, 1907, Jan. 10, 1908; *Polk's Medical Register and Directory of North America*, 10th ed. (Detroit, 1908), p. 345; Harry A. Lee (Colorado commissioner of mines), "Testimony," July 13, 1899, in U.S. Industrial Commission, *Report*, 12:233.

10. New Denver *Ledge*, n.d., rpt. in Sandon *Paystreak*, Sept. 25, 1897, Sept. 17, 1898; Sandon Miners' Union, *By-Laws of Hospital*, p. 4; *Polk's Medical Register*, 7th ed., p. 2065; *MM*, Mar. 1900, p. 24; Sandon *Paystreak*, May 1, 22, July 24, 1897; Martin, "B.C. District Convention Report."

soon ended Neihart's growth and prosperity. Moving on to greener pastures, Dr. Sandow sold his building to the Belt Mountain Miners' Union in 1898.[11] Similarly, when the physician upon whom the North Moccasin Miners' Union depended sold out and abandoned Kendall, Montana, in 1902, Local 111 set out to found its own facility.[12]

Voluntary institutions could be as objectionable as their profit-making counterparts. The two prominent nonprofit hospitals in Salt Lake City—Saint Mark's and Holy Cross—benefited from payroll deductions taken from the mine and mill workers of Park City. Jealously guarding an important source of revenue, these institutions blocked an attempt by Park City residents to build a local facility in the 1880s. In 1902 silver miners complained that "the Salt Lake hospitals were so crowded men could not get proper care and attention." The editor of the *Park Record* scoffed at one operator's claim that miners received excellent care at these institutions. "Men have often left the hospitals before cured, owing to their having been slighted, and given little or no attention by the doctors and attendants. Especially is this true in numerous cases of lead poisoning where doctors have prescribed medicine, and then dropped the case without ascertaining whether patients were improving or not, and showing no interest whatever." Access to the hospitals, located more than twenty miles away, depended on the railroad schedule. When, for example, C. B. Powell accidentally struck dynamite while mucking in the Quincy mine, his face was "literally shot into mincemeat, the left eye being blown out entirely and the eye socket filled with dirt and rock." Powell waited hours for the next train to Salt Lake. Then, "groaning from untold pain, [he] was laid on a blanket and for two hours forced to withstand the jostlings of a trip to the city." Powell survived the journey, but many accident victims did not. In addition, during the winter months snowstorms occasionally cut off rail service through the Wasatch Mountains. Finally, married miners objected to the separation from their families entailed by confinement in a distant hospital.[13]

By the early 1900s, a number of union hospitals were functioning

11. *Neihart Herald*, July 24, 1891, June 4, July 23, 1892; *Medical and Surgical Register of the United States*, 3d ed. (Detroit, 1893), p. 745; *Neihart Miner*, Sept. 8, 1898.

12. *Great Falls Daily Tribune*, Feb. 24, 1902, p. 6, Apr. 29, 1902, p. 3, Sept. 12, 1902, p. 3.

13. *Park Record*, June 28, 1902, Dec. 19, 1903, May 21, 1904, Dec. 13, 1902, Apr. 4, May 9, Nov. 14, Dec. 12, 26, 1903, Jan. 30, 1904; William M. McPhee, *The Trail of the Leprechaun: Early History of a Utah Mining Camp* (Hicksville, N.Y., 1977), pp. 51–52.

successfully. Accordingly, newly organized WFM locals began to take the initiative and build hospitals before company plans could be implemented. In Nevada, where a succession of gold and silver discoveries created instant boom towns in the desert, Western Federation affiliates moved quickly to create health care facilities where none existed. In 1901, the Tonopah miners set the pattern by forming a union during the early days of the gold rush and immediately building a hospital. Miners' organizations in Goldfield, Rhyolite, Rawhide, Silver Peak, and Vernon, Nevada, all established hospitals in the same year they were chartered. Experience had taught workers not to wait for their employers to fill the health care void on the mining frontier. The union approach thus shifted from reaction to preemption.[14]

Some efforts to replace company-dictated programs, however, failed to get off the ground. Members of the Butte Mill and Smeltermen's Union chafed under "a system that compels a workingman to pay a dollar a month for hospitals that are objectional [sic] to him and doctors that he despises and would absolutely object to . . . even at the point of death." Local 74 became interested in health benefit reform in 1901, upon learning that other locals had thriving hospitals. But when the Montana Ore Purchasing Company, the leading operator in the local's jurisdiction, adamantly refused to abolish its mandatory program, the Butte smelter workers' plans aborted. Similarly, the Globe, Arizona, miners abandoned the idea of building their own hospital in the face of employers' determination to maintain elaborate health and welfare programs.[15]

14. Elliott, "Tonopah, Goldfield," pp. 12, 84–85, and passim; Berg, "History of Tonopah," pp. 97, 125, 173; John E. Brinley, Jr., "The Western Federation of Miners" (Ph.D. dissertation, University of Utah, 1972), pp. 220–21 (Brinley erroneously gives the founding of Goldfield's Local 220 as 1905. It was organized in April 1904. See J. A. McLaughlin and A. B. Anderson [Local 220] to Editor, June 27, 1904, *MM*, July 7, 1904, p. 12.); *Tonopah Bonanza*, Nov. 9, 23, Dec. 7, 1901; Glasscock, *Gold in Them Hills*, p. 50; AMA, *American Medical Directory*, 1st ed. (Chicago, 1906), p. 565; Polk's *Medical Register and Directory of North America*, 11th ed. (Detroit, 1910), p. 1170; *Goldfield News*, June 17, 1904, July 14, 1905, p. 4, Feb. 9, 1907; *MSP*, Nov. 26, 1904, p. 362; *Rhyolite Herald*, Sept. 15, 1905; *Rawhide Rustler* (Nev.), Jan. 16, 1907; *Rawhide Daily Press*, Feb. 4, 1908; *Blair Press*, Apr. 18, 1908; *Vernon Review*, Oct. 5, 1907. Across the state line in Death Valley, the Greenwater Miners' Union followed the Nevada boomtown pattern. Local 207 set up a temporary hospital within six months of its founding and before any employer-administered programs were established. See W. H. Culp (Local 207) to Editor, Feb. 2, 1907, *MM*, Feb. 14, 1907, p. 12.

15. Press Committee, Butte Mill and Smeltermen's Union (Local 74) to Editor, n.d., *MM*, Nov. 1901, pp. 41–42; idem, n.d., *MM*, Dec. 1901, pp. 32–35; *American Labor Union Journal* (Butte), Apr. 2, 1903, p. 1; William Wills (Local 60) to Officers and Members

Management of the Treadwell gold mines crushed protest in its fiefdom of Douglas Island, Alaska. Roughly eight hundred members of WFM Local 109 struck in March 1908 over several issues, including compulsory health care fees. The Treadwell miners complained that the fees were exorbitant, that the surplus generated thereby was diverted to antiunion purposes, and that workers had no voice in the expenditure of their "hard-earned money." In addition, local secretary Peter Fisher alleged that "the hospital is such . . . that if you call on the doctor (?) once, you'll scowl at the idea of even sending your DOG for treatment." The union demanded a hospital "controlled for and by the Western Federation of Miners." Taking advantage of the depressed national economy and ethnic divisions among the strikers, management replaced some union members and induced others to break ranks. Treadwell management shattered the strike and preserved its preexisting health care arrangements.[16]

The Douglas Island, Butte, and Globe cases illustrate a general pattern. Wherever the local balance of power strongly favored capital, operators blocked initiatives to reform health care. Such an imbalance commonly arose under two interrelated sets of conditions. First, employers who enjoyed a monopsonistic control over the local labor market created company towns or other quasi-feudal settings antithetical to unions and union health care projects. Second, in the most capital-intensive and technologically sophisticated segments of metals extraction and processing, employers gained leverage by diluting craft skills or rendering them obsolete. As a result, none of the miners' hospitals was located in a copper- or iron-mining district, a smelter town, or in any community in which only one firm operated.[17]

---

of Sandon Miners' Union, July 24, 1907, Mine-Mill Papers, box 156, folder 3; AMA, *American Medical Directory*, 6th ed., p. 204.

16. Peter Fisher to Editor, n.d., *MM*, Dec. 19, 1907, pp. 11 (quotation), 11–13; Committee (Local 109) to Officers and Members of Douglas Island Miners' Union, Mar. 21, 1908, leaflet (in the possession of John Durham, Bolerium Books, San Francisco); Niel McDonald, Yanco Terzich, and Sevald Torkelson (Local 109), "An Appeal from Douglas, Alaska," Apr. 11, 1908, *MM*, Apr. 30, 1908, p. 6; Sevald Torkelson to Editor, June 7, 1907, *MM*, July 11, 1907, p. 14; Yanco Terzich, "Report," in WFM, *Proceedings*, 1908, pp. 313–15; *Douglas Island News* (Alaska), Mar. 25, Apr. 22, June 17, 1908; Charles E. Burke (Local 101, visiting Alaska) to Albert Ryan (Local 101), Apr. 4, 1907, in *MM*, Apr. 18, 1907, p. 14; James C. Foster, "The Western Federation Comes to Alaska," *Pacific Northwest Quarterly* 66 (Oct. 1975): 170–71. In 1907 Local 109 struck unsuccessfully for the more moderate demand of a voice in the disbursement of funds for health benefits and an employees' club. See Yanco Terzich, Report, in WFM, *Proceedings*, 1907, pp. 357–61.

17. Allen, *Company Town*, pp. xi, 33–49; idem, "Company-Owned Mining Town,"

Miners democratically decided to undertake hospital projects. Just as members of the Douglas Island Miners' Union took a vote on their ill-fated strike demands, the membership of those WFM locals that succeeded in founding hospitals participated actively in the decision-making process. In Local 66 in Silver City, the first proposal came from the rank and file: "Suggestions from the Brothers at the Boonville Mine [were] read to the Union. Suggestions were for the erection of a Miners Hospital." Similarly, the *San Miguel Examiner* reported that "the members of the Telluride Miners' Union No. 63 conceived the idea of establishing a modern hospital." Lengthy discussions in union meetings milled and smelted raw ideas. At one special session of the Silver City union devoted to the hospital question, "numerous ideas were advanced by different members."[18] Whereas some groups embarked on reform simply by passing a regular motion in a union meeting, others held special referenda. The referendum in Local 26 produced a strong mandate for action: 1,062 members favored building a hospital; 97 were opposed.[19]

Despite their deliberations and their knowledge of WFM hospitals elsewhere, local unions began the process of planning facilities with only vague notions of their basic features. Hence special rank-and-file committees, union officers, local physicians, and community representatives all played creative roles in shaping the hospitals. The Silver City local voted to have the president appoint a planning com-

---

pp. 194–95; Brown, *Hard-Rock Miners*, pp. 23–26; David J. Bercuson, "Labour Radicalism and the Western Industrial Frontier, 1897–1919," *Canadian Historical Review* 58 (1977): 166–68; Arnold R. Alanen, "The 'Locations': Company Communities on Minnesota's Iron Range," *Minnesota History* 48 (Fall 1982): 94–107; Gates, *Michigan Copper*, pp. 103–15; *MSP*, May 13, 1899, p. 509; Barger and Schurr, *Mining Industries*, pp. 105–41, 222–39; U.S. Work Projects Administration, *Technology, Employment*, pp. 5–29; James E. Fell, Jr., *Ores to Metals: The Rocky Mountain Smelting Industry* (Lincoln, Neb., 1979), pp. 225ff.; Dubofsky, "Western Working Class Radicalism," pp. 133–38. One union hospital did exist for a very short time in the "copper camp" of Greenwater, California. On close inspection, however, this exception proves the rule. A purely speculative by-product of the enthusiasm whipped up by nearby gold discoveries in southern Nevada, the Greenwater boom involved the mining of investors, not minerals. See Stanley W. Paher, *Death Valley Ghost Towns* (Las Vegas, 1973), p. 10; James W. Abbott, "The Greenwater District," *MSP*, Jan. 12, 1907, pp. 52–53; *MSP*, Sept. 14, 1907, p. 316.

18. Silver City Miners' Union, Minute Book, pp. 28 (Sept. 7, 1896) (quotation), 128 (July 5, 1897) (quotation), 28–167 (Sept. 7, 1896-Oct. 11, 1897), Silver City Miners' Union Records, vol. 1; *San Miguel Examiner*, Nov. 8, 1902; Terzich, "Report," in WFM, *Proceedings, 1908*, p. 314; *Kendall Miner*, Jan. 12, 1906; Sandon *Paystreak*, Feb. 4, 11, 1899.

19. Silver City Miners' Union, Minute Book, p. 167 (Oct. 11, 1897), Silver City Miners' Union Records, vol. 1; *Goldfield News*, Sept. 15, 1906, p. 7; *Silverton Weekly Miner*, May 8, 1908; *Lardeau Eagle*, Mar. 6, 1902.

mittee of three "to attend to Hospital Business." Local 26 expanded its committee from three to five members to handle its many duties. In contrast, a single rank-and-file member, working with the building contractors, designed the second North Moccasin Miners' Union Hospital.[20]

In other locals, the officers led the drive to found a hospital. The *San Miguel Examiner* praised the "tireless" work of president Vincent St. John and secretary-treasurer Oscar Carpenter of Local 63. Just as St. John and Carpenter called on Dr. E. D. Allen, other locals turned to physicians to help design their facilities. The Slocan Miners' Union delegated all planning chores to Dr. Alex Forin, the practitioner selected to superintend the hospital upon its completion.[21] In the Lardeau district, the fund-raising committee consisted of representatives of Local 119 and area businessmen. The miners of Rhyolite, Nevada, collaborated with an ad hoc group of women from the community.[22]

Site selection sometimes involved little more than entertaining proposals from individuals trying to sell houses or other vacant buildings. Indeed, a number of locals set up modest facilities in remodeled houses. Local 66, for example, purchased a large residence on "an ideal [site], easy of access at all seasons of the year, and having natural drainage." Donations of parcels of land settled the question in Park City, Ferguson, and Rhyolite. Like their predecessors in the Coeur d'Alene, several locals used temporary facilities until permanent quarters could be erected.[23]

The locals that erected buildings generally hired contractors to do the job. Hence the role of union representatives was to obtain bids, enter into a contract, and see that its terms were met. The Telluride Miners' Union, however, departed from this arrangement to uphold its interpretation of union principles. Having fought a protracted strike during the preceding year over a contracting system that often paid

20. Silver City Miners' Union, Minute Book, p. 162 (Sept. 27, 1897), Silver City Miners' Union Records, vol. 1; *Silverton Weekly Miner*, Mar. 12, May 21, 1909; *Kendall Miner*, Jan. 12, 1906, Mar. 13, 1908; *Lardeau Eagle*, Jan. 16, 1903; *Rawhide Daily Press*, Feb. 14, 1908.

21. *San Miguel Examiner*, Nov. 8, 1902, Jan. 24, 1903; *Slocan Drill*, Feb. 15, 22, 1901; *Park Record*, Nov. 14, 1903.

22. *Lardeau Eagle*, Jan. 23, Feb. 20, May 22, 29, 1902; *Rhyolite Herald*, May 26, 1905.

23. *Owyhee Avalanche*, Oct. 29, Nov. 12, 1897; Silver City Miners' Union, Minute Book, pp. 112 (May 24, 1897), 164 (Oct. 4, 1897), 167 (Oct. 11, 1897), Silver City Miners' Union Records, vol. 1; *Park Record*, Mar. 26, 1904; *Lardeau Eagle*, Mar. 13, 1902; *Rhyolite Herald*, Aug. 4, 1905; *Slocan Drill*, Feb. 15, Mar. 8, 1901; *Kendall Miner*, Jan. 12, 1906; *Goldfield News*, Sept. 15, 1906, p. 7.

inferior piece rates, Local 63 was not about to contradict its position on this still-sore issue. Accordingly, "every stroke of work on the building was done by day's pay and the highest of wages were paid." In contrast, unpaid volunteers performed a significant amount of labor on the Lardeau Miners' Union Hospital.[24]

Above all else, fund-raising preoccupied union activists and their supporters. Most locals boldly commenced construction before accumulating enough money to complete the project. The Silver City miners who suspended construction plans because they "object[ed] to the building of an Hospital without the necessary funds to build it with" were the exception. Other organizations went out on a limb, confident that they would somehow acquire additional funds when their treasuries were empty.[25]

Not surprisingly, the bulk of construction funds came from the miners themselves. Locals relied heavily on special assessments. The Silverton union voted to assess each member "not less than $1.00 per month, nor more than $5.00 per quarter, until the building is free from debt, besides such dues as may be necessary to conduct the hospital without loss."[26] In contrast, the thriving Goldfield local, with over two thousand members, simply allocated $10,000 from its treasury when it decided in 1906 to replace its outgrown facility with a new one capable of accommodating sixty patients. No other miners' body that established a hospital approached Local 220 in size or wealth. In fact, most institutions were founded by small locals. If five organizations with more than 500 members each — Goldfield, Tonopah, Telluride, Silverton, and Park City—are excluded, the remaining twenty

24. *San Miguel Examiner*, Nov. 8, June 7, 1902; *Park Record*, Apr. 23, 30, May 14, 1904; *Kendall Miner*, Jan. 12, Feb. 9, 1906; *Lardeau Eagle*, Apr. 24, May 8, 1902. A very different conflict over union principles interrupted construction of the second Goldfield hospital in 1907. Members of the United Brotherhood of Carpenters and Joiners stopped work to protest the part-time employment of miners on the building. This dispute was part of a larger struggle in the community between the IWW and the AFL over jurisdictional and other concerns. See Jensen, *Heritage of Conflict*, p. 224; Guy L. Rocha, "Radical Labor Struggles in the Tonopah-Goldfield Mining District, 1901–1922," *Nevada Historical Society Quarterly* 20 (1977): 12.

25. Silver City Miners' Union, Minute Book, pp. 132–33 (July 19, 1897), Silver City Miners' Union Records, vol. 1; Press Committee, Local 107, to Editor, n.d., *MM*, July 1901, p. 37; *Tonopah Bonanza*, Oct. 19, 1901; A. Shilland to William D. Haywood, Feb. 6, 1905, Mine-Mill Papers, box 155, folder 13.

26. *Silverton Weekly Miner*, May 8, 1908; James A. Baker (Executive Board, District 6), Report, in WFM, *Proceedings, 1904*, p. 272; *Slocan Drill*, Sept. 4, 1903; W. H. Culp (Local 207) to Editor, Feb. 2, 1907, *MM*, Feb. 14, 1907, p. 12; *Rhyolite Herald*, May 19, 1905; *Kendall Miner*, Dec. 21, 1906; Sandon Miners' Union, *By-Laws of Hospital*, p. 6.

Ymir General Hospital. The Ymir Miners' Union was one of six British Columbia locals that built health-care centers. Local 85 erected this cottage hospital shortly after the turn of the century. (Courtesy of Western Historical Collections, University of Colorado)

Telluride Miners' Union Hospital. Founded in 1902, this facility fell victim to the class war that convulsed southwestern Colorado shortly thereafter. (The Denver Public Library, Western History Department)

hospital sponsors averaged roughly 200 members. The Sandon Miners' Union, for instance, had about 150 members in good standing when it set up its facility in 1899.[27] Self-reliance and grassroots initiative appear to have been strongest in small, close-knit locals.

Only the Telluride Miners' Union turned to the international union for help in meeting construction costs. Local 63 ran out of money after spending $10,000 and appealed to the WFM convention of 1902 for aid. The Telluride miners reminded convention delegates that during the past year their organization not only had lost one tenth of its members through avalanches, fires, and other accidents but also had conducted a prolonged strike without taking any assistance from the general headquarters. The WFM granted Local 63 a donation of $3,000, about half the amount deemed necessary to finish the building.[28]

Hardrock workers raised funds from the general public primarily by hosting social events. Union hospitals were built in small towns, few of which exceeded twenty-five hundred in population, where popular culture was less commercialized than in cities. In this setting, benefit dances on holidays proved particularly popular. The Silverton Miners' Union held four fund-raising balls during 1908—two to celebrate Independence Day, one on Labor Day, and one on New Year's Eve. The Labor Day dance drew "a fine crowd . . ., and the hospital fund received a handsome increase from the proceeds." Apparently a convivial lot, Local 26 also threw a Hard Times ball in February 1909, which brought in over $350. This event displayed a sort of sociable class consciousness. The Silverton Musicians' Union provided the music, the women of the Steam Laundry Union prepared supper, and the miners levied "heavy fines" on those with the temerity to attend in a "boiled shirt" rather than rags.[29]

---

27. Neihart No. 7 (Belt Mountain Miners' Union), "Neihart Notes," *MM*, Jan. 1900, p. 33; Ernest Mills (secretary-treasurer, WFM), "Financial Report," in WFM, *Proceedings, 1908*, pp. 216, 219–21; Thomas D. Tobin (Local 62) to Editor, Apr. 5, 1901, *MM*, May 1901, pp. 32–33; *MM*, Sept. 1902, p. 38; Silver City Miners' Union, Ledger Book, p. 62 (Jan. 1, 1898), Silver City Miners' Union Records, vol. 2; Sandon *Paystreak*, Feb. 4, 1899; Ernest Mills, "Annual Report," in IUMMSW, *Proceedings, 1918*, Appendix, p. 49; idem, "Financial Report," in WFM, *Proceedings, 1911*, p. 198; William Haywood, "Report," in WFM, *Proceedings, 1903*, pp. 88–89; idem, Report, in WFM, *Proceedings, 1905*, p. 208; *Park Record*, Aug. 15, 1903; James Kirwan (acting secretary-treasurer, WFM), "Report," in WFM, *Proceedings, 1907*, pp. 139–40; Press Committee, Local 235, to Editor, Dec. 7, 1905, *MM*, Dec. 21, 1905, p. 11. Needless to say, data on local membership, especially those based on self-reports to the international headquarters, are imprecise.

28. *San Miguel Examiner*, June 7, 1902; WFM, *Proceedings, 1902*, pp. 107–8.

29. *Silverton Weekly Miner*, Sept. 11, 1908, Feb. 12, 1909, June 26, July 3, 10, Dec. 11, 18, 1908, Feb. 5, 19, 1909.

Other locals pursued the same strategy. The Judith Mountain Miners' Union proudly reported that it had raised membership morale as well as money: "Our dance, the proceeds of which will be used in completing our hospital, was a grand success, socially and financially, which makes all our members very enthusiastic as all contributed their mite to make it a success." When the Lardeau miners gave a "sheet and pillow case masquerade" in 1902, they gained not only "a handsome sum" for their health care center but also three dozen sets of bed linens for it.[30] This local also benefited from a dance and food sale put on by its Ladies Auxiliary.[31]

Other labor-intensive forms of community fund-raising were less enjoyable. Frank Holten, a member of the Hospital Committee of Local 119, trekked through snow three feet deep over the divide to gather donations in Camborne, British Columbia. Ordinarily, public canvassing concentrated on the town in which the hospital was to be located. In March 1909 the Silverton organization estimated that it needed an additional $19,000 to complete its facility. The union appealed for public support and circulated a series of subscription lists in the community, one of which produced over $3,000 for hospital furnishings.[32] In general, merchants and others who depended on the miners' business gave generously. Not surprisingly, absentee mining capitalists did not contribute to these fund-raising drives, although many small operators with local ties did.[33]

In British Columbia, community support helped secure government subsidies for construction. In Ferguson, the Hospital Committee reported in February 1902 that "the petition which is being circulated by the committee requesting government aid is being widely signed." Because provincial officials provided such aid on a discretionary basis, the Lardeau hospital was fortunate to receive assistance. Of course, the grantmakers considered this a political as well as a public health

30. Press Committee, Local 107, to Editor, n.d., *MM*, July 1901, p. 37; *Lardeau Eagle*, Nov. 28, 1902; *San Miguel Examiner*, Dec. 7, 1901, Jan. 4, 1902; *Park Record*, Sept. 3, 10, 1904; Alfred Parr, Con Robinson, Archie McDougall (Local 85) to Officers and Members of Sandon Union, June 16, 1902, Mine-Mill Papers, box 153, folder 4.

31. *Lardeau Eagle*, May 22, 29, June 6, 1902; *Rhyolite Herald*, May 19, 26, June 9, July 7, Aug. 4, 1905.

32. *Lardeau Eagle*, Nov. 21, 28, 1902, Jan. 16, 1903; *Silverton Weekly Miner*, Mar. 12, 19, May 21, 28, June 18, July 16, Aug. 6, 27, 1909; *Slocan Drill*, Mar. 8, 1901.

33. Sandon Miners' Union, *By-Laws of Hospital*, p. 6; *Park Record*, Dec. 19, 1903, Feb. 27, Mar. 26, Oct. 1, 1904; *San Miguel Examiner*, July 19, Oct. 18, Nov. 8, 1902; Press Committee, Local 63, to Editor, July 31, 1902, *MM*, Sept. 1902, p. 48; *Tonopah Bonanza*, Nov. 23, 1901.

investment. As the 1903 elections approached, the *Eagle* reminded voters of their indebtedness to the Conservatives: "The Lardeau people should not lose sight of the fact that the McBride government have given a grant of $2,000 to the Miners' Union hospital at Ferguson and that a grant was refused by the previous government." Like Local 119, the organizations in Ymir, Slocan, and Sandon obtained grants to meet building expenses. The Sandon local got help only after William Davidson, a director of the union hospital, won a seat in the Legislative Assembly. Altogether, Victoria made over $14,000 in capital grants to the miners' institutions between 1902 and 1917. South of the border, none of the metal-mining states offered grants for hospital construction.[34]

Some hospital planners addressed the crucial question of diverting check-off revenue from company programs to their own. Anticipating the enormous financial and administrative difficulties of collecting monthly fees, a number of locals pressed for assurances of management cooperation early in their campaigns. Immediately following its decision to establish a health care center, the Silverton union asked the Mine Owners' Association to make deductions for their institution. Four months before the facility in Silver City opened, Simon Harris happily announced that Trade Dollar superintendent James Hutchinson was "willing to collect and turn money into the Union for Hospital instead of paying Doctors." The prospect of improved services and an end to employees' grievances gave management ample incentive to comply with such requests.[35]

Yet operators in Park City strenuously resisted a union proposal to redirect check-off funds. When the miners broached this subject in November 1903, they estimated that local payroll deductions gener-

---

34. *Lardeau Eagle*, Feb. 20, 1902, Aug. 14, 1903, Jan. 23, 1902, June 10, 1904; *Slocan Drill*, Feb. 15, May 10, 1901; J. D. Prentice (provincial secretary) to "Sir," May 2, 1901, Mine-Mill Papers, box 152, folder 2; William Davidson to Anthony Shilland, Jan. 12, 1905, ibid., box 155, folder 12; British Columbia, *Sessional Papers, 1905*, p. B74; idem, *Sessional Papers, 1903*, p. D55; idem, *Sessional Papers, 1907*, p. B57; idem, *Sessional Papers, 1912*, p. C71; idem, *Sessional Papers, 1913*, p. C69; idem, *Sessional Papers, 1915*, p. C86; idem, *Sessional Papers, 1916*, 1:C91; idem, *Sessional Papers, 1917*, 1:C93; idem, *Sessional Papers, 1918*, 1:C97–98. In addition to establishing public hospitals for coal miners, Pennsylvania subsidized voluntary institutions in this period. See Rosemary Stevens, "Sweet Charity: State Aid to Hospitals in Pennsylvania, 1870–1910," *Bulletin of the History of Medicine* 58 (1984): 287–314, 474–95.

35. Silver City Miners' Union, Minute Book, pp. 122 (June 14, 1897), 185 (Nov. 22, 1897), Silver City Miners' Union Records, vol. 1; *Silverton Weekly Miner*, May 8, 1908; *Revelstoke Herald*, n.d., rpt. in *Lardeau Eagle*, Apr. 24, 1902.

ated at least $1,500 per month for Salt Lake hospitals. The *Park Record* encouraged operators to grant this pivotal request because "they have the miners in this camp to thank for their wealth and happiness." The owners initially refused to commit themselves, waiting to see what position the powerful Kearns-Keith interests would take. As the union's scheduled meeting with U.S. Senator Thomas Kearns approached, *Record* editor Samuel Raddon reminded the mining magnate that he had begun his career in this district as a common miner and that "wealth was still pouring into his lap" from his various holdings in Park City. During 1902, for example, Kearns received a major share of the $1.4 million in profits produced by the Silver King property. Because the senator had been the only prominent operator in the area who refused to cut wages during the 1890s, the union had good reason to expect a favorable response from him.[36]

On December 14, 1903, Kearns stunned the delegation from Local 144 by launching a blistering attack on the union proposition. He staunchly defended the quality of care provided at the Salt Lake hospitals and stated that these institutions should not be deprived of revenue because St. Mark's was running a deficit and Holy Cross was "not paying interest on the money invested." Kearns dismissed as foolhardy the idea of a hospital in Park City, arguing that sanitary and climatic conditions were inhospitable. Further, he contended that the miners could not raise enough money to erect an adequate facility. The senator proposed to solve the problem of access by setting up a railway ambulance system, "a hospital car, held in readiness . . . at all times" for the trip to the city.[37]

Local 144 responded to this challenge by mobilizing greater support for its project, both in its own ranks and in the community at large. More than three hundred men attended a "rousing meeting" on Christmas Day to discuss the matter. President Joseph Langford insisted that the fate of the enterprise rested with the rank and file, who had to "be willing at any time to make a sacrifice for the consummation of the proposition." Langford rallied his troops with a recitation of their major grievances against the prevailing system:

> You are all aware of existing conditions. How, at this time, we are compelled to submit to treatment which is not at all satisfactory; our money

36. *Park Record*, Nov. 14, Dec. 12, Nov. 21, 28, 1903, Dec. 27, 1902; Peterson, *Bonanza Kings*, pp. 29–30, 79–80.
37. *Park Record*, Dec. 19, 1903.

taken from us without our consent or approval; the long and tedious journey we have to undertake in order to reach the hospitals; . . . the expense incured [sic] for transportation to and from the city and the danger of never being able to reach our destination safely, especially during the winter months, when . . . there is very great dread on the part of some of our members to taking this journey through fear of further jeopardizing their lives.

Maintaining that "the favorable sentiment of a vast majority of the population of this city is on our side," Langford urged the local to prove Kearns wrong. "This is the time for us to assert our manhood; this is the time for us to show our enemies that we, poor miners as we are, are capable of doing noble things and not dreaming all day long." After several speakers rose to support this position, the Cemetery Committee proposed "a Miners hospital at Park City, to be constructed, owned and operated by an incorporated company." The meeting unanimously adopted this proposal "amid much enthusiasm."[38]

Shortly thereafter, the union formed a nonprofit hospital corporation, which offered stock at $10 per share. Local 144 immediately bought one hundred shares. Individual members purchased single shares on an installment plan. Businessmen and others in the town invested in this venture that promised no dividends. The union soon had the capital required to begin construction. Ground was broken for the Park City Miners' Hospital on April 28, 1904.[39]

As the building neared completion, Local 144 renewed its efforts to alter the check-off arrangement. In July 1904, a union committee met with representatives of the principal mines in the district, who agreed to reconsider their position. Faced with petitions from the majority of their employees and the impending realization of a scheme they had dismissed as fantastic, some operators simply conceded the issue. Kearns and Ernest Bamberger of the Daly-West mine, however, both insisted upon holding referenda on the subject. When Silver King and Daly-West workers voted "almost unanimously in favor of sending [the hospital fee] to the local institution," the matter was resolved. Miners were finally free to support their own hospital.[40]

The facilities and services of the miners' hospitals were modest.

38. Ibid., Dec. 26, 1903.
39. Ibid., Dec. 26, 1903, Jan. 2, Feb. 20, 27, Apr. 30, 1904.
40. Ibid., Oct. 15, July 16, Sept. 3, Oct. 8, 22, Nov. 2, 1904.

They ranged in size from small to very small. The first health care center in Sandon, for instance, had only six beds. At the other end of the spectrum, the Telluride hospital had forty beds, and the union claimed (without specifying how) that in an emergency it could accommodate seventy patients. For the sixteen facilities on which data are available, the average capacity at or near the time of founding was nineteen beds.[41]

Even structures that were not converted houses were essentially residential in design. A common plan consisted of one or two general wards of four to eight beds each, along with a few private rooms for paying patients. Separate wards for infectious disease and maternity cases were exceptional. Hardly efficient in their use of space, the hospitals usually had dining rooms and parlors, as well as kitchens, bathrooms, laundries, physicians' offices, and rooms to house the staff. The miners' institutions thus appear to have been western counterparts of the cottage hospitals of England and New England.[42]

Prevailing notions of hygiene influenced the planning of facilities. The Park City hospital was "carefully arranged so as to get the best light and ventilation [sic] possible, all windows being provided with transoms reaching nearly to the ceiling." The two wards in the Silver City institution were "large and airy." Although admittedly "not sumptuous or expensive," the Slocan Miners' Union General Hospital was "spotlessly clean and neat."[43]

The hardrock hospitals offered a surgical setting that was likely to be safer than the available alternatives—the patient's home, the physician's office, or the county hospital. As late as 1914 more than a

41. *Polk's Medical Register*, 7th ed., p. 1214; *Silverton Weekly Miner*, May 21, 1909; AMA, *American Medical Directory*, 3d ed. (Chicago, 1912), pp. 717, 741; idem, *American Medical Directory*, 1st ed., pp. 546, 565; idem, *American Medical Directory*, 4th ed. (Chicago, 1914), p. 1591; idem, *American Medical Directory*, 13th ed. (Chicago, 1934), p. 1787; *Slocan Drill*, June 7, 1901; *San Miguel Examiner*, Nov. 8, 1902; *Owyhee Avalanche*, Oct. 29, 1897; MM, May 1900, p. 33; *Polk's Medical Register*, 11th ed., pp. 1136, 1170; *Kendall Miner*, Jan. 12, 1906; *Lardeau Eagle*, Sept. 26, 1902; *Park Record*, Oct. 15, 1904, Mar. 4, 1905; Goldfield Miners' Union, "Warranty Deed," Oct. 5, 1911, WFM-IUMMSW Archives, box 1, folder 31; *Polk's Medical Register*, 10th ed., p. 1181; *Rawhide Daily Press*, Feb. 4, 1908.

42. Brian Abel-Smith, *The Hospitals, 1800–1948: A Study in Social Administration in England and Wales* (Cambridge, Mass., 1964), pp. 102–3; Henry C. Burdett, *Cottage Hospitals*, 3d ed. (London, 1896), pp. 327–54, 363–64, and passim; Sandon *Paystreak*, May 26, 1900; see sources cited in the preceding note.

43. *Park Record*, Apr. 30, 1904; *Owyhee Avalanche*, Oct. 29, 1897; *Slocan Drill*, June 7, 1901; *Rhyolite Herald*, June 8, 1906; *San Miguel Examiner*, Nov. 8, 1902; *Manhattan Post*, Nov. 12, 1910.

quarter of California's county institutions lacked any pretense of an operating room, but virtually all the miners' health care centers provided these facilities. Even the tiny Sandon Miners' Union Hospital designated a special room for performing surgery. In addition, by 1900 this hospital had a laboratory. The Silverton, Colorado, facility even possessed x-ray apparatus when it opened in 1909. Most of the other union hospitals, however, apparently acquired neither radiological nor laboratory equipment. More than anything else, lack of funds limited the level of medical technology.[44]

Most of the hospitals admitted patients who were not union members. Of the twenty institutions on which information is available, thirteen served the general public. But even those that restricted admissions opened their doors in emergencies. For instance, the Tonopah Miners' Union Hospital cared for nonunion victims of the 1901–2 pneumonia outbreak. According to the *Tonopah Bonanza*, "No penniless stranger who . . . asked admittance to [this] hospital was ever turned away." In the wake of this epidemic, Local 121 brought policy into line with practice by constructing a larger building, to which "any reputable person paying the monthly fee of $1 will be eligible" for admission. Predictably, the smallest institutions excluded nonmembers so they could guarantee that their handful of beds would be available for union members.[45]

WFM affiliates that established hospitals to serve the general public contributed significantly to community development. Like the creation of schools, churches, and fire departments, the founding of an inpatient health care center was important both materially and symbolically to the progress of a growing community. Despite their ob-

44. California State Board of Charities and Corrections, *Sixth Biennial Report, 1912–14* (Sacramento, 1915), p. 176; *San Miguel Examiner*, Oct. 4, Nov. 8, 1902; *MM*, May 1900, p. 33; *Kendall Miner*, May 18, 1906; *Lardeau Eagle*, Sept. 19, 26, 1902; *Tonopah Miner*, Nov. 28, 1902; Sandon *Paystreak*, Oct. 27, 1900; *Silverton Weekly Miner*, June 18, 1909, Mar. 6, 1903; John Fraser (Local 81) to Provincial Secretary, Feb. 21, 1918, Mine-Mill Papers, box 156, folder 13; see sources cited in note 41.

45. *Tonopah Bonanza*, Feb. 8, 1902; *Tonopah Miner*, Nov. 28, 1902; *Polk's Medical Register and Directory of North America*, 8th ed. (Detroit, 1904), p. 1191; *Silverton Weekly Miner*, May 21, 1909; *Polk's Medical Register*, 9th ed., p. 1263; *Slocan Drill*, June 7, 1901; *San Miguel Examiner*, Apr. 18, 1903; J. C. Barnes (Local 104, American Labor Union, Telluride) to Editor, Dec. 10, 1902, *American Labor Union Journal*, Dec. 18, 1902, p. 3; *Owyhee Avalanche*, Oct. 29, 1897; *MM*, May 1900, p. 33; AMA, *American Medical Directory*, 6th ed., p. 1591; British Columbia, *Sessional Papers*, 1920, 1:C149; *Polk's Medical Register*, 11th ed., pp. 1136–37; *Lardeau Eagle*, Sept. 26, 1902; *Park Record*, Oct. 28, 1905; *Little Rockies Miner*, May 15, 1909; *Polk's Medical Register*, 10th ed., p. 1181; *Rhyolite Herald*, May 19, 1905; *Rawhide Rustler*, Mar. 21, 1908; *Seven Troughs Miner*, Jan. 4, 1908.

vious limitations, the miners' hospitals clearly improved the quality and quantity of health services wherever they were organized. The establishment of these institutions meant, among other things, that less surgery had to be done on kitchen tables. Frontier towns proudly pointed out these facilities in boosting themselves to potential investors. The *Slocan Drill* put it succinctly: "No town of progress or importance is complete without a hospital, and certainly Slocan has reason to be proud of the local institution known as the Miners' Union General Hospital." The founding of a hospital was one of the milestones that marked the transition from mining camp to mining town.[46]

As prime movers in these endeavors, the hardrock unions reaped a harvest of goodwill, winning reputations as industrious and benevolent organizations. The *San Miguel Examiner* hailed the Telluride Miners' Union Hospital as "a monument to the enterprise of organized labor." Even if the facilities did not serve the general public, their founders won praise. The *Owyhee Avalanche* commended the "generosity and noble-heartedness" of the Silver City miners.[47]

As with other WFM mutual benefit activities, the hospitals attracted broad support for organizing efforts and for the union's side in disputes. The *Lardeau Eagle* praised Local 119 as a "good organization for a man to belong to," in part because benefits included "doctor's care and nursing at the Miner's Union hospital." Armed with new inducements, the locals with health care centers intensified their efforts to recruit new members. Shortly after the Slocan facility opened, Local 62 leader Thomas Tobin reported that "with a very few exceptions all the employees [of the mines in the area] are members of the union." Bill Haywood declared that he and his fellow activists in Silver City soon had their jurisdiction "completely unionized." Many, if not most, of the hospital locals became solid union camps.[48]

46. *Slocan Drill*, June 7, 1901; *Park Record*, Oct. 1, 1904, May 20, 1905; Sandon Miners' Union, *By-Laws of Hospital*, pp. 4, 7; *San Miguel Examiner*, Oct. 18, Nov. 8, 1902.

47. *San Miguel Examiner*, July 19, Oct. 18, 1902; *Owyhee Avalanche*, Nov. 12, 1897; Press Committee, Local 66, to Editor, Mar. 13, 1900, *MM*, Apr. 1900, p. 21; *Tonopah Bonanza*, Feb. 8, 1902; George F. Wilson to Editor, n.d., *Park Record*, Nov. 2, 1907; Mrs. R. G. Hemingway, Mrs. S. L. Forsyth, and H. G. Hemingway, "Card of Thanks," *Seven Troughs Miner*, Mar. 20, 1909.

48. *Lardeau Eagle*, Apr. 10, 1903; Thomas D. Tobin to Editor, Apr. 5, 1901, *MM*, May 1900, pp. 32–33; Haywood, *Bill Haywood's Book*, pp. 79, 64–65; Neihart No. 7, "Neihart Notes," *MM*, Jan. 1900, p. 33; Press Committee, Local 81, to Editor, Aug. 10, 1901, *MM*, Sept. 1901, p. 31; *Great Falls Daily Tribune*, Mar. 27, 1902, p. 3; *Kendall Miner*, Dec.

Officials of the international union repeatedly called attention to these humanitarian achievements as they attempted to dispel the stereotypical image of the WFM as a gang of violent anarchists. *Miners' Magazine* editor John O'Neill interpreted the founding of the Park City Miners' Hospital as "another proof that repudiates the slanderous accusation of a mine owners' association, that the Western Federation of Miners is a criminal organization." O'Neill blasted more ore from the same vein five years later when the Silverton, Colorado, hospital opened: "When men in the Western Federation of Miners rear and maintain institutions that care for the unfortunate, it seems blasphemous for the hired writers of subsidized organs to prostitute themselves to such an extent as to hurl calumniations against an organization whose humane efforts are visible in every part of Western America." International president Charles Moyer never tired of publicizing the benevolent work of the hospitals.[49]

On June 25, 1901, Moyer's predecessor, Edward Boyce, attended the annual picnic of the Slocan Miners' Union. Members of Local 62 and other nearby locals paraded down the decorated Main Street of Slocan to the picnic grounds and consumed the usual refreshments. After several British Columbia miners' leaders spoke, the grizzled veteran of the Coeur d'Alene delivered the major address of the day. "Mr. Boyce strongly urged the Unions to work mining properties for themselves," reported the *Slocan Drill*, "even as they were running their own hospitals, etc. Then the men could be their own employers. There was a great duty resting upon labor, and it was time the men got out of the old rut of trade unionism. To merely pay dues was not enough." Thus, for a brief moment at the turn of the century, organized metal miners believed that by grassroots activism they could somehow hold back the rising tide of corporate power. The success of their innovative health care experiments gave the activists grand

21, 1906; Marion W. Moor (Executive Board, WFM), "Report," in WFM, *Proceedings*, 1907, p. 146; *Goldfield News*, Aug. 3, 1907; Press Committee, Local 235, to Editor, Dec. 7, 1905, *MM*, Dec. 21, 1905, p. 11.

49. [John M. O'Neill], Untitled editorial, *MM*, Dec. 29, 1904, p. 5; idem, "The Miners' Union Hospital at Silverton, Colo.," *MM*, June 10, 1909, p. 4; Charles H. Moyer, Testimony, Oct. 9, 1917, in U.S., President's Mediation Commission, "Sessions at Globe," pp. 50, 133, McCluskey Collection, box 4; idem, "Report," in WFM, *Proceedings*, 1911, p. 29.

ideas. The pioneers in Sandon expressed the confidence that self-help fostered: "The hospital is still going on in the good work and the miners are justly proud of it. We have expended over $1,000 in furnishings alone since the fire, and in the near future a large addition will be added to our present premises. There is nothing impossible to the Sandon miner. 'Labor omnia vincit.'"[50]

50. *Slocan Drill,* June 28, 1901; Sandon Miners' Union to Editor, n.d., *MM,* Sept. 1900, p. 38.

6 | *Governing Hospitals*

Local unions faced the ongoing challenge of maintaining the institutions they had created. Miners themselves assumed the responsibilities of hospital governance. They delegated the administration of patient services to physicians and nurses but shouldered the onerous duties of financial management themselves.

The Western Federation activists who ran health care centers were common workingmen who did not know their place. In the late nineteenth and early twentieth centuries, hospital directors were drawn almost exclusively from among the elite of the community. Observing that "the typical hospital trustee is a successful man of business," prominent health care administrator S. S. Goldwater considered trusteeship a responsibility for which only prominent men of affairs were properly suited. "There are certain valuable experiences in life to which the multitude may not reasonably aspire," he sniffed. "One of them is the experience of being a hospital trustee, a privilege which in the United States is reserved for the Republic's best hundred thousand citizens." While medical staff, professionalizing administrators, and lay trustees disputed the proper apportionment of policy-making prerogatives throughout this period, patient representatives played no part in hospital governance. When, for example, in 1903 the central labor body of Boston requested a seat on the board of trustees of Boston City Hospital so it could defend the interests of the working-class patrons of the institution, it ran into what Harry Dowling called a "stone wall of elitism."[1] All that was expected of working-class

1. Sigismund S. Goldwater, "The Privilege of Being a Hospital Trustee," *Modern*

Park City Miners' Hospital. WFM Local 144 in Park City, Utah, built this facility in 1904 despite considerable opposition from leading mine operators. (Courtesy of Western Historical Collections, University of Colorado)

Board of Directors, Park City Miners' Hospital. The first board, elected in 1904, consisted of *(seated, from left)* David Baxter, Joseph Langford, F. C. Getsch, W. J. Kearns, *(standing, from left)* Bartley McDonough, S. E. Pegan, John Patrick, and W. J. Rosevear. (Courtesy of Western Historical Collections, University of Colorado)

patients was that they be compliant and grateful for the benefactions of their betters.

The miners' hospitals were an entirely different affair. Their governance blended participatory and representative democracy. Ultimate responsibility for the institutions rested with the rank-and-file membership. Anthony Shilland reminded his comrades of their powers and obligations in 1910: "The Sandon Hospital is owned, operated and controlled solely by the membership of Sandon Miners Union and as Co-owners, you are with [the board of directors] jointly interested in its success, nor will you be able to avoid your full share of the odium that would attach to the Sandon Miners Union should your Hospital go to the wall for lack of support." The rank and file approved the by-laws under which hospitals operated. They also decided such matters as the appointment of staff and the expansion of facilities by voting on motions at regular union meetings. For example, the membership of the Telluride Miners' Union ratified the selection of Dr. J. G. Shelton as "managing surgeon" in 1902. Silver City miners voted to name Emma Hicks as hospital matron, responsible for nursing and housekeeping, when their facility opened in 1897.[2]

In general, however, the membership as a whole made only the most important decisions. Locals delegated most policy-making authority to their boards of directors. Like all other WFM local officers, hospital directors were chosen every six months by the union membership. The system in Sandon was typical: "This Hospital shall be governed by a Board of Directors, composed as follows: Vice President and Financial Secretary of Sandon Miners' Union, together with seven

Hospital 34 (Apr. 1930): 63; Harry F. Dowling, *City Hospitals: The Undercare of the Underprivileged* (Cambridge, Mass., 1982), p. 40; Vogel, *Invention of the Modern Hospital*, pp. 45–46, 14–16, 111–12; Rosner, *Once Charitable Enterprise*, pp. 16–23, 50–54, 105–7; Charles E. Rosenberg, "The Origins of the American Hospital System," *Bulletin of the New York Academy of Medicine* 55 (1979): 20.

2. Anthony Shilland to Membership of Sandon Miners' Union, Nov. 20, 1910, Mine-Mill Papers, box 157, folder 5; Sandon Miners' Union, Minutes, unpaginated (May 5, Sept. 1, 1900), ibid., box 151, folder 11; Alfred Parr (Local 85) to W. L. Hagler, Feb. 26, 1901, ibid., folder 14; Sandon Miners' Union, *By-Laws of Hospital*, p. 20; *San Miguel Examiner*, Oct. 4, 1902; Silver City Miners' Union, Minute Book, pp. 172–73 (Oct. 25, 1897), 176 (Nov. 8, 1897), 181 (Nov. 15, 1897), 227 (Mar. 7, 1898), Silver City Miners' Union Records, vol. 1; *Owyhee Avalanche*, Sept. 12, 1902; Silverton Miners' Union, Minute Book, p. 127 (May 5, 1923), WFM-IUMMSW Archives, vol. 59; *Lardeau Eagle*, Apr. 10, 1903; *Tonopah Sun*, Apr. 25, 1908; *Tonopah Miner*, Oct. 11, 1913; *Rhyolite Daily Bulletin*, Mar. 8, 1909.

members in good standing, who shall be elected by ballot, at [the] first regular meeting of the Union in each term." Frequent elections by secret ballot kept the boards mindful of the interests of their constituents. Silver City was the exception that proved the rule that leadership required an electoral mandate. A committee appointed by the president ran this local's hospital; the union membership retained only the right to refuse to confirm the appointments. Accordingly, this body had less autonomy than its elected counterparts in other locals.[3]

Besides semiannual elections, other structural safeguards ensured the responsiveness of hospital directors to rank-and-file concerns. Board meetings were open to union members. Hospital locals developed formal procedures for investigating patients' complaints. The by-laws of the Sandon institution obligated the board to hold special meetings to look into all grievances. In addition, trustees were required to make periodic reports of their activities at union meetings. The Silver City local, for instance, instructed its Hospital Committee to report every month.[4]

The actual composition of the boards further displayed the grass-roots democracy of the miners' organizations. A majority of hospital directors were working miners, not members of the union staff. In small locals like Slocan, only the financial secretary was on the union payroll. In larger locals like Telluride, the financial secretary and the president were ordinarily the only officers drawing salaries from the organization. Hence generally all but one or two members of hospital governing bodies labored underground on a full-time basis. Of these, less than half simultaneously held other unpaid offices such as vice president or conductor. To take an extreme case, none of the six men elected in September 1905 to the board of the Goldfield Min-

3. Sandon Miners' Union, *By-Laws of Hospital*, p. 19; WFM, *Constitution*, 1896, p. 25; Alfred Parr to W. L. Hagler, Feb. 26, 1901, Mine-Mill Papers, box 151, folder 14; *San Miguel Examiner*, Jan. 11, 1902; *Slocan Drill*, June 7, 1901; *Kendall Miner*, May 18, 1906; *Park Record*, Jan. 9, 1904, p. 5; *Goldfield News*, Sept. 15, 1905, p. 7; *Rhyolite Herald*, Sept. 15, 1905; *Manhattan News*, Sept. 9, 1906; *Rawhide Daily Press*, Feb. 4, 1908; Silver City Miners' Union, Minute Book, pp. 176 (Nov. 8, 1897), 180–81 (Nov. 15, 1897), and passim, Silver City Miners' Union Records, vol. 1; idem, *Constitution*, 1902, p. 25.

4. Sandon Miners' Union, *By-Laws of Hospital*, pp. 21, 19; idem, Minutes, unpaginated (Apr. 7, Oct. 27, 1900), Mine-Mill Papers, box 151, folder 11; Silver City Miners' Union, Minute Book, pp. 184 (Nov. 22, 1897), 258 (June 13, 1898), 293 (Sept. 12, 1898) Silver City Miners Union Records, vol. 1; idem, *Constitution*, 1902, p. 14; Silverton Miners' Union, Minute Book, pp. 3–4 (May 4, 1918), 8 (June 22, 1918), 15 (Aug. 31, 1918), 20 (Feb. 5, 1919), WFM-IUMMSW Archives, vol. 59; *Park Record*, Oct. 28, 1905.

ers' Union Hospital held any other leadership position in the organization.[5]

Further, high rates of turnover among board members meant widespread participation in hospital governance. On average, local unions replaced over two-thirds of their directors every six months. In some organizations, however, the financial secretary became ensconced in his position and exercised considerable influence over hospital policy as an ex officio director; in other locals, financial secretaries changed frequently. For example, the Bonanza Miners' Union barred members from holding any office for more than two consecutive terms.[6]

Two locals gave nonmembers a limited role in determining hospital policy. As had been the case in the Coeur d'Alene, the Telluride Miners' Union had to grant the district mine owners' association a place on its hospital board to ensure the institution's financial stability. In January 1903, the two parties signed a contract under which employers agreed to deduct a monthly fee from all employees in exchange for the right to select a single representative on the hospital's five-member Board of Control. In recognition of community support of their institution and public use of its services, the Slocan miners allowed "two prominent citizens," one of whom was chosen by the town council, to be appointed to the ten-member board of their facility. This local also deviated from the norm by placing its medical superintendent on the board.[7]

5. *Goldfield News*, Sept. 15, 1905, p. 7; *Silverton Weekly Miner*, Sept. 10, 1909, Dec. 9, 1910, June 7, Dec. 13, 1912, June 11, 1915, June 16, 1916; Silverton Miners' Union, Minute Book, pp. 7 (June 1, 1918), 110 (June 10, 1922), 120 (Nov. 18, 1922), WFM-IUMMSW Archives, vol. 59; *Slocan Drill*, June 7, 1901, Mar. 13, 1903; *San Miguel Examiner*, Mar. 7, Sept. 12, 1903; Silver City Miners' Union, Minute Book, pp. 180 (Nov. 15, 1897), 233 (Mar. 28, 1898), 299 (Sept. 26, 1898) Silver City Miners' Union Records, vol. 1; Sandon Miners' Union, Minutes, unpaginated (Nov. 3, 1900), Mine-Mill Papers, box 151, folder 11; A. Shilland to Membership of Sandon Miners' Union, Nov. 20, 1910, ibid., box 157, folder 5; Sandon Miners' Union, *By-Laws of Hospital*, p. 19; Sandon *Paystreak*, June 10, 1899, Mar. 24, 1900, Jan. 19, 1901; *Great Falls Daily Tribune*, Mar. 27, 1902, p. 3; *MM*, Dec. 29, 1904, p. 8; *Park Record*, May 18, 1907, Jan. 18, 1908; *Rhyolite Herald*, Sept. 15, 1905, Mar. 16, Sept. 7, 1906, Mar. 15, 1907; *Rhyolite Daily Bulletin*, Mar. 9, Sept. 7, 1908, Mar. 8, Apr. 2, 1909; *Manhattan News*, Sept. 9, 1906; *Rawhide Daily Press*, Feb. 4, 1908; *Rawhide Rustler*, Sept. 12, 1908; *Rawhide Press-Times*, Sept. 10, 1909, June 17, 1910, Jan. 20, 1911; *Seven Troughs Miner*, Mar. 20, 1909, June 11, 1910.
6. Alex Halkett and M. Tailleur (Local 235) to Editor, May 3, 1909, *MM*, May 20, 1909, p. 9; see sources cited in the preceding note.
7. Charles A. Chase (secretary, Telluride Mining Association) and Vincent St. John (president, Local 63), "Memorandum of Agreement," Jan. 22, 1903, rpt. in *San Miguel Examiner*, Jan. 24, 1903; *San Miguel Examiner*, Mar. 7, Sept. 12, 1903; *Slocan Drill*, May 24, June 7, 1901, May 9, 1902.

Unions created codes of rules governing eligibility for services. In addressing this elemental issue, the miners drew heavily on their experience in administering disability insurance programs. Immediately after its facility opened in 1897, the Silver City local instructed its Hospital Committee to "draft Resolutions for running the Hospital and present them to this union for action." By the next weekly meeting, the committee had formulated a set of rules, and "each rule was read and adopted by motion separately." Four of these provided criteria and procedures for determining eligibility for admission and discharge. One rule denied services to victims of "venerial [sic] Diseases." Local 81 barred those "afflicted with virulent contagious diseases, or diseases or injury incurred through immoral or unlawful conduct."[8] The customary moralistic restrictions of mutual benefit plans thus shaped hospital policy.

Unlike disability insurance programs, which imposed waiting periods before indemnities were paid, hospital benefits became available to union members immediately upon joining the organization and at the onset of an illness or injury. Moreover, locals sometimes ignored even these minimal admissions regulations. For instance, Henry Hewitt, a miner who had recently arrived from Utah, died at the Silver City facility in May 1902. According to the *Owyhee Avalanche*, "He was not a member of the Miners' Union, but he had made application for membership, and the Silver City Union . . . , with characteristic generosity, gave him all the benefits of the hospital and burial which full membership [entailed]." Nor did the unions limit the length of time that a patient could stay in the hospital. The Sandon institution committed itself to care for patients "until fully recovered."[9]

Some organizations maintained two health plans, one for single men and those married but separated from their families and another

8. Silver City Miners' Union, Minute Book, pp. 181 (Nov. 15, 1897), 184 (Nov. 22, 1897), Silver City Miners' Union Records, vol. 1; Sandon Miners' Union, *By-Laws of Hospital*, p. 21; Silver City Miners' Union, *Constitution and By-Laws*, 1902, pp. 16–17; Sandon Miners' Union to Workmen's Compensation Board, Dec. 5, 1917, Mine-Mill Papers, box 156, folder 12; A. Shilland and Alfred C. Garde (manager, Payne Consolidated Mining Co.), "Sandon Miners' Union Hospital [Agreement]," n.d. [ca. 1901], ibid., box 152, folder 4; Chase and St. John, "Memorandum of Agreement"; *Tonopah Bonanza*, June 21, 1902.
9. *Owyhee Avalanche*, May 16, 1902; Shilland and Garde, "Sandon Miners' Union Hospital," Mine-Mill Papers, box 152, folder 4; J. A. Foley (secretary, Slocan Miners' Union General Hospital) to William Tomlinson, Apr. 9, 1901, ibid., box 151, folder 16; Silver City Miners' Union, *Constitution*, 1902, p. 16.

for married men who lived with their wives and children. The unmarried and immigrant majority received comprehensive inpatient care. The Tonopah Miners' Union, for example, delivered a typical range of hospital services—"bed and board, a nurse and medical attendance." Roderick MacKenzie saw the Silverton Miners' Union Hospital as "a place where . . . the homeless alien in our midst, far removed from loving ones and home, might find in his hour of sickness a refuge where loving hands and trained skill would minister to his needs and aid in prolonging his life as the breadwinner of his dependents beyond the sea." Because men who resided with their wives and families had different needs, some locals made different arrangements for them. In Local 66, an optional indemnity system allowed members to receive nursing from their wives and maintain the household income: "Married men and heads of resident families shall receive $10.00 per week, beginning with the first week, or admittance to the Hospital." In Telluride, married miners and their dependents were entitled to medical and surgical services in their homes. These members forfeited their right to inpatient benefits in exchange for family coverage. Not surprisingly, some locals were less flexible, offering only a uniform set of hospitalization benefits to all members and refusing to cover dependents. Faced with limited means and divergent demands, the miners' organizations could not tailor perfectly appropriate and equitable benefits for every member. Nonetheless, democratic processes led to significant efforts to accommodate the minority who resided with their families.[10]

This worker-designed system of health care functioned reasonably well. The hospitals attempted to deliver care for the wide range of problems found in their communities. Indeed, the five leading categories of cases—mine injuries, typhoid fever, pneumonia, lead poisoning, and appendicitis—accounted for only one fifth of the patients treated by the Park City Miners' Hospital during its initial year of existence. Similarly, other facilities tackled diverse acute and chronic diseases, as well as trauma from many causes.[11]

10. *Tonopah Miner*, Jan. 2, 1904; Roderick MacKenzie to Employees of Silverton Northern Railway, n.d., in *Silverton Weekly Miner*, Mar. 7, 1913; Silver City Miners' Union, *Constitution*, p. 16; *Park Record*, Dec. 3, 1904; Press Committee, Local 235, to Editor, Dec. 7, 1905, *MM*, Dec. 21, 1905, p. 11.

11. *Park Record*, Oct. 28, 1905 (annual report), Oct. 8, 1904–Sept. 30, 1905 (weekly reports); Sandon Miners' Union, *By-Laws of Hospital*, p. 16; *San Miguel Examiner*, Dec. 20, 1902.

Located in small towns where health and welfare institutions could not be narrowly specialized, the hospitals performed a variety of functions beyond those of a general acute-care inpatient facility. They treated a large share of the sick and injured on an outpatient basis. In particular, victims of minor accidents, "outdoor patients," received care such as dispensaries provided in urban centers.[12] At the other end of the spectrum, union health care centers delivered a significant amount of long-term custodial care. Old miners with vague diagnoses, such as "general breakdown" or "general debility," regularly gained admission, especially in the winter. Often the underlying concern was a strong desire to avoid the poorhouse. In March 1901 the Sandon facility took in George Hamilton, "an old man who was sick and in destitute circumstances in a shack in the lower end of town." Thomas Smith spent the last sixteen months of his life at the Slocan Miners' Union General Hospital before succumbing to "a complication of diseases" at age sixty-one. Smith's funeral was held at the hospital.[13]

Aversion to the primitive conditions found in asylums occasionally led to hospitalization of psychiatric patients. In 1900 the Sandon institution offered an alternative to incarceration for one miner who was either mentally ill or merely eccentric: "George Scott, lately employed at the Arlington, had been acting strangely in town, and Sunday evening was locked up. He was to have been committed to Nelson on a charge of insanity, but friends stepped in and took him to the Sandon hospital on Tuesday, the boys at the Arlington raising over $70 for his care."[14] The miners' hospitals were virtually undifferentiated health and welfare institutions.

Hospital staff could do little for victims of the worst accidents. After Carl Johnson was "frightfully mangled" in machinery at the Hercules Consolidated mill in Silverton, he was rushed to the nearby union health care center, but his massive injuries were untreatable, and he died within a few hours. When a Slavic immigrant identified only as "Nick" fell from an ore bucket in Goldfield, he was "promptly taken to the Miners' hospital, but nothing could be done for him." Dying

12. *San Miguel Examiner*, Dec. 20, 1902, Nov. 14, 1903; [Sandon Miners' Union], "Form A, Hospital Act," July 1915, Jan. 1917, Mine-Mill Papers, box 157, folder 8; *Kendall Miner*, Aug. 31, 1906; *Little Rockies Miner*, May 29, 1909.
13. Sandon *Paystreak*, Mar. 23, 1901; *Slocan Drill*, May 6, 1904; *Great Falls Daily Tribune*, Oct. 1, 1904, p. 5; *Silverton Weekly Miner*, July 10, 1914, Dec. 8, 1916; Nelson *Weekly News*, May 25, 1911, p. 6; *Tonopah Bonanza*, Feb. 22, 1902.
14. *Slocan Drill*, Nov. 30, 1900; *Silverton Weekly Miner*, Nov. 19, Dec. 24, 1909.

trauma patients often received only a measure of relief from their pain.[15]

The facilities did effectively handle the flood of less severe injuries incurred in extracting and processing ore. William Connors suffered a broken leg when a slab of rock fell on him at the Barnes-King mine in Kendall, Montana. Co-workers extricated Connors and took him to the North Moccasin Miners' Union Hospital, where Dr. Charles Smith reduced the fracture.[16] Some shattered arms and legs had to be cut off. Swedish immigrant John Finholm had the misfortune to be caught in a cave-in at the Jupiter in Park City: "The left side of his chest was badly crushed, several ribs broken, and the [left] leg was so badly cut and broken that amputation was necessary. He recovered nicely from the operation." Because amputations entailed not only immediate physical risks but also permanent disability, which could well mean destitution, miners submitted to these procedures only as a last resort. As he lay in the Park City Miners' Hospital, amputee Finholm faced a bleak future. "The victim has a wife and family in the old country," reported the *Park Record*, "and of them and their welfare he thinks continually."[17] Less threatening were the innumerable cuts, bruises, sprains, burns, and lacerations that the staff routinely treated. Of course, nurses provided most of the trauma care. On August 12, 1909, Dan Zarcovich arrived at the Tonopah Miners' Union Hospital "peppered with rock" from a premature explosion. Nurses were "busy all day picking bits of rock out of Zarcovich's flesh."[18]

Union physicians occasionally went into the mines to treat or retrieve injury victims. When Silas Cross suffered a dislocated hip and other injuries in the Last Chance near Sandon, Dr. William Gomm "arrived on the scene at 5 A.M. and set the injured limb and brot [sic] the patient to the hospital." Upon receiving word that a boulder had fallen on Peter Macarri at the Butterfly Terrible outside Telluride, the

15. *Silverton Weekly Miner*, Nov. 19, 1909; *Tonopah Daily Sun*, Jan. 26, 1907; *Goldfield News*, Sept. 28, 1907; *Slocan Drill*, Jan. 29, 1904.

16. *Kendall Miner*, Sept. 6, 1907, Apr. 13, Oct. 19, 1906; *Park Record*, July 21, 1906; *Owyhee Avalanche*, May 27, 1898; Sandon *Paystreak*, Oct. 18, 1902.

17. *Park Record*, Dec. 15, 1906; *Tonopah Daily Sun*, July 28, 1905; *Tonopah Miner*, Dec. 23, 1911; *Owyhee Avalanche*, Apr. 21, 1899.

18. *Tonopah Sun*, Aug. 14, 1909, Feb. 8, 1908; *San Miguel Examiner*, Oct. 4, 1902; *Great Falls Daily Tribune*, Aug. 24, 1908, p. 3; *Kendall Miner*, Mar. 26, 1909; *Slocan Drill*, Mar. 8, May 17, 1901.

medical superintendent and head nurse of the hospital immediately secured a horse and rig and raced to the mine. The Bonanza Miners' Union placed a medicine chest and surgical supplies at the Keane Wonder mine and mill to facilitate first-aid work by its physician.[19]

The advent of the telephone and the automobile expedited the delivery of emergency services. When two Silver City miners were "quite severely pounded up" in a blast in 1901, Dr. William Hamilton was quickly summoned to the Sinker tunnel by phone. During a strike of Bell Telephone employees in 1907, the Park City Miners' Union ordered the firm's equipment removed from its hospital. The *Record* criticized the union's shortsightedness: "The removal of one phone is certainly not going to cause the company any over amount of worry, but it may cost several lives, an unnecessary sacrifice." In the 1910s, automobiles began to replace makeshift horse-drawn ambulances. Before Dr. Alex McIntyre purchased his Hupmobile touring car in 1914, a bobsled conveyed some patients to the Manhattan Miners' Union Hospital during the winter. In many areas, however, extremely rough terrain severely limited the use of the horseless carriage.[20]

Typhoid fever sent numerous victims to the hospitals. The primitive sanitary conditions prevalent in mining communities led to recurrent outbreaks of this disorder. At the North Moccasin hospital, admission of several typhoid patients in rapid succession in 1908 led the union physician to urge preventive measures. Together with Dr. William Lakey (who would soon succeed him as medical superintendent of the hospital), Dr. Charles Smith alerted the public through a notice in the *Kendall Miner*: "There are new cases of typhoid at the Hospital, all from the middle of town. You are warned not to drink water or milk, unless boiled." Dr. H. A. Anderson of the Vernon Miners' Union Hospital in the Seven Troughs district of Nevada did not believe in waiting for an epidemic to begin. "The season of typhoid fever is approaching," Anderson warned in July 1907, "and it is the history of all new mining camps that during the first year or two of their existence the mortality from typhoid is very high." He encouraged Vernon residents to burn or bury all garbage, deepen their privies,

19. Sandon *Paystreak*, Nov. 3, 1900; *San Miguel Examiner*, Oct. 3, 1903; *Rhyolite Daily Bulletin*, May 31, 1909; *Silverton Weekly Miner*, Apr. 16, 1915.

20. *Owyhee Avalanche*, Nov. 15, 1901; *Park Record*, June 8, 1907; *Slocan Drill*, June 14, 1901; *Lardeau Eagle*, Aug. 21, 1903; *Manhattan Post*, Feb. 14, 1914, p. 1, May 2, 1914, p. 1; *Silverton Weekly Miner*, Sept. 3, Oct. 8, 1915.

clean their water barrels and tanks, and boil their drinking water. Unfortunately, most efforts to curtail infection were curative, not prophylactic. In the era before antibiotics, proper nursing was the key to surviving an attack of the disease. Patients often spent several weeks in the hospital being fed and cared for. Although mortality from typhoid itself appears to have been low, lengthy confinements sometimes led to pneumonia (then commonly called "typhoid pneumonia"), a nosocomial complication that could prove fatal.[21]

In addition, pneumonia as a primary infection put many hardrock workers in the hospital. Fierce epidemics of this disorder overwhelmed the limited resources of unions on more than one occasion. Dozens died in Tonopah in the outbreaks of 1901–2 and 1904–5. Nor could the Goldfield Miners' Union Hospital prevent more than fifty deaths in 1904–5.[22] As with typhoid, nursing care took on critical importance in the absence of effective medical therapy. Unfortunately, too many victims were brought to the facilities too late for treatment to do any good. Frank Pascoe's friends believed that he was suffering only a "mild attack" of pneumonia and postponed his hospitalization. Hence, "less than ten minutes after he had been put to bed [at the Silverton Miners' Union Hospital], Mr. Pascoe's soul had taken its flight." The lingering stereotype of the hospital as a place to die thus became a self-fulfilling prophecy. But the vast majority of pneumonia patients, who reached institutions in time to benefit from warm beds and hot meals, recovered their health.[23]

Other respiratory ailments helped fill the hospitals during the winter months. The influenza pandemic of 1918 devastated Silverton, Colorado: more than 150 people perished, including 25 members of Local 26.[24] Nurses cared for the multitude of patients with bronchitis, ton-

21. Charles W. Smith and W. J. Lakey, "Warning," *Kendall Miner*, Nov. 6, 1908; H. A. Anderson, "Timely Advice," *Vernon Review*, July 20, 1907; *Kendall Miner*, Dec. 11, 1908; Elliott, "Tonopah, Goldfield," pp. 36, 111–12; *Park Record*, Nov. 26, 1904, Jan. 13, 1906; *Neihart Miner*, Oct. 20, Nov. 24, 1898; *Owyhee Avalanche*, Mar. 9, 1900, Nov. 22, 1901; *San Miguel Examiner*, Dec. 20, 1902, Feb. 21, 1903.

22. Nevada State Board of Health, *Biennial Report, 1903–4* (Carson City, 1905), pp. 7–8; *Tonopah Bonanza*, Feb. 1, 8, 1902; *Tonopah Daily Sun*, Apr. 22, Nov. 15, 1905; Elliott, "Tonopah, Goldfield," pp. 37–38, 95–96, 103.

23. *Silverton Weekly Miner*, Jan. 14, Mar. 11, 1910; *Park Record*, Mar. 4, 1905, May 5, 1906; *Slocan Drill*, Feb. 21, 1902; William E. Gomm to Officers and Members of Sandon Miners' Union, July 13, 1901, Mine-Mill Papers, box 152, folder 4; *Kendall Miner*, Feb. 23, 1906; *Manhattan Post*, Jan. 6, 1912, p. 1; *Rhyolite Daily Bulletin*, Feb. 4, 1908.

24. *MM*, Dec. 1918; *San Miguel Examiner*, Mar. 21, 1903; *Kendall Miner*, Dec. 14, 1906; *Seven Troughs Miner*, Jan. 4, 1908.

silitis, and common colds. In Silver City, matron Mary McGough, the widowed mother of two miners, had a wealth of experience nurturing victims of these disorders. "Mike Brennan is at the hospital nursing a cold," observed the *Owyhee Avalanche* in 1903. "Mother McGough's boys all know where to go when sick, and they appreciate her kindness and good things to eat."[25]

Relatively few cases of either tuberculosis or silicosis reached union health care centers. Victims of these severe disorders commonly fled from mining districts to lower elevations. One silicotic miner, however, returned to Park City to meet his fate: "John Kierce, familiarly known as 'Cast Iron Jack,' died at the hospital yesterday morning from miners consumption. He was taken to the hospital [two days earlier] from a room in the Swede rooming house, but he was too far gone for human aid and the final summons soon came to him. He had been sick for several months and had returned recently from California where he went for his health." Mother McGough's "most tender care and attention" could not save William Williams, who spent months at the Silver City refuge. No therapy could reverse the downward course of silicosis.[26]

Better results were achieved with two other common occupational diseases. Lead poisoning caused frequent admissions in Sandon and Park City. Although information on the specific therapeutic regimen used to combat "lead colic" has not survived, Sandon hospital records indicate that patients invariably left "cured" or at least "improved."[27] Unlike lead poisoning, arthritis ("rheumatism") was incurable, but those who fled cold, wet workplaces and drafty cabins for the warmth of a hospital obtained symptomatic relief from this degenerative disorder.[28]

The scarce extant evidence suggests that overall patient mortality was relatively low despite the extraordinary hazards faced by hardrock

25. *Owyhee Avalanche*, Nov. 6, 1903; Donald Graham to Andrew [sic] Shilland, May 8, 1904, Mine-Mill Papers, box 155, folder 3; *Silverton Weekly Miner*, Dec. 10, 1915; *Kendall Miner*, Jan. 3, 1908; *Manhattan Post*, Nov. 18, 1913, p. 4.

26. *Park Record*, Dec. 3, 1904; *Owyhee Avalanche*, Mar. 13, 1903; *Silverton Weekly Miner*, Jan. 3, Sept. 12, 1913; *Tonopah Miner*, Nov. 19, 1904; *Rhyolite Herald*, Sept. 21, 1906.

27. Sandon Miners' Union Hospital, "Monthly Report," Sept.–Dec. 1902, Mar. 1904, May–July, Dec. 1905, Mine-Mill Papers, box 157, folders 6 and 7; *Park Record*, Oct. 8, 29, 1904, Mar. 11, Apr. 22, 1905.

28. *Silverton Weekly Miner*, Apr. 10, 1914; *Owyhee Avalanche*, Feb. 15, 1901; Sandon Miners' Union Hospital, "Monthly Report," Dec. 1901, Jan., Feb., 1902, Jan., Mar., 1903, Mine-Mill Papers, box 157, folder 6; Sandon *Paystreak*, Feb. 23, 1901.

miners. Of 1,041 patients admitted in Telluride, Sandon, and Park City at various times between 1899 and 1907, only 41 (3.9 percent) died in the hospital. Pneumonia was the leading cause of death at these three facilities, accounting for seventeen (41.4 percent) of the fatalities.[29] Defending its hospital's record of losing nine patients in almost six years, the Sandon union maintained that "three of these nine cases were moribund when admitted." Clearly, some patients died virtually on arrival and received no real care. Others succumbed to desperate surgical procedures. R. R. Scott died at the Bonanza Miners' Union Hospital after "an operation for [a] bowel disorder, from which he had no hope of recovery."[30] Most appendicitis patients apparently came to the hospital only after their appendixes had ruptured. Not surprisingly, a significant share failed to survive surgical intervention.[31] Surgery remained a very perilous ordeal in these small, meagerly equipped facilities, especially when patients refused to submit to procedures until they were on the verge of death.

The Sandon miners believed that their institution's low mortality rate demonstrated "how very efficient our hospital staff is." Yet the administration of patient services in the WFM hospitals primarily embodied not emerging conceptions of bureaucratic efficiency but rather traditional notions of familial nurturing.[32] In small facilities where an elaborate division of labor was out of the question, paternalistic physicians and maternalistic matrons managed the delivery of care.

Physicians directed the day-to-day activities of most miners' hospitals. Bearing such titles as "medical superintendent," "physician in charge," or "hospital manager," these practitioners not only supervised the admission, treatment, and discharge of patients but also

29. *San Miguel Examiner*, Dec. 20, 1902; Sandon Miners' Union, *By-Laws of Hospital*, pp. 15–17; *Park Record*, Oct. 28, 1905, Jan. 18, 1908.

30. Sandon Miners' Union, *By-Laws of Hospital*, p. 16; *Rhyolite Herald*, Mar. 30, 1906; *Silverton Weekly Miner*, Mar. 21, 1913, Nov. 20, 1914; *Park Record*, Oct. 15, 1904.

31. Sandon Miners' Union, *By-Laws of Hospital*, pp. 16–17; *San Miguel Examiner*, Dec. 20, 1902, May 16, 23, 30, 1903; *Kendall Miner*, Jan. 28, 1910; *Lardeau Eagle*, Oct. 9, 1903; *Rhyolite Herald*, July 20, 1906; *Blair Press*, Oct. 8, 1909.

32. Press Committee, Local 81, to Editor, n.d., *MM*, July 1901, p. 36; William H. Walsh, "The Hospital Superintendent, Past, Present and Future," in American Hospital Association, *Transactions of the . . . Sixteenth Annual Conference, 1914* (Kingston, Ont., 1914), pp. 260–69; George Rosen, "The Efficiency Criterion in Medical Care, 1900–1920: An Early Approach to an Evaluation of Health Service," *Bulletin of the History of Medicine* 50 (1976): 28–44.

performed such mundane administrative duties as procuring supplies. The superintendent's powers were circumscribed. An incident in 1912 at the Silverton facility illuminates the peculiar difficulties of asserting medical authority in a democratic institutional setting. When nurse Noma Carter objected to rules set forth by Dr. Alva Burnett, a member of the hospital board supported her, and she defied the superintendent. Burnett gained the upper hand only when the board formally decided to give him "full charge" over matters of patient care. Carter and another nurse quit immediately, taking two patients with them. Paternalism was reinforced when the physician in charge resided in the institution. In January 1903 Dr. W. Edwin Newcombe and his wife moved into quarters in the Lardeau Miners' Union Hospital, where they dined with patients and staff. The modest perquisites of management came at a high price in Kendall, Montana. Dr. Charles Smith, who resided at the North Moccasin Miners' Union Hospital, found himself digging a cellar for the building in the summer of 1906.[33]

Where the local union maintained an open medical staff policy, the matron or head nurse assumed routine administrative responsibilities. In Silver City, Mary McGough told the census taker in 1900 that she was a "hospital manager." Mrs. A. Sommerville served as "hospital keeper" of the Aldridge Miners' Union Hospital. A widow like Mother McGough, Sommerville lived on the premises with her three daughters, the eldest of whom cooked for the hospital. In Sandon, the matron shared administrative chores with the medical superintendent. Whereas the physician serving Local 81 had authority to admit and discharge patients and approve drug purchases, the matron had "charge of inside management . . . and [power to] act in conjunction with the Hospital Board regarding the employment of its employees."[34]

Miners democratically selected matrons, medical superintendents,

33. *Silverton Weekly Miner*, Dec. 20, 27, 1912; *Polk's Medical Register*, 7th ed., p. 1214; *Slocan Drill*, May 15, 1903; *San Miguel Examiner*, Oct. 4, 1902; *Lewistown Argus*, n.d., rpt. in *Great Falls Daily Tribune*, Dec. 10, 1904, p. 3; *Kendall Miner*, Aug. 10, Apr. 20, 1906; *Lardeau Eagle*, Jan. 16, 1903; *Tonopah Miner*, Nov. 28, Dec. 5, 1902, Jan. 9, 1903; *Seven Troughs Miner*, July 16, 1910.

34. U.S. Census Office, "Twelfth Census . . .," Schedule No. 1—Population," 1900, Silver City, Idaho, Sheet A11, Federal Records Center, National Archives and Records Administration, San Bruno, Calif.; ibid., 1900, Aldridge, Mont., Sheet 6A; Sandon Miners' Union, *By-Laws of Hospital*, pp. 20–21; Silver City Miners' Union, Minute Book, pp. 172 (Oct. 25, 1897), 215 (Jan. 31, 1898), Silver City Miners' Union Records, vol. 1; *Tonopah Sun*, Aug. 28, 1909; *Park Record*, Oct. 1, 1904; *Manhattan Post*, Oct. 22, 1910.

and other staff physicians. The by-laws of the Sandon hospital required that both the medical superintendent and head nurse "be confirmed to said positions by a majority vote of Union whenever such offices are to be filled." Physicians in a number of locals had to run for reelection every six months, like any other union officer. In June 1906 three doctors in Rhyolite, Nevada, sought to replace the incumbent at the Bonanza Miners' Union Hospital, Dr. James Wilkinson. According to the *Herald*, "When the vote was counted, it was found that Dr. Grigsby had won by four votes over Dr. Wilkinson, the vote standing 165 to 169. Drs. Mason and Bulette each received seven votes."[35] Individual members in at least three locals were free to select their own physician. All practitioners in Park City, for example, had the right to admit patients to the Miners' Hospital.[36]

Workers used other sanctions besides the threat of electoral defeat to assure the quality of care. The Sandon local gave its board the power "to suspend any member of the staff, for neglect of duty or other misdemeanor, subject to approval of the Union, at first regular or special meeting after such suspension." On April 25, 1902, Local 81 member Isaac Hachey angrily condemned the care he had received from Dr. William Gomm: "When I was ordered out of the hospital I was not better then [sic] the day I came in [;] farther more I was never told to go back for tretement and if I had been attended to I would not be a creple [sic] today." The board of directors investigated this complaint and reported to the local within three weeks:

We find that the Dr. according to his own admission was not explicit enough in forbidding Bro. Hachey from attending Church Christmas night leaving his orders open for misconstruction, and [we] recommended that Bro. J. V. Martin be appointed to wait on the Dr. and caution him to be more careful in the future. We are also of the opinion that Bro. Hachey too deserves some censure inasmuch as he failed to make his complaint to the Hospital Board at their meeting in January, 1902, when asked to do so, and has ever since done his best to bring discredit on the Hospital through Dr. Gomm, this we deem entirely inexcusable on

35. Sandon Miners' Union, *By-Laws of Hospital*, p. 20; *Rhyolite Herald*, June 15, 1906; *San Miguel Examiner*, Oct. 4, 1902; *Kendall Miner*, Apr. 13, 1906; *Tonopah Sun*, Apr. 25, 1908; *Goldfield News*, Sept. 15, 1905, p. 7.
36. AMA, *American Medical Directory*, 2d ed., p. 1160; Silver City Miners' Union, Minute Book, pp. 173 (Oct. 25, 1897), 276 (Aug. 1, 1898), Silver City Miners' Union Records, vol. 1; *Tonopah Sun*, Jan. 22, 1910.

the part of a good Union man, and will leave his case in the hands of the Union to deal with as you may see fit.

Although it is not clear what action, if any, the Sandon organization took against Hachey, the mere fact that the local considered imposing a penalty reveals one way that collective responsibilities limited individual rights in democratically governed enterprises. In contrast to the mild censure given Dr. Gomm, the Tonopah union in 1909 summarily dismissed Dr. Reynolds Mapes after one of his patients died of postoperative blood poisoning.[37]

Overwork increased the possibility of medical error. As a rule, physicians and nurses at miners' hospitals had highly demanding jobs. Physicians shuttled back and forth among as many as four different patient-care settings every day—the hospital, their office, the patients' homes, and the mines. Many doctors in remote areas had neither partners nor colleagues to turn to for assistance. Inevitably, the strain of unrelenting responsibility took its toll. For Victor Hitch, chief surgeon of the Rawhide Miners' Union Hospital, the burden became "so taxing he suffered a nervous breakdown and was forced to go to the coast for a rest." Unlike Dr. Hitch, who returned to Rawhide, most overworked physicians simply quit and left town for good. During the year 1903, the Slocan hospital had three different medical superintendents. Accordingly, unions had to devote considerable time and energy to replacing departed doctors.[38]

Not surprisingly, the physicians recruited to isolated mining towns were a mixed lot. Some had graduated from the medical schools of prominent universities such as McGill and Columbia, others from institutions of uncertain reputation such as the soon-to-be-extinct Chicago College of Medicine and Surgery, Physio-Medical. Many had

37. Sandon Miners' Union, *By-Laws of Hospital*, p. 21; Isaac Hachey to All Members of Sandon Miner [*sic*] Union, Apr. 25, 1902, Mine-Mill Papers, box 153, folder 2; R. J. McLean, W. J. Garbutt, James V. Martin, and Donald Graham, Report, May 10, 1902, ibid., folder 3; *Tonopah Sun*, Dec. 24, 1909; Silver City Miners' Union, *Constitution*, 1902, p. 14.

38. *Rawhide Press-Times*, July 10, 1908; *Slocan Drill*, Apr. 3, Nov. 6, Dec. 11, 1903; D. B. O'Neail to Secretary, [Sandon] Miners' Union, Oct. 13, 1903, Mine-Mill Papers, box 154, folder 7; *MM*, Mar. 18, 1904, p. 13; Silverton Miners' Union, Minute Book, p. 99 (May 28, 1921), WFM-IUMMSW Archives, vol. 59; R. J. Hanlon (secretary, Local 66) to Editor, Oct. 29, 1905, *MM*, Nov. 9, 1905, p. 13; *Tonopah Miner*, Dec. 5, 1902, Jan. 9, 1903; *Little Rockies Miner*, Aug. 22, Sept. 19, 1907; *Vernon Review*, Oct. 5, 1907.

only recently completed their training, which seldom included an internship. A rough comparison of their qualifications (as indicated by medical training, licensure, and experience) with those of company doctors suggests that the quality of care delivered by union physicians probably did not differ markedly from that provided by practitioners who contracted with operators. In Silverton, British Columbia, for example, the miners' hospital retained Dr. Gilbert Hartin, an 1896 McGill graduate, and his partner, William Rose, who had received his medical degree from the same institution in 1898. Hartin and Rose supplanted hospital proprietor Jacob Brouse, an 1892 graduate of McGill. William Gomm, who served as superintendent in Sandon for seventeen years after the union hospital displaced Brouse, was an 1886 graduate of Bellevue Hospital Medical College in New York. It appears that the miners' desire to retain accountable and accessible physicians outweighed their concerns over malpractice by company doctors.[39]

Because of financial constraints, the institutions typically employed only one or two nurses. The stressful combination of heavy workloads and minimal authority led to high turnover among these workers. Some quit to get married. Others fled the mining towns for less arduous jobs in larger institutions. Too small to maintain the training programs that ensured a steady supply of nurses, the WFM hospitals frequently had to cast about for help. In 1904, the secretary of the Ymir General Hospital wrote to his counterpart in Sandon, hoping to locate "a first class Lady Nurse out of employment or two of them."[40] For the most part, however, recruiting and disciplining nurses was left to matrons and medical superintendents. Miners apparently saw

39. *Polk's Medical Register*, 7th ed., pp. 483, 485, 1219, 2068; ibid., 8th ed., pp. 375, 1196, 1223, 2039; ibid., 10th ed., p. 1998; ibid., 11th ed., pp. 1142, 1175; AMA, *American Medical Directory*, 2d ed., pp. 152, 219, 667, 669–70, 690–91, 1162, 1277–79; ibid., 3d ed., p. 742; ibid., 4th ed., pp. 874–75; Nevada, *List of Physicians Registered in Nevada, to May 4, 1909* (N.p., n.d.), pp. 3–15; *Silverton Weekly Miner*, Sept. 27, 1912; *Slocan Drill*, Apr. 17, 1903; *Directory of Owyhee County*, pp. 21–22; *Owyhee Avalanche*, July 7, 1899; *Kendall Miner*, Apr. 13, 1906; *Lardeau Eagle*, Nov. 14, 1901; *Tonopah Miner*, Jan. 9, 1903; *Tonopah Sun*, Jan. 15, 29, 1910; *Little Rockies Miner*, Aug. 22, 1907.

40. W. B. McIsaac to A. Shilland, Jan. 23, 1904, Mine-Mill Papers, box 154, folder 10; Sarah M. Chisholm to Board of Sandon Miners' Union Hospital, July 28, 1902, ibid., box 153, folder 5; *Silverton Weekly Miner*, Mar. 31, May 5, 1911, Feb. 2, 1912, Dec. 25, 1914, Jan. 22, 1915, Dec. 29, 1916; *Owyhee Avalanche*, Dec. 3, 1897; *Kendall Miner*, Sept. 7, 1906, Oct. 11, Nov. 18, 1907; *Lardeau Eagle*, Aug. 14, Nov. 6, 1903; *Rawhide Daily Press*, Feb. 4, 1908.

no contradiction between their opposition to mine operators' paternalism and their acquiescence in paternalistic and maternalistic health care arrangements.

Chronic financial problems plagued the WFM hospitals. The most critical challenge was to ensure a steady flow of income. The unions contained costs by employing physicians on a salaried or capitation basis, hiring few nurses and paying them little more than room and board, and relying on unsophisticated technology. Both the volatility of the metal-mining industry and the general hostility of management to self-help endeavors led to difficulties in generating revenue.

A few locals collected hospital fees from their members in the form of increased monthly union dues,[41] but most sought automatic payroll deductions from management. Looking back over the experience of the previous two decades, international president Moyer observed in 1917 that "we found it impossible to successfully operate without an arrangement with the company whereby we might check off . . . the hospital fee." In the brief period before the Telluride institution gained such an accommodation, it was "a very difficult matter for officials of the union to personally collect hospital dues from a thousand men." Hence administrative exigencies often forced locals to seek the (unpaid) assistance of mine owners.[42]

Most employers cooperated. As previously discussed, some agreed to a system of monthly deductions before the union facilities opened. Others readily complied as soon as the hospital in their area began to deliver services. Miners in Ymir, British Columbia, chose to support the union health care center in a series of referenda. "We have all the mines paying in by cheque even the Ymir [where] our Boys outvoted what few scabs are left," gloated Alfred Parr, secretary of Local 85, in January 1901. "We have a good start and she will cover expenses and leave a surplus from the start." During its first year in existence, the Park City Miners' Hospital received check-off payments from twenty-three different firms, providing 85 percent of its total revenues.[43]

41. *Tonopah Miner*, Jan. 2, 1904; *Rhyolite Daily Bulletin*, Mar. 24, 1909; Silver City Miners' Union, Dues Records, 1901, Silver City Miners' Union Records, envelope 1.
42. Charles Moyer, Testimony, Oct. 9, 1917, in U.S., President's Mediation Commission, "Sessions at Globe," p. 50, McCluskey Collection, box 4; *San Miguel Examiner*, Jan. 10, 17, 1903.
43. Alfred Parr to W. L. Hagler, Jan. 15, 1901, Mine-Mill Papers, box 151, folder 13;

Three months after the founding of the Sandon hospital in March 1899, Local 81 struck to enforce the provincial eight-hour law. This work stoppage lasted several months and involved all major employers in the district. In its immediate aftermath, the union naively assumed that "after the little difficulty that existed here has blown over, there is no doubt that all the mines will pay into the hospital." But the protracted dispute had fostered among many employers an abiding animosity toward the union and all its endeavors. Although some operators agreed to accommodate the miners in this matter, others adamantly refused. In October 1900 a representative of the Queen Bess Proprietary Company bluntly reminded Local 81 that "it is not necessary for our Company to collect Hospital dues at all." In July 1901 employees of the Trade Dollar mine petitioned management to institute check-off deductions. Trade Dollar official G. W. Hughes sent the petitions back to the union secretary. "I beg to inform you," snarled Hughes, "that we have found it much more satisfactory . . . for our employees to pay their obligations themselves." Aware that benevolent activities strengthened the workers' organization, these operators saw no point in doing the union's administrative chores for it.[44]

At the Rambler mine, the employer's opposition to the Sandon Miners' Union Hospital arose from different concerns. In this instance, the company initially checked off the union fee following the 1899–1900 strike. In November 1903, however, superintendent W. E. Zwicky instigated a movement to transfer his employees' patronage to the Victorian Hospital at Kaslo, of which he was a trustee. Local 81 activist

---

Park Record, Oct. 28, 1905; *Slocan Drill*, Apr. 5, 1901; Silver City Miners' Union, Ledger, pp. 59ff. (1897–99), Silver City Miners' Union Records, vol. 2; H. A. Allen, "Hospital Report," *Silverton Weekly Miner*, Oct. 29, 1909. Besides referenda, the Ymir miners built a mandate for check-off with petitions to management. In January 1901, Local 85 alerted Local 2 "to be on the lookout for one Edgar Stevens who is a notorious scab[.] Said party stole a petition from Ymir Union, which they had in circulation for the purpose of supporting a Union Hospital etc." If Stevens showed up in Lead City, Local 85 urged its comrades there "to show him no mercy." See Lead City Miners' Union, Minute Book, pp. 768–69 (Jan. 7, 1901), WFM-IUMMSW Archives, reel 53.

44. [Press Committee, Local 81], "Sandon Miners' Hospital," *MM*, May 1900, p. 33; J. Laing Frocks to W. L. Hagler, Oct. 22, 1900, Mine-Mill Papers, box 151, folder 12; G. W. Hughes to A. Shilland, July 27, 1901, and Trade Dollar Employees to Trade Dollar Mining Company, Petition, July 15, 1901, ibid., box 152, folder 4; Mr. Frocks to Mr. Hagler, Oct. 10, 1900, ibid., box 151, folder 12; Joseph F. McDonald (Local 81) to A. Shilland, July 16, 1901, and Alfred Garde (manager, Payne Consolidated Mining Co.) to A. Shilland, July 25, 1901, ibid., box 152, folder 4.

John Middleton immediately circulated a petition supporting the union institution. After all but one of the Rambler workers had signed this petition, it was presented to management. Undeterred, Zwicky announced that beginning in January 1904, the money deducted for health benefits would be divided equally between the two hospitals. When the union protested this plan, Zwicky discontinued the check-off altogether.[45]

In response to this widespread opposition, Local 81 devised a grass-roots system of collecting fees. A rank-and-file unionist represented the hospital at each mine where check-off had been denied. This agent received payments from his co-workers, issued tickets that verified benefit eligibility, and transmitted the sum collected to the union office. Such a scheme was virtually the only way miners could maintain their benefits at operations like the Queen Bess, where management prohibited Local 81 officers from setting foot on company property. These rank-and-file representatives took many risks. Generally not very businesslike, they stood the losses when individuals obtained tickets but never got around to paying for them. In addition, they absorbed the inevitable criticism of their program's limitations. John Hovey quit in exasperation. "Get someone else in the crew to represent the Hospital here," demanded Hovey. "I am having to take a little too much chin." Although unquestionably inefficient, this system effectively channeled revenue to the hospital and, in turn, retained and recruited members for the organization.[46]

These volunteers also distributed medications provided by the hospital. In fact, their continual demands for medicines and supplies suggest that they were practically administering dispensaries. Alex Murray at the Trade Dollar sent in $13 in fees for October 1902 and requested "some medicine up hear [sic] such as Cough Medicine, Cream Tartar, Cramp Med., Quinine, Liniment, Pills Physic, Vaseline, [and] Red Cloth Plaster for Lame Back." With three feet of snow

45. William H. Adams (general manager, Rambler-Cariboo Mines) to A. Shilland, n.d. [ca. Dec. 1901], Mine-Mill Papers, box 152, folder 9; Henry Tijo (Local 81) to A. Shilland, Nov. 26, 1903, ibid., box 154, folder 8; John Middleton (Local 81) to A. Shilland, Dec. 13, 29, 1903, ibid., folder 9; Middleton to Shilland, Jan. 22, 1904, ibid., folder 10; W. E. Zwicky to A. Silland [sic], Feb. 24, 1904, ibid., folder 11; T. J. Pearson (Local 81) to Dear Sir and Brother, Mar. 23, 1904, ibid., box 155, folder 1.

46. J. C. Hovey to A. Shilland, Feb. 1, 1904, Mine-Mill Papers, box 154, folder 11; Lance H. Porter to A. Shilland, Nov. 17, 1904, ibid., box 155, folder 10; Alex Murray to A. Shilland, Feb. 22, 1902, ibid., box 152, folder 11; John McDougald to A. Shilland, Dec. 14, 1902, ibid., box 153, folder 10.

already on the ground by the beginning of November 1902, W. N. Welsh at the Red Fox prepared for the winter: "Please send us a fresh supply of medicines, we are out of everything, send plenty of salve as that is what is used most." Perhaps as many miners in this district paid their hospital fees so they could obtain supplies for self-care of minor ailments as paid to maintain eligibility for inpatient services for major problems.[47]

The inefficiency of this patchwork system drove the Sandon union to try to win the check-off by political means. In January 1904 miners drafted a bill to close loopholes in the provincial Master and Servants Act "to provide for the compulsory collection of medical fees . . . by employers" when a majority of employees had selected a particular health plan. Committee members from Local 81 encouraged their comrades in New Denver, Silverton, and Slocan to help secure passage of this reform. The committee reported receiving "favorable replies from all the Unions." F. F. Liebscher of Local 95 in Silverton pledged, "We are in complete sympathy with the movement, and we will do all we can to further the good cause." Slocan leader D. B. O'Neail also heartily supported the proposal, noting that it would mean not only more revenue for his organization's hospital but also less "annoyance and friction in collecting the monthly Hospital fees." The unions counted on provincial assembly member William Davidson, still a director of the Sandon Miners' Union Hospital, to carry this bill. Immediately upon reading it, however, Davidson informed his constituents that he opposed the plan. The legislator saw that any advantage gained by a relatively small group of organized miners would be greatly outweighed by the potential for employers to abuse the mass of unorganized workers. This initiative died quietly; the WFM hospitals persevered with time-consuming procedures for collecting fees.[48]

Besides fees from union members, the hospitals derived revenue

47. Alex Murray to A. Shilland, Oct. 15, 1902, Mine-Mill Papers, box 153, folder 8; W. N. Welsh to A. Shilland, Nov. 3, 1902, ibid., folder 9; Alfred Mitchell to A. Shilland, Mar. 14, 1904, ibid., box 155, folder 1.

48. C. H. Richardson, J. A. Caldwell, and W. J. Garbutt to Officers and Members of Sandon Miners' Union, Report, Jan. 23, 1904, F. F. Liebscher (Local 95) to C. H. Richardson, Jan. 18, 1904, and D. B. O'Neail to Secretary, Sandon Miners' Union, Jan. 17, 1904, Mine-Mill Papers, box 154, folder 10; William Davidson to C. H. Richardson, Feb. [n.d.], 1904, ibid., folder 11; British Columbia, *Statutes, 1902* (Victoria, 1902), pp. 157–58.

from a variety of other sources. Some offered prepayment plans to the community at large. The Bonanza Miners' Union announced such a program in August 1905: "The citizens and general public of Rhyolite will be admitted to the Miners' General Hospital at the rate of $2.00 per month, which entitles them to the full benefits of hospital and doctor's services." In addition, the 250 members of the Industrial Workers of the World (IWW) local in Rhyolite enjoyed prepaid benefits at this facility.[49] The institutions also accepted nonunion patients who paid weekly rates for private rooms or ward accommodations. When it opened in 1904, the Park City Miners' Hospital charged $15 per week for a private room and $10 for a bed in a ward, with physician's fees extra.[50]

The provincial government subsidized the general operating expenses of facilities in British Columbia. The Hospital Act of 1902 provided for reimbursement for services rendered at varying per capita per diem rates. The Sandon hospital obtained over $34,000 in grants in the period 1903–27. In addition, both the Sandon and Slocan institutions periodically received assistance from their municipalities in return for caring for charity patients.[51]

Hospitals in the United States, on the other hand, could not count on systematic public assistance. In Rawhide, Nevada, the sheriff routinely dumped indigent patients in the union facility, but the county government refused to assume responsibility for them. "Not one cent has been received from the county funds by those . . . who have cared for the unfortunates that asked for treatment," editorialized the *Rawhide Rustler*. "At the present time the Miners' Union, that glorious

49. *Rhyolite Herald*, Aug. 25, 1905, June 1, 1906; *Slocan Drill*, May 15, 1903; *MM*, May 1900, p. 33; *Tonopah Miner*, Nov. 28, 1902; J. C. Barnes (Local 104, American Labor Union, Telluride) to Editor, Dec. 10, 1902, *American Labor Union Journal*, Dec. 18, 1902, p. 3.

50. *Park Record*, Oct. 22, 1904; *Silverton Weekly Miner*, Nov. 27, 1914; *Slocan Drill*, June 7, 1901; Sandon Miners' Union, *By-Laws of Hospital*, p. 21.

51. British Columbia, *Statutes, 1902*, pp. 115–19; idem, *Sessional Papers, 1903–4*, p. B53; ibid., *1905*, pp. B70–71; ibid., *1906*, p. B54; ibid., *1907*, p. B54; ibid., *1908*, p. B77; ibid., *1909*, p. C59; ibid., *1910*, p. B57; ibid., *1911*, p. C90; ibid., *1912*, pp. C65–66; ibid., *1913*, p. C65; ibid., *1914*, 1:C79; ibid., *1915*, 1:C80–81; ibid., *1916*, 1:C83–84; ibid., *1917*, 1:C85; ibid., *1918*, 1:C91; ibid., *1919*, 1:B81; ibid., *1920*, 1:C149; ibid., *1921*, 1:B167; ibid., 2d sess., *1921*, 1:A183; ibid., *1922*, 1:A188–89; ibid., *1923* (Victoria, 1924), 1:A196–97; ibid., *1924* (Victoria, 1925), 2:O200; ibid., *1925* (Victoria, 1926), 2:O191; ibid., *1926–27* (Victoria, 1927), 1:N176; ibid., [1927] (Victoria, 1928), 2:L171; *Slocan Drill*, Jan. 31, 1902; Sandon *Paystreak*, Aug. 10, Sept. 23, 1899, Jan. 12, 1901.

institution, is out $1,200." Unions thus were forced to provide a significant amount of uncompensated care.[52]

Hospital secretaries handled routine financial chores. Invariably, the financial secretary of the local was saddled with this thankless post as an ex officio responsibility. The miners apparently assumed that the officer who extracted regular union dues, kept financial records, and organized the unorganized could manage hospital finances as well. To a certain extent these duties dovetailed naturally. In April 1900 the Sandon membership encouraged its all-purpose secretary "to initiate any members he may find in McGuigan Basin, on his tour in the interests of the Hospital." More often, however, the combined secretariat meant an overload of administrative minutiae—numerous visits to mines, endless correspondence, regular reports to the union, and innumerable miscellaneous tasks. Duties of the secretary of the Silverton, Colorado, health care center, for instance, included "helping out at the Hospital as much as his time would warrant."[53]

Generally a full-time employee of the local, the hospital secretary received the same wage he had earned underground. Because of the longer hours of the union job, this amounted to taking a pay cut. Inevitably, a small minority gave in to temptation and gave themselves illicit raises. In June 1909 the Bonanza Miners' Union suspended J. J. Kelly for three months and ordered him to restore union dues and hospital fees he had misappropriated. The vast majority of secretaries were honest.[54]

The experience of simultaneously handling the finances of a local union and its health program trained a cadre of miners in skills essential to the success of any complex organization. After serving as

52. *Rawhide Rustler*, Oct. 24, 1908; *Great Falls Daily Tribune*, Aug. 21, 1900, p. 9; *Silverton Weekly Miner*, Sept. 29, 1911; *Tonopah Bonanza*, Feb. 8, 1902.

53. Sandon Miners' Union, Minutes, unpaginated (Apr. 30, 1900), Mine-Mill Papers, box 151, folder 11; Silverton Miners' Union, Minute Book, pp. 124 (Jan. 27, 1923), 3–4 (Apr. 1, 1918), 8 (June 22, 1918), 19 (Jan. 18, 1919), 36 (July 28, 1919), WFM-IUMMSW Archives, vol. 59; *San Miguel Examiner*, Jan. 24, 1903; Silver City Miners' Union, Minute Book, pp. 200–201 (Dec. 20, 1897), Silver City Miners' Union Records, vol. 1; Alfred Parr to W. L. Hagler, Feb. 21, 1901, Mine-Mill Papers, box 151, folder 14; *MM*, June 1919; *Rhyolite Herald*, Dec. 15, 1905.

54. J. B. Williams, Charles B. Cameron, and A. J. Ginglas (Local 235) to Editor, Aug. 12, 1909, *MM*, Aug. 19, 1909, p. 8; Silver City Miners' Union, Minute Book, pp. 200–201 (Dec. 20, 1897), Silver City Miners' Union Records, vol. 1; Jerry P. Shea to Editor, Nov. 23, 1910, *MM*, Dec. 8, 1910, pp. 10–11; Anthony Shilland, "Minutes of Court of Enquiry Meeting," Jan. 20, 1902, Mine-Mill Papers, box 152, folder 10.

financial secretary of Local 66, Bill Haywood became secretary-treasurer of the Western Federation. In 1906 the international executive
board praised his "neatness and business-like methods." Just as a
mastery of organizational skills did not ineluctably turn Haywood into
a stodgy business unionist, the routine of maintaining health care
institutions failed to moderate the radicalism of other activists. In 1919
the Sandon Miners' Union seceded from the IUMMSW and affiliated
with the One Big Union (OBU). These revolutionaries continued to
seek the overthrow of capitalism even as they transacted hospital
business with the Bank of Montreal, the Workmen's Compensation
Board, the provincial secretary, and numerous mining capitalists.[55]

Despite the indefatigable efforts of their secretaries, some WFM
hospitals ran deficits. The locals involved resorted to diverse means
to forestall insolvency. Some asked the general headquarters for assistance, but only once did the international union loan money to an
affiliate (Sandon) to meet maintenance expenses; in all other cases it
left affiliates to their own devices.[56]

Simple transfers of funds from the local treasury and special assessments of the membership were the usual methods of raising money
in an emergency. Anthony Shilland believed that Sandon miners had
only two choices in 1908—to close their hospital or to levy an assessment. "I am in favor of adopting the latter course," argued Shilland, "and am willing to make any kind of sacrifice to keep its doors
open, if for no other reason than that the Mine Owners have made
a special target of it." Between 1909 and 1929, the Silverton Miners'
Union assessed its members $54.25 each to sustain its health care
center. In a few desperate situations the union raised the monthly fee
or curtailed weekly sickness and accident benefits. As dwindling em-

55. Executive Board, WFM, Minute Book, 1:416 (Dec. 15, 1906), WFM-IUMMSW
Archives, vol. 1; Silver City Miners' Union, Dues and Fees Records, 1901, Silver City
Miners' Union Records, envelope 1; Joseph R. Conlin, *Big Bill Haywood and the Radical
Union Movement* (Syracuse, N.Y., 1969), p. 28; Dan McKay (former president, Sandon
Miners' Union) to Manager, Bank of Montreal, Jan. 24, 1920, and [T. B. Roberts (financial
secretary, Sandon Miners' Union, OBU)] to Sam Johnson, Aug. 14, 1920, Mine-Mill
Papers, box 156, folder 14.
56. H. Allen, "Hospital Report," *Silverton Weekly Miner*, Oct. 29, 1909; Frank L. White
and W. W. Calder (president and financial secretary, Local 111) to All Unions, May
20, 1903, Mine-Mill Papers, box 154, folder 2; *Rawhide Press-Times*, Mar. 10, 1908, Sept.
30, 1910; WFM, *Proceedings, 1906*, pp. 149–50, 153; John McIsaac, Anthony Shilland,
and Charles Moyer, Mortgage on Sandon Miners' Union Hospital, Nov. 7, 1907, WFM-
IUMMSW Archives, box 1, folder 21.

ployment thinned the ranks of Local 62 in 1903, the Slocan miners voted to suspend disability insurance payments for three months "to preserve our Union funds so as to be able to carry our Hospital along."[57]

WFM locals also frequently turned to the general public for aid. As they had done to raise construction funds, the hardrock workers relied heavily on social events to bring in contributions. In June 1913 the *Tonopah Miner* illuminated both the predicament of the local hospital and the success of its community fund-raising strategy: "The only way in which the place is kept free from debt is . . . through dances and such affairs have always been well attended." Just as the Tonopah miners scheduled a dance for the eve of Independence Day, most locals sought to capitalize on the celebration of major holidays. For over twenty-five years the Sandon union held a Hospital Ball on St. Patrick's Day, which roughly coincided with the anniversary of the founding of the institution. Several locals held dances on Labor Day. The Silverton, Colorado, organization made its Hard Times Ball an annual extravaganza preceded by a parade of ragged revelers. In addition to the efforts of the hospital secretary and board members, the membership as a whole took an active role in planning and carrying out these events.[58]

Although miners themselves put on most public fund-raising activities, community groups occasionally sponsored charitable events. Employees of the Silverton Northern Railway donated the proceeds of their annual ball to the miners' hospital. Roderick MacKenzie expressed the gratitude of Local 26 for this "big hearted donation" and appealed for more support: "We cordially invite and respectfully solicit the cooperation of all, and wish each member of the community to feel and say with us, 'Our Hospital,' where friend and foe shall receive the same tender care and attention." Accordingly, this facility benefited from a dance given by the American Legion in 1920. Ad hoc

57. Anthony Shilland to Martin S. Caine, June 3, 1908, Mine-Mill Papers, box 156, folder 4; D. B. O'Neail to A. Shilland, Jan. 29, 1903, ibid., box 153, folder 11; Silverton Miners' Union, Minute Book, pp. 19 (Jan. 18, 1919), 111 (July 1, 1922), 146 (Sept. 14, 1929), WFM-IUMMSW Archives, vol. 59; *Rhyolite Daily Bulletin*, Mar. 24, 1909.

58. *Tonopah Miner*, June 14, 1913; *Silverton Weekly Miner*, Sept. 3, Dec. 24, 1909, Mar. 18, 1910, May 5, 1911, July 4, 1913; *Slocan Drill*, Mar. 7, 1902, May 13, 1904; *Sandon Paystreak*, Feb. 23, 1901; J. A. Moir (Sandon Miners' Union Hospital), "Net Balance from A[nnual] Ball," Mar. 31, 1927, Receipt Book 32, Mine-Mill Papers, box 157, folder 10; *Kendall Miner*, Mar. 16, 1906, Sept. 3, 1909; *Rhyolite Herald*, June 23, 1905, Mar. 16, 1906; *Manhattan Post*, Oct. 15, 1910.

committees, usually made up of women, also raised money through minstrel shows, teas, dramas, basket socials, and other fund-raising events.[59]

Despite these exertions, most WFM hospitals were relatively short-lived. All but three of the miners' unions had either sold or closed their facilities by the early 1920s. Only the hospitals in Ainsworth and Sandon, British Columbia, and Silverton, Colorado, survived past 1930. Data from twenty-two institutions show that the average hospital ran for roughly twelve years under union control.[60]

More than any other factor, geology doomed the hospitals. The life of a mining town was highly precarious: when paying ore gave out, the community collapsed. The Nevada boom towns of the 1900s offer the most dramatic evidence of brutal geological determinism. For instance, the life span of the Rawhide Miners' Union Hospital—born in 1908, died in 1912—is fully explained by the trend in ore production in the surrounding district: in 1907 the value of ore produced was zero; in 1908, $147,189; 1909, $202,715; 1910, $177,395; 1911, $93,266; and again in 1912, zero. The population of Rhyolite plummeted from approximately 5,000 in 1907 to 675 in 1910. This community's WFM local and its health care center were gone by 1912. Indeed, in the Nevada desert, where building materials were extremely scarce, structures in busted towns were often dismantled and their parts recycled elsewhere. Some miners' hospitals literally disappeared overnight.[61]

59. Roderick MacKenzie to Employees of the Silverton Northern Railway, Mar. 7, 1913, in *Silverton Weekly Miner*, Mar. 7, 1913; *Silverton Weekly Miner*, Jan. 27, 1911, May 3, Dec. 27, 1912, Feb. 21, 1913; Silverton Miners' Union, Minute Book, pp. 59 (Jan. 31, 1920), 98 (May 21, 1921), WFM-IUMMSW Archives, vol. 59; *Owyhee Avalanche*, Mar. 2, 9, 1900; *Little Rockies Miner*, Feb. 27, 1909.

60. Brinley, "Western Federation of Miners," pp. 212–24; U.S. Bureau of the Census, *Benevolent Institutions, 1904*, pp. 172–73; AMA, *American Medical Directory*, 16th ed. (Chicago, 1940), pp. 1943, 1944; ibid., 4th ed., p. 899; ibid., 5th ed. (Chicago, 1916), pp. 922, 923; Silverton Miners' Union, Minute Book, p. 196 (June 19, 1937), WFM-IUMMSW Archives, vol. 59; *CIO News—Mine, Mill and Smelter Workers Edition*, Mar. 6, 1939, p. 2; *Polk's Medical Register and Directory of North America*, 13th ed. (Detroit, 1914), pp. 997, 1024; British Columbia, *Sessional Papers, 1926–27*, 1:N176; ibid., 1922, 1:A188; ibid., 1907, pp. B54–55; *San Miguel Examiner*, Jan. 6, 1906; Julia C. Welch, *Gold Town to Ghost Town: The Story of Silver City, Idaho* (Moscow, Ida., 1982), p. 94; *Manhattan Post*, Nov. 8, 1913, p. 2; Fifield, ed., *American and Canadian Hospitals*, p. 1228; Ernest Mills, "Annual Summary of Financial Reports," in IUMMSW, *Official Proceedings of the Twenty-fourth Consecutive and Fourth Biennial Convention, 1920* (Denver, n.d.), p. 130; *Goldfield News*, Aug. 29, 1908; Executive Board, WFM, Minute Book, 3:95 (July 31, 1912), 4:10 (Nov. 22, 1915), WFM-IUMMSW Archives, vols. 3 and 4.

61. Elliott, "Tonopah, Goldfield," pp. 269, 84; U.S. Bureau of the Census, *Thirteenth Census, 1910*, vol. 3: *Population* (Washington, 1913), pp. 78–79; Ernest Mills, "Financial

Of course, most metal-mining communities declined somewhat less precipitously than Rawhide and Rhyolite. In Silver City, a more representative case, the veins of heavily worked mines gradually pinched out and new ones could not be found. In February 1914 WFM secretary-treasurer Mills recorded the fate of Local 66: "Defunct . . . mines closed down." Here as elsewhere, miners managed to keep their hospital open until the union disbanded. A typical fatal problem was that as the population of a district shrank, it became increasingly difficult for the union physician to piece together a living from a meager hospital salary, private practice, and other miscellaneous contract work. Unlike the socialist doctors who staffed the health programs of German unions in this period, most WFM physicians were not ideologically committed to the miners' cause. Hence, when their financial prospects dimmed, they joined the general exodus, leaving the community with no doctor.[62]

Two hospitals were casualties of class warfare. In September 1903 the Telluride Miners' Union struck the principal mines within its jurisdiction over wages and hours. Initially, the union considered the health care center part of its armamentarium. "For the care of men during the strike," reported the *San Miguel Examiner*, "the union has a hospital, store, coal mine, lodging-houses and restaurant. Officials claim that the men can hold out for an indefinite period." But as the battle wore on, the facility became more of a burden than an asset. With "revenue for its maintenance . . . so decreased that it will hardly pay the salary of one nurse," Local 63 closed the hospital in November 1903.[63]

Report," in WFM, *Official Proceedings of the Eighteenth Annual Convention, 1910* (Denver, 1910), p. 203; Paher, *Nevada Ghost Towns*, p. 32; idem, *Death Valley Ghost Towns*, p. 10; Hugh A. Shamberger, *The Story of Seven Troughs* (Carson City, Nev., 1972), pp. 27–28, 43; Executive Board, WFM, Minute Book, 3:95 (July 31, 1912), WFM-IUMMSW Archives, vol. 3; Mills, "Financial Report," in WFM, *Official Proceedings of the Twentieth Annual Convention, 1912* (Denver, 1912), pp. 105, 169; see also sources cited in preceding note.

62. [Ernest Mills], "Defunct Unions and New Unions," p. 18, WFM-IUMMSW Archives, vol. 43; Welch, *Gold Town*, p. 94; William D. Haywood, Report, in WFM, *Proceedings, 1905*, p. 204; *Slocan Drill*, Sept. 4, Nov. 6, 1903; Ernest Mills, "Annual Report," in IUMMSW, *Proceedings, 1918*, Appendix, p. 49; O. W. Freeman, "Gold Mining in the Judith Mountains, Montana," *MSP*, June 10, 1916, pp. 864–65; British Columbia Minister of Mines, "Annual Report," 1909, pp. K115–18; *MM*, Mar. 18, 1904, p. 13, June 9, 1910, p. 11; AMA, *American Medical Directory*, 3d ed., p. 742; Donald W. Light, Stephan Liebfried, and Florian Tennstedt, "Social Medicine versus Professional Dominance: The German Experience," *American Journal of Public Health* 76 (1986): 78–83; see also sources cited in note 60.

63. *San Miguel Examiner*, Sept. 19, Nov. 21, Sept. 5, Dec. 19, 1903.

Like their predecessors in the Coeur d'Alene, the Telluride miners soon discovered the limitations of local solidarity in waging industrial conflict. Whereas Local 63 had staunch solidarity within its ranks, the mine owners had military power. The union could not prevent the imposition of martial law, which, in turn, permitted the wholesale importation of strikebreakers. The strikers converted their idle health care center into a rooming house, and federal troops used its rival, Dr. Hall's hospital, as barracks. Mass arrests, deportations, and vigilante violence broke the strike in the winter of 1903–4. In the bitter aftermath, the union facility reopened for only a brief interval before succumbing to a blacklist of all who dared to patronize it.[64]

The health care program in Goldfield, Nevada, also fell victim to an ill-fated work stoppage. In November 1907, Local 220 struck over the introduction of scrip pay. Federal troops and state police smashed the strike during the winter of 1907–8 and all but destroyed the militant IWW-dominated miners' organization. The Goldfield Miners' Union Hospital was sold to Roman Catholic nuns, who renamed it St. Mary's Hospital.[65]

Taken together with the other major setbacks of this decade, the shattering defeats at Telluride and Goldfield had broad ramifications for WFM health policy. The federation lost more than two hospitals in these battles: it was forced to abandon its general commitment to such initiatives. At the 1908 convention, Roderick MacKenzie, executive board member for the district that included Colorado, reviewed the organization's recent record in conducting big strikes and found it "a complete failure." MacKenzie denounced "the wanton extravagance of local unions squandering their funds through investment . . . in palatial halls and hospitals." After conceding that he was "not opposed to a union owning a hall or a hospital when it can afford to," he described the locals in his district that had overextended themselves:

64. ibid., Nov. 28, 1903–Apr. 9, 1904; George G. Suggs, Jr., *Colorado's War on Militant Unionism: James H. Peabody and the Western Federation of Miners* (Detroit, 1972), pp. 118–45; *San Miguel Examiner*, Nov. 4, 1905, Jan. 6, 1906; Executive Board, WFM, Minute Book, 1:290 (June 10, 1905), 326 (Dec. 12, 1905), WFM-IUMMSW Archives, vol. 1; Charles H. Moyer, Testimony, Oct. 9, 1917, in U.S., President's Mediation Commission, "Sessions at Globe," pp. 49, 133–34, McCluskey Collection, box 4.

65. Jensen, *Heritage of Conflict*, pp. 229–35; *Goldfield News*, Aug. 29, 1908; *Polk's Medical Register*, 11th ed., p. 1175; Executive Board, WFM, Minute Book, 3:97 (Aug. 1, 1912), 105 (Jan. 8, 1913), WFM-IUMMSW Archives, vol. 3; Mother Mary Agnes to Charles Moyer, June 2, 1913, ibid., box 1, folder 31.

In Telluride the union built a hospital into which the general organization had to sink nearly seventeen thousand dollars or lose the hospital. This building represents an investment of about $40,000. It is lying idle and the organization has to meet the tax bill.

In Park City the union invested its every cent in a hall and hospital. The salary of the secretary had to be stopped because otherwise they could not meet their bills, as the treasury is empty. . . .

In Silverton . . . at this moment excavations are going on for the erection of a twenty to thirty thousand dollar hospital, which, under favorable conditions, it is true, will not take No. 26 long to pay for; but . . . one unsuccessful scrap with the mine owners, it is more than possible, would place them in the same position as Telluride. . . .

With the money represented by those dead monuments within its treasury, the Western Federation of Miners would be a power instead of being almost helpless and financially bankrupt, as it is to-day.

MacKenzie proposed that "it be made illegal for any union to invest in any property without the approval of the Executive Board or the convention." This proposal aimed to ensure the financial stability of locals so that they could both win strikes in which they themselves became involved and pay assessments to support other locals on strike.[66]

Although the convention did not adopt this proposal, delegates did instruct the executive board to advise locals to exercise "greater care" before entering into such ventures. MacKenzie's analysis contributed to a growing movement to centralize power within the loose federation. Further impetus came at the next convention. Secretary-treasurer Mills reported that as of June 30, 1909, delinquencies on strike assessments levied by the general headquarters totaled more than $22,000. Nearly half of this amount was owed by locals burdened by hospitals, six of which were each over a thousand dollars in arrears. Because these assessments were the only way the central organization could help striking affiliates financially, the failure of hospital locals to pay their share crippled the WFM's capacity to sustain work stoppages.[67]

66. Roderick MacKenzie, "Report," in WFM, *Proceedings, 1908*, pp. 293–94 (quotations), 282–95.

67. WFM, *Proceedings, 1908*, pp. 393–94; Ernest Mills, "Financial Report," in WFM, *Proceedings, 1909*, pp. 58–59; J. A. Baker (Executive Board), Report, in WFM, *Proceedings, 1904*, p. 272.

This financial crisis had a chilling effect on further health care initiatives. Besides the facility already under construction in Silverton, Colorado, only the hospitals in Ainsworth and Silverton, British Columbia, were established after 1908. Although this experiment in democracy was reasonably successful in delivering health services, it did not escape the onslaught of larger forces. By hard experience the unionists came to realize the fatal limitations of a decentralized strategy for resisting the power of capital. The Western Federation could no longer afford to encourage local projects that diverted resources from the crucial effort to support affiliates embroiled in disputes that threatened the very existence of the union as a whole.

7 | *The Politics of Prevention*

It is now being conceded by some of the employers that it is unjust to place the responsibility for industrial accidents on the victims, or on the wives and children of the victims, of such accidents, and while we welcome these admissions, let us endeavor to protect ourselves and those depending upon us, by having laws enacted which will protect us from the viciousness of a system which makes it profitable for the master class to enforce conditions which render accidents, not only liable, but certain. To do this, and get the best possible results, laws must be enacted and enforced which will make accidents unprofitable.

—Committee on the President's Report,
WFM convention, 1911

After the panic of 1907, the Western Federation of Miners adopted a more aggressive health policy. The primary focus of the union's efforts shifted from coping with the effects of occupational hazards to preventing them. Increasingly, provision of services and benefits by local affiliates gave way to political agitation for protective legislation on the state and provincial levels.

This activism embodied a distinctive brand of political self-help. The preamble to the WFM constitution adopted in 1907 boldly proclaimed that "the working class, and it alone, can and must achieve its own emancipation. We hold . . . that an industrial union and the concerted political action of all wage workers is the only method of attaining this end." Whereas middle-class Progressives played a critical role in effecting reform in other regions, western miners had relatively few supporters among the professional and technical stratum. The absence of Progressive allies in the mining states necessitated workers' self-reliance.[1]

---

1. WFM, *Constitution and By-Laws*, 1907, rpt. in Jensen, *Heritage of Conflict*, p. 189;

WFM activists saw government intervention as a form of self-reliance because they intended to control the state apparatus themselves. Above all else, political self-help meant electing miners to office. Reflecting on the role of trade unions in politics in the December 1901 issue of the *Miners' Magazine*, Edward Boyce argued that workers' "interests are more secure when men from their own ranks handle the affairs of government." Numerous Western Federation leaders served as state and provincial legislators. J. J. Bennett, president of the DeLamar Miners' Union, introduced the first eight-hour bill into the Idaho legislature. William Davidson of Sandon carried a substantial amount of legislation for British Columbia mine, mill, and smelter workers. Hardrock workers in Montana, Arizona, and Nevada sent several local leaders to their legislatures.[2]

Clearly, the 1907 constitution conceived miners' self-interest in class terms. Yet in practice the WFM adopted a political strategy that displayed only a secondary commitment to class solidarity. Throughout this period, the union devoted most of its attention to advocating narrow measures to reform conditions within its own industry. The extraordinary, peculiar hazards of underground work drove the miners to pursue protection for themselves alone. The rhetoric of class politics thus veiled the persistent pursuit of special-interest legislation.

The Western Federation's growing preoccupation with legislative reform after 1907 represented not the discovery of politics but a shift in emphasis. The union had launched its first major health-related political campaign in the 1890s in instigating a movement for the eight-hour day. "We are unanimously in favor of eight hours constituting a day's work and we demand that an eight hour law be enacted by our legislators," declared the founding convention. Any such protection for adult male workers was difficult to enact and virtually

---

Guy E. Miller, Reply to Michigan Mine Operators, in *MM*, Aug. 14, 1913, p. 13; Perlman and Taft, *Labor in the U.S.*, 4:169, 178.

2. [Edward Boyce], "Trade Unions in Politics," *MM*, pp. 12–13; Committee on President's Report, Report, in WFM, *Proceedings, 1910*, p. 310; *Idaho Avalanche*, Jan. 15, Feb. 5, 1897; *Idaho State Tribune*, n.d., rpt. in *Owyhee Avalanche*, July 1, 1898; *MM*, July 1919; J. T. Saywell, "Labor and Socialism in British Columbia: A Survey of Historical Developments before 1903," *British Columbia Historical Quarterly* 15 (1951): 148; *Slocan Drill*, Sept. 18, Oct. 9, 1903, Nov. 18, 1904; *Tonopah Miner*, Nov. 9, 1912; *Nevada Socialist*, Sept. 1914, p. 2, Oct. 26, 1914, p. 4. Building trades unionists in San Francisco held the same belief and adopted a similar political strategy at this time. See Kazin, *Barons of Labor*, pp. 136–202.

impossible to defend in the courts in this laissez-faire era. To surmount these obstacles, the union shrewdly concentrated on the indisputable health and safety aspects of the hours question.[3]

The Utah constitution of 1895 empowered the state government to guard the health and safety of mine and smelter workers. Citing the unique risks of their employment, members of the WFM local in Park City and other groups of workers petitioned the 1896 legislature for an eight-hour measure. Lawmakers responded by passing an act covering metal mines and smelters, the first such protection in North American history for male workers in the private sector. Two years later, the U.S. Supreme Court upheld the constitutionality of this law in the landmark case of *Holden v. Hardy*. By restricting individual freedom to make employment contracts, Utah miners had made a small but significant clearing in the Darwinist jungle of industrial relations.[4]

This breakthrough helped bring about the passage of similar laws throughout the region. British Columbia granted a shorter day for hardrock miners in 1899 and extended protection to smelter employees in 1907. Feverish competition for labor's political support forced the warring Montana copper kings to concede an eight-hour measure in 1901. Arizona and Nevada followed suit two years later. By the end of the decade, metal miners in Idaho (1907), Oregon (1907), and California (1909) had also won this reform. The last western stronghold of the long workday fell when Colorado operators finally ran out of political tricks in 1913.[5]

The Western Federation was deeply involved in every aspect of this

3. WFM, "Proceedings," 1893, p. 20, Labor Collection, Berkeley; Elizabeth Brandeis, "Hour Laws for Men," in John R. Commons et al., *History of Labor in the United States*, vol. 3 (New York, 1935), pp. 540–63; David L. Lonsdale, "The Movement for an Eight-Hour Law in Colorado, 1893–1913" (Ph.D. dissertation, University of Colorado, 1963), pp. 4–11.

4. Utah, *Constitution*, 1895 (Salt Lake City, 1896), p. 66; Utah, *Laws*, 1896 (Salt Lake City, 1896), p. 219; Brandeis, "Hour Laws," pp. 551–53; John H. Murphy, "Utah and Colorado's Eight-Hour Law," *American Federationist*, July 1899, pp. 103–4; Florence Kelley, "The United States Supreme Court and the Utah Eight-Hours Laws," *American Journal of Sociology* 4 (1898): 21, 25–30; Wyman, *Hard-Rock Epic*, pp. 207–9; Marion C. Cahill, *Shorter Hours: A Study of the Movement since the Civil War* (New York, 1932), pp. 116–28.

5. Brandeis, "Hour Laws," pp. 551–52, 562; Wyman, *Hard-Rock Epic*, pp. 209–25; Jensen, *Heritage of Conflict*, pp. 100–117; Schwantes, *Radical Heritage*, p. 123; British Columbia, *Statutes*, 1907 (Victoria, 1907), p. 85; David L. Lonsdale, "The Fight for an Eight-Hour Day," *Colorado Magazine* 43 (1966): 352–53; [John M. O'Neill], "The Eight Hour Day," *MM*, Nov. 16, 1905, p. 10.

movement. The union challenged operators' economic conception of the problem, arguing that the eight-hour day was essentially a public health matter. Butte miners advocated remedial legislation as a "sanitary measure" as early as 1891. The Randsburg, California, local rallied support with the contention that "the occupation of miners, millmen and smeltermen is both dangerous and unhealthy." The Cobalt Miners' Union called on the Ontario government to enact legislation in 1911, stating that it was "hardly necessary to enumerate the reasons for demanding this act of justice." Nevertheless, Local 146 listed the "unhealthy conditions" justifying reform — "powder, gas, smoke, impure air, dust, etc." Deemphasizing other economic, political, and social arguments, the WFM pleaded that its members' unique risks warranted special protection.[6]

Opponents of shorter hours never tried to deny that metal mining was extraordinarily dangerous. The union thus set the terms of public debate. For example, in the winter of 1899 the Lincoln Miners' Union of Delamar induced Representative W. J. Dooley to sponsor Nevada's first eight-hour bill. Dooley's introductory speech to the assembly stressed health considerations:

It means less hours in life-taking powder smoke; less hours in the damp and desolate underground; less hours in the poisonous roasters and smelters; less hours in the deadly mill; less hours throughout the path and walk of labor, and more employed and longer generations.

It means less paid out for doctors' bills and medicine and more paid out for education and advancement. . . .

Indulge me for a few moments in an illustration, and let us visit a once prosperous mining camp. We are awe stricken at the deserted appearance of the once live streets and byways, and stand breathless in our gaze at the abandoned business buildings and the homes of the once happy miner, and as we roam around we are attracted to a number of white spots on yonder hillside; as we approach we are soon sensible of the

6. Lingenfelter, *Hardrock Miners*, p. 191; P. Mertz, G. C. Nebeker, and E. M. Arandale (Local 44), "For the Eight-Hour Day," *MM*, Oct. 23, 1908, p. 9; William DuFeu et al. (Local 146) to J. P. Whitney (premier, Ontario), Resolutions, Feb. 19, 1911, in *MM*, Mar. 16, 1911, p. 9; Charles A. McKay (president, Local 96) to J. F. Hume (B.C. minister of mines), Apr. 1, 1899, in British Columbia, *Sessional Papers, 1900*, pp. 466–67; Vincent St. John and A. G. Dingwell (president and recording secretary, San Juan District Union), "[Resolutions] Against Present Measures," in *San Miguel Examiner*, Feb. 21, 1903; Terry *News-Record*, Mar. 21, 1907.

solemnity of the spot; a few steps more and we are within the walls of the mining town of the dead. Ask this slab of plain white pine wood its story and it answers: My victory is powder smoke. Its companion takes up the question and answers: My victory is arsenic and lead, and so on through the line until the sad story is told.

The *Great Falls Daily Tribune* applied the same union-made logic to smelting: "The work in smelters is of a most trying character. It is dangerous to health and even to life. If eight hours are demanded anywhere they certainly should be among the heat and the gases of the smelters." Based on the Utah precedent, hours reform passed as health and safety legislation. The title of the Colorado law declared "Certain Employments Injurious to Health and Dangerous to Life and Limb."[7]

Federation members and staff wrote and introduced a number of eight-hour bills. The union's attorney helped draft the laws adopted in Idaho and Oregon, among others. Representative John J. Quinn, a leader of the Butte Miners' Union, sponsored the measure enacted in Montana. According to the *Miners' Magazine*, Quinn "more than any other man in Montana . . . labored tirelessly for an eight-hour law." Miner-legislator William Davidson was the father of British Columbia's eight-hour limitation on smelter work.[8]

Hardrock workers used a variety of tactics to secure passage of hours legislation. They bombarded lawmakers with petitions. In 1899, Local 72 obtained more than seven hundred signatures on its petitions and pledged to aid cooperative legislators "by all honorable means." Union delegations frequently testified at committee hearings on pending proposals. During the 1903 session of the Colorado legislature, Guy Miller of the Telluride local rounded up sponsors for an ill-fated plan to grant shorter hours to mill workers as well as miners. In the California session of 1909, three WFM lobbyists won reform by giving their "undivided attention to the measure."[9]

7. W. J. Dooley, quoted in *DeLamar Lode*, Mar. 7, 1899; *Great Falls Daily Tribune*, Sept. 21, 1900, p. 2; Colorado, *Laws, 1913* (Denver, 1913), p. 305; *Owyhee Avalanche*, Mar. 1, 1901.

8. [John M. O'Neill], Untitled eulogy, *MM*, July 11, 1912, p. 4; Lingenfelter, *Hardrock Miners*, p. 191; William Davidson to Anthony Shilland, Feb. 15, 20, 1905, Mine-Mill Papers, box 155, folder 13; *MM*, Oct. 1901, p. 24, July 1919; Press Committee, Local 121, to Editor, Feb. 6, 1903, *MM*, Mar. 1903, p. 45.

9. Committee on Resolutions, Local 72, "Resolutions," Nov. 29, 1900, *MM*, Jan. 1901, pp. 36–37; *MM*, Mar. 18, 1909, p. 6, Feb. 16, 1905, p. 4, Mar. 11, 1909, p. 10,

Obviously, the fate of these campaigns depended to a great extent on the amount of resistance offered by mining capitalists and their representatives. Deriding the state legislature as a "subsidized body of toadies," Edward Boyce complained in 1901 that "no eight hour law for miners or any other body of workingmen will pass in Idaho, for it is without exception the worst corporation-ridden state in the Union." In general, three factors softened employers' opposition enough to permit enactment of legislation—the need of politically ambitious operators to cultivate labor support, the WFM's success in cutting hours through collective bargaining and strikes, and labor shortages that led some firms to make unilateral concessions to attract workers.[10]

Employers also conceded hours legislation because they retained hopes that the judiciary would invalidate it. Even after the decisive federal ruling in 1898, operators continued to challenge the constitutionality of eight-hour statutes. The Western Federation's attorney, John H. Murphy, made a career of defending these reforms. A former locomotive fireman who studied law after being blacklisted for his involvement in the American Railway Union, Murphy argued the miners' case for the Utah law before the U.S. Supreme Court. By rebuffing similar attacks in several other states, he earned the nickname "Eight-Hour Murphy."[11]

This legislation often became a reality only in areas where unions had the strength to enforce it. Many employers either brazenly ignored or cleverly circumvented hours restrictions. Miners frequently struck to implement legislation. The British Columbia minister of mines reportedly assured operators that he would not enforce the law "unless the pressure in its favor became so strong that he could not ignore it." The miners' movement quickly applied such pressure, culminating in a long work stoppage. Like many others, this particular dispute

Apr. 4, 1912, p. 8; *DeLamar Lode*, Jan. 24, 1899; Mertz, Nebeker, and Arandale, "For the Eight-Hour Day," p. 9; *Silverton Weekly Miner*, Mar. 20, 1903; Dan Evans (Local 42) to Editor, Oct. 21, 1907, *MM*, Oct. 31, 1907, p. 12.

10. [Edward Boyce], "Eight Hour Legislation," *MM*, Apr. 1901, p. 3; Malone, *Battle for Butte*, p. 151; *MM*, Mar. 9, 1905, p. 3, Aug. 9, 1906, p. 4, Dec. 20, 1906, p. 7, Jan. 10, 1907, p. 3, Oct. 31, 1912, p. 10; Executive Board, WFM, Minute Book, 1:417–18 (Dec. 15, 1906), WFM-IUMMSW Archives, vol. 1.

11. John M. O'Neill, "Memorial Address," in IUMMSW, *Proceedings, 1920*, pp. 78–79; Lonsdale, "Fight for Eight-Hour Day," pp. 341–43; *MM*, Jan. 21, 1904, p. 7; Executive Board, WFM, Minute Book, 1:322–26 (Dec. 11, 1905), 338 (Dec. 14, 1905), WFM-IUMMSW Archives, vol. 1; John H. Murphy, "Report," in WFM, *Proceedings, 1907*, p. 282.

centered on the issue of whether decreased hours would be accompanied by corresponding decreases in wages. District 6 invoked the "dangerous and unhealthy nature of our calling" to justify retention of the $3.50 wage. In the summer of 1903, the WFM led a strike by three thousand miners in the Morenci district to force compliance with Arizona's new statute.[12]

Where eight hours had been won, the federation began agitation for a six-hour limitation. Executive board member Fred Clough broached this subject in 1909 with a vague proposal that the international officers "do all in their power" to secure shorter shifts for workers who faced underground temperatures exceeding ninety degrees. According to Clough, "In some of the mines of Nevada and Arizona men are working in 'hot boxes' . . . where the temperature is hotter, by far, than where scab miners go after leaving this earth." In the 1911 session of the Montana legislature, the WFM sought a six-hour law "in mines where the heat was excessive and other unsanitary conditions existed." The union convention that year formally endorsed the six-hour day in hot mines. Recognizing that in some smelters "the fumes and gases [were] equally injurious," the Mine-Mill convention of 1920 called for similar protection for metallurgical workers as well. Nothing came of these initiatives, however, except heightened consciousness of exploitation.[13]

A body of legislation that aimed to eradicate hazards, not merely to limit the duration of exposure to them, gradually evolved in the late nineteenth and early twentieth centuries. Initially, piecemeal regulation of particular risks proliferated. As late as 1908 only four states— Colorado, Missouri, Montana, and New York—had general safety laws for metal mining,[14] but fragmentary legal provisions eventually grew into comprehensive codes of hazard control.

The miners' movement led the campaign to expand the scope of these reforms. In the preamble to its first constitution, the WFM

---

12. Sandon *Paystreak*, Apr. 8, 1899; Alfred Parr and A. J. Hughes (secretary and president, District 6), Resolution to Provincial Government, in ibid., Feb. 3, 1900; *MM*, Aug. 1903, p. 40; Moyer and Haywood, "An Appeal for an Eight-Hour Fund," *MM*, Aug. 1903, pp. 2–3; O. N. Wood (Local 192) to Editor, Jan. 30, 1905, *MM*, Feb. 9, 1905, p. 4; J. F. Hutchinson (Executive Board), "Report," in WFM, *Proceedings, 1909*, pp. 285–86.

13. Fred Clough, "Report," in WFM, *Proceedings, 1909*, p. 267; Committee on Good and Welfare, Report, in WFM, *Proceedings, 1911*, pp. 350–51; Committee on President's Report, "Report," in IUMMSW, *Proceedings, 1920*, pp. 69, 71.

14. *EMJ*, Dec. 5, 1908, pp. 1088–95.

committed itself to securing "such protection from the law as will remove needless risk to life and health." The federation's first efforts focused on improving conditions in and around mine shafts. To this end, the 1903 convention endorsed a standard code of bell signals for hoisting cages. In addition, the union agitated for sweeping safety reforms in jurisdictions where no protective laws whatsoever existed. The Tonopah local had a broad-gauge inspection bill introduced in 1903; it died quietly. Persistence paid off six years later, however, when Nevada finally passed a general mine-safety act.[15] Heavy pressure from the union forced the Arizona legislature to enact a comprehensive safety code in 1912. In contrast, lawmakers in California and Utah ignored miners' demands until the enactment of workers' compensation had created new incentives for employers to agree to safer working conditions. Overall, the union had only limited success in obtaining safety regulations in this period.[16]

The WFM did, however, make one major breakthrough in the struggle to prevent occupational diseases. By the second decade of the twentieth century, unionists recognized that silicosis disabled and killed more miners than all accidents combined and set their priorities accordingly. The union led the fight to eliminate exposure to silica dust throughout the western mining region.

Inspired by reforms obtained by coal miners in eastern states, hardrock activists initially advocated state standards for mine ventilation. In February 1894 the *Butte Bystander* (the union's official organ at that time) published two letters on this subject by Vice President John Duggan, a former coal digger. Duggan argued that metal mining was "far more fatal [than coal mining], not only in the number of deaths caused by accident so-called, but by miners' consumption." He held up for emulation Pennsylvania's requirement that operators supply

15. WFM, "Constitution," in "Proceedings," 1893, p. 4, Labor Collection, Berkeley; *Slocan Drill*, Apr. 27, 1900; *MM*, Jan. 1901, pp. 10–11, Dec. 31, 1908, pp. 5–6, 7–8; Press Committee, Local 121, to Editor, Feb. 6, 1903, *MM*, Mar. 1903, p. 45; WFM, *Proceedings*, 1903, pp. 202–3; WFM, *Proceedings, 1908*, p. 398; *Tonopah Sun*, Aug. 22, 1908; Nevada, *Statutes, 1909* (Carson City, 1909), pp. 218–23; Wyman, *Hard-Rock Epic*, pp. 186–89.

16. Arizona, *Acts, Resolutions and Memorials, 1912, Regular Session* (Phoenix, 1912), pp. 87–111; John Gallagher and Albert Ryan (president and secretary-treasurer, Arizona State Miners' Union) to Officers and Members of the Arizona State Miners' Union, Nov. 1, 1905, in *MM*, Nov. 16, 1905, p. 12; Bingham Miners' Union, Minute Book, 2:193 (Nov. 21, 1908), unpaginated end page (Dec. 19, 1908), WFM and IUMMSW Records, box 2; Executive Board, WFM, Minute Book, 3:57 (Jan. 6, 1911), WFM-IUMMSW Archives, vol. 3; H. M. Wolflin (California chief mine inspector), "Mine Inspection in California," *MM*, Mar. 1919.

their workings with two hundred cubic feet of air per minute per worker. Before the end of the decade, a weak version of his suggestion had become the public policy of British Columbia. Union demands led to amendment of the Inspection of Metalliferous Mines Act in 1899, mandating "not less than seventy-five cubic feet of air per minute . . . for every man and beast employed."[17]

Montana miners faced more formidable obstacles to progress. As the 1909 session of the legislature approached, WFM organizer John Lowney mordantly assessed the prospects for reform:

> We have humane societies for the protection of animals with agents paid by the state, but there is no society, humane or otherwise, which deems it worth while to inquire into the conditions under which human beings work in the mines of Butte. They take no notice of the daily processions on the streets of Butte, wending their way to the cemeteries, and those who are borne in those processions to their last resting place have been the very flower of physical manhood stricken in their prime by that dread disease known as miners' consumption. . . .
>
> Those conditions can be changed to a great extent by proper ventilation and better sanitary methods, but those things cost money and human life, here as elsewhere, is the cheapest thing in all the world. We need legislation to enforce better sanitary conditions in our mines, but the working men of Butte, who are vastly in the majority, selected as their representatives in the legislature at the recent election, mine owners, mine superintendents and business men whose interests are directly opposed to the working man's interests and they will naturally get what they voted for.

This dismal prediction proved accurate. Lowney reported four months later that WFM lobbyists for a ventilation law had been "unceremoniously turned down."[18]

At the next session, legislator P. J. Duffy, former president of the Butte Miners' Union, secured the appointment of a joint committee to investigate underground working conditions. Lowney and repre-

---

17. John Duggan to Editor, n.d., *Butte Bystander*, Feb. 17, 1894; Duggan to Editor, Feb. 19, 1894, ibid., Feb. 24, 1894; British Columbia, *Statutes, 1899* (Victoria, 1899), p. 154. The British Columbia law of 1897 included a meaningless provision for an "adequate amount of ventilation." See British Columbia, *Statutes, 1897* (Victoria, 1897), p. 279.

18. John C. Lowney to Editor, Nov. 23, 1908, *MM*, Dec. 10, 1908, pp. 10–11; Lowney to Editor, Mar. 16, 1909, *MM*, Mar. 25, 1909, p. 11; "Wage Slave" to Editor, n.d., *MM*, Jan. 13, 1910, p. 10.

sentatives of Local 1 testified on the magnitude of the silicosis problem and called for improved ventilation, the six-hour day, and other hazard-control measures. Nevertheless, after touring the mines and taking statements from mine managers, physicians, and state inspectors, the investigators lamely concluded that "the companies in Butte are doing all in their power to perfect their ventilation and sanitary conditions." On the committee's recommendation, the legislature passed a token remedial measure to appease the miners. This act set no quantitative standard for underground air supply, requiring only that in workings deeper than three hundred feet "a suitable and practical method for ventilating" be provided "where necessary, feasible and practicable." Reflecting on this illusory reform, Lowney (a man who had much to be cynical about) reminded his brothers that "workingmen may expect nothing from legislators controlled by corporate interests."[19]

Miners in other states refused to follow the Montana example. Instead, the WFM advocated mandatory installation and use of wet methods for drilling and handling dry ore. The superiority of this approach to dust abatement was abundantly clear by 1910. In 1903 the *Mining and Scientific Press* reported technological progress in this area: "It is quite possible to prevent [miners' consumption] entirely by the injection of water through the drill still [steel], or by forcing it through a tube which is placed alongside of the steel, and which is connected to a common bicycle foot pump." The following year the *Engineering and Mining Journal* published "The Prevention of Miners' Phthisis" by J. S. Haldane and R. Arthur Thomas, which made a strong case for wet-methods reform. Water-injection drills, especially those produced by the Leyner Engineering Works of Denver, provided technically and economically feasible alternatives to dry drills. In addition, by the second decade of this century, recommendations of wet methods by government commissions in England, Australia, and South Africa had received widespread publicity on this continent. Although North American operators continued to assert that only ventilation legislation, or no legislation at all, was needed to curtail the dust

19. Joint Committee to Investigate Sanitary Conditions, "Proceedings," 1911, rpt. in U.S. Commission on Industrial Relations, *Final Report and Testimony*, 4:3981 (quotation), 3901–82; Montana, *Laws, Resolutions and Memorials, 1911* (Helena, n.d.), pp. 136 (quotation), 135–37; J. C. Lowney to Editor, Mar. 10, 1911, *MM*, Mar. 23, 1911, pp. 10–11.

threat, union activists sought to import newly formulated reform proposals to their states and provinces.[20]

The union made its initial attempt to obtain wet-methods legislation in Arizona. In 1909 the territorial governor had appointed a commission, which included Peter Whipple of the Globe Miners' Union, to draft a mining code. At the first legislative session of the new state government in 1912, this commission offered a comprehensive safety code which contained a provision requiring water sprays on machine drills. Perry Hall, chairman of the House Mines and Mining Committee and former president of Local 118 in McCabe, promptly introduced a bill embodying this proposal. The measure picked up urban support when a legislator "drew the attention of the members to the ever-large number of tuberculosis victims hawking and spitting on the streets of Phoenix, nine-tenths of whom were miners." At a joint meeting of the House and Senate committees on mines, however, employers forced the substitution of weaker language. In its amended form, the Hall bill required spray equipment only "where necessary," without specifying what constituted a necessity. This insubstantive reform became law in May 1912 as a section of the general mine-safety statute.[21]

Upon determining that this regulation was indeed worthless, Robert A. Campbell, secretary-treasurer of the Arizona State Federation of Labor and former president of the Bisbee Miners' Union, procured a working model and the blueprints of a spray device that had proven effective in combating the dust problem. When a special legislative session opened in February 1913, Perry Hall introduced an amendment to the mining code to make spraying mandatory wherever power drills were used in dry rock. House member J. Tom Lewis boasted of his success in building support for Hall's bill:

20. *MSP*, May 9, 1903, p. 303; J. S. Haldane and R. Arthur Thomas, "The Prevention of Miners' Phthisis," *EMJ*, June 23, 1904, p. 994; *MSP*, Sept. 5, 1903, pp. 152–53, Dec. 17, 1910, p. 818; Charles A. Hirschberg, "History of the Water Leyner Drill," *MSP*, Oct. 29, 1910, p. 596; *EMJ*, May 25, 1905, p. 1010; Treve Holman, "Historical Relationship of Mining, Silicosis, and Rock Removal," *British Journal of Industrial Medicine* 4 (1947): 9–16.

21. Joseph D. Cannon, "What Has the Western Federation . . . Done?" *MM*, Aug. 17, 1916; Arizona, *Acts, Resolutions and Memorials, 1912, Regular Session*, p. 105; J. Tom Lewis to Members of Organized Labor, n.d., *Arizona Labor Journal*, Sept. 8, 1916, p. 2; Arizona, *Journals of the First Legislative Assembly, 1912, Regular Session* (Clifton, Ariz., 1912), pp. 65, 250, 279, 344–45, 423, 441; *Arizona Gazette* (Phoenix), May 7, 1912, p. 1; *Daily Arizona Silver Belt*, Jan. 10, 1912, p. 4, May 14, 1912, p. 1.

Bro. Campbell and myself made arrangements with a stone cutting firm in Phoenix for the use of their compressor to demonstrate the practical side of the spray. The Mines and Mining Committee, the Labor Committee, several members of both House and Senate and the Law and Legislative Committee of the Arizona State Federation of Labor were present at the demonstration, the result being that the amendment passed and became part of the code in 1913.

Arizona miners had altered the development of productive technology to prevent disease.[22]

In Nevada the Western Federation sought to broaden the scope of dust abatement. During the summer of 1912, the Tonopah Miners' Union drafted a bill requiring not only that drills be supplied with water but also that "dry ores, in ore shoots [sic] and ore houses or ore pockets . . . be sprinkled with water . . . sufficient in degree to overcome, allay and settle the dust." The union thus aimed to minimize the silica hazard for shovelers and other laborers who raised considerable amounts of dust in performing routine tasks. This initiative received strong bureaucratic support from a state government that had only minimal professional and technical expertise. At its meeting in July 1912, the State Board of Health (with only one physician on its staff) recommended the adoption of wet drilling and ore-handling processes. The state inspector of mines also lent his authority to the reform campaign. In an annual report issued on the eve of the 1913 legislative assembly, inspector Edward Ryan shrewdly cast his concerns about the spread of silicosis in pragmatic terms. "Strong young men will . . . feel themselves gradually wasting away," he observed, "and at an age when a man is ordinarily at his best he finds himself unfit to work underground, and the knowledge gained by years of experience is lost to himself and the industry." Citing recent findings on the alarming prevalence of this disorder among Australian gold miners, Ryan argued that "what is true in regard to the mines of Western Australia is equally true of the mines of this State." He endorsed protective legislation "to stop this withering blight."[23]

22. Lewis to Members of Organized Labor; Arizona State Mine Inspector, *Annual Report, 1912* (Phoenix, n.d.), pp. 3–21; Arizona, *Revised Statutes, 1913* (Phoenix, 1913), 1:1371.
23. Stephen S. Clark and Thomas McManus, Communication No. 15, in WFM, *Proceedings, 1912*, pp. 190–91; Nevada State Inspector of Mines, *Annual Report, 1912* (Carson City, 1913), pp. 10–11; Nevada State Board of Health, *Biennial Report, 1911–12* (Carson City, 1913), p. 38.

Meanwhile, the international union made its own preparations for the upcoming session. The 1912 convention had instructed the executive board "to use all possible means to have the proposed law enacted." The board sent Neil McGee to a legislative conference of the Nevada Socialist party in January 1913, where he secured the socialists' commitment to work on behalf of reform. The WFM board then instructed McGee "to remain in Carson [City] in the interest of labor legislation such time as may be directed by the President."[24]

The Nevada locals probably did not need any help from international headquarters. George Cole, a former secretary of the Tonopah local, introduced a wet-drilling proposal into the assembly and had it referred to the Committee on Mines and Mining, which he himself chaired. This measure passed both houses without a single dissenting vote and was signed into law on St. Patrick's Day.[25] A companion bill requiring the spraying of broken ore became law only with deleterious amendments. One loophole exempted mines with fewer than ten employees. Another allowed the state inspector to waive the requirement where he deemed it to be impracticable.[26] Nonetheless, the WFM had made significant progress toward the eradication of silica dust through the enactment of these laws.

The advances in Arizona and Nevada inspired union activists in other areas to demand the same protection. The convention of 1914 recommended that all locals agitate for legislation to create "a better system of ventilation, sprinkling and general sanitary conditions, as a preventative against the diseases prevalent among workers in the mining industry, especially miners' consumption." Although the federation was weak in Missouri, it indirectly influenced the passage of wet-methods legislation in that state in 1915. Ongoing organizing drives in the Joplin district pressed operators to acquiesce in reforms so as to deny the union an important issue for recruiting members.[27]

24. WFM, *Proceedings, 1912*, p. 191; Executive Board, WFM, Minute Book, 3:127 (Jan. 20, 1913), 96 (Aug. 1, 1912), 115–16 (Jan. 13, 1913), after 131 (Jan. 23, 1913), WFM-IUMMSW Archives, vol. 3; Socialist Party, "Socialist Legislators at Work," *MM*, Feb. 27, 1913, p. 10.

25. Nevada, Assembly, *Journal, 1913* (Carson City, 1913), pp. 9, 78, 90, 146, 275, 312; Nevada, Senate, *Journal, 1913* (Carson City, 1913), pp. 69, 124, 129, 178, 201; Nevada, *Statutes, 1913* (Carson City, 1913), pp. 167–68.

26. Nevada, Assembly, *Journal, 1913*, pp. 127, 163, 174, 176, 363, 368, 378; Nevada, Senate, *Journal, 1913*, pp. 153, 240, 256, 263; Nevada, *Statutes, 1913*, p. 305.

27. Committee on Good and Welfare, Report, in WFM, *Official Proceedings of the Twenty-First Consecutive and First Biennial Convention, 1914* (Denver, 1914), p. 82; Charles

Similarly, a combined effort of the miners' movement and the state mine inspector resulted in the enactment of a wet-process measure in Idaho in 1917.[28] In other states during this decade, however, dust-abatement initiatives were either defeated or gutted.[29]

Both Canadian district affiliates scored victories in this battle. District 6 led the campaign for dust prevention in British Columbia. At its 1916 convention, District President Frank Phillips called for intervention to end the silicosis epidemic:

> The Provincial Government proposes enlarging Tranquille Sanatorium, but I am convinced that prevention is better than doubtful cure, and I would urge that an amendment be made to the metalliferous mines inspection act providing that in every case where this class of drill is used, a spray system capable of keeping down the excessive dust be installed and that its use be made obligatory. I understand that in Nevada and Arizona an efficient, inexpensive and simple system has been developed and is giving every satisfaction.

During the 1918 deliberations of the provincial legislature, Marcus Martin of Local 96 lobbied hard for such an amendment while serving on the legislative committee of the British Columbia Federation of Labor. District 6 considered the law passed at this session to be "the direct result of our activity."[30]

Moyer, "Address," in ibid., p. 37; W. J. Edens (Local 217) to Editor, Apr. 4, 1913, *MM*, Apr. 17, 1913, p. 13; *Missouri Trades Unionist*, Feb. 11, 18, 25, Mar. 4, 1914; U.S. Bureau of Mines, *Pulmonary Disease in Joplin*, pp. 32, 42–44; Missouri, *Laws, 1915* (Jefferson City, n.d.), pp. 329–30. Along with the 1913 declaration of support for the Nevada wet-methods bill, the resolution of the 1914 convention disproves James Foster's contention that when the 1904 convention dealt with a desperate request for assistance by a silicotic member, it was "the only official mention of lung disease in more than twenty years" of WFM convention proceedings." See Foster, "Western Miners and Silicosis: 'The Scourge of the Underground Toiler,' 1890–1943," *Industrial and Labor Relations Review* 37 (1984): 371.

28. Idaho State Inspector of Mines, *Eighteenth Annual Report*, 1916 (N.p., n.d.), p. 13; *EMJ*, Sept. 15, 1917, p. 498; Idaho, *General Laws, 1917* (Boise, 1917), pp. 302–3.

29. *MM*, Mar. 13, 1913, p. 6, June 12, 1913, pp. 6–7, Apr. 1917; Lewis H. Eddy, "Tentative Mine-Safety Rules in California," *EMJ*, June 12, 1915, p. 1043; *EMJ*, July 17, 1915, p. 121; *MSP*, Aug. 7, 1915, pp. 202–3; California Industrial Accident Commission, *Mine Safety Rules* (Sacramento, 1915), p. 50; Utah Industrial Commission, *General Safety Orders Covering Underground Metal Mining Operations, 1919* (Salt Lake City, n.d.), pp. 33–34.

30. Frank Phillips, Report, in *MM*, Apr. 6, 1916; Marcus Martin, "B.C. Convention Report," *MM*, Mar. 1919; G. Marshall and George Dingwall (Local 38), "Report of the Rossland Miners' Union Delegates . . .," Feb. 9, 1917, *MM*, Mar. 1917; *MM*, Oct. 1917; British Columbia, *Statutes, 1918* (Victoria, 1918), pp. 159–60.

Miners in Ontario soon followed suit. Agitation by District 17 culminated in 1919 in amendments to the provincial Mining Act that not only mandated wet technology but also restricted blasting so that "workmen shall be exposed as little as practicable to dust and smoke."[31]

Hardrock unionists realized that enforcement of protective legislation was always problematic. Accordingly, the Western Federation devoted as much time and energy to the implementation of safety and health regulations as it did to their enactment. The founding convention resolved to seek "the election of competent, practical miners as mine inspectors." The two key tenets embodied in this resolution—the election of inspectors and the requirement of mining experience—guided attempts to enforce safe and healthful working conditions for the next quarter-century. Here again, democratic values governed union policy.[32]

The WFM strongly advocated the election of inspectors. Unionists believed that mining capitalists invariably had much more influence over governors than they did. Hence gubernatorial appointment predisposed against pro-miner candidates. The Legislative Committee of the Miami Miners' Union pleaded its case to Arizona governor George Hunt in 1912 in terms of lofty principles:

> Government by the people can only be maintained and democratically executed, when the people choose and dismiss their public officers, [and] special stress is placed against the appointment of mine inspector, who, unless he can be under the control of the people, can be made the bulwark over which the toilers in the mines will be forced to prevail, before they can obtain redress or conditions beneficial to them.
>   . . . Any office deemed important enough by the people to disburse their hard earned dollars in the maintenance thereof is important enough for them to control.

Bowing to this demand, the Arizona legislature passed and Hunt signed a measure requiring that the inspector be chosen every two years at the general election. Most other states, territories, and provinces, however, denied such proposals to extend democracy. Idaho

---

31. Ontario, *Statutes, 1919* (Toronto, 1919), pp. 67 (quotation), 66–67; Porcupine Miners' Union No. 145, "Why Join the Union?" *MM*, Mar. 1917.
32. WFM, "Proceedings," 1893, p. 19, Labor Collection, Berkeley.

and Nevada were the only other major mining jurisdictions to elect safety officials during this period.[33]

The union generally won its demand that inspectors be "practical miners," but too often this victory proved to be a hollow one. The pioneering Colorado law of 1889, for which the Leadville union made strenuous efforts, required that the governor appoint a man who had "a practical knowledge of the best methods of working, ventilating and timbering mines, and he must have had an experience of at least five years in mining." Subsequent legislation was drawn along the same lines.[34]

To be sure, this criterion prevented the post from becoming a haven for unqualified political hacks in need of a salary. Yet it did not prevent the selection of mine managers who opposed vigorous pursuit of safe working conditions. Although some inspectors did serve as "the conscience of the West," as Mark Wyman put it, others were notoriously soft on operators. Lenient enforcement policies prevailed in South Dakota after Governor Coe Crawford rejected the candidate proposed in 1907 by WFM locals in the Black Hills:

> Henry Lemon had the endorsement of all the labor unions for mine inspector, but Reformer Crawford never looked at the miners' petition. All they wanted to know was, who does the Homestake company want? And of course, that company wanted their old foreman, [Nicholas] Treweek, so that when men were killed or injured through the greed or carelessness of the management, the subservient mine inspector can endorse that stereotyped phrase, "no blame attaches to the company."

Overall, the federation had little success in securing the appointment or election of hardrock workers as regulators.[35]

33. Legislative Committee, Miami Miners' Union to Governor George W. P. Hunt, n.d., in *Daily Arizona Silver Belt*, Apr. 7, 1912, p. 5; Arizona, *Acts, Resolutions and Memorials, 1912, Regular Session*, p. 88; *Coeur d'Alene Miner*, July 28, 1894; *Park Record*, Nov. 3, 1906; *Tonopah Sun*, Feb. 9, 1907; O. T. Hansen, "Idaho's Dual-Purpose State Geologist," *Journal of the West* 10 (1971): 151; Nevada, *Statutes, 1909*, p. 223.

34. Colorado, *Laws, 1889* (Denver, 1889), p. 255; Idaho, *General Laws, 1893* (Boise, 1893), p. 153; Wyman, *Hard-Rock Epic*, pp. 187–88; Montana, *Laws, Resolutions and Memorials, 1889* (Helena, 1889), p. 160; South Dakota, *Laws, 1890* (Pierre, 1890), p. 263; British Columbia, *Statutes, 1897* (Victoria, 1897), p. 273; Nevada, *Statutes, 1909*, p. 218; Arizona, *Acts, Resolutions and Memorials, 1912, Regular Session*, pp. 88–89.

35. Wyman, *Hard-Rock Epic*, pp. 190 (quotation), 190–95; *Deadwood Lantern* (S.D.), n.d., rpt. in *MM*, Feb. 14, 1907, p. 5; *Coeur d'Alene Miner*, Apr. 29, 1893, p. 5; *Owyhee Avalanche*, Sept. 10, 1897, Dec. 9, 1898; Lead City Miners' Union, Minute Book, pp.

The Politics of Prevention 171

No matter who held the inspectorship, local unions insisted on rigorous enforcement of the law. In 1894 the Idaho inspector failed to respond to repeated requests to investigate thoroughly a series of fatal cave-ins in the Bunker Hill and Sullivan mine. Union activists in the Coeur d'Alene gathered more than seven hundred signatures on a petition calling for the removal of W. S. Haskins for gross negligence and incompetence. Governor William McConnell not only left mining entrepreneur Haskins at his post but also gave the protest petition to Bunker Hill management, which used it as a blacklist. Disgusted with the performance of both public servants, the WFM convention of that year appealed to "all true citizens of Idaho to unite with the common purpose . . . of relegating such capitalistic minions . . . to the oblivion their action so justly merits."[36]

Where officials wanted to ameliorate working conditions, they generally had sufficient police power to do so. Inspectors in most jurisdictions could impose fines or stop production until hazards were corrected. In Montana, however, the law of 1889 gave state agents only the power to issue notices that victims of subsequent accidents could use in court to demonstrate employer negligence. John Duggan dismissed this toothless system as "of little practical value." State Inspector of Mines John Byrne concurred. Byrne lamented restrictions forced on his office by "large mining corporations," which defeated all proposals to make him more a regulator than a spectator in the mines. He drew a dark conclusion from laissez-faire public policy: "To think that the law protects the mine owner in the right to expose his employees to dangers which constantly threaten their lives, after such dangers have been pointed out and official warning served on him, is to imagine a government that holds human life as its cheapest possession. But such is the law." As a rule, the strength of enforcement

181 (Dec. 6, 1892), 184 (Jan. 2, 1893), WFM-IUMMSW Archives, reel 53; Silver City Miners' Union, Minute Book, pp. 271–300 (July 18-Sept. 26, 1898), Silver City Miners' Union Records, vol. 1; *San Miguel Examiner*, Dec. 3, 1898; Guy E. Miller, "The Western Federation of Miners," *MM*, Mar. 27, 1913, p. 7; Dickinson, "Bisbee Warren District," p. 30. In West Virginia during this period, the United Mine Workers denounced mine inspectors as puppets of the coal operators. See David A. Corbin, *Life, Work, and Rebellion in the Coal Fields: The Southern West Virginia Miners, 1880–1922* (Urbana, Ill., 1981), pp. 16–17.

36. WFM, "Proceedings," 1894, pp. 9–10, Labor Collection, Berkeley; Ed Boyce et al. to Editor, n.d., *Butte Bystander*, Jan. 13, 1894; *Coeur d'Alene Miner*, Feb. 24, 1894, p. 1; Clancy Miners' Union, Minute Book, p. 61 (June 25, 1895), Small Collection 270, folder 1; Alfred Parr and A. J. Hughes (secretary and president, District 6), "Eight Hour Law," *Ferguson Eagle*, Feb. 14, 1900.

provisions depended upon the strength of miners' unions in the state or province. For example, rather than merely giving inspectors the option to close down unsafe operations, the WFM-sponsored law in Arizona required that they do so.[37]

A severe shortage of staff and other resources curtailed regulation throughout the region. Testifying before the U.S. Industrial Commission in 1899, Colorado miner John Sullivan claimed that he had seen only one inspector underground during the past ten years. Sullivan estimated that this official "went through a mine where there were about 200 men working in about twenty minutes." The Idaho inspector had no deputies, yet the game warden in that state had four assistants during this period. In desperation, WFM District 14 offered to pay the salary and expenses of an inspector to be stationed in its area. The state attorney general killed this plan as unconstitutional. Idaho lawmakers adamantly refused to authorize a deputy: one official had to maintain surveillance over mines separated by as much as four hundred miles. In neighboring Montana, over ten thousand metal miners were protected by an inspector with only one deputy. Fish and game in the state were protected by a warden with twenty deputies.[38]

Even under these constraints, government regulators eliminated or reduced significantly many safety hazards. Aggregate data clearly demonstrate a decline in the rate of fatal accidents following implementation of inspection laws. Inspectors ordinarily forced abatement of the most flagrant threats to life and limb such as unguarded chutes and shafts, lack of a protective cage for hoisting, improper storage of dynamite, and inadequate timbering.[39]

37. John Duggan to Editor, Feb. 19, 1894, *Butte Bystander*, Feb. 24, 1894; Montana State Inspector of Mines, *Annual Report*, *1902*, pp. 11 (quotation), 18 (quotation), 9–18; James Doyle (mine operator, Victor, Colo.), "Testimony," July 18, 1899, in U.S. Industrial Commission, *Report*, 12:369; Montana, *Laws, Resolutions and Memorials, 1889*, p. 162; idem, *Laws, Resolutions and Memorials, 1903* (Helena, 1903), p. 180; Arizona, *Acts, Resolutions and Memorials, 1912, Regular Session*, p. 92; Colorado, *Laws, 1889*, p. 257; Idaho, *General Laws, 1893*, p. 154; British Columbia, *Statutes, 1897*, p. 275.

38. John C. Sullivan, "Testimony," July 18, 1899, in U.S. Industrial Commission, *Report*, 12:358; *Idaho Avalanche*, Feb. 19, 1897; *Owyhee Avalanche*, June 16, 1899; Idaho State Inspector of Mines, *Eighth Annual Report, 1906* (N.p., n.d.), pp. 13–14; idem, *Annual Report, 1913*, pp. 7–8; idem, *Twentieth Annual Report, 1918* (N.p., n.d.), pp. 26, 31; Leslie Lurnes, Henry Rutz, and Sam Kilburn (District 14) to Walter H. Hanson (Idaho state senator), Oct. 20, 1913, in *MM*, Nov. 6, 1913, pp. 9–10; Montana Department of Labor and Industry, *Biennial Report, 1913–14*, pp. 263, 265; District Association 6 to E. G. Pryor (premier of B.C.), May 28, 1903, Mine-Mill Papers, box 154, folder 2; Moudy, "Cripple Creek Miner," p. 382; Wyman, *Hard-Rock Epic*, pp. 188–89.

39. U.S. Bureau of Mines, *Metal-Mine Accidents, 1920*, pp. 73–75; Montana Inspector

Inspectors even made some progress in controlling underground air contamination. Edward Ryan shut down a section of the Belmont mine in Tonopah in 1912 and "personally compelled the management to connect air pipes into the bad places."[40] Nevada officials also enforced the wet-methods laws. Reporting in 1914 that "very little trouble has been experienced in getting the operators to comply," inspector Ryan enumerated the remedial measures he had ordered in a number of mines. But he unhappily conceded that in some instances workers "have shown no disposition to take advantage of this humane law, but continue eating dust." Addressing the inevitable conflict between the pressure to produce and the time-consuming task of hauling water for spraying, Ryan urged managers both to allow their employees enough time to use prescribed procedures and to make water more readily accessible. Arizona unions not only demanded strict adherence to wet-methods regulations but also challenged productivity demands that undermined healthful work practices. WFM leader Charles Tanner confronted the hard realities of enforcement:

> We have a law . . . providing that a spray must be furnished when required and the law is generally complied with, but the poor devil who has a family to support and a job to hold knows full well that if he protects his lungs by fooling with a spray, he won't get as much work done as the manager has told the foreman to tell his shifters to tell him he must do if he wants to work there, and so it goes. . . .
>
> Above all, we need organization to speak for the worker on the job, so that when the manager tells the foreman to tell the shifter to tell the men what constitute [sic] a day's work that the men will have an organization to tell the shifter to tell the foreman to tell the manager that we are going to have something to say about what constitutes a day's work: that we intend to have something to say about the conditions under which men work.

As always, implementation of government regulations depended critically on the ability of workers' organizations to resist intimidation of and discrimination against those who exercised their rights.[41]

of Mines, *Report, 1902*, p. 22; Nevada State Inspector of Mines, *Report, 1913–14*, pp. 9, 15–26; idem, *Report, 1917–18*, pp. 14–17; Arizona State Mine Inspector, *Annual Report, 1912* (Phoenix, n.d.), pp. 4–21.

40. *Manhattan Post*, Sept. 21, 1912, p. 4; Nevada State Inspector of Mines, *Report, 1912*, p. 64; Arizona State Mine Inspector, *Report, 1912*, pp. 3–4; idem, *Annual Report, 1914* (Phoenix, n.d.), p. 7.

41. Nevada State Inspector of Mines, *Report, 1913–14*, pp. 8 (quotation), 8–9, 17–24;

Workers' compensation also stimulated advances in accident prevention. By compelling employers to pay insurance premiums to cover
a share of their injured employees' lost wages and medical expenses,
compensation laws introduced a significant financial incentive for the
amelioration of working conditions. Obviously, this system of social
insurance was not limited to the mining, milling, and smelting of
metals; it clearly resulted from larger social and political forces outside
the industry. Hence a thorough discussion of this subject is beyond
the scope of this study.[42] Nonetheless, the miners' important contribution to the initiation, enactment, and implementation of compensation reform in the West merits attention.

In the dark age before workers' compensation, the costs of mine
injuries and illnesses were borne almost entirely by the victims, their
families, their unions and other mutual benefit organizations, and the
community at large. The only course of remedial action open to the
disabled worker or the surviving dependents of a deceased worker
was to file a lawsuit for damages against the employer. In doing so,
however, plaintiffs confronted formidable, if not insurmountable, obstacles to recovering damages.

The most important source of evidence for a legal action involving
a fatality came from the inquest conducted by the county coroner's

Charles H. Tanner to Editor, n.d., *MM*, May 4, 1916; Nevada State Inspector of Mines,
Report, 1915–16, pp. 9, 13, 41; idem, *Biennial Report, 1919–20* (Carson City, 1921), pp.
13, 31, 41–42; *Arizona Labor Journal*, n.d., rpt. in *MM*, July 1918; Alice Hamilton, "[Notes
on meeting with] Dean Scarlett, Phoenix," Jan. 12, 1919, Alice Hamilton Papers, box
2, folder 37, Schlesinger Library, Radcliffe College, Cambridge, Mass.; Idaho State
Inspector of Mines, *Report, 1917*, pp. 13–14; idem, *Twentieth Annual Report, 1918* (N.p.,
n.d.), p. 49; *EMJ*, Sept. 15, 1917, p. 498; British Columbia Minister of Mines, "Report,"
1919, in British Columbia, *Sessional Papers, 1920*, 2:N287–91; H. I. Young and A. J.
Lanza, "Underground Mine Sanitation," in National Safety Council, *Proceedings of the
Sixth Annual Safety Congress, 1917* (N.p., n.d.), p. 1351. For a useful contemporary study
of the role of shopfloor organization in minimizing dangerous intensification of labor,
see Leon Grunberg, "The Effects of the Social Relations of Production on Productivity
and Workers' Safety: An Ignored Set of Relationships," *International Journal of Health
Services* 13 (1983): 621–34.

42. I concede that by limiting my analysis of workers' compensation in this way I
preclude the possibility of revealing the classwide political alliances that I contend the
WFM-IUMMSW eschewed in favor of special-interest campaigns. Unquestionably, in
most instances the drive for compensation legislation involved the union in broader
alliances. Yet even these movements encompassed less than the entire working class,
ignoring the interests of agricultural laborers and workers in industries deemed not
"especially dangerous." For examples of truncated compensation laws which covered
only mining and other selected industries, see British Columbia, *Statutes, 1902* (Victoria,
1902), pp. 317–18; Nevada, *Statutes, 1911* (Carson City, 1911), pp. 363–64; Arizona,
Laws, Resolutions and Memorials, 1912, Special Session (Phoenix, 1912), pp. 23–24; Montana, *Laws, Resolutions and Memorials, 1915* (Helena, n.d.), pp. 175–77.

jury. Mine owners manipulated these investigations either by influencing the coroner (who was often the company doctor) or by intimidating witnesses. In 1894, a committee of Coeur d'Alene miners denounced a jury that had failed even to visit the site of a fatal accident. The committee also lambasted the acting coroner for refusing to select experienced miners as jurors, damning him as "an apostate from justice and active, subservient tool in the hands of the mine managers." Noting the exonerative reports of two recent inquests, John Duggan questioned the universal tendency to blame the victim. "Tis somewhat strange that nobody is ever to blame for these accidents," observed Duggan, "unless it be the unfortunate victims who of course are beyond the possibility of blaming anybody." Although individual lapses of judgment and inescapable dangers of underground work unquestionably accounted for a share of accidents, mine operators and their agents alleged that these two factors caused virtually all injuries.[43]

Prevailing legal doctrines made operators virtually invulnerable. In the late nineteenth century, three common-law principles provided potent defenses—assumption of risk, contributory negligence, and negligence of fellow employees. Employers contended that merely by accepting a job the worker assumed all the risks thereof. For instance, the Oliver Iron Mining Company asked applicants for employment in the 1900s an apparently innocuous question: "Are you familiar with the nature of the work, the manner of its performance, and the duties which, if employed, you will be called upon to perform?" By giving the affirmative answer necessary to obtain a job, the applicant took responsibility for any subsequent injuries deemed somehow inherent in "the nature of the work." Moreover, regardless of his own role in causing an accident, the operator could defend himself by pointing to any aspect of the victim's behavior that in any way contributed to his mishap. In addition, defendants escaped liability by identifying negligent actions of the victim's co-workers, including foremen and

43. Edward Boyce et al. to Editor, n.d., *Butte Bystander*, Jan. 13, 1894; John Duggan to Editor, Jan. 10, 1894, ibid.; *Butte Daily Miner*, Mar. 4, 22, 1887; [Edward Boyce], "The Dangers of Mining," *MM*, Jan. 1901, pp. 10–11; Montana State Inspector of Mines, *Report, 1902*, p. 18; Coroner's Jury, Kaslo, B.C., Report, Mar. 21, 1907, Mine-Mill Papers, box 156, folder 3; South Dakota, State Inspector of Mines, *Annual Report for the Year Ending November 1, 1908* (Sioux Falls, S.D., 1908), pp. 14–18; William Thompson, Thomas Collins, and Sam Birce (Local 145), "In Memoriam," *MM*, Feb. 6, 1913, p. 14; *San Miguel Examiner*, Feb. 17, 1906.

other low-level managers, whom the law considered merely "fellow servants" of the mine owner. Besides these ideological advantages, employers usually hired superior legal experts. Sam Kilburn of the Wallace Miners' Union complained that Coeur d'Alene operators were "able to command the best legal talent by reason of their wealth . . ., [but] the widow and orphans have difficulty in getting a good lawyer." Miners and their survivors received little compensation through the courts.[44]

The WFM joined the growing movement to abrogate these legal barricades. In 1901 union attorney Murphy attacked the outmoded defenses as "monstrous and barbarous." "The time is ripe," he asserted, "since the courts are so loth to change or modify the doctrine, to do so by carefully drawn statutes." The Tonopah local drew up an employers' liability bill and presented it to the 1903 Nevada legislature. Despite backing from two lawmakers who were members of Local 121, the measure failed. Four years later Nevada joined several other mining states in invalidating traditional bulwarks against liability. The 1910 convention ordered the executive board to "have a comprehensive employers' liability law drawn and submitted to the local unions of the Federation to the end that concerted political action may be taken by the membership." Delegates at this convention also urged local and district affiliates to sue employers on behalf of members "where gross negligence has resulted in death or injury."[45]

But increasing employers' vulnerability to lawsuits did relatively little for accident victims. The judicial process still meant lengthy

44. Oliver Mining Company, Application Blank, rpt. in *MM*, May 6, 1909, p. 7; Sam Kilburn to Our Fellow Workmen, n.d., *MM*, Apr. 15, 1909, p. 11; *Great Falls Daily Tribune*, May 1, 1903, p. 8; *Silverton Weekly Miner*, Apr. 22, 1904; *Park Record*, June 22, 1907; Montana Department of Labor and Industry, *Report*, *1913–14*, p. 16; Wyman, *Hard-Rock Epic*, p. 123; Phipps, "Bull Pen," pp. 139–40. Needless to say, workers in other industries had the same problem with the legal system. See Gersuny, *Work Hazards and Industrial Conflict*, pp. 45–97; Brody, *Steelworkers in America*, pp. 91–92; Licht, *Working for the Railroad*, pp. 197–201.

45. John H. Murphy, "The Law of Negligence," *MM*, Aug. 1901, pp. 8 (quotation), 8–11; WFM, *Proceedings, 1910*, pp. 279 (quotation), 280 (quotation), 25–26, 279–80, 352–53; Press Committee, Local 121, to Editor, Feb. 6, 1903, *MM*, Apr. 1903, p. 45; *MM*, Dec. 31, 1908, p. 3; Executive Board, WFM, Minute Book, 2:83–84 (Jan. 11, 1909), WFM-IUMMSW Archives, vol. 2; Joe F. Hutchinson to Editor, Mar. 2, 1909, *MM*, Mar. 18, 1909, p. 11; Charles H. Moyer, "Report," in WFM, *Proceedings, 1911*, p. 29; British Columbia, *Statutes, 1891* (Victoria, n.d.), pp. 25–35; Colorado, *Laws, 1901* (Denver, 1901), pp. 161–62; Montana, *Laws, Resolutions and Memorials, 1903* (Helena, 1903), pp. 156–57; Nevada, *Statutes, 1907* (Carson City, 1907), pp. 437–38; Idaho, *General Laws, 1909* (Boise, 1909), pp. 34–38.

delays and uncertain awards. Further, workers who took their employers to court lost any hope of returning to their old jobs. The management of the Great Falls smelter routinely suspended workers pending settlement of their accident claims. Managers at this plant also helped their claims agents reach inexpensive out-of-court settlements by estimating the likelihood of the employee's destitution. Specifically, the accident reporting forms used by Anaconda in 1910 included the item: "If a family man, the probable condition of his family as to being needy or otherwise." Although some victims or their survivors took advantage of employers' new liability to win substantial awards, the majority still recovered little or nothing. A decade after the enactment of liability legislation in Montana, the Department of Labor and Industry concluded that "only a small percentage of the victims . . . are receiving adequate and proportionate compensation for the loss sustained."[46]

Together with other unions, the WFM began to press for a no-fault system of compensation. In 1902 British Columbia adopted a Workmen's Compensation Act modeled after the British act of 1897. Unlike the German arrangement under which a fixed schedule of benefits became the exclusive remedy for injured workers, the Canadian plan permitted accident victims a choice. Those who believed they could establish their employer's culpability were free to sue; defendants were restricted in their use of the assumption-of-risk and fellow-servant doctrines. Alternatively, those unwilling to gamble on a suit could collect half pay for disability. The act granted three years' wages to surviving dependents of workers killed on the job. If there were no dependents, the law covered only medical and burial expenses. Despite the limitations on its automatic benefits, this law heralded a new approach to accident compensation.[47]

Miners in the United States did not immediately seize upon this innovation. Along with the rest of the labor movement in this country at the turn of the century, the WFM considered workers' compensation

46. James O'Grady (manager, Great Falls smelter), Accident Reporting Rules, Jan. 8, 1910, Anaconda Records, box 210, file 601–1; Montana Department of Labor and Industry, *Report, 1913–14*, p. 16; J. C. Tallon, "Unpaid Accident Claims," Dec. 17, 1908, Anaconda Records, box 208, file 397–3; *San Miguel Examiner*, Dec. 13, 1902; Idaho State Inspector of Mines, *Fourteenth Annual Report, 1912* (N.p., n.d.), p. 13.

47. British Columbia, *Statutes, 1902*, pp. 314 (quotation), 313–22; Harold F. Underhill, "Labor Legislation in British Columbia" (Ph.D. dissertation, University of California, Berkeley, 1935), p. 65.

doomed to judicial invalidation on grounds of unconstitutionality. By 1910, however, the union was ready to try to import this reform. In part, the same financial crisis that had curtailed the federation's hospital program impelled it to seek relief from the onerous burden of disability and death benefit payments. In 1909 Charles Bunting of District 6 made an invidious comparison between the policy of the United Mine Workers (UMW) and that of his own organization. "The U.M.W. of A. have . . . abolished sick benefits from their unions and have several paid officers in the field continuously," observed Bunting. "They also strictly enforce the workmen's compensation act, having collected about $70,000 for their members up to date in British Columbia, while we have done nothing in this respect." Bunting closed his argument by pointing out that enforcement of this law had driven employers to adopt safety measures, which, in turn, had significantly reduced the injury rate in the coal mines of the province. District 6 responded to this challenge by retaining an attorney to pursue compensation matters. This lawyer not only handled individual cases but also worked with the UMW to win the right of nonresident dependents to benefits.[48]

WFM leaders encouraged emulation of the Canadian plan in 1910. "The compensation act which has been a law in British Columbia for some time has, to a large extent, protected the life and limb of the mine workers in that locality," concluded the executive board. "We believe that agitation for similar laws in the different states should be started." Before the year was over, the union and its allies had scored a major victory on this issue in Arizona. Bringing strong pressure to bear on delegates framing the new state constitution, the WFM-dominated territorial labor movement secured constitutional provisions compelling the first session of the Arizona legislature to enact laws giving the injured worker the option of automatic benefits or the right to sue his employer, who was barred from invoking traditional defenses. Appropriate measures were duly enacted in 1912. President Moyer singled out the Arizona constitution as "a living example of

48. Charles Bunting, "Report of Fraternal Delegate Bunting of District 6," *MM*, Apr. 8, 1909, p. 10; John A. McKinnon, "The Annual Convention of District Association No. 6," *MM*, Feb. 10, 1910, p. 10; L. P. Eckstein (District 6 attorney) to A. Shilland, May 21, 1910, Mine-Mill Papers, box 157, folder 4; A. Shilland (secretary-treasurer, District 6), Report on Meeting of Mar. 15, 1914, ibid., box 156, folder 9; L. P. Eckstein, Report to District 6, July 17, 1911, in WFM, *Proceedings, 1911*, pp. 234–38.

what can be accomplished by concerted action of the working class on the political field."[49]

The union pressed forward with attempts to enact legislation on the English-British Columbian model elsewhere. The executive board proudly reported to the 1911 convention that a union-supported measure "modeled after the British Compensation Act" had passed in Nevada. At the same time the board acknowledged a recent setback in Montana: "An effort was made to have a Compensation Act along the lines of the English Compensation Act passed, but the corporate interests were so strongly entrenched in the legislature of Montana that our efforts were defeated." They then reminded local activists of "the necessity of continuing efforts to . . . place the task of caring for those who have been maimed and crippled and the dependents of those who have lost their lives in the mad race for profits, where it properly belongs, as a part of the cost of production."[50]

Despite its early inroads, the English version of workers' compensation did not prevail in the hardrock mining region (or anywhere in the United States). Under mounting pressure from organized labor and its allies, employers largely abandoned their adamant opposition to social insurance. In 1914 socialist leader A. Grant Miller summarized this shift in policy: "The master class did all they could to prevent it for many years . . ., but finally they perceived that legislation was inevitable and they changed their tactics and got in to make the law and make it as harmless to themselves as they could." Capitalists in mining and other major western industries accepted legislation pro-

49. Executive Board, "Report," in WFM, *Proceedings, 1910*, p. 220; Charles Moyer, "Report," in WFM, *Proceedings, 1911*, p. 42; Executive Board, "Report," Jan. 14, 1911, *MM*, Jan. 26, 1911, p. 8; Arizona, *Constitution*, 1910 (N.p., n.d.), pp. 33–34; idem, Constitutional Convention, *Minutes* (Phoenix, n.d.), pp. 62, 67, 382–84; *MM*, July 7, 1910, p. 11; Tru A. McGinnis, "The Influence of Organized Labor on the Making of the Arizona Constitution" (M.A. thesis, University of Arizona, 1931), pp. 70–73; James D. McBride, "Henry S. McCluskey: Workingman's Advocate" (Ph.D. dissertation, Arizona State University, 1982), pp. 178–80; Arizona, *Acts, Resolutions and Memorials, 1912, Regular Session*, pp. 491–95; idem, *Acts, Resolutions and Memorials, 1912, Special Session*, pp. 23–25.

50. Executive Board, "Report," in WFM, *Proceedings, 1911*, pp. 48–49; Charles Moyer, "Report," in ibid., pp. 42–43; ibid., pp. 285–86, 318–19, 350–51; Charles H. Tanner (WFM lobbyist, Carson City, Nev.), "Report," Mar. 18, 1911, *MM*, Apr. 6, 1911, p. 11. Tanner and the Executive Board either were ignorant of or chose to overlook flaws in the Nevada statute that made the compensation option less than automatic in cases where the contributory negligence of the employee was more than "slight." See Nevada, *Statutes*, 1911, pp. 362–67.

viding meager benefits, long waiting periods, and other restrictions designed to minimize their financial obligations. Employers also insisted upon making compensation an exclusive remedy for injured workers, eliminating the option of suing for damages. Unlike the more urbanized eastern and midwestern states, the Rocky Mountain states lacked sizable numbers of middle-class Progressive reformers sympathetic to workers' needs in this matter. For example, in 1912 not one of the sixty-one members of the General Administrative Council of the American Association for Labor Legislation resided between Minneapolis and San Francisco. Hence, there was no one like John B. Andrews in Idaho or Montana. By 1917, the leading western mining states had established stingy programs based on the German system. Labor activists were able to force this issue onto the political agenda, but they lacked the power to determine the structure and substance of the reforms enacted.[51]

Workers' compensation plans ordinarily excluded occupational disease. The WFM made a pioneering effort to extend coverage to include work-related diseases, especially silicosis. Once again, British Columbia miners broached the issue. In January 1913 District 6 resolved to demand "such amendments to the Workmans Compensation Act as will bring within the scope of its benefits those men suffering from

---

51. A. Grant Miller, "Proposed Amendments to the Compensation Law," *Nevada Socialist*, Oct. 26, 1914, p. 4; American Association for Labor Legislation, *Proceedings of the Fifth Annual Meeting, 1911*, in *American Labor Legislation Review* 2 (1912): 156–57 and passim; Richard B. Roeder, "Montana Progressivism: Sound and Fury and One Small Tax Reform," *Montana* 20 (Oct. 1970): 18–26; Michael P. Malone and Richard B. Roeder, *Montana: A History of Two Centuries* (Seattle, 1976), p. 202; James Cuthbertson (Local 105) to Officers and Delegates of District Association No. 6, n.d., *MM*, Apr. 24, 1913, p. 9; California, *Statutes, 1913* (San Francisco, 1913), pp. 279–320; Nevada, *Statutes, 1913*, pp. 137–53; Colorado, *Laws, 1915* (Denver, 1915), pp. 515–87; Montana, *Laws, Resolutions and Memorials, 1915*, pp. 168–218; Idaho, *General Laws, 1917* (Boise, 1917), pp. 252–94; Utah, *Laws, 1917* (Salt Lake City, n.d.), pp. 306–38. For states in which labor found greater support from middle-class Progressives, see John D. Buenker, *Urban Liberalism and Progressive Reform* (1973; rpt. New York, 1978), pp. 42–79; Robert F. Wesser, "Conflict and Compromise: The Workmen's Compensation Movement in New York, 1890s–1913," *Labor History* 12 (1971): 345–72; Irwin Yellowitz, *Labor and the Progressive Movement in New York State, 1897–1916* (Ithaca, 1965), pp. 107–27; Robert Asher, "Workmen's Compensation in the United States, 1880–1935" (Ph.D. dissertation, University of Minnesota, 1971), pp. 229ff.; idem, "Communications," *Labor History*, 13 (1972): 312–16. The National Civic Federation, which in James Weinstein's loose interpretation decisively shaped compensation policy for both capital and labor, may have influenced the attitudes of some major western mining firms but hardly preempted debate over this issue. Needless to say, the federation's seduction of Samuel Gómpers (if indeed it can be credited with such a seduction) did nothing to moderate the radicalism of the WFM on this issue. Cf. James Weinstein, *The Corporate Ideal in the Liberal State: 1900–1918* (Boston, 1968), pp. 43–55.

such diseases as lead poisoning, miners Pthisis [sic] et cetera." This demand was probably a response to both the enactment the preceding year of the Miners' Phthisis Compensation Act in South Africa and the growing agitation for disease compensation in the United States by the American Association for Labor Legislation.[52]

Unionists in both British Columbia and Ontario carefully tracked legislative developments throughout the British Empire. District 14 achieved an important breakthrough in 1914, when the Ontario legislature passed "An Act to provide for Compensation to Workmen for Injuries sustained and Industrial Diseases contracted in the course of their Employment." Copied directly from the English law of 1906, the short schedule of six compensable illnesses included two significant afflictions of metal mining and smelting—lead poisoning and hookworm disease. But, as in Britain, silicosis was not on the list. Two years later, British Columbia adopted an identical schedule. In 1917 Ontario followed the South African model by making "miners' phthisis" a compensable condition. Despite repeated efforts by District 6, British Columbia did not authorize silicosis benefits until 1936.[53]

Union advocacy of compensation for occupational disease proved to be fruitless in the United States. The WFM convention of 1914 went on record in favor of "a compensation act covering all diseases as well as the life and limb of workers" and encouraged locals to agitate on this matter. But the federation's politically active affiliates were preoc-

---

52. F. C. Campbell, W. F. Fleming, and James Cuthbertson (delegates, District 6 convention), "Resolution No. 5," n.d. [Jan. 1913], Mine-Mill Papers, box 156, folder 8; *MM*, Jan. 23, 1913, p. 6; *British Columbia Federationist*, n.d., rpt. in *MM*, Feb. 6, 1913, p. 14; *EMJ*, Sept. 28, 1912, p. 603; John B. Andrews, "Legal Protection for Workers in Unhealthful Trades," in Second National Conference on Industrial Diseases, *Proceedings, 1912*, rpt. in *American Labor Legislation Review* 2 (1912): 359; *MM*, Mar. 13, 1913, p. 8. My interpretation of the origins of occupational disease compensation differs from that of James Foster in *"The Western Dilemma*: Miners, Silicosis, and Compensation," *Labor History* 26 (1985): 275. Foster's emphasis on English developments is misleading: England was merely following the South African example of 1912. Before 1918, English policy actually obscured the issue of silicosis compensation. Thomas Legge frankly acknowledged that the Committee on Compensation for Industrial Diseases, appointed in 1906 to determine which disorders to include under England's reformed compensation law, decided to exclude silicosis so as to prevent mass discharges of incipient silicotics. See Thomas Legge, "Industrial Diseases under the Workmen's Compensation Acts," *Journal of Industrial Hygiene* 2 (1920): 26, 29–32; idem, *Industrial Maladies* (London, 1934), pp. 21, 31.

53. Ontario, *Statutes, 1914* (Toronto, 1914), pp. 150–88; idem, *Statutes, 1917* (Toronto, 1917), p. 213; Porcupine Miners' Union, "Why Join the Union?" *MM*, Mar. 1917; British Columbia, *Statutes, 1916* (Victoria, 1916), pp. 344, 372; idem, *Statutes, 1936, 2d Session* (Victoria, 1936), pp. 191–94; Underhill, "Labor Legislation," p. 78; Moyie Miners' Union (Local 71, B.C.), "Resolution No. 7," *MM*, Mar. 1919.

cupied with winning, retaining, or enforcing more rudimentary concerns such as increased benefits for accidents and shorter waiting periods. To be sure, some militants demanded reform. Charles Tanner repeatedly urged that Arizona's plan be extended to "throw the mantle of protection over the wasted form and dependent family of the worker stricken with miners' consumption or other industrial disease." Yet this state did not compensate victims of work-induced disease until 1943. With the defeat in 1921 of a union-supported bill to include silicosis under Nevada's insurance program, the last of the early initiatives ended in futility.[54]

Failure to control occupational diseases through workers' compensation partly explains the union's increasing interest in comprehensive health insurance and related welfare measures to ameliorate the plight of the sick and injured. In response to a request from the American Association for Labor Legislation, the 1916 convention voted to endorse the principle of compulsory health insurance and urged union officials to "cooperate with the various organizations working . . . for the enactment of such a law." The IUMMSW convention two years later went further, demanding "the enactment of adequate universal workmen's health insurance laws, . . . [under] democratic administration, with commercial insurance companies excluded." The *Miners' Magazine* buttressed this position by publishing a steady stream of propaganda for health insurance legislation. Nonetheless, among major mining centers only California (where the union's influence was inconsequential) and British Columbia seriously considered such legislation.[55] The WFM-dominated Arizona State Federation of Labor led the initiative campaign that in 1914 created the first state old-age pensions in the United States. This law was instantly declared unconstitutional.[56]

54. WFM, *Proceedings, 1914*, pp. 82 (quotation), 82–83; Charles H. Tanner to Editor, n.d., *MM*, May 4, 1916; Tanner to Editor, June 1, 1915, *MM*, July 1, 1915, p. 4; McBride, "McCluskey," pp. 214, 270–86; Foster, "*Western Dilemma*," pp. 278–81; Frank W. Ingram (Nevada labor commissioner) to Henry S. McCluskey, Mar. 1, 1921, McCluskey Collection, box 3, folder 8. I have found no evidence that the 1915 amendments to the California law, incorporating all diseases, had any immediate practical benefit for mine, mill, and smelter workers.

55. WFM, *Proceedings, 1916*, pp. 156–57, 94; IUMMSW, *Proceedings, 1918*, pp. 22–23; Socialist Party, "The National Platform," *MM*, June 6, 1912, p. 7; *MM*, Apr. 6, 1916, p. 1, Feb. 1917, Mar. 1917, Sept. 1918; John B. Andrews, "Bringing Medical Science to the Aid of the Wage Earner," *MM*, May 1918.

56. Thomas A. French, "History of the Arizona State Federation of Labor," *Arizona*

Campaigns to establish public hospitals for miners also generally failed. During the 1890s the WFM considered building its own "home or retreat for disabled miners, especially those afflicted with 'miners' consumption'"; but this plan died because of insufficient interest.[57] The union then sought to emulate coal miners' success in obtaining state hospitals in eastern states.[58] Movements for special nursing facilities emerged throughout the metal-mining region in the years before World War I. Campaigns in Arizona, British Columbia, Nevada, Utah, Idaho, and California all went down to defeat. The Arizona legislature in 1915 rejected a proposal by Western Federation activists to establish a hospital "especially devoted to the reception, care and treatment of miners afflicted with occupational diseases."[59] Nevertheless, the WFM and its allies did manage to score two small victories. The territorial government of Alaska founded the Pioneers' Home at Sitka in 1913, "primarily . . . for aged and infirm prospectors," and added a hospital wing in 1918.[60] In Montana, "agitation for years by the Miners' Union and citizens of Butte" culminated in 1912 in an act providing a state sanitarium near Warm Springs for victims of tuberculosis and miners' consumption.[61] Overall, very few metal miners with chronic disease or other serious impairments found refuge in special state long-term care facilities in the early twentieth century.

Labor Journal, n.d., rpt. in *MM*, July 1920, p. 2; Charles H. Tanner to Editor, June 1, 1915, *MM*, July 1, 1915, p. 4; Arizona, *Acts, Resolutions and Memorials, 1915* (N.p., n.d.), pp. 10–11.

57. *Butte Bystander*, May 24, 17, 1896, June 5, 1897, p. 5; Gold Hill Miners' Union, Minute Book, p. 571 (Aug. 10, 1896), Gold Hill Miners' Union Records, Nevada Historical Society; Haywood, *Bill Haywood's Book*, p. 71; Lead City Miners' Union, Minute Book, pp. 427 (Aug. 17, 1896), 604–6 (Jan. 2, 1899), WFM-IUMMSW Archives, reel 53; Edward Boyce, "President's Report," in WFM, *Proceedings, 1901*, p. 13.

58. Alexander Trachtenberg, *The History of Legislation for the Protection of Coal Miners in Pennsylvania, 1824–1915* (New York, 1942), pp. 96–98; Stevens, "Sweet Charity," pp. 304–5; *United Mine Workers Journal*, Sept. 12, 1912, p. 2; U.S. Bureau of the Census, *Benevolent Institutions, 1910*, pp. 362–63; *Arizona Labor Journal*, June 10, 1915, p. 1.

59. Miners' Hospital Bill, rpt. in *Arizona Labor Journal*, June 17, 1915, p. 1; *Arizona Labor Journal*, Apr. 1, 1915, pp. 1, 3, June 10, 1915, p. 1, June 17, 1915, pp. 1, 2, June 24, 1915, pp. 1, 2, July 1, 1915, p. 1, Jan. 26, 1917, p. 1, Feb. 9, 1917, p. 1; H. S. McCluskey, "Report," Feb. 26, 1919, *MM*, Mar. 1919; Julius Hadley and J. J. Bennett to Editor, Jan. 18, 1897, *Idaho Avalanche*, Jan. 22, 1897; *Tonopah Miner*, Feb. 23, 1907; *Tonopah Sun*, Jan. 2, 1909; John A. McKinnon (President, District 6), "Report," *MM*, Feb. 10, 1910, p. 11.

60. *American and Canadian Hospitals*, 2d ed. (Chicago, 1937), p. 1297; *Miners' Union Bulletin*, Dec. 6, 1909.

61. *EMJ*, June 29, 1912, p. 1289; Montana Legislative Council, *Montana Code Annotated* (Helena, 1983), 7:378; *Kendall Miner*, Mar. 2, 1906; *EMJ*, Oct. 5, 1912, p. 661; *Great Falls Daily Tribune*, Jan. 19, 1913, p. 3.

The WFM pursued no consistent parliamentary strategy. On some issues its spokesmen maintained extreme positions, holding to demands that were impossible to attain in view of the prevailing balance of forces. For example, the organized miners backed Populist demands for employers' liability and eight-hour legislation in the Rocky Mountain states in the early 1890s. The Socialist party of America, on whose platform numerous union leaders ran, advocated comprehensive social insurance as early as 1904. The 1902 platform of the Socialist party of British Columbia went beyond insurance proposals, demanding "government hospitals throughout the province, and free medical attendance to all needing such." Throughout this period, radical groups shaped the union's political positions to a considerable extent.[62]

But even impossibilism had pragmatic uses. Radical demands served, on occasion, to broaden the political spectrum and thereby make liberal proposals look more reasonable. In the 1913 session of the Nevada legislature, Democrat George Cole's wet-methods bill appeared innocuous when juxtaposed to Socialist I. F. Davis's far more stringent measure. Mining capitalists acquiesced in the passage of Cole's bill. Extreme propositions sometimes had more than just heuristic value.[63]

Third-party ventures achieved mixed results. Candidates from Socialist and other minor parties divided the working-class vote and occasionally helped defeat Democrats sympathetic to reform. But if the reality of third-party slates was at times deleterious, the threat of such undertakings gave miners and their allies in the labor movement considerable clout. The Goldfield Miners' Union helped force the compromise that led to Nevada's eight-hour law. "Yes, unionism and socialism accelerated the action taken," boasted Local 220, "the former urging the eight-hour bill and the latter demanding a constitutional amendment, [so that] the astute politician U.S. Senator [Francis G.]

62. *Lardeau Eagle*, Feb. 20, Jan. 30, 1902; Lonsdale, "Eight Hour Law in Colorado," p. 33; Thomas A. Clinch, *Urban Populism and Free Silver in Montana* (Missoula, Mont., 1970), pp. 47ff.; *Coeur d'Alene Miner*, July 28, 1894; Underhill, "Labor Legislation," p. 65; WFM, *Proceedings, 1905*, p. 324; Executive Board, "Report," Minute Book, 1:419 (Dec. 15, 1906), WFM-IUMMSW Archives, vol. 1; *Park Record*, Nov. 3, 1906; *Nevada Socialist*, Sept. 1914, p. 4; Phipps, "Bull Pen," pp. 83–84; Socialist Party, "The National Platform. . .," *MM*, June 6, 1912, p. 7; *MM*, Nov. 1901, p. 29, Dec. 3, 1903, p. 6, July 14, 1904, p. 5; W. F. Burlison to Editor, n.d., *Arizona Labor Journal*, Oct. 6, 1916, p. 1; Dubofsky, "Western Working Class Radicalism," pp. 140–43, 151–53.

63. *MM*, Feb. 13, 1913, p. 10; Socialist Party, "Socialist State Legislators at Work," *MM*, Feb. 27, 1913, p. 10; Nevada, Assembly, *Journal*, 1913, p. 146; Nevada, *Statutes*, 1913, pp. 167–68, 305; F. A. Campbell, W. F. Fleming, and James Cuthbertson, Resolution No. 5, n.d. [Jan. 1913], Mine-Mill Papers, box 156, folder 8.

Newlands guarantee[d] the latter providing the Socialists refrained from putting in a ticket to embarrass his chances for election as senator."[64]

The transition to statehood afforded Arizona miners an unparalleled opportunity to use this threat. Immediately upon the passage of federal legislation enabling statehood, organized labor set out to help write the state constitution. The Bisbee Miners' Union organized a conference in July 1910 to formulate a set of labor articles. In their conference call, Local 106 leaders Thomas Stack and W. E. Stewart gave unionists a strong inducement to participate. "The working class . . . has the power to make this constitution to its own liking," they contended, "and if it is properly drafted, our economic struggles of the future will be greatly simplified, and our efforts to better our conditions rendered much easier." This meeting not only agreed upon a long list of demands but also created a Labor party to run a slate in the election of delegates to the constitutional convention. The WFM loaned the new party money to publish a newspaper to disseminate its demands. This initiative immediately forced the Arizona Democratic party to agree to labor's program in exchange for dissolution of the independent slate. The resulting coalition swept the election of convention delegates and wrote a constitution that mandated strong mine safety, workers' compensation, and other protections. The first session of the state legislature had no choice but to pass the specified reforms.[65]

The union also influenced mainstream parties, especially the Democrats, in more mundane ways. Despite the consistent socialist policy of the international union and the strength of radical sentiment in many locals, the hardrock miners remained a politically diverse group. Throughout the early twentieth century, far more western miners

64. Press Committee, Local 220, to Editor, Aug. 5, 1904, *MM*, Aug. 18, 1904, p. 12; Press Committee, Local 121, to Editor, Feb. 6, 1903, *MM*, Apr. 1903, p. 45; *EMJ*, Nov. 5, 1910, p. 924; *Idaho Avalanche*, Oct. 30, 1896; *Slocan Drill*, Apr. 27, Oct. 26, 1900, Sept. 18, 1903, Nov. 18, 1904; Sandon *Paystreak*, Sept. 22, Dec. 8, 1900; Schwantes, *Radical Heritage*, pp. 163–67.
65. Thomas Stack and W. E. Stewart, "To All Working Class Organizations in Arizona," June 29, 1910, rpt. in *MM*, July 7, 1910, p. 10; Unnamed Bisbee miner to Editor, June 30, 1910, *MM*, July 7, 1910, p. 11; Byrkit, *Forging the Copper Collar*, p. 41; Labor Party of Arizona, *Labor's Declaration of Independence* (N.p., n.d. [1910]); Executive Board, WFM, Minute Book, 3:48 (Aug. 3, 1910), WFM-IUMMSW Archives, vol. 3; McGinnis, "Arizona Constitution," pp. 30–36, 70–78, 96; McBride, "McCluskey," pp. 175–78; Moyer, "Report," in WFM, *Proceedings, 1911*, p. 42; *Daily Arizona Silver Belt*, Jan. 21, 1912, p. 1.

voted for the Democratic party than the Socialist party. Many local leaders worked as Democratic activists and ran as Democratic candidates. After the turn of the century, Democrats routinely advocated such measures as mine inspection and shorter hours: a politician did not need be a Socialist to support the eight-hour day. Hence, in large part the reforms won in this period can be viewed simply as modest rewards to a significant Democratic constituency within the mining districts.[66]

The WFM set up state and provincial organizations to serve as levers for moving politicians of all parties. In 1902 the accomplishments of District 6 led the *Miners' Magazine* to advocate the creation of analogous bodies in the United States. "If the unions in each state had a state miners' union . . . to promote legislation," speculated President Boyce, "the time would soon come when each state would have upon its statute books laws calculated to protect the miner in his dangerous occupation and in his rights against the attacks of corporations." State and district organizations proliferated wherever the union maintained more than a handful of locals. Their primary functions were to coordinate lobbying, endorse candidates, draft bills, and help launch independent slates. During the electoral campaign of 1908, the state union in California extracted commitments from candidates to support pending eight-hour legislation. Officers of the group then followed through with a lobbying effort that brought about hours reform in the next legislative session.[67]

WFM locals also actively participated in state and provincial labor federations. James Cuthbertson reported to District 6 that the 1913 convention of the provincial federation had approved all the resolu-

66. Jensen, *Heritage of Conflict*, pp. 70, 102; Wyman, *Hard-Rock Epic*, pp. 250–51; Laslett, *Labor and the Left*, pp. 255, 267–68; *Silverton Weekly Miner*, Nov. 14, 1902, Oct. 23, Nov. 13, 1908, Nov. 8, 1912; *Owyhee Avalanche*, Sept. 12, 1902; Press Committee, Telluride Miners' Union, to Editor, Nov. 10, 1902, *MM*, Dec. 1902, pp. 46–47; Frank Holten to A. Shilland, July 19, 1903, Mine-Mill Papers, box 154, folder 4; *Kendall Miner*, Nov. 9, 1906; *Tonopah Miner*, Aug. 22, 1908; *Park Record*, Oct. 10, Nov. 7, 1903; W. Ashton Taylor (Local 45) to Editor, Mar. 2, 1908, *MM*, Mar. 19, 1908, p. 7; *Rawhide Press-Times*, June 3, 1910; *MM*, Mar. 11, 1909, p. 10.

67. [Edward Boyce], "State Miners' Unions," *MM*, Jan. 1902, pp. 13–14 (quotation), 13–15; P. Mertz, G. C. Nebeker, and E. M. Arandale (Local 44), "For an Eight-Hour Day," *MM*, Oct. 23, 1908, p. 9; *MM*, Mar. 18, 1909, p. 6; Lead City Miners' Union, Minute Book, pp. 547 (Apr. 18, 1898), 609 (Jan. 9, 1899), WFM-IUMMSW Archives, reel 53; John Gallagher and Albert Ryan (president and secretary-treasurer, Arizona State Miners' Union) to Officers and Members of Arizona State Miners' Union, Nov. 1, 1905, rpt. in *MM*, Nov. 16, 1905, p. 12; *Park Record*, Oct. 17, 1903, Oct. 8, 1904.

tions he had introduced, including a demand for renovation of the compensation system. Cuthbertson boasted that "the Unionists of the coast are pretty well satisfied that the miners of the interior form the backbone of the B.C. Provincial Federation of Labor." The Rawhide Miners' Union called the conference in 1910 that formed the Nevada State Labor League. The league, which assumed the political functions of a state labor body, elected Rawhide miner John H. Malloy its president. After the WFM reaffiliated with the AFL in 1911, it became more deeply involved in the federations throughout the region. Hardrock unionists played a prominent role in founding the Arizona State Federation of Labor in 1912, electing E. B. Simonton of the Globe local as the organization's first president.[68]

Clearly, the WFM was deeply committed to seeking political remedies to health and safety problems. This review of almost thirty years of political activism supports the view that too much should not be made of the union's two-year involvement with the Industrial Workers of the World. The real syndicalism of the Western Federation derived from its bedrock assumption that local unions represented the fundamental institutional building blocks of socialist society, not from a rejection of politics. Even some locals that sympathized with the IWW remained committed to parliamentary reform. For example, the Press Committee of the Porcupine, Ontario, local gave only qualified support to the Wobblies: "We do not agree with the tactics as a whole of the I.W.W. We are strong advocates of political action, but do not intend to lose sight of the economic power."[69]

68. James Cuthbertson, "Report," *MM*, Apr. 24, 1913, p. 9; *Silverton Weekly Miner*, Mar. 20, 1903; *Rawhide Press-Times*, June 3, 10, 1910; William S. Lunsford (secretary, Nevada State Labor League), "The Nevada Labor Convention," *MM*, July 7, 1910, p. 12; *Daily Arizona Silver Belt*, Jan. 21, 1912, p. 1; Thomas A. French, "History of the Arizona Federation of Labor," *Arizona Labor Journal*, n.d., rpt. in *MM*, July 1920, p. 2; *MM*, Sept. 3, 1903, p. 4; Arizona State Federation of Labor, *Preamble, Declaration of Principles, and Constitution, 1916* (N.p., n.d.), p. 3.
69. Harold E. Bothy, James D. Cluney, and F. Mahoney to All Local Unions, Mar. 10, 1912, *MM*, Apr. 11, 1912, p. 7; Jensen, *Heritage of Conflict*, pp. 169–70; Wyman, *Hard-Rock Epic*, pp. 235–38, 241–42; Laslett, *Labor and the Left*, pp. 257–58, 264. Jensen, Laslett, and Wyman all circumscribe the union's commitment to syndicalism and discuss the federation's commitment to politics. Wyman does, however, argue that setbacks suffered in Colorado in the years 1903–5 "proved to be the final blow in propelling the federation away from supporting political action" (p. 233) for the period 1905–7. Even this contention is too strong. After all, the gubernatorial candidate of the Colorado Socialist party in 1906 was WFM Secretary-Treasurer Bill Haywood (see Haywood, *Bill Haywood's Book*, p. 202). In any case, the syndicalist stereotype has persisted because

Faced with exceedingly dangerous working conditions, miners could not afford to ignore any approach that might eliminate or minimize hazards. Unionists realized that even small regulations such as requiring lids on ore chutes could save many lives. Still, they had no illusions about the many limitations and pitfalls of preventing hazards through state intervention. As a committee of the convention of 1914 put it, "We realize that it is impossible to secure adequate protection under the present system, yet we are not unmindful of the many laws for the protection of labor upon the Statute Books . . ., placed there through the power of our economic organization."[70] Whereas desperation bred anarchosyndicalism in some miners, it merely intensified reformism in a far larger number of them. Hence, despite innumerable setbacks and illusory gains, the WFM persisted in its attempts to ameliorate working conditions through political agitation.

---

of the WFM's leadership in founding the IWW, not because of simplistic interpretations by historians of the union.

70. Committee on President's Report, "Report," in WFM, *Proceedings, 1914*, p. 244; W. S. Reid to Editor, Feb. 26, 1909, *MM*, Mar. 11, 1909, p. 9.

8 | *The New Paternalism*

A is for *accident* which we try to avoid.
B is for *bandage* which should be employed.
C is for *care* and for *carelessness* too.
D is for *damage* which from the latter ensue.
E is for *eyes* which goggles protect.
F is for *feet* you must not neglect.
G is for *ginmill* which we do abhor.
H is for *habit* throw it out at the door.
I is for *insurance* which you do collect.
J is for *Jay* who insurance does neglect.
K is for *kindness* which cannot be bought.
L is for *laborer* which 'sistance is sought.
M is for *manager* whose friendship you make.
N is for *noodle* which you must not break.
O is for *optimist* be glad your alive.
P is for *pension* for which all do strive.
Q is for *quarrels* which we do not like.
R is for *ringleader* a good man to spike.
S is for *superintendent* not a bad guy.
T is for *town* to keep it spotless we try.
U is for *united* which we all strive to be.
V is for *villain* who will not agree.
W is for *willing* this our men we do find.
X is for *xylophone* played by some at night time.
Y is for *yap* who always is late.
Z is for *zealous* for this you get great.
— American Smelting and Refining Company, 1915

During the first quarter of the twentieth century, the old paternalism of company doctors and bunkhouses gave way to a new

welfare capitalism of corporate health plans and safety engineers. Safety and workers' compensation legislation stimulated increased efforts by managers of mines, mills, and smelters to eliminate hazards. At the same time, elaborate employer-sponsored health care and welfare programs developed in this industry. These reforms attacked not merely health care and safety problems but the "labor problem" itself. By the 1920s union traditions of self-help had been undermined and, in large measure, eclipsed.

Bureaucratic methods of managing labor grew out of profound economic changes. The extraction and processing of metal-bearing ores became increasingly oligopolistic after the turn of the century. The decisive turning point was 1899, the year the organization of the American Smelting and Refining Company (ASARCO) and the Amalgamated Copper Company greatly accelerated the centralization of capital. By the end of World War I, 63 enterprises accounted for 70 percent of U.S. ore production. The balance within the industry swung sharply away from precious metals and toward industrial commodities, especially copper, lead, and zinc. Capital invested in extracting base metals more than tripled between 1909 and 1919, surpassing $1 billion, while investment in gold and silver mining declined. Large enterprises such as Phelps Dodge, Nevada Consolidated Copper, Calumet and Hecla, and Anaconda dominated production of industrial metals. By 1920 most mine, mill, and smelter workers toiled for companies with more than five hundred employees.[1]

Economic rationalization fostered more enlightened labor policies among leading corporations. Beyond the need to comply with legal requirements, farsighted managers saw a strategic advantage in preventing occupational hazards. Employers hoped that a new image of benevolence would attract and retain better employees, undercut unionism, and eliminate class conflict. The American Mining Congress proclaimed in 1915 that the "day of 'rough neck' tactics has passed." From this perspective, management had to reduce friction by communicating with workers. "Nine tenths of all strife is due to misunderstanding," insisted the *Mining Congress Journal*. "The fraction is even greater when applied to labor strife." Benevolent despot James

---

1. U.S. Bureau of the Census, *Fourteenth Census, 1920*, vol. 11: *Mines and Quarries, 1919* (Washington, 1922), pp. 364–69; idem, *Fourteenth Census, 1920*, vol. 10: *Manufactures, 1919* (Washington, 1923), pp. 849–54; Fell, *Ores to Metals*, pp. 218–76; Marcosson, *Metal Magic*, pp. 57–113; idem, *Anaconda*, pp. 95–166.

Douglas of Phelps Dodge contended that "the great mass of the . . . wage earners must be converted from strikers and slaves to the present system of unionism." ASARCO announced that its wide-ranging welfare endeavors sought "to earn [the employees'] loyalty and confidence, and to give them sound reasons for believing that the Company's interest is their interest."[2]

Some corporate leaders also believed that welfare programs could directly increase productivity and profits. "The provision of good board, lodging, medical treatment, and means of recreation for mine workers is no longer regarded by wise managers as philanthropy or paternalism, but as good business," contended Telluride mine superintendent L. F. S. Holland. Addressing the American Institute of Mining Engineers in 1915, J. Parke Channing of Miami Copper promoted the industrial service movement in narrow business terms. "The inevitable tendency of the day," observed Channing, "is toward 'industrial betterment,' 'safety,' 'industrial education,' 'efficiency,' and many other things which have become so familiar to progressive employers. There is no longer any question that these things are worth while from both the human and economic standpoints. They 'pay' in dollars and cents." Conservation of human resources became an economic necessity during the acute labor shortages of World War I.[3]

The first two decades of the twentieth century witnessed a proliferation of new types of welfare measures by mine, mill, and smelter operators. Besides influences outside the industry, the long-standing paternalism of the Michigan copper barons and of firms like the Homestake Mining Company helped guide these initiatives. Company housing projects expanded beyond the erection of crude bunkhouses to include construction of tracts of family homes. Operators built elaborate recreational facilities and clubhouses, as well as subsidizing

2. Editorial, "Day of 'Rough Neck' Tactics Has Passed," *Mining Congress Journal*, Oct. 1915, p. 544; James Douglas, quoted in H. H. Langton, *James Douglas, A Memoir* (Toronto, 1940), p. 114; ASARCO, Circular 344, Mar. 7, 1917, rpt. in *EMJ*, Mar. 21, 1917, p. 507; Editorial, "Taking Care of the Workman," *MSP*, Nov. 16, 1912, pp. 616–17; Sam Lewisohn (Miami Copper Co.) to Editor, Oct. 18, 1920, *MSP*, Nov. 6, 1920, pp. 651–53; Division of Industrial Cooperation, American Mining Congress, "Platform," *Mining Congress Journal*, Sept. 1923, p. 187.

3. L. F. S. Holland, "Welfare Work among Mine Workers," *MSP*, Nov. 14, 1914, p. 747; J. Parke Channing, "Enlarging the Worth of the Worker and the Perspective of the Employer," in American Institute of Mining Engineers, *Transactions* 51 (1916): 365; Charles F. Willis, "Physical Examination prior to Employment," in ibid. 63 (1920): 599; *EMJ*, Nov. 6, 1915, p. 759; *Great Falls Daily Tribune*, Jan. 13, 1918, sec. 2, p. 1; Alanen, "The 'Locations,'" p. 98.

YMCA branches in their communities. Bunker Hill and Sullivan in 1911 built an industrial YMCA in Kellogg, Idaho, on the exact site on which twelve years earlier the military had erected a bull pen to incarcerate union supporters. Unlike its predecessor, the YMCA had a swimming pool, bowling alleys, and reading and class rooms. It also held the offices of the company union. In their ambitious efforts to Americanize immigrants, employers offered instruction in the English language, modern homemaking skills, and a host of other subjects. Some firms even experimented with pseudo-democratic employee representation schemes.[4]

The Safety First movement formed an essential part of the new welfare capitalism. In fact, campaigns to protect workers against occupational hazards were among the most common welfare provisions, both in metal mining and in other industries.[5] Unlike most other components of corporate welfarism, this program penetrated into daily social relations on the job. Safety First had a special strategic value to employers: it vitiated the union's traditional role as the guardian of working conditions.

U.S. Steel provided an influential model for the safety crusade in nonferrous metals. The giant steelmaker began to systematize the accident-prevention activities of its subsidiaries in 1906. This work culminated in the formation of a Bureau of Safety, Sanitation, and Welfare in 1911. A wide-ranging program of inspection, education, administrative reform, and technological change produced immediate results: the number of serious accidents at the firm fell 43 percent in four years.[6] The contiguity of the ferrous and nonferrous metals in-

---

4. Gates, *Michigan Copper*, pp. 93–115; James MacNaughton, "Welfare Work of the Calumet and Hecla," *EMJ*, Sept. 26, 1914, pp. 575–77; W. H. Moulton, "The Sociological Side of the Mining Industry," *EMJ*, Oct. 30, 1909, pp. 860–63; Reed, *Medical Service of Homestake*, passim; John A. Goodell, "Friendliness versus Friction at the Bunker Hill and Sullivan," *MSP*, Jan. 9, 1915, pp. 57–58; Phipps, "Bull Pen," p. 141; A. M. Heckman, "Social Betterment in Arizona," *MSP*, Feb. 1, 1919, pp. 158–60; Leifur Magnusson, "A Modern Copper Mining Town," *Monthly Labor Review* 7 (1918): 278–84; Marcosson, *Metal Magic*, pp. 262–81; T. A. Rickard, "Men and Machinery," *MSP*, Apr. 6, 1918, pp. 471–72; *Park Record*, June 20, 1903; Smith, *Song of the Hammer and Drill*, p. 158; *Arizona Silver Belt*, Feb. 16, 1908, p. 4; Garcia, *Desert Immigrants*, pp. 221–22.

5. U.S. Bureau of Labor Statistics, *Welfare Work for Employees in Industrial Establishments in the United States*, Bulletin 250 (Washington, 1919), pp. 16–18; Gerd Korman, *Industrialization, Immigrants and Americanizers: The View from Milwaukee, 1866–1921* (Madison, 1967), pp. 110–35; Graebner, *Coal-Mining Safety*, pp. 146–48; Brody, *Workers in Industrial America*, p. 59; *MSP*, June 21, 1913, p. 941; B. F. Tillson, "Accident Prevention by the New Jersey Zinc Co.," *EMJ*, Dec. 12, 1914, p. 1034.

6. Brody, *Steelworkers*, pp. 165–68; Lew R. Palmer, "History of the Safety Movement,"

dustries facilitated dissemination of this plan. "The mining industry in particular has gained from the example set by [U.S. Steel] in the splendid work of humanizing industry," noted the *Engineering and Mining Journal.* "The two metal-mining subsidiaries, the Oliver Iron Mining Co. . . . and the Tennessee Coal, Iron and Railroad Co. . . . have set the safety standards now followed by several other mining companies." Phelps Dodge, for instance, set up a safety department after sending a representative to tour U.S. Steel plants. Programs in smelting, such as the one initiated by ASARCO in 1913, drew their inspiration from the same source.[7]

Although a few companies introduced safety work before the advent of workers' compensation, most were driven to take up this activity only by the passage of legislation. Surveying recent developments, the Montana Industrial Accident Board concluded in 1919 that "compensation laws brought the Safety First crusade." Phelps Dodge miner W. E. Holm unappreciatively explained his employer's newfound interest in accident prevention: "Shortly after the organized workers of Arizona forced the capitalist lawmakers to place on the statute book a compulsory compensation and employers' liability law this mighty BOSS deemed it advisable to form what is known as the 'safety first,' or in other words, 'save the dollar first' organization." The *Engineering and Mining Journal* reported in 1914 that compensation laws increased employers' costs "without doubt" and cited the case of a large Nevada mining and smelting concern whose expenditures for its injured employees had more than tripled since the enactment of legislation. "In such circumstances," editorialized the *Journal,* "the cheapest way to pay for accidents is not to have them. This is the economic basis of the 'Safety First' movement."[8]

Annals of the American Academy of Political and Social Science 123 (Jan. 1926): 9–12, 18–19; Dianne Bennett and William Graebner, "Safety First: Slogan and Symbol of the Industrial Safety Movement," *Journal of the Illinois State Historical Society* 68 (1975): 244–46; U.S. Bureau of Labor Statistics, *The Safety Movement in the Iron and Steel Industry, 1907 to 1917,* by Lucian W. Chaney and Hugh S. Hanna, Bulletin 234 (Washington, 1918); ASARCO *Safety Review,* Aug. 1915.

7. *EMJ,* July 31, 1920, p. 217, July 19, 1913, p. 120; Marcosson, *Metal Magic,* p. 265; *MSP,* Feb. 7, 1914, p. 266, Oct. 17, 1914, p. 617; Editorial, "Accident Prevention in Smelting Works," *EMJ,* Sept. 11, 1915, p. 448.

8. Montana Industrial Accident Board, *Report, 1919,* p. 68; W. E. Holm (Local 106) to Editor, Apr. 13, 1914, *MM,* Apr. 23, 1914, p. 11; Editorial, "Workmen's Compensation Laws," *EMJ,* Aug. 15, 1914, p. 320; Arizona State Mine Inspector, *Second Annual Report, 1913* (N.p., n.d.), pp. 4–5; Ed Ryan, "Accident Prevention in Mining," *MSP,* Mar. 21, 1914, p. 499; California Industrial Accident Commission, *Merit Rating California's Mines*

The movement spread by diverse means. Trade journals widely publicized and heartily supported developments in the field. Emblazoned on the cover of the first issue of the *Mining Congress Journal* in January 1915 were the motto "Safety-Efficiency-Conservation" and a declaration, "Our Mission," which began with the vow "to reduce, so far as humanly possible, the numbers of killed and injured in mining operations." Conferences held by engineering and management groups featured numerous presentations on safety topics. The National Safety Council maintained an active mining section. Needless to say, managers communicated informally as well, often visiting one another's facilities to observe innovations.[9]

Government officials played a prominent role throughout the campaign. State and provincial mine inspectors persistently advocated the establishment and expansion of private sector programs. In January 1914 the Nevada Industrial Commission and the University of Nevada presented a Safety First conference attended by six hundred representatives of mining and other industries. Inspectors' offices served primarily as clearinghouses, gathering and distributing information on exemplary programs both within and outside their own jurisdictions. Montana authorities illuminated the successful efforts of Anaconda, ASARCO, and other leading firms in the state. The Department of Mines in British Columbia called attention to innovators like the Granby Consolidated Mining and Smelting Company and organized first-aid training classes for miners. Inspections afforded opportunities to advise or coerce management to adopt protective measures. Charged with collecting accident and compensation data, government officials publicized all indications of declining injury rates.[10]

for Compensation Insurance, by H. M. Wolflin, Bulletin 6 (Sacramento, 1917), pp. 3, 13–16; Horace F. Lunt, "Accidents in Metal Mines," *MSP*, Jan. 28, 1922, p. 117. The same forces operated in steel and coal. See Brody, *Steelworkers*, pp. 167–68; Graebner, *Coal-Mining Safety*, p. 148.

9. *Mining Congress Journal*, Jan. 1915, front cover, Feb. 1915, p. 84, Feb. 1916, p. 61; *MSP*, June 21, 1913, p. 941, Oct. 18, 1913, p. 634, Dec. 20, 1913, p. 955; Tillson, "Accident Prevention by New Jersey Zinc," pp. 1034–39; Edwin Higgins, "The Safety Movement in the Lake Superior Iron Region," in American Institute of Mining Engineers, *Transactions* 50 (1915): 755–70.

10. *MSP*, Feb. 7, 1914, pp. 266 (quotation), 266–67; Montana Department of Labor and Industry, *Report, 1913–14*, pp. 43–44; Montana Industrial Accident Board, *Third Annual Report, 1918* (Helena, n.d.), pp. 121–25; idem, *Report, 1920*, pp. 131–55; Arizona State Bureau of Mines, *State Safety News*, Apr. 1917, p. 8, Feb. 1918, pp. 2–8; Nevada State Inspector of Mines, *Report, 1913–14*, pp. 9–11; H. M. Wolflin (chief mine inspector,

The U.S. Bureau of Mines stimulated a great deal of safety work. According to the *Mining Congress Journal*, "The spread of the Safety-First idea through the mining fields was undoubtedly hastened and materially aided and advanced through the creation of the Bureau of Mines." Established in 1910, the BOM had, as its first director put it, "no authority to do anything except conduct inquiries and investigations, publish reports, and give advice." Making a virtue of necessity, the agency soon came to see education as a panacea. When, for instance, BOM engineer Edward Steidle encountered "very crude" conditions around Park City in 1917, he blithely assumed that the problem was "purely a lack of education" on the part of operators. The bureau's first report from Joplin observed that "students of safety work in mining and other industries regard educational work as the chief factor in the prevention of accidents."[11]

Aided by physicians transferred from the U.S. Public Health Service, the BOM produced a flood of informational literature — bulletins, technical papers, journal articles, circulars, and reports. Like their counterparts in state government, federal officials emphasized corporate accomplishments and technological advances. Its two major studies of silicosis notwithstanding, the agency was preoccupied with preventing injuries. Federal authorities thus reinforced the prevailing notion that occupational disease remained a relatively unimportant matter.[12]

Safety Department, California Industrial Accident Commission) to All Safety Bears, Mar. 28, 1917, *Safety Bear Letter No. 7* (N.p., n.d. [1917]); Idaho Inspector of Mines, *Report, 1918*, pp. 33, 40; *EMJ*, Nov. 4, 1916, pp. 815–16; British Columbia Minister of Mines, "Report," 1919, in British Columbia, *Sessional Papers*, 1920, 2:N291.

11. *Mining Congress Journal*, Jan. 1915, p. 17; Joseph A. Holmes, "The Work of the United States Bureau of Mines," *American Labor Legislation Review* 2 (1912): 125 (quotation), 125–30; Edward Steidle to Mr. [H. M.] Wolflin, July 21, 1917, U.S. Bureau of Mines Records, RG 70, General Records, 1910–50, box 330, file 702; U.S. Bureau of Mines, *Pulmonary Disease in Joplin*, p. 43; D. A. Lyon, "Preface," in U.S. Bureau of Mines, *Review of Safety and Health Conditions in the Mines at Butte*, by G. S. Rice and R. R. Sayers, Bulletin 257 (Washington, 1925), p. iii; Hotchkiss, "Occupational Diseases," p. 139.

12. T. T. Read (safety service director, BOM), "Some Problems of Mine Safety," *Mining Congress Journal*, Oct. 1924, pp. 473–74; U.S. Bureau of Mines, *Safety and Efficiency in Mine Tunneling*, by D. W. Brunton and J. A. Davis, Bulletin 57 (Washington, 1914); idem, *Organizing and Conducting Safety Work in Mines*, by Herbert M. Wilson and James R. Fleming, Technical Paper 103 (Washington, 1917); idem, *Metal-Mine Accidents, 1911–20* (series of annual reports); idem, *Safety Organization of Old Dominion Mine at Globe, Arizona*, by E. D. Gardner, Report of Investigation 2260 (N.p., 1921); idem, *Miners' Safety and Health Almanac for 1919*, by R. C. Williams, Miners' Circular 24 (Washington, 1918).

The BOM also administered an extensive training program in rescue and first-aid work. Using a fleet of specially equipped railroad cars, federal officials taught thousands of western miners and smelter workers the rudiments of emergency services during the 1910s and 1920s. The agency institutionalized this activity by forming chapters of the Joseph A. Holmes Safety-First Association in districts where it had trained a substantial number of workers. It also helped organize contests among rescue teams from different firms.[13]

Embracing essentially the same approach, mine, mill, and smelter management set out to teach safety to workers. Of the three major components of the accident-prevention campaign — education on work habits, administrative reform, and technological controls—education clearly predominated. In 1916 the *Engineering and Mining Journal* reported that the top priority of Anaconda's Bureau of Safety was "the elimination of dangerous practices or carelessness, and the education of the foremen and men to think and act safely." George Douglass, safety inspector at ASARCO, estimated that hazard-control technology could prevent no more than 40 percent of smelter accidents. Douglass considered eradication of the remaining 60 percent a matter of "education and right thinking."[14]

More than anything else, Safety First was a crusade against "carelessness." In the new no-fault era of workers' compensation, employers sorely needed to renovate the outmoded legalistic ideology of individual negligence. Incessant reiteration of safety messages provided a suitable new strategy of blaming the victim. Exhortations to "put safety first" and to "think" constituted a substantial share of the educational content of many programs. Signs, posters, banners, bulletins, pamphlets, leaflets, and speeches hammered away with simple slogans and platitudes. At a dinner hosted by the Liberty Bell Mining

13. U.S. Bureau of Mines, *Experiment Stations of the Bureau of Mines,* by Van H. Manning, Bulletin 175 (Washington, 1919), pp. 12–15; A. J. Lanza to Assistant Surgeons, Rescue Cars 1, 2, and 5, Sept. 13, 1917, U.S. Bureau of Mines Records, RG 70, General Records, 1910–50, box 239, file 58566; John Boardman (BOM) to Western Federation of Miners, July 16, 1914, in WFM, *Proceedings, 1914,* p. 18; *EMJ,* July 17, 1915, p. 122, July 8, 1916, p. 106; *Mining Congress Journal,* Feb. 1916, p. 61, May 1925, p. 228; C. W. Goodale and John L. Boardman, "Bureau of Safety of Anaconda Copper Mining Company," in American Institute of Mining and Metallurgical Engineers, *Transactions* 68 (1923): 12, 14.

14. *EMJ,* Feb. 26, 1916, p. 382; George M. Douglass, "Safety Appliances in Smelteries and Refineries," *EMJ,* July 20, 1918, p. 105; *Anode,* Feb. 1915, p. 11; *MSP,* Mar. 25, 1916, p. 450; W. H. Parker (Safety First Department, Great Falls smelter) to A. E. Wiggin (general superintendent), June 19, 1918, Anaconda Records, box 233, file 1311.

Company of Telluride, 135 employees were treated to an evening of oratory "warning them against thoughtlessness and carelessness." The back of the menu for this event bore inspirational messages, such as "I will think before I act" and "I will do all I can to make Liberty Bell the safest and best mine to work in." At the other extreme, messages that focused on practical solutions to specific hazards tended to belabor the obvious. The precautions suggested in one poem were hardly necessary:

> When you're loading up your round,
> In the stope or on the ground. Safety First.
> Cut your fuses plenty long,
> For your powder's good and strong,
> Or you may be a long time gone. Safety First.
>
> . . . . .
>
> So now, boys, it's up to you
> In whatever you may do
> Always keep in mind the rule—Safety First.
> If you disregard the same
> You will surely be to blame,
> And you'll land down where you cannot quench your thirst.

Blunt admonitions to obey company rules were central to this approach to worker education.[15]

Concomitant administrative reforms did, however, mitigate victim blaming. Corporate leaders placed much of the responsibility for accident prevention on their subordinates in the management hierarchy. In the inaugural issue of the *Anode*, Anaconda's monthly safety magazine, C. F. Kelley, vice president, and C. W. Goodale, director of the Bureau of Safety, declared that the company "expects all Superintendents and Foremen to make every effort to prevent injury to employees." Safety engineer J. J. Carrigan illuminated the culpability of low-level supervisors: "Statistics show that nearly eighty percent

15. *EMJ*, May 8, 1915, p. 810; John A. Stevens, "Safety First," *Anode*, Mar. 1915, p. 16; Chauncey L. Berrien, "Safety First in the Mines," ibid., p. 1; W. C. Capron, "Discipline and Education to Prevent Accidents," ibid., pp. 10–11; Mine Inspector, Arizona Copper Co., "Report for Six Months Ending Mar. 31, 1914," Arizona Copper Co. Records, box 110, folder 1; idem, "Report . . . for the Year Ending September 30, 1919," ibid., folder 3; *MSP*, Feb. 28, 1914, p. 394, Oct. 17, 1914, p. 617; Nevada Consolidated Copper Co., *Safety Bulletin*, Apr. 1914, rpt. in *EMJ*, May 23, 1914, p. 1069; *EMJ*, Mar. 14, 1914, p. 587.

of mine accidents are the result of carelessness of the employee. From these figures it must not be inferred that the employee is entirely responsible, as a man may become thoughtless and careless owing to the attitude displayed by his foreman or shift boss, in not watching or insisting that a man works carefully and keeps his place in a clean and tidy condition." Long accustomed to blaming foremen in order to escape legal liability for injuries, top management adapted the obsolete fellow-servant doctrine to the new realities of accident prevention.[16]

Foremen had to try to enforce lengthy codes of rules. Employees received rule books which prescribed and proscribed a myriad of work practices; foremen received incentives to see that regulations were followed. Anaconda awarded cash prizes to supervisors whose crews incurred the fewest accidents. ASARCO presented gold watches to foremen credited with completing a year without an injury to any of their workers. Corporate bureaucrats used the stick as well as the carrot. Anaconda's general mine superintendents reprimanded foremen and shift bosses under whose command preventable mishaps occurred. According to those in control of the firm's safety program, "This kept the foremen and bosses well lined up on the safety work." Employers also tried to discipline workers who broke rules with reprimands, layoffs, or dismissal. The efficacy of these sanctions, however, depended on the state of the labor market. During the labor shortage created by World War I, management had to abandon efforts to apply regulations strictly.[17]

16. C. F. Kelley and C. W. Goodale, "Announcement," *Anode*, Jan. 1915, p. 3; J. J. Carrigan, "Notes on Prevention of Mine Accidents," ibid., p. 4; Thomas Cowperthwaite (safety inspector, Calumet and Arizona Mining Co.), "Safety Organization and Method of Operating and Maintaining Interest among Shift Bosses and Foremen," in National Safety Council, *Proceedings of the Tenth Annual Safety Congress, 1921* (N.p., n.d.), pp. 459–62; Edward Ryan, "Accident Prevention in Mining," *MSP*, Mar. 21, 1914, pp. 498–99; W. J. Olcott, "General Instructions from the President," in Oliver Iron Mining Company, *Safety Regulations* (N.p., 1912), pp. 6–7.

17. Goodale and Boardman, "Bureau of Safety," pp. 25–26 (quotation), 16–27; Montana Department of Labor and Industry, *Report, 1913–14*, p. 310; U.S. Bureau of Mines, *Rules and Regulations for Metal Mines*, by W. R. Ingalls, James Douglas, J. R. Finlay, J. Parke Channing, and John H. Hammond, Bulletin 75 (Washington, 1915), pp. 9, and passim; Oliver Iron Mining Co., *Safety Regulations*, pp. 4, 6–7, and passim; Douglass, "Safety Appliances," p. 109; *EMJ*, Mar. 21, 1914, p. 629, Mar. 20, 1915, p. 542, Feb. 26, 1916, p. 382, Jan. 13, 1917, p. 125; Arizona, *State Safety News*, May 1916, pp. 8–11; Great Falls Reduction Department, Anaconda Copper Mining Co., *Instructions and Rules to Prevent Accidents to Employees*, 1914 (N.p., n.d.). The bonus system offered foremen an inducement to cover up accidents. See U.S. Bureau of Mines, *Safety Organizations in Arizona Copper Mines*, Technical Paper 452 (Washington, 1929), p. 5.

The Safety First movement led to technological safeguards for many common hazards. Such simple measures as erecting guardrails, shielding the moving parts of machinery, and providing splashguards for furnaces prevented innumerable injuries. Mining and smelting concerns also made significant advances in systematically ventilating their facilities. Not all hazard-control technologies involved reengineering the workplace; many, if not most, required workers to wear personal protective equipment. ASARCO covered its smelter workers with felt hats, goggles, woolen shirts, aprons, and leggings to avoid burns from spills and splashes of matte and slag. Safety shoes and respirators came into widespread use.[18]

Although engineering measures were generally less important than educational and administrative initiatives, engineers directed most safety programs. Montana's Industrial Accident Board reported in 1918 that a new corporate bureaucracy was emerging "under the direction of specialists." Safety departments in major corporations made rules, produced educational materials, inspected facilities, and collected accident data. Smaller operators obviously could not mount such ambitious efforts. The California Metal Producers Association hired BOM engineer Edwin Higgins to oversee its Mother Lode Mine Safety Association. Members of the association shared Higgins's services, and each retained its own mine inspector. Based on his investigation of the Calumet and Arizona Mining Company, A. W. Allen concluded in 1922 that "the safety engineer has become an integral part of the modern industrial machine." Thus entrenched, the role of these engineers and the nature of their programs remained essentially unchanged for the next half-century.[19]

Safety committees aided the engineers. Although arrangements var-

18. Douglass, "Safety Appliances," pp. 105–9; ASARCO *Safety Review*, Aug. 1915, Oct. 1915, Aug. 1916; Boardman, "Safety in Mining," pp. 102–4; John W. Luther, "Industrial Hygiene as Practiced at Palmerton, Pennsylvania," *MSP*, May 16, 1914, p. 810; *MSP*, Feb. 28, 1914, p. 394, Apr. 24, 1915, p. 658; Charles A. Mitke (Phelps Dodge Corp.), "Practice of Mine Ventilation," in National Safety Council, *Proceedings of the . . . Seventh Annual Congress, 1918* (N.p., n.d.), pp. 1089–93; U.S. Bureau of Mines, *Underground Ventilation at Butte*, by Daniel Harrington, Bulletin 204 (Washington, 1923), passim; Cash, "Labor in the West," p. 241.

19. Montana Industrial Accident Board, *Report, 1918*, pp. 121 (quotation), 121–25; A. W. Allen, "Accident Prevention at the Calumet and Arizona Mines and Smelter," *MSP*, Feb. 18, 1922, pp. 227 (quotation), 227–31; Marcosson, *Metal Magic*, p. 264; Cash, "Labor in the West," p. 239; *EMJ*, Mar. 3, 1917, p. 395; *MSP*, July 19, 1913, p. 86, Apr. 11, 1914, p. 626, Apr. 3, 1920, p. 502; Arizona State Mine Inspector, *Report, 1913*, pp. 4–5; U.S. Bureau of Mines, *Safety Organizations in Arizona*, pp. 3–4.

ied among enterprises, the most common plan had two tiers—a central committee of upper-echelon managers and a number of workplace committees composed of managers and workers. The central bodies set policy. Their primary function, however, was to symbolize the commitment of top executives to this issue. In contrast, the committees based at a particular mine, mill, or smelter attacked specific hazards through periodic inspections. The ASARCO *Safety Review* boasted in October 1915 that committees at its plants were "devoting their efforts to a 'fine tooth' campaign": "Where a fence should be put up, a safety chain attached, new walk ways laid, warning notices erected, safety guards . . . placed on dangerous machinery, . . . the Safety Committees have tackled the job with a vim and spirit that shows that they are genuine 'Johnnies on the Spot,' and that the Safety First movement MOVES." Though acknowledging the worth of hazard-control proposals generated by these inspections, B. F. Tillson of New Jersey Zinc emphasized that committee participation both educated the workers involved and gave a "subtle spur to the supervision of the bosses, caused by the inspection and possible criticism of their territories by a workmen's committee." Some companies also installed suggestion boxes to elicit ideas for correcting hazards. Employees suggested most of the safety devices installed at the Phelps Dodge smelter in Douglas, Arizona.[20]

Shrewd managers appropriated workers' services as well as their knowledge. Rescue and first-aid crews organized as part of the safety drive took over mutual aid functions customarily performed by informal work groups. Anaconda boasted in 1916 that its rescue corps of two hundred was the largest in the world. By 1922 the company claimed to have trained more than two thousand employees in emergency services.[21] Anaconda's C. W. Goodale and John Boardman recognized the broad ramifications of employee involvement, observing

20. ASARCO *Safety Review*, Oct. 1915; Tillson, "Accident Prevention by New Jersey Zinc," p. 1037; Marcosson, *Metal Magic*, pp. 264–67; Montana Industrial Accident Board, *Report, 1918*, p. 124–25; Dickinson, "Bisbee Warren District," pp. 41–44; *MSP*, June 21, 1913, p. 941, Dec. 19, 1914, p. 942, Apr. 24, 1915, p. 658; *EMJ*, Mar. 3, 1917, p. 395; Albert Tallon, "Maintaining Safety Interest at the Old Dominion Company," in National Safety Council, *Proceedings of the Twelfth Annual Safety Congress, 1923* (N.p., 1924), p. 656.

21. *EMJ*, Oct. 7, 1916, p. 685, Mar. 3, 1917, p. 395; Goodale and Boardman, "Bureau of Safety," pp. 13–14; *MSP*, Apr. 18, 1914, p. 670, Oct. 17, 1914, p. 617; *Great Falls Daily Tribune*, May 15, 1915, p. 5, July 23, 1915, p. 12; Idaho State Inspector of Mines, *Report, 1913*, p. 37.

that "first-aid work has . . . served the purpose, to a great extent, of popularizing the safety work." Contests between teams from different firms and different departments within a firm became major community events. Almost twenty thousand people turned out for the first Safety First Field Day in Butte on July 29, 1918. The Southwestern Mine Safety Association in Arizona held its annual mine-rescue and first-aid meet before large crowds on Labor Day, a tactic calculated to undercut union celebrations of the holiday.[22]

Overall, the Safety First movement significantly reduced injury rates. Both Anaconda and Phelps Dodge reported cutting accidental death rates roughly in half during the initial year of their safety programs. The accident rate at ASARCO's plants for the first quarter of 1915 dropped 19 percent from that of the same period in the preceding year. For all metal mines in the United States, the fatality rate declined from 4.0 per thousand full-time workers in the period 1911–15 to 3.7 for the years 1916–20. This change is remarkable considering that the World War I boom brought an influx of inexperienced workers into this industry. During the interval 1921–25, the fatal injury rate continued to fall, averaging 3.2 per thousand workers.[23]

Safety First placed the WFM-IUMMSW in a difficult, if not untenable, position. The union could hardly complain when employers installed ventilation equipment and enclosed dangerous machinery. Because it had no engineers on its staff to address the technical aspects of controlling hazards in increasingly complex industrial settings, the IUMMSW was incapable of proposing constructive alternatives to or advances beyond the plans put forward by employers. This absence of staff expertise also helped assure that it had almost no relationship with the U.S. Bureau of Mines. Instead, after 1910 the union's scarce resources had to be allocated to an endless series of desperate strikes and lockouts. Vernon Jensen's description of the federation's plight in 1914 aptly conveys its declining fortunes: "The W.F.M. never got

22. Goodale and Boardman, "Bureau of Safety," pp. 14 (quotation), 13–14, 29–30; *MSP*, July 11, 1914, p. 41, Sept. 18, 1915, p. 452, Aug. 10, 1918, p. 200; *Anode*, Sept. 1920, p. 13; *EMJ*, Aug. 19, 1916, p. 362; Arizona *State Safety News*, Apr. 1917, p. 8.

23. *EMJ*, Oct. 30, 1915, p. 734, Apr. 8, 1916, p. 659; *MSP*, Apr. 18, 1914, p. 670, Jan. 30, 1915, p. 188; ASARCO *Safety Review*, Aug. 1915; Dickinson, "Bisbee Warren District," pp. 49–50; Brown, *Hard-Rock Miners*, p. 174; Idaho State Inspector of Mines, *Eighteenth Annual Report, 1916* (N.p., n.d.), p. 5; U.S. Bureau of Mines, *Metal-Mine Accidents*, 1920, p. 75; U.S. Bureau of the Census, *Historical Statistics*, 1:607. As discussed in Chapter 2, extant data on nonfatal injuries are profoundly flawed, if not worthless. Hence this analysis is confined to fatalities.

out of trouble. If it wasn't one thing it was something else." The self-destruction of the huge Butte local and other disasters caused the WFM to lose two-thirds of its members between 1911 and 1915. Beset by intensified opposition from employers and growing internal dissension, the metal miners' organization remained too preoccupied with more pressing matters to commit itself to reshaping the safety movement.[24]

Whereas at the turn of the century the Western Federation had thoroughly criticized the institutions and ideology of early welfare capitalism, no comparable outcry met the more sophisticated safety programs and propaganda. To be sure, a handful of stalwarts denounced the limitations of employers' efforts and their ulterior anti-union motives. In a letter to the *Miners' Magazine* in 1914, W. E. Holm of Local 106 dismissed employees participating in the Phelps Dodge program as "a few pets." Yet five years later the union newspaper published without comment an article on the Miners' Safety Bear Club of California, reporting that the club's constitution was "Safety First" and its by-laws were "Think Before You Act." By October 1920 the *Miners' Magazine* was reduced to reprinting doggerel from Anaconda's safety magazine. Most surprisingly, the union failed to emphasize the simple argument that organized labor had forced the enactment of the legislation that had catalyzed most private sector reforms. Thus the accident-prevention crusade resulted in a sweeping ideological victory for its proponents.[25]

Not all union activists, however, were willing to leave the prevention of occupational hazards entirely to management. Many locals maintained an adversarial approach to cleaning up the workplace.

24. Jensen, *Heritage of Conflict*, pp. 369, 248ff; *EMJ*, Feb. 7, 1914, p. 267; *Mining Congress Journal*, Feb. 1916, p. 61, Apr. 1916, pp. 155–56; *Great Falls Daily Tribune*, June 1, 1919, p. 3; Charles Moyer, "Report," in WFM, *Proceedings, 1914*, p. 30; William D. Ryan, Address, in ibid., pp. 116–17; IUMMSW, *Proceedings, 1920*, p. 92; Wolman, *Ebb and Flow*, pp. 172–73. Similarly, the efforts of the Textile Workers Union of America to curtail the byssinosis epidemic suffered from a lack of professional staff and a substantial decline in union strength. See Charles Levenstein, Dianne Plantamura, and William Mass, "Labor and Byssinosis, 1941–1969," in Rosner and Markowitz, eds., *Dying for Work*, pp. 210, 215–20.

25. W. E. Holm to Editor, Apr. 13, 1914, *MM*, Apr. 23, 1914, p. 11; H. M. Wolflin, "Mine Inspection in California," *MM*, Mar. 1919; P. J. Holohan, "Present-Day Mining," *MM*, Apr. 16, 1916; Ben Goggin (IUMMSW organizer) to Editor, Feb. 26, 1917, *MM*, Mar. 1917; Guy E. Miller (IUMMSW organizer), "Think It Over," *MM*, Mar. 1917; *Anode*, n.d., rpt. in *MM*, Oct. 1920, p. 5; Lewis H. Eddy, "California First-Aid Meet," *EMJ*, Oct. 10, 1914, p. 646.

The Great Falls Mill and Smeltermen's Union took its complaints not to the management-dominated safety committee at the plant but rather to the Montana Industrial Accident Board. When the release of arsine gas in November 1918 killed five Great Falls workers and sickened others, Local 16 intervened. It challenged the company doctor's diagnosis of influenza and pneumonia in one fatal case and attempted to win workers' compensation for all those poisoned. More important, the union called for a state investigation of the disaster. A delegation from the local accompanied state authorities on their inspection of the smelter.[26]

Workers still occasionally resorted to strikes over hazards after the advent of Safety First programs. Beginning with a major confrontation on the Michigan copper range in 1913–14, the WFM challenged the introduction of one-man machine drills. Strikers protested the new technology on the grounds that it often forced miners to work alone, so that no partner was available to assist the victim in the event of an accident. Fluorospar miners in Rosiclare, Illinois, demanded improved ventilation when they walked out in 1916. In the aftermath of the catastrophic Speculator fire in Butte, the Metal Mine Workers' Union, a hastily organized independent group, struck for better conditions underground, including bulkheads with manholes through which workers could escape in an emergency. Finally, the IUMMSW began to negotiate agreements for increased wage payments for hazardous work. In November 1919, Local 26 and mine operators around Silverton signed a contract providing a bonus of fifty cents per day for miners sinking shafts.[27]

The structure of health care programs for employees changed considerably during the early twentieth century. Arrangements under which an independent practitioner delivered medical services and maintained his own small proprietary hospital were inadequate for

26. Great Falls Mill and Smeltermen's Union, Minute Book, 8:217 (Dec. 2, 1918), 219–20 (Dec. 9, 1918), unpaginated (Apr. 21, May 19, 1919), 9:3 (July 14, 1919), 23 (Sept. 8, 1919), WFM-IUMMSW Archives, vols. 248–49; Montana Industrial Accident Board, *Report, 1919*, pp. 93–97; *Great Falls Daily Tribune*, Nov. 9, 1918, p. 8, Nov. 11, 1918, p. 9, Nov. 13, 1918, p. 8, Nov. 16, 1918, p. 2, May 16, 1919, p. 13, June 1, 1919, p. 13.

27. Charles H. Moyer, "Address," in WFM, *Proceedings, 1914*, Appendix, p. 26; Jensen, *Heritage of Conflict*, pp. 275–88; John H. Walker, "The Rosiclare Strike," *MM*, July 6, 1916; Gutfeld, "Speculator Disaster," pp. 30–38; *EMJ*, Aug. 25, 1917, p. 363; *MSP*, Nov. 1, 1919, p. 653.

the large operations that had come to dominate metals extraction and processing. Hence many firms became involved in delivering health care through their own medical departments and company hospitals. Others devised comprehensive programs with community hospitals and physician groups.

Copper operators in northern Michigan began to build company-owned hospitals in the early 1860s. The Homestake Mining Company erected the first facility at its gold mine at Lead, South Dakota, in 1879 but continued for many years to rely on contract practitioners. In 1906 the company required that the members of its medical staff become full-time employees, forcing them to discontinue their private practices. Only a small minority of firms, however, ran their own inpatient facilities before 1900.[28]

After the turn of the century, a number of copper producers took over the delivery of health services to their workers. By 1909 there were at least ten company hospitals in Arizona. The largest of these was the Copper Queen Hospital in Bisbee, with one hundred beds. Although the Southwest was the primary locus of this trend, operators in other areas ventured into the field. The Hidden Creek mine in northern British Columbia maintained a hospital that the provincial minister of mines described as "well equipped" and "thoroughly modern" in 1917. The Kennecott Copper Company Hospital commenced operations in Latouche, Alaska, in 1910. Three district associations of mine operators set up institutions in Nevada between 1905 and 1918. Bureau of Mines surgeon Arthur Murray advised operators in 1920 that "where practical a hospital, fully equipped, should be maintained at the mine" to increase labor efficiency.[29]

28. Cash, "Labor in the West," pp. 165–68, 234–36; Gates, *Michigan Copper*, p. 104; *Medical and Surgical Register*, 3d ed., p. 745; U.S. Bureau of the Census, *Benevolent Institutions, 1904*, pp. 128–29, 162–67, 208–9.

29. British Columbia Minister of Mines, "Report," 1917, p. F370; U.S. Bureau of Mines, *The Efficiency of Mine Labor with Special Consideration of Industrial Medicine and Health Conservation*, by Arthur L. Murray, Report of Investigation 2117 (N.p., 1920), p. 4; AMA, *American Medical Directory*, 2d ed., pp. 69, 97, 689; AMA, *American Medical Directory*, 6th ed., pp. 203–4, 241, 975; *Polk's Medical Register*, 14th ed., pp. 225, 228, 265; U.S. Commissioner of Labor, *Report, 1908*, p. 624; Adolph Lewisohn (president, Miami Copper Co.), "Statement," in U.S. Commission on Industrial Relations, *Final Report and Testimony*, 9:8359; Arizona Copper Co., "Record of Patients Admitted to Hospital," 1916–17, Arizona Copper Co. Records, box 108, folder 1; L. A. Parsons, "The United Verde Smelter," *MSP*, Oct. 16, 1920, p. 548; Dickinson, "Bisbee Warren District," pp. 50–52; *EMJ*, July 12, 1913, p. 56, May 9, 1914, p. 965, July 31, 1920, p. 223; *MSP*, May 9, 1914, p. 965, July 18, 1914, p. 116; Rikard, "Experiment in Welfare Capitalism," pp. 205–38.

Most employers, however, continued to arrange with autonomous providers to care for their workers. Solo practitioners retained the business of smaller mines but were not capable of handling large groups of employees. Hence managers of sizable operations turned increasingly to capitation agreements with community hospitals. In Great Falls, Anaconda contracted with a group of physicians who, in turn, arranged for inpatient services with the Protestant and Catholic institutions in the community. Surveying the industry in the late 1920s, Pierce Williams found that "the majority of the mining companies in the [Rocky Mountain] region contract with independent hospitals to provide care to injured or sick employees at a fixed rate per employee per month, deducted from wages."[30]

The new plans increasingly brought physicians into the workplace. First-aid stations and dispensaries became commonplace at major mines, mills, and smelters. Nevada Copper maintained "emergency hospitals" at all its camps to deal with occupational accidents. The medical group responsible for the Great Falls smelter kept a physician at the plant for at least two hours per day. In a period when professional specialization was only beginning, the incumbent of this position practiced both clinical medicine and industrial hygiene. Assigned to this post in 1918, Dr. E. R. Fouts not only identified cases of lead and arsenic poisoning but also proposed a plan for eliminating these hazards. Yet as a hard-headed member of the management team, Fouts felt compelled to trivialize the very problem he was addressing: "Among the workers of the Bag House and Reverbatory [reverberatory furnace], [I] found some slight symptoms of leading, but you have to take their complaints with a grain of salt, as they are all anxious to be transferred." (Of course, the workers sought transfers primarily to escape the lead risk.) Company physicians also trained managers and workers in first aid.[31]

Preemployment medical examinations became an important part of

30. Williams, *Purchase of Medical Care*, pp. 96 (quotation), 98–109; Dr. J. H. Irwin (Great Falls), "Medical Services for Employees and Members of Their Families," July 1, 1925, Anaconda Records, box 209, file 585–9; J. T. Roberts (assistant secretary, Anaconda) and Sister Constantia (St. Ann's Hospital, Anaconda, Mont.), "Contract and Agreement," June 29, 1915, ibid., box 245, file A53.

31. Williams, *Purchase of Medical Care*, p. 101; E. R. Fouts to M. W. Krejci (assistant manager, Great Falls smelter), May 4, 1918, Anaconda Records, box 219, file 1002–1; U.S. Bureau of Mines, *Efficiency of Mine Labor*, p. 4; Holland, "Welfare Work among Mine Workers," p. 753; *MSP*, Apr. 18, 1914, p. 670, Apr. 24, 1915, p. 658; *EMJ*, July 12, 1913, p. 56; Tillson, "Accident Prevention by New Jersey Zinc," p. 1036.

corporate programs after 1910. *Mining and Scientific Press* published an editorial in 1913 entitled "Safety and Health First," which observed that "examinations are now the rule with many of the mining and smelting companies." Charles Willis of Phelps Dodge also viewed the practice as "a part of the general plan for the improvement of conditions for workmen due to its relation to the safety movement. In no other industry is the safety of a man more interwoven with that of his fellow workmen than in mining." Here again, the enactment of workers' compensation enlightened management. *Mining and Scientific Press* considered the screening practices at Phelps Dodge "the natural and inevitable result of the newer laws regarding compensation for accidents." In theory, examinations not only helped contain compensation costs but enabled management to place workers in jobs for which they were best suited physically. Some managers used medical findings to make efficient use of partially disabled individuals when labor was scarce.[32]

This system also had a dark side. When employers were not desperate for labor, they often used examinations to deny jobs to workers with insignificant health problems or with no impairments. Because the examiner's responsibility included verifying age statements on job applications, the cult of efficiency sometimes led to systematic age discrimination. A worker at Nevada Copper doubted management's assurances that those already employed had nothing to fear from such a policy: "The age limit was placed at 44 years and the examination was so severe that one-half to two-thirds could not pass it satisfactorily. The employees felt that it was only a question of time when the older men and physical incompetents would be gradually weeded out." When WFM Local 233 and other labor organizations at its Ely operations threatened to strike over this issue in October 1915, Nevada Copper abandoned examinations. Of course, by themselves examinations did nothing to aid those found to be unfit for work. In co-

---

32. Editorial, "Safety and Health First," *MSP*, Dec. 20, 1913, p. 955; Charles F. Willis, "Physical Examination Previous to Employment," in American Institute of Mining Engineers, *Transactions* 63 (1920): 601 (quotation), 598–605; Editorial, untitled, *MSP*, Mar. 28, 1914, p. 518; Luther, "Industrial Hygiene at Palmerton," p. 809; U.S. Bureau of Mines, *Efficiency of Mine Labor*, pp. 1–2; A. J. Lanza to Daniel Harrington, Apr. 15, 1918, U.S. Bureau of Mines Records, RG 70, General Records, 1910–50, box 364, file 71317. Medical examinations became widely prevalent among major employers in many industries in this period. See Angela Nugent, "Fit for Work: The Introduction of Physical Examinations in Industry," *Bulletin of the History of Medicine* 57 (1983): 578–95.

operation with the BOM, the Metropolitan Life Insurance Company, and the local post of the American Legion, the Tri-State Zinc and Lead Ore Producers Association ran a diagnostic clinic in Picher, Oklahoma, during the 1920s. This facility administered thousands of preemployment and annual screenings of mine employees. Not integrated into any comprehensive health plan and located in a depressed area where no other viable opportunities for work existed, the Picher clinic in effect treated silicosis with a dose of unemployment.[33]

Workers objected to medical evaluations as an invasion of personal privacy. In 1919 the Mine-Mill local at ASARCO's plant in Pueblo, Colorado, struck to put an end to a procedure it considered "only a humiliating farce." Anaconda refused to adopt preemployment examinations for this reason. Frederick Laist, superintendent of the smelter at Anaconda, Montana, voiced his principled opposition to A. E. Wiggin, his counterpart in Great Falls: "I have always been convinced that such prying into men's personal affairs is extremely objectionable and in the long run works much more injury than benefit to the Company's interest." Wiggin agreed, speculating that screening would cause "a great deal of complaint on the part of the men."[34]

Preemployment examinations provided a means of denying work to unionists without the appearance of discrimination. When Alice Hamilton enumerated some of the objections to health supervision at the 1915 conference of the National Safety Council, she started with "the effort to get rid of the so-called agitator." Arizona operators had to be ingenious because state law barred the use of blacklists. In 1916 the *Arizona Labor Journal* complained that medical screening gave management "an ideal 'Blacklist,' entirely within the law." After reflecting

33. "Miner" to Editor, Nov. 11, 1915, *EMJ*, Nov. 27, 1915, p. 889; U.S. Bureau of Mines, *Silicosis and Tuberculosis among Miners of the Tri-State District of Oklahoma, Kansas and Missouri—I*, by R. R. Sayers, F. V. Meriwether, A. J. Lanza, and W. W. Adams, Technical Paper 545 (Washington, 1933), pp. 26 (quotation), 4, and passim; *Manhattan Post*, Dec. 27, 1913, p. 1; A. J. Lanza to Surgeon General, Nov. 13, 1914, U.S. Public Health Service Records, RG 90, General Files, 1897–1923, box 500-L, file 5153; *EMJ*, Nov. 6, 1915, p. 759; *MM*, Feb. 3, 1916. Similarly, textile manufacturers do not take chances on new workers whose examinations disclose findings suggestive of incipient byssinosis. See Janet M. Bronstein, "The Effect of Public Controversy on Occupational Health Problems: Byssinosis," *American Journal of Public Health* 74 (1984): 1135.

34. H. S. Blackler et al. (committee, Local 43) to Editor, Sept. 20, 1919, *MM*, Oct. 1919; Frederick Laist to A. E. Wiggin, Aug. 21, 1919, and Wiggin to Laist, Aug. 23, 1919, Anaconda Records, box 236, file 1391–3.

on the peculiar difficulties of substantiating such discrimination, Thomas Quinnan of the Bisbee Miners' Union argued from circumstantial evidence against the Copper Queen and other local employers:

> Men have been rejected by these doctors and inside of one week were accepted in the United States army, where we are told the highest physical qualifications are necessary to secure acceptance.
>
> Again we have a number of cases where a man has been examined under his right name and been rejected, but again appearing under another name before the doctors, has been accepted. . . . What conclusion is left for you here? Only one, and that is, there is a blacklist.

Putting an end to these examinations became a prominent issue in the Bisbee work stoppage of 1917. The crucial encounter in this dispute occurred on July 12, 1917, when more than eleven hundred union supporters were rounded up, loaded into boxcars, transported 170 miles to Columbus, New Mexico, and left in the desert. By defeating this strike, the copper barons remained free to practice their own version of preventive medicine.[35]

Whereas the WFM-IUMMSW sought the outright abolition of medical examinations, it pursued a less aggressive policy with regard to corporate health plans as a whole. Throughout the 1890s and 1900s the federation had insisted that company programs be replaced by union hospitals. But by the 1910s, the miners' organization demanded instead that it be given a role in governing employer-administered plans.

Together with the alleged inadequacies of these programs, the autocratic nature of the wage-deduction system caused the most discontent among hardrock workers. Although some employers subsidized their programs, the bulk of revenue came from employees' check-off payments. With some exceptions, these deductions continued to be mandatory. The union convention of 1914 reiterated the democratic position that "those whose contributions maintain hos-

---

35. Alice Hamilton, "Some of the Objections to Health Supervision," in National Safety Council, *Proceedings of the . . . Fourth Annual Safety Congress, 1915* (N.p., n.d.), p. 425; Thomas Quinnan, "Miners Required to Pass Examination—Workers Claim Blacklist Is Maintained," *Arizona Labor Journal*, June 22, 1916, p. 1; Editorial, "Importance of Mine Inspector," ibid., Mar. 16, 1916, p. 4; Byrkit, *Copper Collar*, pp. 200, 158, 190, and passim; Philip Taft, "The Bisbee Deportation," *Labor History* 13 (1972): 3–40; Kluger, *Clifton-Morenci Strike*, p. 72.

pitals should decide their management and those who pay for the physician's service should have the power to hire and fire." The convention urged all locals "to take up this matter with other labor organizations or the various states and provinces and agitate for the enactment of legislation giving to the labor organization of the industry control of funds for hospital and medical attendance." Thus subsumed under the quest for state health insurance, this seed bore no legislative fruit in any mining state or province.[36]

Most reforms came through collective bargaining and direct action. Local 253 in the Silver Peak district of Nevada set precedent by negotiating a jointly controlled health care plan. A hospital administered solely by the union had failed shortly after its founding in 1907, a year of economic panic. The first-aid station maintained by the Pittsburg-Silver Peak Gold Mining Company did not meet the miners' needs. Accordingly, the local and the company signed an agreement in February 1910 to establish a fund based on wage deductions of $1.50 per month. The plan provided for a small company-built hospital, a physician to staff it, and services of "a good hospital at Tonopah or Goldfield if necessary" in serious cases. A committee of three, two of whom were chosen by Local 253, governed this program. "The union really controls the policy of this committee, which is empowered to employ and discharge a physician and to adjust all grievances which may occur," observed the *Blair Press*. Further, Pittsburg-Silver Peak agreed in 1912 to dispense with check-off contributions and pay the full cost of this program.[37]

Employers in the Southwest were not so accommodating. The health plan was one of the issues at stake when laborers at the ASARCO smelter in El Paso walked out spontaneously in April 1913. The strike committee demanded "the removal of the physician in charge of the hospital department, as this union of workers is not satisfied neither with his medical services nor with any other treatment that they receive at his hands." WFM organizer Charles Tanner arrived shortly

36. WFM, *Proceedings, 1914*, p. 63; Charles H. Moyer, Testimony, Oct. 9, 1917, in U.S., President's Mediation Commission, "Sessions at Globe," pp. 131–32, McCluskey Collection, box 4; Leifur Magnusson, "A Modern Copper Mining Town," *Monthly Labor Review* 7 (1918): 283; *EMJ*, July 12, 1913, p. 56, Apr. 22, 1916, p. 723; *MSP*, Apr. 24, 1915, p. 658, June 5, 1920, p. 847; Dickinson, "Bisbee Warren District," pp. 50–51; Montana Department of Labor and Industry, *Third Biennial Report, 1917–18* (Helena, n.d.), pp. 10–11.

37. *Blair Press*, Feb. 11, 1910, Dec. 31, 1909; Charles H. Varney et al. (Locals 252 and 253) to Editor, May 6, 1912, *MM*, June 13, 1912, pp. 10–11.

after the strike began and organized the El Paso Mill and Smeltermen's Union. The new local reformulated its demands to include union recognition. The smeltermen also broadened their health benefit proposal, seeking a "voice in the management of the hospital they support." ASARCO crushed this protest by importing trainloads of strikebreakers. The El Paso workers won no health concessions.[38]

Hardrock workers in Arizona found their employers equally resistant to democracy. Roughly eight thousand miners stopped work in the Clifton-Morenci district in September 1915 in a dispute over wages and other issues. The principal operators—Arizona Copper, Detroit Copper (a Phelps Dodge subsidiary), and Shannon Copper—rejected demands for the abolition of both preemployment examinations and supplemental charges by the company hospitals beyond the check-off. The settlement reached four months later required strikers to disaffiliate from the WFM. This agreement established employee committees to meet with management "to discuss any matters pertaining to the welfare of the men." These matters included "complaints against Hospital or Medical Departments." Needless to say, union leaders were disgusted. Organizer Henry McCluskey predicted the futility of this sort of representation. "Grievance committees on the company payroll without an organization behind (if they are foolish enough to act) can be controlled," McCluskey argued, "and if they become too active can be discharged without redress." Thomas Quinnan of Local 106 excoriated a similar arrangement at Phelps Dodge in Bisbee:

We are only too familiar with these appointed committees who must respond to their employers every whim or [receive] a request to leave the service of the company, as a person discontented with his position is a menace to the peace of the board. These appointed boards are a joke. In the first place they have no powers conferred on them more than that of a mutual admiration society, but are used by these employers to mislead inquiring minds, by posing as humane and intelligent employers who have the interests of their employes at heart.

38. J. W. C. Ibarra et al. (employees committee) to Officers of the El Paso Smelting Works, Apr. 21, 1913, in *MM*, May 8, 1913, p. 8; C. H. Tanner to Editor, Apr. 29, 1913, *MM*, May 15, 1913, p. 11; *MM*, July 17, 1913, pp. 9–10; WFM, "Defunct Unions and New Unions," p. 29, WFM-IUMMSW Archives, vol. 43; Garcia, *Desert Immigrants*, pp. 107–8. Tanner's letter and the WFM record of chartering this local indicate that, contrary to Garcia's account, the strikers did join the WFM.

The committees accomplished their mission: they did nothing to reform the policies to which the miners objected.[39]

Workers in the nearby Globe-Miami district resented many common
practices of the Old Dominion Hospital, which was run by the Old
Dominion Copper Company, and the Miami-Inspiration Hospital,
which was leased to Dr. John Bacon by the Miami Copper Company.
When Alice Hamilton visited this area in 1919, she found the medical
practitioners deeply committed to their employers. "There are no
neutrals anywhere," concluded Hamilton. "I asked the hotel clerk in
Globe about the physicians in the camp . . . whom I could interview,
only to be told: 'All doctors here are copper, but they say there is one
labor doctor in Miami.' . . . Only one labor doctor could I find in all
that region; the rest were deeply dyed copper, some of them more
royalist than the king." By mid-1917, Local 60 in Globe and Local 70
in Miami had amassed countless complaints against the company
hospitals. The *Miners' Magazine* summarized these accusations: "The
methods of the companies in conducting the hospitals have become
unendurable. Men receive less consideration, medically, than that
accorded to mules. A list of cases showing practically maltreatment
of patients is being prepared which will astound its readers. Carelessness, neglect and actually wrong diagnosis are frequent, and the
sending of the men back to work before their hurts are healed, that
compensation need not be paid, has become a common practice."[40]
Specifically, unionists asserted that hospital staff frequently discharged patients just before the expiration of the fourteen-day waiting
period for compensation benefits. In addition, workers criticized the

39. Arizona Copper Co., Detroit Copper Mining Co., Shannon Copper Co. and
Employees' Committee, *Agreement in Regard to Industrial Conditions in the Clifton-Morenci-
Metcalf District* (N.p., n.d. [1916]), p. 7; H. S. McCluskey, "Labor Forward," *Arizona
Labor Journal*, May 4, 1916, p. 4; Thomas Quinnan, "Miners Required to Pass Exami-
nation," ibid., June 22, 1916, p. 1; ibid., Sept. 16, 1915, p. 1, Jan. 13, 1916, p. 1; Kluger,
Clifton-Morenci Strike, pp. 22–23, 72, 78, and passim; *EMJ*, Oct. 9, 1915, pp. 605–7; R.
L. Byrd, "The Strike of Miners in the Clifton-Morenci Copper Mining District," n.d.
[ca. Oct. 1915], and Hywel Davies and Joseph S. Myers (U.S. commissioners of con-
ciliation) to Governor George W. P. Hunt, Feb. 10, 1916, Clifton-Morenci Strike, 1915–
16, File, Special Collections Department, University of Arizona Library, Tucson; *Polk's
Medical Register*, 14th ed., p. 228. When in 1983 a member of the staff of the Phelps
Dodge hospital in Morenci, Dr. Jorge O'Leary, refused to stop treating striking miners
and their families, he was discharged. O'Leary and the strikers established the People's
Clinic in Clifton. See *AFL-CIO News*, Dec. 3, 1983, p. 5; Carol Ann Bassett, "Fired for
His Pro-Union Stand, a Doctor Treats Strikers for Free in an Arizona Company Town,"
People, Jan. 16, 1984, pp. 68, 71.
40. Hamilton, *Exploring the Dangerous Trades*, pp. 210–11; *MM*, July 1917.

outright denial of services. Union organizer Joseph Cannon recounted one case of an injured miner who was taken to the Old Dominion Hospital. When the physician arrived, he "informed the man that nothing was the matter with him but that he was lazy, and . . . to get up and out of there, to which the victim replied that he was badly injured, was not able to leave the hospital, and sorely in need of medical attention, to which, however, the doctor snapped his fingers and told him laziness was his only complaint. Three hours later this victim was dead."[41]

Because the check-off to support these programs was mandatory, the IUMMSW saw this situation as "taxation without representation." On July 2, 1917, approximately seven thousand miners struck for union representation in general and a role in health plan governance in particular. They demanded a measure of industrial democracy: "First—Recognition of the grievance committee of the local unions of the Mine, Mill and Smelter Workers International Union and those of the other organized trades now represented in the mining industry in the Globe and Miami district. . . . Fourth—Equal representation on the board of control of the hospital." Although the presence of the IWW in the district made Mine-Mill appear moderate by comparison, Globe-Miami employers staunchly opposed these proposals. The time-worn scenario was played out once again: the U.S. cavalry arrived on July 5; vigilantes organized; both sides resorted to violent tactics; union activists were arrested wholesale; strikebreakers were brought in from Texas and New Mexico; production slowly began to resume.[42]

Unlike past disputes, however, federal officials intervened with more than just troops this time. The exigencies of the world war had temporarily given the central government a stronger role in settling

41. Joseph D. Cannon, "The Grievances at Miami and Globe, Arizona," *MM,* Aug. 1917; idem, Testimony, Oct. 9, 1917, in U.S., President's Mediation Commission, "Sessions at Globe," pp. 31–52, McCluskey Collection, box 4; *MM,* Aug. 1917; *Arizona Silver Belt,* June 23, 1907, p. 2, July 7, 1907, p. 2.

42. Joseph D. Cannon, "Speech," June 30, 1917, in U.S., President's Mediation Commission, "Sessions at Globe," pp. 333 (quotation), 30–31, McCluskey Collection, box 4; Locals 60 and 70, Strike Demands, July 1917, in *MM,* Aug. 1917; Executive Committees, Globe and Miami Miners' Unions, "Response to the Circular Entitled 'Your Duty Any Time,'" n.d., in *MM,* July 1917; *Arizona Labor Journal,* June 15, 1917, pp. 1–2, Sept. 28, 1917, p. 1; George D. Smith et al. (Locals 60 and 70) to Local and International Unions, July 27, 1917, ibid., Aug. 3, 1917, p. 1; Jensen, *Heritage of Conflict,* pp. 391–99, 407–8; Daphne Overstreet, "On Strike!: The 1917 Walkout at Globe, Arizona," *Journal of Arizona History* 18 (1977): 199–215.

industrial conflicts. The President's Mediation Commission, headed by Secretary of Labor William B. Wilson, came to Globe in October 1917 to investigate and resolve this dispute. The commission held lengthy hearings at which numerous strike participants and observers testified. Mine-Mill President Moyer focused on the hypocrisy of patriotic employers who supported the the war effort. "The great employer of America surely may no longer declaim for world-wide democracy and in the next moment deny it to be the method of dealing with its employees," Moyer argued. "He crys out against autocracy in government; he crys for paternalism in industry." Joe Cannon presented a detailed indictment of the prevailing health care arrangements.[43]

After listening to both sides of the story, the commission immediately recommended terms for resolving the dispute. This proposal called for "workmen's committees" such as the union had been rejecting for months. The representation scheme prohibited participation by members of the Mine-Mill staff. In addition, it gave the committees no real policy-making power over health programs: "The workmen's committee may make such investigations of the hospital department on behalf of the employes as it may from time to time deem necessary, and make such recommendations to the trustees relative to improvements as it may find desirable." Nonetheless, faced with a deteriorating strike, the union had no choice but to accept this settlement. Employers, on the other hand, saw no reason to abide by the commission's plan. They either blatantly ignored or surreptitiously circumvented it. Thus workers lost another battle in the war to make the Arizona copper industry safe for democracy.[44]

43. Charles Moyer, Testimony, Oct. 9, 1917, in U.S., President's Mediation Commission, "Sessions at Globe," pp. 166 (quotation), 122–75, McCluskey Collection, box 4; Joseph Cannon, Testimony, Oct. 9, 1917, in ibid., pp. 6–7, 30–52; MM, Oct. 1917; Jensen, *Heritage of Conflict*, pp. 411–16; Melvyn Dubofsky, "Abortive Reform: The Wilson Administration and Organized Labor, 1913–1920," in James E. Cronin and Carmen Sirianni, eds., *Work, Community and Power: The Experience of Labor in Europe and America, 1900–1925* (Philadelphia, 1983), pp. 208–9.

44. U.S., President's Mediation Commission, to Charles H. Moyer et al., Oct. 19, 1917, rpt. in MM, Nov. 1917; MM, Nov. 1917; "A Striker" to Editor, Aug. 8, 1917, *Arizona Labor Journal*, Aug. 17, 1917, pp. 1–2; Henry S. McCluskey, Report, in IUMMSW, *Proceedings, 1918*, p. 95; Charles H. Moyer, "Report," in ibid., Appendix, p. 7; Jensen, *Heritage of Conflict*, pp. 416–17, 421–22, 424–25. In Bisbee the presidential commission only watered the seeds of company unionism. The antiunion employees' committees that had previously dealt only with problems at the company hospital expanded to cover other grievances. In 1920 this system grew into a full-blown representation

Local unions had more success when they intervened in less ambitious ways in the administration of benefits. When, for example,
the Miami-Inspiration Hospital refused to admit Mike Tussup because
it had no room for him, the secretary of the Miami Miners' Union
went to the institution and helped the superintendent find a bed for
the sick miner. A delegation from the Globe local extracted from Old
Dominion the concession that its physicians discontinue the practice
of charging "an unreasonable fee" for completing disability certificates.[45]

The Sick Committee of the Great Falls Mill and Smeltermen's Union
devoted considerable time to monitoring Anaconda's health benefit
program. The smeltermen frequently pursued grievances on the un-
availability and negligence of contract physicians. Company officials
formally recognized the local's right to participate in quality assurance
in 1902 by posting this notice: "Any complaint of the employees regarding the performance of the contract must be made to the Sick
Committee of the Mill and Smeltermen's Union within thirty days of
the occurance calling for complaint." Yet the committee was continually hamstrung because the union was not formally a party to the
health services contract. Nonetheless, the local redressed the most
blatant abuses either by pressing management to discipline its physicians or by confronting the doctors. The same methods forced physicians and hospitals to cancel or reduce inappropriate bills.[46]

---

scheme. See *MSP*, Aug. 20, 1921, pp. 248–49; H. C. Henrie (manager, Labor Department, Copper Queen), "A Metal Mine Employees' Representation Plan," *Mining Congress Journal*, June 1923, p. 195.

45. P. C. Renaud (Local 60), Testimony, Oct. 12, 1917, in U.S., President's Mediation
Commission, "Sessions at Globe," p. 608, McCluskey Collection, box 4; *MM*, Aug.
1917; Nelson *Weekly News*, Dec. 22, 1910.

46. Chief clerk (Boston and Montana smelter, Great Falls) to B. Asemann (chief
timekeeper), Apr. 26, 1902, Anaconda Records, box 209, file 585–1; C. W. Goodale
(manager), "Memorandum," Mar. 24, 1909, ibid., box 210, file 585–3; James Lithgow
(chair, Sick Committee, Local 16) to J. T. Morrow (superintendent), Feb. 10, 1913,
Morrow to Lithgow, Feb. 24, 1913, and A. F. Longeway (contract physician) to Morrow,
Mar. 12, 1903, ibid., box 226, file 1150–3; V. W. Mullery (recording secretary, Local 16)
to James O'Grady (general manager), Apr. 19, 1915, O'Grady to Drs. Longeway and
Adams, Apr. 23, 1915, F. J. Adams to O'Grady, Apr. 24, 1915, and O'Grady to Mullery,
Apr. 26, 1915, ibid., file 1150–1; Great Falls Mill and Smeltermen's Union, Minute Book,
2:155 (July 28, 1900), 392 (Apr. 19, 1902), 451–52 (Aug. 16, 1902), 471 (Oct. 11, 1902),
5:217 (Sept. 22, 1908), 219 (Sept. 29, 1908), 221 (Oct. 6, 1908), 231 (Oct. 27, 1908), 7:84
(Apr. 27, 1915), WFM-IUMMSW Archives, vols. 242, 245, 247; *Great Falls Daily Tribune*,
July 20, 1902, p. 12. Local 2 pressed similar grievances against physicians retained by
the Homestake Mining Company. Like its counterpart in Great Falls, the Lead City
local was not a direct party to the medical services contracts governing the benefit plan

In 1919 Local 16 tried to expand its limited powers to remedy grievances by attempting to integrate the benefit plan into its collective bargaining agreement. Anaconda management adamantly maintained a paternalistic stance, however, rejecting the union's proposal that it become a direct party to the negotiation and administration of all future contracts covering health services. In contrast, during the same year, employers in Porcupine, Ontario, offered to negotiate benefits. As a result, operators and Mine-Mill Local 145 agreed to a hospitalization plan and a disability insurance program, the latter funded entirely by employers. Thus by 1920 labor and management had begun to integrate the determination of health and welfare benefits into the general collective bargaining process.[47]

This offer of employer-financed insurance reflected an emerging trend in corporate policy. Rather than become entangled in delivering services, employers increasingly turned to monetary benefits. To be sure, mine operators had provided sickness and accident coverage through commercial insurance carriers and self-insured funds, financed by payroll deductions, for decades. But like the company doctor supported by check-off, these schemes seldom won the goodwill of employees.[48] Hence enlightened operators began to subsidize programs wholly or in large part. The Montana Industrial Accident

and, accordingly, met considerable frustration. See Lead City Miners' Union, Minute Book, pp. 71–72 (Apr. 13, 1891), 74 (Apr. 20, 1891), 133 (Feb. 8, 1892), 134 (Feb. 15, 1892), 144 (Apr. 19, 1892), 409 (Apr. 13, 1896), 410 (Apr. 20, 1896), WFM-IUMMSW Archives, reel 53.

47. Albert E. Wiggin (general superintendent, Great Falls smelter), "Memorandum," Feb. 24, 1919, and Anaconda Copper Mining Co., Great Falls Reduction Department, "Medical Services for Employees and Members of Their Families," Nov. 1, 1919, Anaconda Records, box 209, file 585–9; Great Falls Mill and Smeltermen's Union, Minute Book, 9:5–6 (July 17, 1919), 46 (Nov. 24, 1919), WFM-IUMMSW Archives, vol. 249; *Northern Miner* (Porcupine, Ont.), n.d., rpt. in *MM*, Aug. 1919. Of course, the Porcupine situation was exceptional. Elsewhere in Ontario, employers refused to bargain over hospital and doctor fees. See Joseph Gorman (secretary, Local 146), "Why Cobalt Miners Are on Strike," *MM*, Sept. 1919.

48. *Butte Bystander*, July 19, 1896; *MM*, Apr. 1903, p. 3; Victor D. Brannon, "Employers' Liability and Workmen's Compensation in Arizona" (M.A. thesis, University of Arizona, 1932), p. 2; U.S. Industrial Commission, *Report*, 12:xv; Moudy, "Cripple Creek Miner," p. 381; W. Gintzburger (manager, Monitor and Ajax Fractions) to A. Shilland, Apr. 16, 1904, Mine-Mill Papers, box 155, folder 2; *EMJ*, Feb. 11, 1893, p. 132, May 25, 1901, p. 671; J. C. Lowney to Editor, Apr. 26, 1916, *MM*, May 4, 1916; Wyman, *Hard-Rock Epic*, pp. 143–44. For a survey of disability and death benefit plans administered by railroad and steel firms which illuminates employee resentment of their coercive features, see Robert Asher, "The Limits of Big Business Paternalism: Relief for Injured Workers in the Years before Workmen's Compensation," in Rosner and Markowitz, eds., *Dying for Work*, pp. 19–33.

Board reported in 1920 that "many of the employers are securing free of any charge to workmen what is termed 'Group Insurance.'" ASARCO in 1917 instituted a company-paid death benefit of $1,000 for married workers and $500 for single workers, with increases based on seniority. Other firms quickly followed suit, eager to blunt union organizing appeals and to retain employees during the war. Although management completely controlled most of these insurance programs, some had elected or appointed boards of employees (always in a nonunion setting).[49]

ASARCO and a few other large corporations established old-age pension plans after 1910. One union supporter in Bisbee grudgingly acknowledged that pensions accomplished their purpose, that is, "to delude laborers and keep them contented." In large part these undertakings responded to the growing movement for social insurance legislation. Farsighted corporate leaders hoped that the establishment of private welfare programs would end agitation for public programs. Phelps Dodge announced the creation of its pension fund at the same banquet at which it declared its intention to repeal Arizona's workers' compensation law, a statute on the dreaded English model.[50]

In January 1916 James Price, safety engineer at the Great Falls smelter, surveyed the broad ramifications of recent reforms in industrial relations. He found that "the industries of today are slowly, but nevertheless surely evolving a man who is distinctly worth while. He is wide awake, thoughtful, resourceful, efficient." Two years later, Anaconda promoted one such man to assist him. Edwin Young, a twenty-eight-year employee at the plant and longtime leader of the Mill and Smeltermen's Union, was appointed to the newly created position of

49. Montana Industrial Accident Board, *Report, 1920*, p. 155; W. H. North to Editor, Dec. 7, 1910, *MSP*, Jan. 22, 1910, p. 163; *EMJ*, Feb. 3, 1912, p. 282, July 10, 1920, p. 87, July 31, 1920, p. 230; *Engineering and Mining Journal-Press*, May 30, 1925, p. 898; MacNaughton, "Welfare Work of Calumet and Hecla," p. 575; Copper Queen Consolidated Mining Co., *Benefit Plan for the Employees, 1916* (N.p., n.d.); ASARCO, *Regulations Governing the System of Death Benefits in the Nature of Life Insurance, 1917* (N.p., n.d.); idem, Circular 344, Mar. 7, 1917, rpt. in *EMJ*, Mar. 21, 1917, p. 507; Ballard Dunn, "Group Insurance Plan," *EMJ*, July 31, 1920, p. 215.

50. W. E. Holm to Editor, Nov. 29, 1913, *MM*, Dec. 11, 1913, p. 9; Copper Queen Consolidated Mining Co., *System of Pensions, 1913* (N.p., n.d.); Marcosson, *Metal Magic*, pp. 268–72; *MM*, July 31, 1913, pp. 8–9, Mar. 12, 1914, p. 11; South Dakota, State Mine Inspector, *Annual Report, 1917* (N.p., n.d.), p. 8; *Engineering and Mining Journal-Press*, May 19, 1923, p. 907.

welfare engineer. The company safety magazine described this latest advance in the bureaucratization of welfare work: "The duties of the office will be to keep a close look-out over the plant for things that need attention in order that the general welfare of the men may be best protected. [He is] to visit the hospitals, or homes of the men who may be off duty because of illness, and to bring to the men the knowledge that the company which employs them is interested in their welfare and wants to cheer them if they are suffering because of illness or injury." Moreover, management urged employees to take their health benefit grievances to Young.[51] Progressive employers thus not only incorporated the union's programs but also co-opted its leaders.

Still, the new paternalism never wholly extirpated the old fraternalism. Long after Young's appointment, the Sick Committee of Local 16 continued to visit the sick and protest the errors of the company's health care providers. On April 21, 1919, the union warned smelter management that if the welfare engineer meddled in its affairs, it would demand his removal.[52] Local 16 believed that welfare engineering meant not the end of class conflict but rather a fresh offensive in the ongoing struggle.

Nonetheless, by 1925 the era of self-help had ended. By this time even die-hard groups like the Great Falls Smeltermen sought only bilaterally controlled health care programs. Indeed, the 1920s was a time of abject helplessness for the IUMMSW, which shrank into virtual extinction. In addition to its bitter rivalry with the IWW, the union had to contend with a Canadian secessionist movement led by the One Big Union. During the paralytic postwar depression, employers' opposition to Mine-Mill intensified. Anaconda dealt the union a crushing blow by peremptorily canceling all its collective bargaining agreements in January 1921. The organization failed even to hold a

51. [James Price], "'Safety Jim' Says," *Anode*, Jan. 1916, pp. 10–11; *Anode*, Aug. 1918, p. 14; Albert E. Wiggin, "Appointment of Welfare Engineer," Memorandum, July 19, 1918, Anaconda Records, box 236, file 1391–1; Anaconda, Great Falls Reduction Department, "Medical Services for Employees and Members of Their Families," Nov. 1, 1919, ibid., box 209, file 585–9; *MSP*, Dec. 26, 1914, p. 1005; Dickinson, "Bisbee Warren District," p. 98; Augustus Locke to Editor, Apr. 5, 1918, *MSP*, Apr. 27, 1918, p. 573; *Great Falls Daily Tribune*, Sept. 3, 1919, p. 4, Apr. 16, 1920, p. 4.

52. Great Falls Mill and Smeltermen's Union, Minute Book, 8:unpaginated (Apr. 21, 1919), 9:75 (Feb. 9, 1920), 139 (June 28, 1920), WFM-IUMMSW Archives, vols. 248–49; H. E. Gallaher (secretary, Local 16) to A. E. Wiggin, Apr. 12, 1924, Anaconda Records, box 226, file 1150–3.

convention between 1920 and 1926. The handful of locals that survived the decade were too weak to mount any initiatives for democratic health and welfare reform.[53]

Yet employer dominance in matters of health and welfare never became absolute. Employee participation in safety committees, welfare fund elections, and general representation plans created aspirations and expectations that could not always be fulfilled within the constraints of paternalism. Employers could not hide the fundamental fact that power to make the most important decisions regarding working conditions and health and welfare benefits rested with a few managers, not the mass of employees. Moreover, some workers remembered that it had been their struggles that had forced employers to adopt ameliorative measures in the first place.

Accordingly, the resurgence of nonferrous metals unionism in the 1930s brought renewed efforts to democratize the determination of working conditions and welfare provisions. The IUMMSW led the fight for workers' compensation coverage of silicosis in the leading mining centers. Manipulating the threat of federal regulation, the union and its allies won limited benefits for this and other work-induced disorders in Utah, Arizona, and other states, beginning in the early 1940s.[54] When it became clear that insurance premiums and state legislation gave operators insufficient incentive to eradicate health hazards, Mine-Mill sought federal intervention. Persistent agitation culminated in 1966 in the passage of the Federal Metal and Nonmetallic Mine Safety Act, which imposed uniform limits on exposure to major hazards in underground and open pit operations.[55]

53. Jensen, *Heritage of Conflict*, pp. 452–65; John Clark (secretary, Local 16) to Wesley Morgan (secretary, Local 18, Kellogg, Ida.), Feb. 13, 1940, WFM-IUMMSW Archives, box 384, folder 1.

54. Montana Industrial Health Committee, "Mr. Taxpayer, Are You Tired of Paying Industry's Industrial Health Bill," leaflet, n.d. [1952], Anaconda Records, box 210, file 605–5; IUMMSW, *Official Proceedings of the Thirty-Second Convention, 1935* (N.p., n.d.), pp. 44, 146–47, 151; idem, *Official Proceedings of the Thirty-Fourth Convention, 1937* (N.p., n.d.), pp. 32, 116; *CIO News—Mine, Mill and Smelter Workers Edition*, Mar. 27, 1939, p. 2; Robert C. Brown and Thomas Murray, "Progressive Bloc in Montana Legislature Passes Important Bills," ibid., Mar. 20, 1939, p. 2; McBride, "McCluskey," pp. 285–86; Utah, *Laws, 1941* (Kaysville, Utah, 1941), pp. 79–87; Arizona, *Acts, Memorials and Resolutions, 1943* (N.p., n.d.), pp. 34–65; Montana, *Laws, Resolutions and Memorials, 1959* (Helena, n.d.), pp. 272–317.

55. *EMJ*, Mar. 1964, p. 20; A. C. Skinner (international president), "Report," in IUMMSW, *Official Proceedings of the Fifty-Ninth Convention, 1965* (N.p., n.d.), Appendix I, p. 11; Brett Englund (aide to Senator Lee Metcalf), Address, in ibid., p. 30; U.S., *Statutes at Large, 1966* (Washington, 1967), 80:772–85.

The union also bargained with employers for improved health and welfare benefits and a role in managing these benefits. Mine-Mill became an early advocate of paid sick leave, health insurance for retirees, and substantial pensions, successfully negotiating concessions from the major corporations within its jurisdiction. In addition, the union used the grievance process, work stoppages, and other means to oppose employer-administered medical examinations and to improve working conditions.[56] When the International Union of Mine, Mill and Smelter Workers merged into the United Steelworkers of America in 1967, it left a long record of activism in ameliorating the well-being of its members.

56. George G. Suggs, Jr., *Union Busting in the Tri-State: The Oklahoma, Kansas, and Missouri Metal Workers' Strike of 1935* (Norman, Okla., 1986), pp. 29–44; *EMJ*, Aug. 1945, p. 106, Oct. 1945, p. 129, Feb. 1947, p. 151, May 1954, pp. 92–93; *CIO News—Mine, Mill and Smelter Workers Edition*, Jan. 23, 1939, p. 2, Mar. 6, 1939, p. 1, Apr. 10, 1939, p. 7; Hospital Committee, Butte Miners' Union, Report, Apr. 17, 1940, WFM-IUMMSW Archives, box 384, folder 1; IUMMSW, *Official Proceedings of the Fifty-first Convention, 1956* (Denver, n.d.), pp. 109–11.

Epilogue

Workers in the industrializing era were more than so much hamburger, haplessly ground up by new machinery. The western miners' activism reveals a clear pattern of strenuous, often efficacious, resistance to victimization by occupational accidents and diseases. A strong ethos of fraternalism led hardrock workers to be their brother's keeper on the job. This code of self-preservation through mutual protection formed an integral part of craftsmanship in the late nineteenth century. Agitation for legislative protection significantly ameliorated numerous threats to health and safety. These workers thus aggressively responded to the onslaught of technological change with a wide-ranging effort to prevent injury and illness.

The miners' experience also elucidates formidable obstacles to democratizing the determination of working conditions. The industrial revolution thoroughly eroded direct workers' control of the underground workplace. Protective legislation proved to be difficult to enact and still more difficult to enforce. The rise of sophisticated employer safety programs left the WFM-IUMMSW in a defensive stance.

Contemporary advocates of workers' health and safety can assume that they will face similar problems. Corporate leaders fully recognize the threat to managerial prerogatives posed by employees' demands for a meaningful role in deciding how to eliminate workplace hazards. Further, industrialization has vitiated traditional skills and workers' control throughout the economy as a whole. In addition, technological innovation has given rise to new types of work in which no tradition of craft independence exists. Needless to say, the degradation of labor holds strong negative implications for rank-and-file movements to clean up the workplace. In particular, the ongoing application of computer technology to diverse occupations serves, on balance, to subdivide labor even further and to narrow the scope of employees' freedom to avert occupational stress and a host of other threats to health and safety. In the face of these sweeping changes, workers possess neither the autonomy to direct their own risk-eradication campaigns nor the leverage over their employers to force engineering and administrative reforms. The entrenchment of welfare capitalist institutions and the growing imbalance of power between labor and capital make it difficult to foresee any substantial increase in workers' decision-making power in this area during the foreseeable future. No worthwhile purpose is served by romanticizing the prospects for workplace democracy.[1]

The western miners' health-care experiments demonstrated that opposition to employer paternalism could assume new forms. Deeply ingrained values and habits of independent action and long experience administering disability insurance benefits lay the groundwork for planning and maintaining worker-controlled hospitals throughout the mining region. These democratic institutions went beyond mere protest to offer a practical system for delivering primary-care services on a nonexploitive basis. Their moment of success gave their founders self-confidence and dreams of wider freedom from corporate domination. Only larger forces—the volatility of the nonferrous metals industry and the escalation of industrial conflict—prevented further advance of this democratic approach to providing health services.

Pure self-help of this nature is almost certainly a thing of the past. In light of both the current situation of North American unions and the dramatic upheavals convulsing the health care industry, it is virtually impossible to envision a resurgence of union-governed hos-

1. Harry Braverman, *Labor and Monopoly Capital: The Degradation of Work in the Twentieth Century* (New York, 1974); Andrew Zimbalist, ed., *Case Studies on the Labor Process* (New York, 1979); David F. Noble, *Forces of Production: A Social History of Industrial Production* (New York, 1984); Harley Shaiken, *Work Transformed: Automation and Labor in the Computer Age* (New York, 1985); William Serrin, "Work Rules Overtaking Pay as Key Labor Issue," *New York Times*, Oct. 26, 1986, p. 17; Zoe E. Clayson and Jane L. Halpern, "Changes in the Workplace: Implications for Occupational Safety and Health," *Journal of Public Health Policy* 4 (1983): 279–97; Steven Deutsch, "Extending Workplace Democracy: Struggles to Come in Job Safety and Health," *Labor Studies Journal* 6 (1981): 127–28. There is also a danger in making a panacea of workplace democracy. On the miserable safety record of the plywood cooperatives of the Pacific Northwest, see Edward S. Greenberg, *Workplace Democracy: The Political Effects of Participation* (Ithaca, 1986), pp. 84–87.

pitals. Nonetheless, worker representatives can assume a larger role in the governance of hospitals, health maintenance organizations, and other health centers without unilaterally shouldering the onerous responsibilities of founding and maintaining their own institutions. Presently, the governance of facilities funded in large part by employee benefits remains almost entirely in the hands of business leaders and physicians.[2] Arguments based on democratic principles might well gain places for unionists on the boards of directors of public and voluntary hospitals, from which they have been virtually excluded. If moral suasion failed, the labor movement could press for legislation like that enacted in West Virginia in 1983, which requires that hospital boards include representatives of workers and other segments of the community.[3] In addition, as Frank Goldsmith and Lorin Kerr pointed out in a recent essay, "The establishment of [union-controlled] occupational health clinics in industrial areas is a feasible goal in many parts of the country."[4]

Like the delivery of hospital services, the less ambitious welfare programs mounted by local mine, mill, and smelter workers' organizations had an important impact on their members' lives. These workers, especially immigrants and others separated from family and kin, recognized that in the event of misfortune only the union stood between them and the poorhouse or potter's field. Grassroots self-help

2. Trustee Magazine and Arthur Young, *The Hospital Governing Board Chairman: Profile and Opinions* (N.p., 1983), pp. 6–8, 25, 37–39; Kenneth Kaufman, Stephen Shortell, Selwyn Becker, and Duncan Neuhauser, "The Effects of Board Composition and Structure on Hospital Performance," *Hospital and Health Services Administration* 24 (1979): 50–51; Theodore Goldberg and Ronald Hemmelgarn, "Who Governs Hospitals?" *Hospitals* 45 (Aug. 1, 1971): 79; Ian Berger and Robert Earsy, "Occupations of Boston Hospital Board Members," *Inquiry* 10 (1973): 42–46; Anthony Kovner, "Hospital Board Members as Policy-Makers: Role, Priorities, and Qualifications," *Medical Care* 12 (1974): 974. On the minimal representation given unions on the boards of Blue Cross associations, see Sylvia A. Law, *Blue Cross: What Went Wrong?* (New Haven, 1974), p. 29.

3. H. Robert Cathcart, "Including the Community in Hospital Governance," *Hospital Progress* 51 (Oct. 1970): 72–76; West Virginia, *Acts, 1983* (Beckley, W.Va., n.d.), pp. 473–74; "Court Upholds Labor Role on Local Hospital Boards," *AFL-CIO News*, Jan. 19, 1985, pp. 1, 6.

4. Frank Goldsmith and Lorin Kerr, "Worker Participation in Job Safety and Health," *Journal of Public Health Policy* 4 (1983): 463; *Labor Notes*, Feb. 1985, p. 9; David H. Wegman, Gilles P. Theriault, and John M. Peters, "Worker-Sponsored Survey for Asbestosis," *Archives of Environmental Health* 27 (1973): 105–9. On union-governed outpatient facilities dealing with nonoccupational problems, see Thomas Herriman, "Union Health Clinics," in Richard H. Egdahl, ed., *Background Papers on Industry's Changing Role in Health Care Delivery* (New York, 1977), pp. 40–47.

activities such as lay nursing and friendly visiting complemented disability benefit payments in ways that built loyalty to unionism. Funeral rituals supplemented burial insurance payments in the same manner. Fraternalism forged abiding solidarity, helping to explain both the militance of the WFM and its resilience in the wake of setback after setback.

As AFL-CIO leaders consider innovative benefit programs such as legal services and health insurance for the unemployed, they might find encouragement in the metal miners' success in binding members to their movement with similar methods. By addressing unmet needs for protection against insecurity, unions can demonstrate in new ways the breadth of their concern for the well-being of working people. Surely, Samuel Gompers, who held that "those unions having . . . the most complete beneficial features have been best able to hold their membership in the most adverse times," would approve of these experiments.[5]

The main lesson of the hardrock unionists' initiatives is the certainty of hard struggle in any attempt to extend the frontier of democracy. The dim prospects in the near term for a democratic transformation of working conditions and health care services need not deter efforts to win incremental improvements. Even small gains help to curtail the sense of powerlessness that is one of the most pervasive and pernicious health hazards threatening workers today.[6]

The hardrock miners' battles suggest that it will take the most persistent, innovative efforts in the workplace, in the community, and in the political arena to overcome the adverse effects of corporate authoritarianism on workers' well-being. In all likelihood, workers engaged in these struggles will benefit most from building coalitions

5. Samuel Gompers, "The Next Step toward Emancipation," *American Federationist*, Dec. 1899, p. 248; AFL-CIO Committee on the Evolution of Work, *The Changing Situation of Workers and Their Unions* (N.p., 1985), p. 20; William Serrin, "Unions' Race with Change," *New York Times*, Feb. 22, 1986, p. 22; AFL-CIO Union Privilege Benefit Programs, *New Horizons*, n.d. [ca. Feb. 1987]; *AFL-CIO News*, June 21, 1986, p. 5; James L. Medoff and Nina A. Mendelson, "Unions of the Past," ibid., May 25, 1985, pp. 11–12.

6. Daniel M. Berman, *Death on the Job: Health and Safety Struggles in the United States* (New York, 1978), pp. 195–96 and passim; Deutsch, "Extending Workplace Democracy," pp. 127–30; Bruce L. Margolis, William H. Kroes, and Robert P. Quinn, "Job Stress: An Unlisted Occupational Hazard," *Journal of Occupational Medicine* 16 (1974): 659–61; Jon Garfield, "Alienated Labor, Stress, and Coronary Disease," *International Journal of Health Services* 10 (1980): 551–61.

with progressive health care providers and other professionals, not from going it alone as the miners did. Nonetheless, the long heritage of grassroots self-help that began with organizations like the Coeur d'Alene Miners' Union can offer some encouragement, if not inspiration, to both labor activists and their allies.

Bibliography

Primary Sources

Manuscripts

Berkeley, California. University of California. Bancroft Library.
    Bodie Miners' Union (Calif.). Records, 1890–1913.
    Gold Hill Miners' Union (Nev.). Organizational Papers, 1876–1921.
    Goldfield Mining Companies (Nev.). Records, 1904–25.
    Silver City Miners' Union (Idaho). Records, 1896–1902.
    Silver Lake Mines (Silverton, Colo.). Letterbook, 1896–98.
    Trade Dollar Consolidated Mining and Milling Company (Silver City, Idaho).
        Records, 1891–1947.
——. University of California. Graduate Social Science Library. Labor Collection.
    Executive Board, Western Federation of Miners. Minutes, 1893–95. Microfilm.
    Western Federation of Miners. Convention Proceedings, 1893–95. Microfilm.
Boise, Idaho. Idaho State Historical Society.
    Ernest P. Orford. Letterbook, 1897–98.
    Trade Dollar Consolidated Mining and Milling Company (Silver City, Idaho).
        Papers, 1891–1908.
Boulder, Colorado. University of Colorado. Norlin Library. Western Historical Collections.
    Western Federation of Miners–International Union of Mine, Mill and Smelter
        Workers Archives, 1893–1967.
Cambridge, Massachusetts. Radcliffe College. Schlesinger Library.
    Alice Hamilton. Papers.
Goldfield, Nevada. Esmeralda County Courthouse.
    Esmeralda County Recorder. Records, 1904–11.
Helena, Montana. Montana Historical Society.
    Anaconda Copper Mining Company. Records.
    Clancy Miners' Union (Mont.). Minute Book, 1894–96.

Edith R. Maxwell. "Great Falls Yesterday." 1939.
Ithaca, New York. Cornell University. New York State School of Industrial and Labor Relations. Catherwood Library. Labor-Management Documentation Center.
    Western Federation of Miners and International Union of Mine, Mill and Smelter Workers Records.
Nevada City, California. Rood Administrative Center.
    Nevada County Recorder. Records, 1873–1925.
Reno, Nevada. Nevada Historical Society.
    Gold Hill Miners' Union. Records, 1889–96.
——. University of Nevada Library. Special Collections Department.
    Gold Hill Miners' Union. Records, 1866–68, 1872–75.
    Tenabo Mill and Mining Company (Cortez, Nev.). Records.
San Bruno, California. National Archives and Records Administration. Federal Records Center.
    U.S. Census Office. Manuscript Census, 1900. Microfilm.
Spokane, Washington. Eastern Washington State Historical Society.
    Edward Boyce. Papers.
Suitland, Maryland. National Archives and Records Administration. Washington National Records Center.
    U.S. Bureau of Mines. Records.
Tempe, Arizona. Arizona State University Library. Arizona Collection.
    Henry S. McCluskey. Collection.
Tonopah, Nevada. Nye County Courthouse.
    Nye County Recorder. Records, 1887–1923.
Tucson, Arizona. University of Arizona Library, Special Collections Department.
    Arizona Copper Company. Records, 1882–1921.
    Clifton-Morenci Strike, 1915–16. File.
    Samuel C. Dickinson. "A Sociological Survey of the Bisbee Warren District." 1917.
Vancouver, British Columbia. University of British Columbia Library. Special Collections Division.
    International Union of Mine, Mill and Smelter Workers. Papers.
Washington, D.C. National Archives.
    U.S. Public Health Service. Records.

Newspapers, Journals, and Other Periodicals

American Federationist. New York. 1894–1916.
American Institute of Mining Engineers *Transactions*. 1890–1925.
American Labor Union Journal. Butte, Mont. 1902–03.
American Smelting and Refining Co. *Safety Review*. New York. 1915–19.
Anaconda Copper Mining Co. *Anode*. Butte, Mont. 1915–23.
Arizona Labor Journal. Phoenix. 1915–19.
Arizona Silver Belt. Globe. 1907–08.

Arizona State Bureau of Mines *State Safety Bulletin*. Tucson. 1916.
Arizona State Bureau of Mines *State Safety News*. Tucson. 1916–19.
Blair Press. Nev. 1908–10.
Butte Bystander. Mont. 1892–97.
Butte *Daily Inter Mountain*. Mont. 1887, 1889–90.
Butte Daily Miner. Mont. 1887–89.
California Industrial Accident Commission, Safety Department, Mining Division *Safety Bear Letter*. 1916–17.
Carthage Press. Mo. 1914–17.
Coeur d'Alene Miner. Wallace, Idaho. 1892–94.
Colorado Medicine. Denver. 1908–20.
Daily Arizona Silver Belt. Globe. 1911–12.
DeLamar Lode. Delamar, Nev. 1895–1903.
Denver Medical Times and Utah Medical Journal. 1910–14.
Douglas Island News. Alaska. 1907–08.
Engineering and Mining Journal. New York. 1890–1922.
Engineering and Mining Journal-Press. New York. 1922–25.
Fairbanks Daily News-Miner. Alaska. 1909.
Fairbanks Daily Times. Alaska. 1907–08.
Ferguson Eagle. B.C. 1900.
Goldfield News. Nev. 1904–10.
Great Falls Daily Tribune. Mont. 1895–1920.
Idaho Avalanche. Silver City. 1895–97.
Idaho Daily Statesman. Boise. 1891.
Industrial Worker. Spokane, Wash. 1911–13.
Kendall Miner. Mont. 1905–11.
Lardeau Eagle. Ferguson, B.C. 1900–04.
Little Rockies Miner. Zortman, Mont. 1907–09.
Lyon County Times. Yerington, Nev. 1907.
Manhattan News. Nev. 1906–7.
Manhattan Post. Nev. 1910–14.
Miners' Magazine. Butte, Mont., and Denver. 1900–21.
Miners' Union Bulletin. Fairbanks, Alaska. 1908–10.
Mining and Scientific Press. San Francisco. 1888–1922.
Mining Congress Journal. New York. 1915–25.
Missouri Trades Unionist. Joplin. 1914–18.
National Safety Council *Proceedings of the . . . Annual Safety Congress*. 1913–25.
Neihart Herald. Mont. 1891–92.
Neihart Miner. Mont. 1898.
Nelson Weekly Miner. B.C. 1898–99.
Nelson *Weekly News*. B.C. 1909–13.
Nevada Socialist. Reno. 1914, 1916.
New North-West. Deer Lodge, Mont. 1889.
Owyhee Avalanche. Silver City, Idaho. 1897–1904.
Park Record. Park City, Utah. 1902–08.

Pueblo Courier. Colo. 1898.
Rawhide Daily Press. Nev. 1908.
Rawhide Press-Times. Nev. 1908–11.
Rawhide Rustler. Nev. 1907–08.
Reese River Reveille. Austin, Nev. 1909–12.
Rhyolite Daily Bulletin. Nev. 1908–9.
Rhyolite Herald. Nev. 1905–7.
San Miguel Examiner. Telluride, Colo. 1897–1906.
Sandon *Paystreak*. B.C. 1896–1902.
Seven Troughs Miner. Vernon/Mazuma, Nev. 1907–10.
Silverton Weekly Miner. Colo. 1902–16.
Slocan Drill. B.C. 1900–5.
Spokane Review. Wash. 1891–93.
Tanana Leader. Alaska. 1909–10.
Tanana Miner. Chena, Alaska. 1907–8.
Tanana Miners' Record. Fairbanks, Alaska. 1907.
Terry *News-Record*. S.Dak. 1906–9.
Tonopah Bonanza. Nev. 1901–5.
Tonopah Daily Bonanza. Nev. 1921–22.
Tonopah Daily Sun. Nev. 1905. Weekly mining edition, 1906–10.
Tonopah Miner. Nev. 1902–5, 1911–13, 1920–21.
Tonopah Mining Reporter. Nev. 1921–22.
U.S. Public Health Service *Public Health Reports*. Washington. 1912–20.
U.S. Steel Corporation, Committee of Safety *Bulletin*. 1910–1920.
Vernon Review. Nev. 1907.
Virginia City *Daily Territorial Enterprise*. Nev. 1876–78.
Wallace Press. Idaho. 1890–92, 1895–96.
Wardner News. Idaho. 1888–95.
Webb City Register. Mo. 1910, 1914.
Weekly Missoulian. Missoula, Mont. 1886–92.
Wood River Times. Hailey, Idaho. 1882–84.
Yerington Times. Nev. 1907–10.

Labor Publications

Arizona State Federation of Labor. *Preamble, Declaration of Principles and Constitution, 1916*. N.p., n.d.
——. *Proceedings of the Sixth Annual Convention, 1917*. N.p., n.d.
Bodie Miners' Union (Calif.). *Constitution, By-Laws, Order of Business and Rules of Order, 1899*. N.p., n.d.
Bourne Miners' Union (Oregon). *Constitution, By-Laws and Rules of Order, 1902*. Denver, n.d.
Burke Miners' Union (Idaho). *Constitution, By-Laws, Order of Business, and Rules of Order*. Wallace, Idaho, n.d.
Butte Miners' Union (Mont.). *Constitution, By-Laws, Order of Business, and Rules of Order, 1902*. Butte, 1902.

Central Executive Miners' Union of Coeur d'Alenes. *Constitution, By-Laws, Order of Business, and Rules of Order.* Wallace, Idaho, 1895.

Cloud City Miners' Union (Leadville, Colo.). *Constitution and By-Laws, Order of Business and Rules of Order.* Leadville, n.d.

Cornucopia Miners' Union (Oregon). *Constitution, By-Laws and Rules of Order.* Butte, Mont., 1900.

Globe Miners' Union (Ariz.). *Constitution and By-Laws,* 1902. Girard, Kan., 1903.

Granite Miners' Union (Mont.). *Constitution, By-Laws, Order of Business and Rules of Order.* Philipsburg, Mont., n.d. (ca. 1888).

Grass Valley Miners' Union (Calif.). *Constitution, By-Laws and Rules of Order,* 1902. Grass Valley, 1903.

Great Falls Mill and Smeltermen's Union (Mont.). *Constitution and By-Laws,* 1931. Great Falls, n.d.

International Union of Mine, Mill and Smelter Workers. *Official Proceedings of the Twenty-Third Consecutive and Third Biennial Convention, 1918.* Denver, n.d.

——. *Official Proceedings of the Twenty-Fourth Consecutive and Fourth Biennial Convention, 1920.* Denver, n.d.

Jackson Miners' Union (Calif.). *Constitution and By-Laws,* 1903. N.p., n.d.

Lead City Miners' Union (S.D.). *Constitution and By-Laws,* 1900. N.p., n.d.

Marysville Miners' Union (Mont.). *Constitution, By-Laws, Order of Business and Rules of Order,* 1901. Butte, 1901.

Randsburg Miners' Union (Calif.). *Constitution and By-Laws, Rules of Order and Order of Business.* Pueblo, Colo., n.d.

San Juan District Union (Colo.). *Constitution and By-Laws,* 1900. Telluride, Colo., n.d.

Sandon Miners' Union (B.C.). *By-Laws and Sketch of Sandon Miners' Union Hospital.* N.p., n.d. [1905].

Silver City Miners' Union (Idaho). *Constitution and By-Laws.* Silver City, 1902.

Tintic District Miners' Union (Utah). *Constitution, By-Laws, Order of Business and Rules of Order,* 1902. Eureka, Utah, n.d.

Tonopah Miners' Union (Nev.). *Constitution and By-Laws.* N.p. [Tonopah], n.d.

Trail Mill and Smeltermen's Union (B.C.). *Constitution and By-Laws.* 1907. Trail, B.C., n.d.

Two Bit Miners' Union (S.D.). *Constitution and By-Laws.* Deadwood, S.D., 1898.

Virginia City Miners' Union (Nev.). *Constitution and By-Laws.* Reno, 1911.

——. *Constitution, By-Laws, Order of Business and Rules of Order.* Virginia City, 1879.

Weaver Miners' Union (Octave, Ariz.). *Constitution and By-Laws,* 1902. Denver, n.d.

Western Federation of Miners. *Constitution and By-Laws,* 1896. Butte, Mont. n.d.

——. *Constitution and By-Laws,* 1912. Denver, n.d.

——. *Constitution*, 1914. Denver, n.d.
——. *Official Proceedings of the Annual Convention*, 1901–12. Pueblo, Colo., and Denver, 1901–12.
——. *Official Proceedings of the Twenty-First Consecutive and First Biennial Convention*, 1914. Denver, 1914.
——. *Official Proceedings of the Twenty-Second Consecutive and Second Biennial Convention*, 1916. N.p., n.d.

Published Articles, Books, and Pamphlets

"Accident Record of the Anaconda Copper Mining Company." *Monthly Labor Review* 13 (Oct. 1921): 176–77.
"Accident Relief of the United States Steel Corporation." *Survey*, April 23, 1910, pp. 136–39.
"Accurate Death Certificates." *Journal of the Missouri State Medical Association* 14 (1917): 251.
American and Canadian Hospitals. 2d ed. Chicago, 1937.
The American Hospital Digest and Directory. Chicago, 1923.
American Medical Association. *American Medical Directory*. 1st–17th eds. Chicago, 1906–42.
——, Council on Medical Education and Hospitals. "Hospital Service in the United States." *Journal of the American Medical Association* 76 (1921): 1083–1103.
——. "Hospital Service in the United States." *Journal of the American Medical Association* 92 (1929): 1043–1118.
Andrews, John B. "Legal Protection for Workers in Unhealthful Trades." *American Labor Legislation Review* 2 (1912): 356–62.
Arizona Copper Company, Detroit Copper Mining Company of Arizona, Shannon Copper Company, and Employees' Committee. *Agreement in Regard to Industrial Conditions*. N.p., n.d. [1916].
Bassett, Carol Ann. "Fired for His Pro-Union Stand, a Doctor Treats Strikers for Free in an Arizona Company Town." *People*, Jan. 16, 1984, pp. 68, 71.
Betts, William W. "Chalicosis Pulmonum, or Chronic Interstitial Pneumonia Induced by Stone Dust." *Journal of the American Medical Association* 34 (1900): 70–74.
Bradshaw, George. *Safety First*. New York, 1913.
Bruner, Firmin. *Some Remembered, Some Forgot: Life in Central Nevada Mining Camps*. Carson City, Nev., 1974.
Burdett, Henry C. *Cottage Hospitals*. 3d ed. London, 1896.
Butler, Samuel W. *The Medical Register and Directory of the United States*. 2d ed. Philadelphia, 1877.
Close, Charles L. "Safety in the Steel Industry." *Annals of the American Academy of Political and Social Science* 123 (1926): 86–92.
Crampton, Frank A. *Deep Enough: A Working Stiff in the Western Mine Camps*. 1956. Reprint. Norman, Okla., 1982.

DeQuille, Dan [William Wright]. *The Big Bonanza.* 1876. Reprint. Las Vegas, 1974.

Drach, Gustave W. "The Hospital of the Tennessee Coal, Iron, and Railroad Company." *Modern Hospital* 17 (1921): 95–99.

Eastman, Crystal. *Work-Accidents and the Law.* New York, 1910.

Fifield, James C., ed. *American and Canadian Hospitals.* Minneapolis, 1933.

Frazier, Russell G. "Bingham Canyon through the Eyes of a Company Doctor." *Utah Historical Quarterly* 33 (1965): 283–88.

Goldwater, S. S. "The Privilege of Being a Hospital Trustee." *Modern Hospital* 34 (Apr. 1930): 63–64.

Gompers, Samuel. *Labor and the Employer.* Compiled and edited by Hayes Robbins. New York, 1920.

——. *Seventy Years of Life and Labor.* 2 vols. New York, 1925.

Gunn, Herbert. "Hookworm Disease in the Mines of California." *California State Board of Health Monthly Bulletin* 6 (1910): 408–13.

Hamilton, Alice. *Exploring the Dangerous Trades.* Boston, 1943.

——. "Lead Poisoning in Illinois." In First National Conference on Industrial Diseases, *Proceedings,* 1910, pp. 27–33. New York, 1910.

——. "Lead-Poisoning in Illinois." *Journal of the American Medical Association* 56 (1911): 1240–44.

——. "A Mid-American Tragedy." *Survey Graphic,* Aug. 1940, pp. 434–37.

Hammond, John Hays. *The Autobiography of John Hays Hammond.* 2 vols. New York, 1935.

Harriman, Job. *The Class War in Idaho.* 3d ed. New York, 1900.

Haywood, William D. *Bill Haywood's Book: The Autobiography of William D. Haywood.* New York, 1929.

Hickey, Thomas A. *The Story of the Bullpen at Wardner, Idaho.* New York, 1900.

Historical, Descriptive, and Commercial Directory of Owyhee County, Idaho. 1898. Reprint. Seattle, 1966.

Hollander, Jacob H., and George E. Barnett, eds. *Studies in American Trade Unionism.* New York, 1907.

Holmes, Joseph A. "The Work of the U.S. Bureau of Mines." *American Labor Legislation Review* 2 (1912): 125–30.

Hotchkiss, Samuel C. "Occupational Diseases in the Mining Industry." *American Labor Legislation Review* 2 (1912): 131–39.

Kelley, C. F. *Insurance and Compensation Laws: Address before the Committees of Labor and Capital of the Senate and House of Representatives, Thirteenth Assembly, Helena, Montana, February 7, 1913.* N.p., n.d.

Kelley, Florence. "Eight-Hour Law of Utah, and the U.S. Supreme Court." *American Journal of Sociology* 4 (1898): 21–34.

Kennedy, James B. *Beneficiary Features of American Trade Unions.* Baltimore, 1908.

Lanza, Anthony J. "Miners' Consumption in Southwestern Missouri." *Journal of the Missouri State Medical Association* 13 (1916): 251–54.

——, ed. *Silicosis and Asbestosis.* New York, 1938.

Lee, Mabel Barbee. *Cripple Creek Days.* Garden City, N.Y., 1958.

Legge, Robert T. "Miners' Silicosis: Its Pathology, Symptomatology and Prevention." *Journal of the American Medical Association* 81 (1923): 809–10.

Legge, Thomas M. "Industrial Diseases under the Workmen's Compensation Act." *Journal of Industrial Hygiene* 2 (1920): 25–32.

——. *Industrial Maladies*. London, 1934.

Luther, John W. "Industrial Hygiene as Practiced at Palmerton, Pennsylvania." *MSP*, May 16, 1914, pp. 809–12.

Lynch, James M. "Trade Union Sickness Insurance." *American Labor Legislation Review* 4 (1914): 82–91.

Magnusson, Leifur. "A Modern Copper Mining Town." *Monthly Labor Review* 7 (1918): 278–84.

Medical and Surgical Directory of the United States. 1st ed. Detroit, 1886.

Medical and Surgical Register of the United States. 2d–4th eds. Detroit, 1890–96.

Montana-Tonopah Mining Company. *Report for the Fiscal Year 1909–1910*. N.p., n.d.

Moudy, Ross B. "The Story of a Cripple Creek Miner." *Independent*, Aug. 18, 1904, pp. 380–82.

Oliver Iron Mining Company. *Safety Regulations, 1912*. N.p., n.d.

Palmer, Lewis R. "History of the Safety Movement." *Annals of the American Academy of Political and Social Science* 123 (1926): 9–19.

Pearson, R. Raymond. *Philosophy of a Mucker*. Ridgecrest, Calif., 1960.

Polk's Medical Register and Directory of North America. 8th–13th eds. Detroit, 1904–14.

Polk's Medical Register and Directory of the United States and Canada. 7th ed. Detroit, 1902; 14th ed. Detroit, 1917.

Raymond, Rossiter W. "The Hygiene of Mines." In American Institute of Mining Engineers, *Transactions* 8 (1880): 97–120.

Reed, Louis S. *The Medical Service of the Homestake Mining Company*. Chicago, 1932.

Rickard, Thomas A. *The Bunker Hill Enterprise*. San Francisco, 1921.

Ross, Malcolm. *Death of a Yale Man*. New York, 1939.

Sayers, R. R., E. R. Hayhurst, and A. J. Lanza. "Status of Silicosis." *American Journal of Public Health* 19 (1929): 635–40.

Shinn, Charles H. *Mining Camps: A Study in American Frontier Government*. 1884. Reprint. New York, 1965.

Sinclair, Upton. *The Jungle*. 1906. Reprint. New York, 1960.

Standard Medical Directory of North America, 1903–4. Chicago, 1903.

Stevens, Albert C. *The Cyclopedia of Fraternities*. 2d ed. 1907. Reprint. Detroit, 1966.

Toner, J. M. "Statistics of Regular Medical Associations and Hospitals of the United States." *Transactions of the American Medical Association* 24 (1873): 285–333.

Tri-State Survey Committee. *A Preliminary Report on Living, Working and Health Conditions in the Tri-State Mining Area*. New York, 1939.

Walsh, William H. "The Hospital Superintendent, Past, Present and Future."

In American Hospital Association, *Transactions of the . . . Sixteenth Annual Conference, 1914*, pp. 260–69.

Weed, Walter H. *The Mines Handbook.* 12th ed. New York, 1916.

Williams, Wayne C. "The Colorado Workmen's Compensation Act." *Colorado School of Mines Quarterly* 10 (Dec. 1915): 3–13.

Government Publications

Arizona. *Acts, Resolutions and Memorials.* 1912–19.

——. *Constitution.* 1910.

——. *Revised Statutes.* 1913.

——, Constitutional Convention. *Minutes.* 1910.

——, State Mine Inspector. *Annual Report.* 1912–18.

British Columbia. *Revised Statutes.* 1911, 1924.

——. *Sessional Papers.* 1895–1938.

——. *Statutes.* 1891, 1897–1919.

——, Committee on Workmen's Compensation Laws. *Report.* 1916.

——, Workmen's Compensation Board. *Annual Report.* 1916.

California. *Labor Laws.* 1921.

——. *Statutes.* 1881, 1911–15.

——, Industrial Accident Commission. *Mine Safety Rules.* 1915.

——, Industrial Accident Commission. *Safety and Efficiency in Mines.* 1916–17.

——, Senate and Assembly. *Appendix to the Journals of the Senate and Assembly.* 1895.

——, State Board of Charities and Corrections. *Biennial Report.* 1903–18.

——, State Mining Bureau. *Mining Laws, United States and California.* 1917.

Canada, Department of Agriculture, Census Office. *Fourth Census of Canada.* 1901.

——, Department of Labour. *Report on Labour Organisation in Canada.* 1911–25.

——, Department of Pensions and National Health. *Directory of the Hospitals of Canada*, by Canadian Medical Association. 1929.

——, Department of Trade and Commerce, Census and Statistics Office. *Fifth Census of Canada.* 1911.

——, Department of Trade and Commerce, Dominion Bureau of Statistics. *Sixth Census of Canada.* 1921.

Colorado. *Laws.* 1889, 1893, 1901, 1913–19.

Idaho. *General Laws.* 1893, 1909, 1917.

——, State Inspector of Mines. *Annual Report.* 1905–20.

Missouri. *Laws.* 1915.

——, Workmen's Compensation Commission. *Report.* 1914.

Montana. *Laws, Resolutions and Memorials.* 1889, 1903, 1911–19.

——, Department of Labor and Industry. *Biennial Report.* 1913–20.

——, Industrial Accident Board. *Annual Report.* 1915–20.

——, Inspector of Mines. *Annual Report.* 1896–97, 1901–2.

——, Legislative Council. *Montana Code Annotated.* 1983.

——, State Board of Health. *Biennial Report*. 1901–22.
Nevada. *List of Registered Physicians in Nevada*. 1909.
——. *Statutes*. 1903, 1907–19.
——, Industrial Commission. *Report*. 1913–24.
——, State Board of Health. *Biennial Report*. 1903–20.
——, State Inspector of Mines. *Annual Report*. 1910, 1912.
——. *Biennial Report*. 1913–22.
New Mexico. *New Mexico Statutes, 1978, Annotated*. 1978.
Ontario. *Statutes*. 1914–19.
South Dakota, State Mine Inspector. *Annual Report*. 1901–25.
U.S., Bureau of Labor. *Twenty-Third Annual Report of the Commissioner of Labor, 1908: Workmen's Insurance and Benefit Funds in the United States*. 1909.
U.S., Bureau of Labor Statistics. *Beneficial Activities of American Trade Unions*. Bulletin 465. 1928.
——. *Comparison of Workmen's Compensation Insurance and Administration*, by Carl Hookstadt. Bulletin 301. 1922.
——. *Comparison of Workmen's Compensation Laws of the United States and Canada*, by Lindley D. Clark and Martin C. Frincke, Jr. Bulletin 272. 1920.
——. *Comparison of Workmen's Compensation Laws of the United States up to December 31, 1917*, by Carl Hookstadt. Bulletin 240. 1918.
——. *The Cost of American Almshouses*, by Estelle M. Stewart. Bulletin 386. 1925.
——. *Industrial Accident Statistics*, by Frederick L. Hoffman. Bulletin 157. 1915.
——. *Lead Poisoning in the Smelting and Refining of Lead*, by Alice Hamilton. Bulletin 141. 1914.
——. *Michigan Copper District Strike*. Bulletin 139. 1914.
——. *Mortality from Respiratory Diseases in Dusty Trades*, by Frederick L. Hoffman. Bulletin 231. 1918.
——. *Proceedings of the Conference on Social Insurance*. Bulletin 212. 1917.
——. *The Safety Movement in the Iron and Steel Industry, 1907–1917*, by Lucian W. Chaney and Hugh S. Hanna. Bulletin 234. 1918.
U.S., Bureau of Mines. *Accident Prevention in the Mines of Butte, Montana*, by Daniel Harrington. Technical Paper 229. 1920.
——. *Accidents at Metallurgical Works*, by William W. Adams. Technical Paper 297. 1922.
——. *Control of Hookworm Infection at the Deep Gold Mines of the Mother Lode*, by James G. Cumming and Joseph H. White. Bulletin 139. 1917.
——. *Development of Workmen's Compensation Insurance for Metal Mines*. Report of Investigation 2590. 1924.
——. *The Efficiency of Mine Labor with Special Consideration of Industrial Medicine and Health Conservation*, by Arthur L. Murray. Report of Investigation 2117. 1920.
——. *Experiment Stations of the Bureau of Mines*, by Van H. Manning. Bulletin 175. 1919.
——. *Influence of Age and Occupation on Frequency and Severity of Disability*, by W. W. Adams. Report of Investigation 2116. 1920.

——. *Lead Poisoning in the Mining of Lead in Utah*, by Arthur L. Murray. Technical Paper 389. 1926.

——. *Lessons from the Granite Mountain Shaft Fire, Butte*, by Daniel Harrington. Bulletin 188. 1922.

——. *Metal-Mine Accidents in the United States*, by Albert H. Fay. Technical Papers 40, 61, 94, 129, 168, 202, 224, 252. 1911–18.

——. *Metal-Mine Accidents in the United States*, by William W. Adams. Technical Papers 286, 299. 1919–20.

——. *Metal-Mine Ventilation and Its Relation to Safety and Efficiency in Mining Operations*, by Daniel Harrington. Report of Investigation 2133. 1920.

——. *Miners' Consumption in the Mines of Butte, Montana*, by Daniel Harrington and Anthony J. Lanza. Technical Paper 260. 1921.

——. *Mining and Treatment of Lead and Zinc Ores in the Joplin District, Missouri, A Preliminary Report*, by Clarence A. Wright. Technical Paper 41. 1913.

——. *Morbidity Studies as an Aid in Preventing Illness among Miners*, by R. R. Sayers. Report of Investigation 2453. 1923.

——. *Organizing and Conducting Safety Work in Mines*, by Herbert M. Wilson and James R. Fleming. Technical Paper 103. 1917.

——. *Prevention of Illness among Miners*, by R. R. Sayers. Report of Investigation 2319. 1922.

——. *Pulmonary Disease in the Joplin District, Missouri, and Its Relation to Rock Dust in the Mines, a Preliminary Report*, by Anthony J. Lanza and Edwin Higgins. Technical Paper 105. 1915.

——. *Relation of Lead Poisoning in Utah to Mining*, by Arthur L. Murray. Report of Investigation 2274. 1921.

——. *Review of Literature on Effects of Breathing Dusts with Special Reference to Silicosis*, by Daniel Harrington and Sara J. Davenport. Bulletin 400. 1937.

——. *Review of Safety and Health Conditions in the Mines at Butte*, by George S. Rice and R. R. Sayers. Bulletin 257. 1925.

——. *Rules and Regulations for Metal Mines*, by W. R. Ingalls, James Douglas, J. R. Finlay, J. Parke Channing, and John Hays Hammond. Bulletin 75. 1915.

——. *The Safety and Health Campaign in the Mining Camps of Utah*, by C. A. Allen and A. L. Murray. Report of Investigation 2245. 1921.

——. *Safety Organization of Old Dominion Mine at Globe, Arizona*, by E. D. Gardner. Report of Investigation 2260. 1921.

——. *Safety Organizations in Arizona Copper Mines*, by E. D. Gardner and D. J. Parker. Technical Paper 452. 1929.

——. *Siliceous Dust in Relation to Pulmonary Disease among Miners in the Joplin District, Missouri*, by Edwin Higgins, Anthony Lanza, F. B. Laney, and George S. Rice. Bulletin 132. 1917.

——. *Silicosis among Miners*, by R. R. Sayers. Technical Paper 372. 1925.

——. *Silicosis and Tuberculosis among Miners of the Tri-State District of Oklahoma, Kansas, and Missouri—Part I*, by R. R. Sayers, F. V. Meriwether, A. J. Lanza, and W. W. Adams. Technical Paper 545. 1933.

——. *Silicosis and Tuberculosis among Miners of the Tri-State District of Oklahoma,*

Kansas, and Missouri—Part II, by F. V. Meriwether, R. R. Sayers, and A. J. Lanza. Technical Paper 552. 1933.

——. *Underground Hygiene and Sanitation*, by R. R. Sayers. Report of Investigation 2391. 1922.

——. *Underground Ventilation at Butte*, by Daniel Harrington. Bulletin 204. 1923.

U.S., Bureau of the Census. *Benevolent Institutions, 1904.* 1905.

——. *Benevolent Institutions, 1910.* 1913.

——. *Fourteenth Census, 1920.* Vol. 10: *Manufactures, 1919.* 1923.

——. *Fourteenth Census, 1920.* Vol. 11: *Mines and Quarries, 1919.* 1922.

——. *Historical Statistics of the United States, Colonial Times to 1970.* 2 vols. 1975.

——. *Mines and Quarries, 1902.* 1905.

——. *Thirteenth Census, 1910.* Vols. 2 and 3: *Population.* 1913.

U.S., Census Office. *Compendium of the Eleventh Census, 1890.* Part I: *Population.* 1892.

——. *Eleventh Census, 1890.* Vol. 1: *Population.* 1895.

——. *Report on Mineral Industries in the United States at the Eleventh Census.* 1892.

——. *Tenth Census, 1880.* Vol. 13: *Statistics and Technology of the Precious Metals*, by S. F. Emmons and G. F. Becker. 1885.

——. *Twelfth Census, 1900.* Vol. 1: *Population.* 2 parts. 1901–2.

U.S., Commission on Industrial Relations. *Final Report and Testimony.* 64th Congress, 1st sess., Senate Document 415. 11 vols. 1916.

U.S., Department of Labor, Division of Labor Standards. *Conference on Health and Working Conditions in the Tri-State District.* N.d. [1940].

U.S., Geological Survey. *Comstock Mining and Miners*, by Eliot Lord. 1883.

U.S., House of Representatives. *Papers Relative to Labor Troubles at Goldfield, Nevada.* 60th Cong., 1st sess., Document 607. 1908.

——, Committee on Military Affairs. *Coeur d'Alenes Labor Troubles.* 56th Cong., 1st sess., Report 1999. 1900.

U.S., Immigration Commission. *Reports.* Vol. 16: *Immigrants in Industries.* 1911.

U.S., Industrial Commission. *Report.* Vol. 12: *Relations and Conditions of Capital and Labor Employed in the Mining Industry.* 1901.

U.S., Public Health Service. *Miners' Consumption: A Study of 433 Cases of the Disease among Zinc Miners in Southwestern Missouri*, by Anthony J. Lanza and Samuel B. Childs. Bulletin 85. 1917.

——, Surgeon General. *Annual Report.* 1912–25.

U.S., Senate. *Coeur d'Alene Mining Troubles.* 56th Cong., 1st sess., Document 24. 1899.

——. *Coeur d'Alene Mining Troubles.* 56th Cong., 1st sess., Document 25. 1899.

——. *A Report on Labor Disturbances in the State of Colorado, from 1880 to 1904, Inclusive*, by Carroll D. Wright. 58th Cong., 3d sess., Document 122. 1905.

——. *Review of the Labor Troubles in the Metalliferous Mines of the Rocky Mountain Region.* 58th Cong., 1st sess., Document 86. 1904.

——, Committee on Military Affairs. *Home for Miners.* 57th Cong., 1st sess., Report 877. 1902.

U.S., Work Projects Administration, National Research Project. *Technology, Employment, and Output per Man in Copper Mining*, by Y. S. Leong, Emil Erdreich, J. C. Burritt, O. E. Kiessling, C. E. Nighman, and George C. Heikes. Report E–12. 1940.

Utah. *Constitution*. 1895.

——. *Laws*. 1896, 1917.

——, Industrial Commission. *General Safety Orders Covering Underground Metal Mining Operations*. 1919.

Selected Secondary Sources

Books

Allen, James B. *The Company Town in the American West*. Norman, Okla., 1966.

Barger, Harold, and Sam H. Schurr. *The Mining Industries, 1899–1939: A Study of Output, Employment and Productivity*. New York, 1944.

Berman, Daniel M. *Death on the Job: Occupational Health and Safety Struggles in the United States*. New York, 1978.

Brandes, Stuart D. *American Welfare Capitalism, 1880–1940*. Chicago, 1976.

Brody, David. *Steelworkers in America: The Nonunion Era*. 1960. Reprint. New York, 1969.

——. *Workers in Industrial America: Essays on the Twentieth-Century Struggle*. New York, 1980.

Brown, Ronald C. *Hard-Rock Miners: The Intermountain West, 1860–1920*. College Station, Tex., 1979.

Brykit, James W. *Forging the Copper Collar: Arizona's Labor-Management War of 1901–1921*. Tucson, Ariz., 1982.

Fahey, John. *The Days of the Hercules*. Moscow, Idaho, 1978.

Fell, James E., Jr. *Ores to Metals: The Rocky Mountain Smelting Industry*. Lincoln, Neb., 1979.

Garcia, Mario T. *Desert Immigrants: The Mexicans of El Paso, 1880–1920*. New Haven, Conn., 1981.

Gates, William B., Jr. *Michigan Copper and Boston Dollars: An Economic History of the Michigan Copper Mining Industry*. Cambridge, Mass., 1951.

Gersuny, Carl. *Work Hazards and Industrial Conflict*. Hanover, N.H., 1981.

Glasscock, Carl B. *Gold in Them Hills: The Story of the West's Last Wild Mining Days*. Indianapolis, Ind., 1932.

Graebner, William. *Coal-Mining Safety in the Progressive Period: The Political Economy of Reform*. Lexington, Ky., 1976.

Gutman, Herbert G. *Work, Culture, and Society in Industrializing America*. New York, 1976.

Jenkin, A. K. H. *The Cornish Miner*. 3d ed. London, 1962.

Jensen, Vernon H. *Heritage of Conflict: Labor Relations in the Nonferrous Metals Industry up to 1930*. Ithaca, N.Y., 1950.

——. *Nonferrous Metals Industry Unionism, 1932–1954: A Story of Leadership Controversy*. Ithaca, N.Y., 1954.

Kazin, Michael. *Barons of Labor: The San Francisco Building Trades and Union Power in the Progressive Era.* Urbana, Ill., 1987.

Kluger, James R. *The Clifton-Morenci Strike: Labor Difficulty in Arizona, 1915–1916.* Tucson, Ariz., 1970.

Laslett, John H. M. *Labor and the Left: A Study of Socialist and Radical Influences in the American Labor Movement, 1881–1924.* New York, 1970.

Licht, Walter. *Working for the Railroad: The Organization of Work in the Nineteenth Century.* Princeton, N.J., 1983.

Lingenfelter, Richard E. *The Hardrock Miners: A History of the Mining Labor Movement in the American West, 1863–1893.* Berkeley, Calif., 1974.

Malone, Michael P. *The Battle for Butte: Mining and Politics on the Northern Frontier, 1864–1906.* Seattle, Wash., 1981.

Mann, Ralph. *After the Gold Rush: Society in Grass Valley and Nevada City, California, 1849–1870.* Stanford, Calif., 1982.

Marcosson, Isaac F. *Anaconda.* New York, 1957.

———. *Metal Magic: The Story of the American Smelting and Refining Company.* New York, 1949.

Montgomery, David. *Workers' Control in America: Studies in the History of Work, Technology, and Labor Struggles.* New York, 1979.

Paher, Stanley W. *Death Valley Ghost Towns.* Las Vegas, Nev., 1973.

———. *Nevada Ghost Towns and Mining Camps.* Berkeley, Calif., 1970.

Paul, Rodman. *Mining Frontiers of the Far West, 1848–1880.* New York, 1963.

Perlman, Selig, and Philip Taft. *History of Labor in the United States, 1896–1932.* Vol. 4: *Labor Movements.* New York, 1935.

Peterson, Richard H. *The Bonanza Kings: The Social Origins and Business Behavior of Western Mining Enterpreneurs, 1870–1900.* Lincoln, Neb., 1977.

Reverby, Susan, and David Rosner. *Health Care in America: Essays in Social History.* Philadelphia, 1979.

Rosen, George. *The History of Miners' Diseases: A Medical and Social Interpretation.* New York, 1943.

Rosner, David. *A Once Charitable Enterprise: Hospitals and Health Care in Brooklyn and New York, 1885–1915.* New York, 1982.

Rowe, John. *The Hard-Rock Men: Cornish Immigrants and the North American Mining Frontier.* New York, 1974.

Salvatore, Nick. *Eugene V. Debs: Citizen and Socialist.* Urbana, Ill., 1982.

Schwantes, Carlos A. *Radical Heritage: Labor, Socialism, and Reform in Washington and British Columbia, 1885–1917.* Seattle, Wash., 1979.

Smith, Duane A. *Rocky Mountain Mining Camps: The Urban Frontier.* Bloomington, Ind., 1967.

———. *The Song of the Hammer and Drill: The Colorado San Juans, 1860–1914.* Golden, Colo., 1982.

Smith, Robert W. *The Coeur d'Alene Mining War of 1892.* Corvallis, Oreg., 1961.

Todd, Arthur C. *The Cornish Miner in America.* Truro, England, 1967.

Vogel, Morris J. *The Invention of the Modern Hospital: Boston, 1870–1930.* Chicago, 1980.

Williams, Pierce. *The Purchase of Medical Care through Fixed Periodic Payment*. New York, 1932.

Wolman, Leo. *Ebb and Flow in Trade Unionism*. New York, 1936.

Wyman, Mark. *Hard-Rock Epic: Western Miners and the Industrial Revolution, 1860–1910*. Berkeley, Calif., 1979.

Young, Otis E., Jr. *Western Mining*. Norman, Okla., 1970.

Articles and Essays

Alanen, Arnold R. "The 'Locations': Company Communities on Minnesota's Iron Ranges." *Minnesota History* 48 (1982): 94–107.

Allen, James B. "The Company-Owned Mining Town in the West: Exploitation or Benevolent Paternalism?" In *Reflections of Western Historians*, ed. John A. Carroll, pp. 177–97. Tucson, Ariz., 1969.

Dubofsky, Melvyn. "The Origins of Western Working Class Radicalism, 1890–1905." *Labor History* 7 (1966): 131–54.

Emmons, David M. "Immigrant Workers and Industrial Hazards: The Irish Miners of Butte, 1880–1919." *Journal of American Ethnic History* 5 (1985): 41–64.

Foster, James C. "*The Western Dilemma*: Miners, Silicosis, and Compensation." *Labor History* 26 (1985): 268–87.

Frisch, Paul A. "Labor Conflict at Eureka, 1886–97." *Utah Historical Quarterly* 49 (1981): 145–56.

Gutfeld, Arnon. "The Speculator Disaster in 1917: Labor Resurgence at Butte, Montana." *Arizona and the West* 11 (1969): 27–38.

Rosenberg, Charles E. "And Heal the Sick: The Hospital and the Patient in Nineteenth Century America." *Journal of Social History* 10 (1977): 428–47.

——. "Inward Vision and Outward Glance: The Shaping of the American Hospital, 1880–1914." *Bulletin of the History of Medicine* 53 (1979): 346–91.

Stevens, Rosemary. "Sweet Charity: State Aid to Hospitals in Pennsylvania, 1870–1910." *Bulletin of the History of Medicine* 58 (1984): 237–314, 474–95.

Townley, John M. "The Delamar Boom: Development of a Small One-Company Mining District in the Great Basin." *Nevada Historical Society Quarterly* 15 (1972): 3–19.

Dissertations and Theses

Berg, Lucile R. "A History of the Tonopah Area and Adjacent Region of Central Nevada, 1827–1941." M.A. thesis. University of Nevada, Reno, 1942.

Brinley, John E. "The Western Federation of Miners." Ph.D. dissertation. University of Utah, 1972.

Cash, Joseph H. "Labor in the West: The Homestake Mining Company and Its Workers, 1877–1942." Ph.D. dissertation. University of Iowa, 1966.

Elliott, Russell R. "The Tonopah, Goldfield, Bullfrog Mining Districts, 1900–

1915: History of a Twentieth Century Boom." Ph.D. dissertation. University of California, Berkeley, 1963.

Michalski, Thomas A. "A Social History of Yugoslav Immigrants in Tonopah and White Pine, Nevada, 1860–1920." Ph.D. dissertation. State University of New York, Buffalo, 1983.

Phipps, Stanley S. "From Bull Pen to Bargaining Table: The Tumultuous Struggle of the Coeur d'Alene Miners for the Right to Organize, 1887–1942." Ph.D. dissertation. University of Idaho, 1983.

Rikard, Marlene H. "An Experiment in Welfare Capitalism: The Health Care Services of the Tennessee Coal, Iron and Railroad Company." Ph.D. dissertation. University of Alabama, 1983.

Robinson, James C. "Work and Health: An Economic and Policy Analysis." Ph.D. dissertation. University of California, Berkeley, 1984.

Index

241

Library of Congress Cataloging-in-Publication Data

Derickson, Alan.
  Workers' health, workers' democracy.

  Bibliography: p.
  Includes index.
    1. Miners—Health and hygiene—Rocky Mountain Region—History. 2. Trade-
unions—Hospitals—Rocky Mountain Region—History. I. Title.
RC965.M48D47 1988   331.89   88-47722
ISBN 0-8014-2060-1 (alk. paper)